TURN-OF-THE-CENTURY CABARET

TURN-OF-THE-CENTURY CABARET

Paris, Barcelona, Berlin, Munich, Vienna, Cracow, Moscow, St. Petersburg, Zurich

HAROLD B. SEGEL

Columbia University Press
New York 1987

Library of Congress Cataloging-in-Publication Data

Segel, Harold B.
Turn-of-the-century cabaret.

Bibliography: p.
Includes index.
1. Music-halls (Variety-theaters, cabarets, etc.)—Europe—History. I. Title.
PN1969.C3S44 1987 792′.094 86-31699
ISBN 0-231-05128-X

Columbia University Press
New York Guildford, Surrey

Printed in the United States of America

Book design by Ken Venezio

To my wife Jeannette and my son Abbott

CONTENTS

ACKNOWLEDGMENTS

In the spring of 1960 I published an article on the Cracow Green Balloon in *The Polish Review*. At the time, my interest in cabaret had a limited, localized focus. I had no idea that that modest interest in one particular cabaret would eventually develop into a near obsession. A book on the spread of cabaret throughout turn-of-the-century Europe was furthest from my mind.

By the mid-1970s my interest in the early history of the cabaret had become more serious and certainly broader in scope. The first real evidence of this came in the form of a lecture on "The Turn-of-the-Century European Cabaret and Art" at the Graduate Center of the City University of New York in December 1975. The lecture, which was repeated at Northwestern University in May 1976, became an article, "Fin-de-Siècle Cabaret," which was published in the *Performing Arts Journal* in the spring of 1977.

By 1982, a book on cabaret was definitely in progress, although the scope of it was still unresolved. That issue would be settled a little later on. Two lectures on cabaret in Vienna—"The Beginnings of Cabaret in Austria, 1906–1912," in Solomon Wank's Vienna Seminar at Concordia University in Montreal in March 1982, and on "Fin-de-Siècle Vienna Cabaret," at Columbia University in April that same year—were based on a rough draft of the chapter on Vienna in the present book. An invitation to participate in a conference on theater and literature in Russia from 1900 to 1930 in Stockholm in late April 1982 provided me with an opportunity to test reaction to what I had managed to complete by then on the prerevolutionary Russian cabaret. Suggestions by my Swedish hosts, and friends, Nils Åke Nilsson, Bengt Jangfeldt, and Lars Kleberg of the Slaviska Institutionen of Stockholm University helped improve the lecture which was published under the title "Russian Cabaret in the European Context: Preliminary Considerations" in *Theatre and Literature in Russia, 1900–1930* (Stockholm, 1984). The chapter on Moscow and St. Petersburg/Petrograd cabaret is an expansion of that paper.

Much of the research for the book was conducted necessarily in Europe. I had much hospitality and help along the way, which I am happy to acknowledge here: in Helsinki, at the Slavic Library, where an excellent collection of early twentieth-century Russian newspapers and journals was of inestimable value; in Paris, at the Bibliothèque de la Ville de Paris and the Musée de Montmartre, where I was fortunate to arrive in time for the centenary of the Chat Noir; in Munich, at the Bayrische Staatsbibliothek, the Stadtbibliothek, Monacensia Abteilung, with its wealth of material on turn-of-the-century Munich, the Theatermuseum, and the Stadtmuseum, where Miss Reichenwallner and Dr. Düvigneau exerted themselves on my behalf; in Mainz, at the superb Deutsches Kabarettarchiv, where its founder and curator Reinhold Hippen was gracious and solicitous during a whirlwind visit; in Vienna, at the Österreichische Nationalbibliothek, the Bildarchiv of the Nationalbibliothek, the Theatersammlung, and the Hochschule and Museum für angewandte Kunst; and in Barcelona, at the Museu del Teatre, where my clumsy Catalan was tolerated with bemused patience.

My visits to Barcelona were especially pleasant thanks to the great courtesy and assistance of the Maragall family, above all Sra. Marta Maragall i Montaner and Sr. Joan Antoni Maragall, who permitted me to work in the private collection of the Sala Parés, which was so much a part of turn-of-the-century Catalonian modernism. The afternoons on Petritxol, especially when soft guitar music wafted up from that sliver of a street, will stay long in my memory. Sr. Jacint Reventos of Barcelona was gracious in his reply to a request for information about Jaime Sabartés, and Dr. Josep M. Carbonell of the Departament de Titelles of the Institut del Teatre of the Diputació de Barcelona went out of his way to try to find material on Juli Pi.

I would also like to express my gratitude to several personal friends who helped at key points. George Collins of Columbia University provided leads in Barcelona; Mrs. Asunta Carballeira was the one who first put me in touch with the Maragalls; Dr. Ludmilla Hellgren, a dear friend from the old days in Stockholm, sent me copies of Hanns von Gumppenberg's *Überdramen* at a time when I needed them badly and they were unavailable to me; Maria Kańska of the Wydawnictwo Literackie of Cracow who, together with her delightful family, extended me hospitality and also helped with photographs; Stanisław Jaworski, Tomasz Weiss, and Andrzej Nowakowski of the Instytut Filologii Polskiej of the Jagiellonian University of Cracow who, together with Pani Jaworska at the Biblioteka Jagiellońska, arranged for me to have reproductions of Green Balloon invitations; and my former student, Frank Sciacca, who dug up rare material on the Moscow Letuchaya mysh and its American tours as the Chauve-Souris of Paris.

The late and much missed Bernard Beckerman of Columbia University invited me once to talk on cabaret before the lively Drama Circle that he founded and looked after like an anxious parent. The comments of colleagues and students at that session helped me understand the need for further clarification of certain points. Bernie Beckerman's interest in and valuable comments on the "cabaret project" were a source of encouragement, especially when other professional commitments pulled me away from what became a true labor of love for painfully long periods of time. I deeply regret that he is no longer here to pass a keen eye over the final product.

I wish to express my gratitude to the following publishers for permission to quote from the sources listed:

INTRODUCTION

This is a book about cabaret. More specifically, it is a detailed account of the rise and spread of what was a veritable cabaret mania throughout Europe in the late nineteenth and early twentieth centuries, in that period known as the turn-of-the-century, or, to use the common French term, the *fin-de-siècle.*

Whatever the antecedents or progenitors of cabaret in taverns or cafés where entertainment of one type or another, often impromptu, accompanied drink more often than food, the fact is that the cabaret as a distinct cultural phenomenon has a precise—and relatively recent—chronology.[1] It began in Paris on November 18, 1881, the year in which the first and most famous cabaret of all, the Chat Noir (Black Cat), was established. Paris, during what the French like to call the *Belle Epoque,* was the cultural capital of Europe, the mecca of the arts to which admirers and young hopefuls flocked from one end of Europe to the other, and indeed from still farther away. If something caught on in Paris, the immense reputation of the city as the source of fashion and innovation insured its rapid diffusion across the Continent and beyond.

This is surely what happened in the case of cabaret. The novelty and extraordinary popularity of the Chat Noir—the mystique with which it was invested, the legend that grew up about it—launched a fashion which before long had all of Europe in its grasp.

Besides giving rise to many cabarets in Paris itself, in its own time and after it had become history, the Chat Noir also inspired the introduction of cabaret in major centers throughout Europe in the late nineteenth and early twentieth centuries: Amsterdam in 1895, Barcelona in 1897, Berlin, Munich, and Vienna in 1901, Cracow, Poland, in 1905, Budapest in 1907, Warsaw in 1908, Moscow and St. Petersburg in 1908, Prague in

1911, Christiana (as Oslo was then known) in 1912, after the failure of a dismal earlier attempt as early as 1892, London in 1912, and Zurich in 1916.

Now how do we explain the mercurial rise of cabaret in turn-of-the-century Europe?

Today, cabaret has lost most of its original meaning and purpose. In our own culture, "cabaret" is distinguished from "nightclub" almost wholly on the basis of size and atmosphere. Indeed, the two terms are often used synonymously, further blurring distinctions. Generally, the nightclub is perceived as physically large, the cabaret, by contrast, small and intimate. The entertainment offered in the nightclub tends toward the gaudier and more in the tradition of the revue: a raised stage, an orchestra, a chorus of dancers, singers, and a standup comedian or two. The audience is seated at tables, food and drink are served, and the space separating audience from performer usually serves the customers as a dance floor in between "sets" or programs. Admission to the nightclub is open to anyone and the performers are all paid professionals.

The contemporary cabaret retains most of these features, but in scaled down form; it is, in effect, a miniature nightclub. The premises are as a rule considerably smaller (rarely permitting dancing by the public), the entertainment dominated by just one or a few performers, with a bias often toward singers. Unlike the nightclub, the cabaret aims at an atmosphere of intimacy and this is achieved both by the reduced number of entertainers and a spatial configuration that brings performer and audience into relatively close contact. Like nightclubs, however, cabarets generally seat people at tables at which food and drink are served and are open to anyone willing to pay the price. Performers are also paid professionals who move from cabaret to cabaret or appear in other places of entertainment such as nightclubs, theaters, and concert halls.

In the beginning, and for most of its history before the end of World War I, cabaret had an entirely different character. It arose, in the first place, as an informal grouping of artists—painters, poets, musicians, and theater people—who felt a need to come together, preferably away from the eye of public and critic alike, in order to enjoy the company of those of similar interests and attitudes, to share their creative efforts, to experiment in any way the spirit moved them, and, most important, to feel free to mock and deride the values and cultural monuments of a society they condemned as hopelessly bourgeois and philistine.

At its origin, the cabaret had, therefore, a certain elitist character; it existed only or primarily for artists and their closest friends. It was also intended as something essentially private, although this tended to vary from one location to another. In general, however, the public was not actively sought and the cabaret proprietor, usually an artist himself, derived income—at best, a secondary consideration—from drinks (beer or wine) served the cabaret "regulars." The small premises of the early cabarets, usually capable of holding no more than a hundred people, if that, guaranteed that even when members of the public were admitted, both as a concession to insatiable curiosity and, in some instances, for purely commercial reasons, their numbers would be small. In this first brilliant period in the history of the European cabaret, from 1881 to 1917, audiences were made up predominantly of artists who with the growing fame of the cabarets attracted other artists, their friends, and a variety of cultural fellow-travelers. This left little physical space to accommodate a paying public at any one time, so that the admission of the public did not pose any real threat of commercialization. In post-World War I Europe, by which time cabaret had ceased to be a novelty and by and large had fulfilled its function as a locus of an emerging avant-garde, the situation changed considerably. Cabarets were now viewed as places of entertainment; their facilities were expanded and enhanced, their doors thrown open to an ever larger paying public, their programs more professionally arranged and managed, and their spirit transformed from artistic exclusivity and experimentation to commercial divertissement.

In chronicling the rise and spread of cabaret from its beginning in Paris in 1881 up to and including the birth of the Dada movement at the Cabaret Voltaire in Zurich in the years 1916 and 1917, this book seeks to demonstrate that rather than a marginal cultural activity in the turn-of-the-century period, the cabaret was very much at the center of the upheaval in the arts then taking place in Europe. As the nineteenth century drew to a close dissatisfaction with prevailing forms of artistic expression, and with the state of culture in general, intensified into an urgent restlessness and desire for change. Artists and intellectuals felt an overwhelming sense of alienation from a society they chose to view as irretrievably mired in the status quo of convention and tradition. It was a society dominated by the bourgeois and the philistine and as the century approached its end, belief in the inevitability of violent change became widespread. Since the orderly reconstitution of society and its values seemed ever more impossible to achieve, the perception took hold that if change was to come it would be only in the wake of some great upheaval, of an apocalypse. Cracks in the pillars of the despised society were becoming more and more visible and the greater the awareness of them the keener the sense of imminent fragmentation and disintegration. World War I, of course, with its awesome devastation, its transformation of the political map of Europe, and its redistribution of power, lay just around the corner. When it erupted, it was greeted by many with foreboding and exhilaration as the long anticipated cataclysm that would finally bury the old century beneath the dust and rubble of its outmoded institutions and monuments.

In the climate of that growing sense of fragmentation and imminent collapse, artists and intellectuals became increasingly bolder in their questioning—and ultimate rejection—of authority, increasingly more willing to challenge conventions and traditions. It was this ever widening contempt for authority, in whatever form, that gave rise to the avant-garde. As European culture entered a period of transition toward the end of the nineteenth century, as if in anticipation of the coming of the avant-garde, the cabaret emerged as a focal point of experimentation and innovation.[2] By serving as a gathering place for restless, disaffected, and defiant artists and their fellow-travelers, the cabaret rapidly developed into a kind of sanctuary within whose privacy and safety barbs could be hurled with impunity at the enemies of authority and philistinism just outside the gates, and forms of art cultivated which by their very nature flouted the accepted and approved. Far from being just a marginal activity, the cabaret occupied a forward position on the barricades of the great revolution that was then in the making. Indeed, it emerged *when* it did because of the undeniable appropriateness of the role it came to fulfill.

It is the contention of this book that the art both cultivated *and* represented by the cabaret is what the Germans call, in a single word, *Kleinkunst.* Literally translated, *Kleinkunst* means "small art." The phenomenon referred to is best understood as an "art of small forms," that is, an art consisting of genres traditionally regarded as minor, or marginal, in terms of so-called high culture. With hardly an exception, the genres of *Kleinkunst* cultivated in the turn-of-the-century European cabarets had already been in existence for some time. This is certainly true of the French popular song, the chanson. In some instances—pantomime, puppet, marionette, and shadow shows, for example—they go back to antiquity. By the late nineteenth century, when cabaret first began to appear, most, if not all, forms of *Kleinkunst* were associated in people's minds with popular culture, with the entertainment offered at fairs, circuses, musical halls (for which those in London often provided the model), or variety theaters (*variété,* in French), which enjoyed great popularity at the time in Paris, Rome, and Naples. These "small" forms, or genres, included: the popular song (chanson), generally sentimental, romantic, or patriotic; puppet and marionette shows, sometimes derived from a particular domestic tradition such as the Catalonian *putxinel-lis* or the Polish *szopka;* shadow shows (what the French call *ombres chinsoises,* "Chinese shadows," because of their presumed Oriental origin), consisting of the silhouettes of figures and scenes cut out of cardboard or some other material and projected onto a small screen by means of a background light; poems of a humorous, frequently satiric character, at times related to popular tradition such as the German *Bänkelsang* and *Moritat,* which dealt mostly with sensational happenings and were sung by street performers who set up shop on benches, often accompanying themselves on a fiddle or illustrating their songs by means of a poster-like canvas with scenes painted on it; dances, folk or popular in origin; one-act plays and dramatic sketches, often satirical or parodic; monologues, and other forms of recitation.

The preference for "small forms" on the part of the turn-of-the-century cabaretists was hardly coincidental. Quite the contrary; it was by means of the cultivation of genres long regarded as minor or marginal that the artists who created the great European cabaret culture of the late nineteenth and early twentieth centuries sought not only to break with tradition and convention, but to defy them. By turning to folk and popular culture for inspiration, by merging "high" and "low" art, by narrowing—or eliminating—the distance between spectator and performer, they signalled their disdain for the art of a society that had increasingly become less relevant to them. At the same time, they pointed the way to a revolution in taste that would set the stage for a new art. If cabarets were at the outset elitist virtually by definition, the art for which they became best known was anything but that. It drew much of its nourishment from popular sources and aimed, above all, at ending the hegemony of art that was either elitist by virtue of patronage or audience, or bourgeois by virtue of its standards and conventions.

The cabaret's nose-thumbing at contemporary art and society gave prominence to forms of *Kleinkunst* such as the chanson, the marionette and shadow show, and the short parodic play, which came to enjoy virtually universal cultivation wherever cabaret existed. But as cabaret spread, forms initially given their greatest impetus by the Parisian experience, such as the chanson—which was not everywhere assimilable with the same ease—were modified by local traditions and augmented by forms more characteristic of the indigenous culture. Although cabarets outside of Paris took the Parisian Chat Noir as their point of departure and often resembled each other in theme and style, the most renowned were shaped by, and accommodated, phenomena of distinctly local character. Thus, whatever the links between them and frequent similarities, no two were alike either in focus or formal preferences.

This was very much the case with the chanson, which was widely imitated throughout Europe but rarely successfully. The great revival of the genre in late nineteenth- and early twentieth-century France—to which its vigorous espousal by the Parisian cabaret contributed so importantly—had demonstrably French social, economic, and political stimuli. Cultivated especially by poets who came out of the antibourgeois, anti-establishment Bohème of the time and who were no strangers to poverty and human wretchedness, the chansons often sought to jar and shock by their pictures of urban misery, crime, and social injustice. Collectively representing a poetry of both the underworld and the "other world" of a Paris of want and degradation from which the well-fed and well-dressed chose to turn their eyes, the turn-of-the-century chansons had such a high degree of French, and Parisian, specificity that they crossed national boundaries only with considerable difficulty.

Satire and parody were also forged into effective weapons in the cabaret offensive against pretensiousness in high culture, smugness in society, and conservatism in politics. There was hardly a turn-of-the-century cabaret in which the reigning literary modes of naturalism and symbolism were not deflated, above all by means of parody. The principal targets were the acknowledged high priests of European naturalism, neoromanticism, and symbolism: the German Gerhart Hauptmann (1862–1946), whose drama about Silesian weavers, *Die Weber* (The Weavers, 1892), written originally in Silesian dialect, was regarded as the acme of European Naturalist drama, the Italian Gabriele D'Annunzio (1863–1938), viewed as ludicrous for his highly theatrical neoromantic posturing, and the Belgian Maurice Maeterlinck (1862–1949), an easy butt of cabaret parody for his eerie otherworldliness and exaggerated solemnity. In the strongly theatrically oriented cabarets of prerevolutionary Moscow and St. Petersburg, for example, satire and parody also took aim at such universal targets as Hauptmann, D'Annunzio, and Maeterlinck, but reserved their sharpest bite for such domestic phenomena as the widely esteemed but philosophically shallow playwright and prose writer Leonid Andreev (1871–1919) and for the Moscow Art Theater, respected abroad but at home regarded as a bastion of naturalism. Significantly, some of the leading figures in early twentieth-century Russian cabaret—the directors Vsevolod Meyerhold (1870–1940) and Nikolai Evreinov (1879–1953) and the critic Aleksandr Kugel (1864–1928)—were in the forefront of the campaign to resolve the contemporary "crisis" of the Russian stage by ending the hegemony of the imperial theater system, on the one hand, and the dominance of Stanislavsky's ultra-naturalistic methods of production and system of acting, on the other. Although conventionally not so regarded, the prerevolutionary Russian cabaret deserves to be accorded an important role in the movement to breathe fresh life into the stodgy Russian theater of the period by championing the cause of theatricality, or "re-theatricalized" theater.

Disaffection toward, at times outright defiance of, the established social and political order frequently accompanied repudiation of the established order in art. In the face of stern Prussian and Bavarian state censorship, the Berlin and Munich cabarets of the turn-of-the-century period had to be ever mindful of the programs they assembled, even when, as in the case especially of the Munich Elf Scharfrichter (Eleven Executioners), the most famous pre-World War I cabaret in all Germany, the private club status of the cabaret was as much an attempt to circumvent police surveillance as to preserve the ambience of an authentic circle of artists. Despite this need for caution, and the pressure of state and community against it, the early German cabaret articulated concern not only over the situation in contemporary art, but over numbing social conservatism, especially in the Bavarian context, and over the specter of rising nationalism and militarism embodied, above all, in Prussian ambitions and policies. In attempting to assert its right to challenge authority, the Munich cabaret hastened its own demise. At the same time, however, it paved the way for the dynamic cabaret culture of Weimar Germany whose fame rested, in large measure, on the extent to which it functioned as a microcosm of the sharpening social, economic, and political tensions of the 1920s and '30s.

Social rather than political conservatism engaged the satiric and parodic energies of the artists who established and frequented the most important cabaret of turn-of-the-century Poland, the Zielony Balonik (Green Balloon). Located in the old Polish capital of Cracow, in that part of Poland that had fallen to Austria in the Partitions of the late eighteenth century, the Green Balloon had even less latitude with respect to political satire than the contemporary German or Austrian cabarets. Always watchful for signs of nationalism among its Slavic minorities, especially the Poles, the imperial Hapsburg authorities kept close tabs on private undertakings such as cabarets, making it virtually impossible for the pre-World War I Polish cabaret to mount anything capable of being construed, or misconstrued, as an offense or challenge to Hapsburg authority. But despite this limitation, the Cracow cabaret, which was the most outstanding in Eastern Europe at the time, still found ample material for its programs in the conservatism and class-consciousness of Cracow and the paradoxical situation in which the tradition-bound ancient capital then found itself as the reluctant seat of a vigorous turn-of-the-century modernist movement referred to as "Young Poland." By and large supportive of modernism, the Cracow cabaret assigned itself the role of admonishing excesses in the development of this modernism just as it held up to ridicule the smug conservatism so vehemently opposed to it.

The close association of cabaret with progressive developments in the arts in Europe in the late nineteenth and early twentieth centuries was demonstrated on more than a single occasion. The Barcelona cabaret Els Quatre Gats (The Four Cats) and the later Vienna Fledermaus (Bat) enjoyed an even more intimate relationship with modernism than the Polish Green Balloon. In the case of the Cracow cabaret, a certain distance, even detachment, was kept as much from "Young Poland" modernism as from traditional Cracow conservatism. This way, the cabaret could feel free to aim its satiric barbs wherever it chose. The situation was different, however, in both Barcelona and Vienna. The most famous cabaret in Spanish history, Els Quatre Gats, was established by Catalonian artists who had spent time in France and identified with the new currents in French art. They had also become part of contemporary Parisian bohemian life as well as the world of the Montmartre cabaret.

When they returned to their native Catalonia, they were determined to advance the cause of modernist art, above all of a native Catalonian modernist painting—which included a figure such as Pablo Picasso—and toward this end founded the first cabaret in Barcelona on the model of the Parisian Chat Noir which they knew firsthand. Moreover, the promotion of Catalonian modernism by artists of the caliber of Santiago Rusiñol (1861–1931), Miguel Utrillo (1862–1934), the father of Maurice Utrillo, and Ramon Casas (1866–1932) became an integral aspect of the ardent championship of an emerging Catalonian nationalism. The late nineteenth century witnessed a resurgence of Catalonian political and cultural nationalism after a long period of repression and slumber. Identifying Catalonian modernism as a valuable component of a nationalist movement aimed at a restoration and enhancement of regional privileges within the framework of the Spanish administrative system, the Barcelona cabaret placed itself in the forefront of the most artistically and politically significant development in modern Catalonian history.

Located in the capital of the Hapsburg Empire, the Vienna cabaret lacked the nationalist dimension of the Quatre Gats of Barcelona. But its place in the evolution of a preeminent Austrian modernism was also important. At first an offshoot of the then defunct Munich Elf Scharfrichter, the Vienna cabaret took a little while to find its authentic Viennese identity. When it did, in the Fledermaus, the most brilliant of Viennese cabarets, it attracted the talents of almost every major artist of the period—the writers Karl Kraus, Hugo von Hofmannstahl, Hermann Bahr, Alfred Polgar, and Egon Friedell, the painters Gustav Klimt and Emil Orlik, the painter and dramatist Oskar Kokoschka, the caricaturist Carl Hollitzer, the graphic artist Berthold Löffler, the architects Adolf Loos and Josef Hoffmann, the stage and costume designers R. Josef Divéky, Kolo Moser, E. J. Wimmer-Wisgrill, and Fritz Zeymer, the dancers Gertrude Barrison and the Wiesenthal sisters. Apart from reflecting the ascendancy of the Vienna Secession, the Fledermaus cabaret drew heavily on the talents of artists associated with the vibrant school of Viennese applied art, the Wiener Werkstätte (Vienna Workshops), becoming not just an outlet for the Werkstätte, but, to all intents and purposes, an extension of them. Furthermore, the production of Kokoschka's little play *Sphinx und Strohmann* (Sphinx and Strawman) by the Fledermaus in 1909 gave the cabaret a place in the development of German-language Expressionist drama.

Although cabarets such as those in Cracow, Barcelona, and Vienna bore a close relationship to modernism in their respective countries, the Zurich Cabaret Voltaire, which was established by artists from other countries who were seeking a safe haven from the horrors of the World War, enjoys a special renown in the history of twentieth-century art as the birthplace of the Dada movement. The Cabaret Voltaire is the last to be dealt with in this book, both because it was the last major cabaret to appear before the end of the war and because it was the most extreme, the most revolutionary in its assault on the conventions and traditions of the bourgeois nineteenth century. In the bizarre violence of its mockery and rejection of the past, the Cabaret Voltaire became the logical culmination of the entire turn-of-the-century cabaret movement. No aspect of nineteenth-century society, no genre or style of traditional art was spared the lashes of Dadaist rebuke, and when rational discourse, language, and even meaning were brought under attack it was obvious that the turn-of-the-century European cabaret had played its role well in that transformation of sensibility that laid the groundwork for the avant-garde of the twentieth century.

The art of the cabaret was previously characterized as an art of "small forms." But the cabaret itself ought to be viewed as a "small form" art, a phenomenon of European cultural development which arose in a period of transition when a breakup, a fragmentation of the traditional structures of nineteenth-century art both accompanied and heralded the emergence of the avant-garde. Characteristic of this dismantling of the forms of nineteenth-century art, which paralleled the enthusiasm of turn-of-the-century artists and intellectuals for a dismantling of society itself, was a clear preference for smaller forms. Indeed, to speak of a decided tendency toward miniaturization would not at all be wide of the mark. This cultivation of small forms expressed itself in phenomena already marked: the chanson, the puppet, marionette, and shadow show, all of which could be easily accommodated by, and in fact were designed for, miniature stages; one-act plays and dramatic sketches, monologues, and so on. Elsewhere, the growing taste for small forms was reflected in a new interest in chamber music, in the spread of the little theater movement (the establishment of small chamber, or intimate theaters), in the loosening of novel and play structure through a type of segmentation in which unity gives way to the looser linkage of smaller, relatively more autonomous units, in the emergence of the feuilleton, the witty and pithy journalistic essay on any subject of interest to the author, so handsomely represented in Austria, for example, by such writers as Theodor Herzl (1860–1904), Herman Bahr (1863–1934), and Alfred Polgar (1873–1955), and in the cultivation of highly laconic writing, which typified the style of one of the outstanding characters in the turn-of-the-century Vienna cabaret, the archetypical bohemian Peter Altenberg (1899–1919), and reached the level of a *reductio ad absurdum* in the theory and practice of the Italian Futurists in the teens of the present century; it was in the programmatic *Il teatro futurista sintetico* (The Futuristic Synthetic Theater, 1915), after all, that its authors, Marinetti, Settimelli, and Cora, declared that "É stupido scrivere cento pagine dove ne basterebbe una" (It's stupid to write a hundred pages where one would suffice).[3]

In a period when accelerated change in many spheres of life intensified impatience with conventions and traditions now considered hindrances to progress, a restlessness with grand artistic designs and, in literature, with verbiage and stately periods would not have been unusual. A sense of imminent sweeping change, of tumultuous upheaval, also gave rise to a sense of impermanence. The result was not only the cultivation of laconicism, but of ephemerality as well, all epitomized in the art of the cabaret and in the cabaret itself as an art form. With few exceptions, the turn-of-the-century cabarets were short-lived, as transient as much of the art they presented. Adding to this sense of transience and expendability was their almost universal disavowal of commitment in art, a clear rejection of the social, moral, and other obligations imposed on art throughout the nineteenth century. To the cabaretists of the turn-of-the-century, art could best free itself from the tyranny of commitment by vigorously asserting its right to purposelessness, its freedom not to have meaning in any conventionally representational sense, its legitimacy as play. In its rejection of authority, its defiance of convention and tradition, its pursuit of the small and the fleeting, its eschewal of commitment, its spirit of play, the cabaret of the late nineteenth and early twentieth centuries was thus far more than a marginal diversion of the time. It could be viewed as the very symbol of those forces of change in sense and sensibility out of which the new art of the twentieth century was born.

A word now about the organization of this book. As an account of the emergence and spread of cabaret in turn-of-the-century Europe, it follows a logical chronological progression: it begins with the establishment of the first cabaret, the Chat Noir, in Paris in 1881, then traces the subsequent development of the cabaret movement throughout Europe, ending with the Cabaret Voltaire in Zurich in 1916–1917. As the birthplace of Dada, the Cabaret Voltaire is seen as the watershed reached by the development of the turn-of-the-century cabaret as an intimate, elitist, largely nonprofessional, minimally commercial, and artistically experimental performance environment. Cabaret continued to grow and even to flourish after World War I; in one form or another, it has survived to our own time. But with the exception of certain post-World War II cabarets, mostly student undertakings and notably in Germany and East Central Europe (where they arose primarily as a form of protest), the cabaret culture that developed after World War I became increasingly more commercial. Whatever the quality of the entertainment offered and however interesting as a mirror of (and outlet for) contemporary social and political antagonisms, as in interwar Germany (and so well depicted in the film *Cabaret* of 1972), the cabaret ceased to be the embodiment of a changing sensibility, the manifest anticipation of a new art, of the avant-garde.

When cabaret first emerged in turn-of-the-century Europe, in most instances on the initiative of artists themselves, it was an outgrowth of far-reaching transition in society and art; not only did it reflect and participate in that transition, it emerged from it as perhaps the most characteristic form of a dissolution of old structures which necessarily preceded the advent of the new. When that period of transition, that process of change had run its course and the old Europe of the nineteenth century had gone to its destruction in the hell fires of the first "world" war, the cabaret, as it existed in the turn-of-the-century, had also run its course. That it would continue to exist on the foundation of what had been built in the late nineteenth and early twentieth centuries was certainly to be expected; but that later cabaret would not be, indeed could not be, what it had been before should also come as no surprise.

For the sake of thoroughness, I would have liked, of course, to cover every significant manifestation of cabaret in turn-of-the-century Europe; however, that would have been patently out of the question, and not only for reasons of space. The cabarets included for discussion were not only the most important in their respective cultures, but among the most vibrant and interesting in Europe as a whole. Both necessity and selectivity governed my choices. Apart from Paris, Barcelona, Berlin, Munich,

Vienna, Moscow, St. Petersburg, and Zurich demanded inclusion for reasons of importance and representativeness. With respect to East Central Europe, my preference was for the most outstanding cabaret of one particular country, since coverage of the development of cabaret in such cities as Cracow, Warsaw, Prague, and Budapest would have made the final book grossly imbalanced. My choice fell on Cracow, on the Green Balloon, for several reasons: my strong personal interest in Polish culture, the earlier establishment and relatively greater significance of cabaret in Poland than elsewhere in East Central Europe, its curious relationship to its environment, its place in the development of Polish modernism, and the role played in it by one of the most engaging personalities of twentieth-century Polish literature, Dr. Tadeusz Żeleński ("Boy," 1874–1941).

Among major European cultures, England and Italy may seem surprisingly absent. Italy, in fact, had no significant turn-of-the-century cabaret—a fact acknowledged by the *Enciclopedia dello spettacolo* (Encyclopedia of the Stage)[4]—possibly because of cultural decentralization and regionalism and a relationship between artist and society that would have encouraged far more public forms of confrontation than cabaret. Moreover, the place of cabaret was taken, to a considerable extent, in my judgment, by the Futurist movement initiated by Filippo Tommaso Marinetti (1876–1944) in 1909. In its defiant, outrageous demolition of the conventional and traditional, its assault on the expectations and sensibilities of audiences, its embrace of novelty, its emphasis on speed and brevity (*simultaneità*), its advocacy of variety theater as the model for a new art of the stage, and its cultivation of small forms (the *sintesi,* or extremely short theatrical work, for example), futurism shared much in common with the turn-of-the-century cabaret. The Futurists also represented a type of community of artists bound together by a similarity of outlook and goals. If the Futurists performed for the most part in public places, the better to outrage their audiences, their *serate,* or "evenings," often had something of the quality of cabaret programs.

Cabaret came relatively late to England, and never seemed to enjoy the eager embrace of the form characteristic of its reception on the Continent. It was also alien from its very inception, another factor possibly contributing to its self-consciousness and tentativeness. The first English cabaret, called the Cabaret Theatre Club or the Cave of the Golden Calf, was opened in June 1912 by Frida (or Freda) Strindberg, the Swedish dramatist's second wife, an Austrian journalist whose maiden name was Maria Friedrike Cornelia Uhl (1872–1943). After the breakup both of her marriage to Strindberg and her liaison with the German poet, dramatist, and cabaretist Frank Wedekind (1864–1918)—from whom her interest in cabaret may well have derived—Frida Uhl Strindberg settled in London between 1910 and the approach of World War I, when she left for what proved to be a short stay in the United States. While in London, she established the Cabaret Theatre Club as a "modernist nightclub," in part motivated by an obsessive desire to stage Strindberg's plays in the English capital. Among the artists who helped decorate the premises of the Cave on Heddon Street, off Regent, were the sculptor Sir Jacob Epstein (1880–1959), the portrait painter Augustus John (1878–1961), with whom the ever romantic Frida had an affair,[5] and the avant-garde painter and writer Wyndham Lewis (1882–1957)—another, this time unsuccessful, target of Madame Strindberg's affections—a close associate of Ezra Pound and the founder of vorticism, a movement in art similar in certain respects to cubism and futurism. Wyndham Lewis, who painted the Club's murals (in what Violet Hunt calls "raw meat designs")[6] and also designed a brochure for it,[7] offers this description of its founding in his *Rude Assignment:*

> Strinberg [*sic*], the Swedish dramatist, had a number of wives, one being a Viennese. This very adventurous woman . . . rented an enormous basement. Hence the term "Cave." She had it suitably decorated with murals by myself, and number of columns by Jacob Epstein: hired an orchestra—with a frenzied Hungarian gypsy fiddler to lead it—a smart corps of Austrian waiters and an Austrian cook: then with considerable amount of press-promotion she opened as a night-club.
>
> With the Epstein figures appearing to hold up the threateningly low ceiling, the somewhat abstract hieroglyphics I had painted round the walls, the impassioned orchestra, it must have provided a kick or two for the young man about town of the moment. It was my first job . . . I did not receive a great deal for my night-club murals (actually £60). I was quite unknown, however, and would have done them for nothing.[8]

Clearly designed as a nightclub principally for the artists Frida Strindberg enjoyed cultivating rather than as a cabaret, in any strict sense, the Cave of the Golden Calf offered intimacy in an ambience of art where dining and dancing seemed to take precedence over any entertainments presented. The writer Sir Osbert Sitwell, a frequent visitor to the Cave, confirms its character in his autobiographical *Great Morning:*

the Cabaret Club, where the lesser artists of the theatre, as well as the greater, mixed with painters, writers, and their opposite, officers in the Brigade of Guards. This low-ceilinged night club, appropriately sunk below the pavement of Beak Street, and hideously but relevantly frescoed by the then mature Wyndham Lewis, appeared in the small hours to be a super-heated vorticist garden of gesticulating figures, dancing and talking, while the rhythm of the primitive forms of ragtime throbbed through the wide room. . . . Dancing more than conversation was the art which occupied the young men of the time in the Cabaret Club (I had taken with ease and delight to modern ballroom dancing).[9]

From a copy of the program[10] as well as from contemporary accounts, the Cave of the Golden Calf evidently did retain something of the character of a turn-of-the-century cabaret. Dances of different types, songs, including German lieder, "gypsy folklore," and "amateur plays" were presented.[11] So, too, were shadow shows, as we learn from a draft of a letter of Wyndam Lewis to the artist Cuthbert Hamilton dated Paris 1913:

I was concerned the other day at your ruffled state during the shadow-picture bustle. I hope that beastly Cabaret, that has been the cause of so many ridiculous vexations to me, is not going to add lessening of our good camaraderie to the number of its senseless misdeeds.[12]

The ubiquitous Marinetti, who also was to carry the banners of futurism to the St. Petersburg cabaret Brodyachaya sobaka (The Stray Dog) in early 1914, visited London frequently between 1912 and 1914 and graced the Cave of the Golden Calf with his presence in the fall of 1913. Wyndham Lewis describes the occasion briefly in a letter to Mrs. Percy Harris: "I was sorry you did not come to the Cabaret Club last night, as Marinetti declaimed some particularly bloodthirsty concoctions with great dramatic force."[13] Marinetti's more important appearances in London took place, however, not at the Cave, but at the Doré Galleries—which was a far more significant center of avant-garde art at the time—where he held forth on November 20, 1913, and again several times during 1914.

Thus, England, too, was affected by the cabaret fever to which the rest of Europe succumbed from 1881 to 1916. But whatever the participation in its activities by the likes of Sir Jacob Epstein, Augustus John, and Wyndham Lewis, the Cave of the Golden Calf never came to assume the place in contemporary art and society that the major cabarets of the Continent did. Whether because of her personality and foreign background, or because of the timidity and nonconfrontational nature of the English avant-garde of the time, Frida Strindberg's Cabaret Theatre Club—which lasted only as long as she remained in London to preside over it—faded away with little resonance, hardly more than a footnote in the history of twentieth-century English culture.

Two final technical notes about the book. Where good translations of non-English-language materials were available, I have chosen to use them for the sake of convenience; otherwise, all translations are my own except where indicated. Additionally, transliteration from Russian in the chapter on the Moscow and St. Petersburg cabaret conforms to a common, if imperfect, transliteration system.

ILLUSTRATIONS

TURN-OF-THE-CENTURY CABARET

CHAPTER ONE

PARIS: BLACK CATS AND REED PIPES

The Chat Noir, or Black Cat, with which the story of the cabaret begins, became a legend in its own time. From its opening in 1881 until its closing in 1897—a longevity itself remarkable in the history of the cabaret—it was a landmark of Montmartre, as familiar a part of the landscape of that then rustic village on the hill overlooking Paris as its windmills. The great success of the Chat Noir, as often happens, inspired a number of imitations in *fin-de-siècle* Paris giving rise to a veritable cabaret fever. But whatever success any of them achieved—and there were a few, like Aristide Bruant's Le Mirliton (The Reed Pipe), that came to enjoy much renown in their time—none developed the mystique of the Chat Noir. To the Parisian of the time and the many foreigners who sought it out on their visits to Paris, the Chat Noir was cabaret and cabaret was the Chat Noir.

The circle of artists who made up the cabaret were hardly unaware of the legend of which they were rapidly becoming a part and seldom missed an opportunity to enhance it. It was partly for that reason, for example, that the cabaret began to publish its own weekly magazine appropriately called *Le Chat Noir,* on January 14, 1882, less than a year after the cabaret itself had been established. Mainly as an outlet for literary compositions by writers associated with the cabaret, the magazine appeared every Saturday at a price of 15 centimes. Before long, *Le Chat Noir,* which consisted of only a few pages, was as successful in its own way as the parent cabaret; its title page illustration of a huge black cat, tail held high, its head cocked at a wry angle against the background of Montmartre and its windmills—the most prominent of which bears the name of the popular dance hall La Moulin de la Galette—became a familiar sight in the kiosks and cafés of Paris.

In addition to literary compositions by contemporary writers and those of past generations viewed as kindred spirits, *Le Chat Noir* also carried occasional articles about doings in Montmartre, of which it considered itself the voice, and about the Chat Noir cabaret. In its issue of May 27, 1882, a humorous announcement appeared which says much about the legend that had begun to grow up about the cabaret and the way the Chat Noir took delight in fostering its own image. Under the heading "Justice Has Been Done," the announcement proceeds to inform in mock-serious tone that

> By a huge majority, the Chamber of Deputies has declared the Cabaret of the Black Cat of public worth and has added it to the number of historical monuments of France. This unique thing in the world will thus not have to endure the ravages of time. The prefect of the Seine has received the order to isolate this cabaret in the middle of a square planted with exotic trees on which poets could hang their lyres.
>
> This cabaret is the most Astonishing, Wondrous, Bizarre, Magnificent, Astounding, Vibrant Creation of ages that have long since fallen to the Scythe of Time.
>
> Founded by Julius Caesar, one can behold it in the glasses with which were served Charlemagne, Villon, Rabelais, Cardinal Richelieu, the Duchess de Chevreuse, Mme. de Rambouillet, Mlle. de Scudery, Louis XIV, Mme. de la Vallière, Voltaire, Diderot, Robespierre, Bonaparte, Mme. de Stael and Mme. Récamier, Baudelaire, Baour-Lormain, George Sand, Sapeck, Goudeau.
>
> Ask to see the lyre of Victor Hugo and the sonorous lute of Charles Pitou and Clovis Hugues, the pockmarked poet.[1]

Its tongue-in-cheek bombast and humor notwithstanding, the Chat Noir had indeed become something of a national monument. That its success far exceeded even the lofty aspirations of its founder, Rodolphe Salis (1852–1897), goes without saying.

The son of a conservative and mildly prosperous distiller in Châtellerault, in the Department of Vienne, Salis decided as a young man that his future lay in art, for which he displayed some talent, rather than in the family distillery business. Despite the stern objections of his father, for whom the career of a painter lacked respectability, young Rodolphe was firm in his resolve to pursue his muse. Consequently, he left Châtellerault to study painting in Paris at the Ecole des Beaux-Arts. With only a little money from his mother to support him (200 francs, to be exact), Salis had to work while pursuing his studies. He managed to earn modest sums by painting landscapes for a dealer named Borniche who bought cheap and sold high, mostly to Americans, or mass producing, together with three friends in similar financial straits, "Stations of the Cross" paintings for a store selling religious objects in the vicinity of the Saint-Sulpice.[2] The later enterprise was concealed beneath a cloak of artistic integrity in the form of a school of art called "l'École Vibrant" "founded" by Salis for the purpose of reforming pictorial art; hardly was the "school" founded than its name was changed from "l'École Vibrant" to the more fanciful "École Iriso-Subversive de Chicago."

The change of name did nothing, alas, to improve the financial position of Salis and his comrades-in-brush. The market for religious paintings, particularly the sort turned out by the "École Vibrant"/"École Iriso-Subversive de Chicago," was then sluggish and before too much time elapsed the whole enterprise was dropped and the four-way partnership dissolved. Desperate for funds, Salis returned to his native Châtellerault in the hope that time had healed all wounds and his father might now look more benevolently upon his errant son. But the old man proved as stubborn as ever and were it not for the limited largesse of his mother, Salis would have left with nary a sou. The visit produced another gain in the form of a local beauty who agreed to become his wife. But the fair Hélène was of frail constitution and unable to withstand the rigors and privations of her husband's bohemian life style in Paris. Her failing health necessitated a return visit to Châtellerault by a now desperate Salis wholly dependent on his family for the money needed to provide proper care for his wife. It was too late, however, and Hélène, whom he had left behind in Paris while he was away, died. What followed now for Salis was a period of mourning, a tour of military service during the Franco-Prussian War of 1870–71, and a prodigal-like conciliatory reunion in Châtellerault with *père* Salis who at last agreed to help his son with the proviso that he remarry and find some "useful" occupation. Bowing perhaps to the inevitable, Salis accepted his father's terms, renouncing painting and becoming affianced to a red-haired beauty of property whom he had met in the house of his parents.

Following his marriage in the town hall of Montmartre on the Rue des Abbesses in 1880 and the setting up of a modest household on the Rue Germaine-Pilon, Salis again had to wrestle with the problem of how to earn a living. He finally decided to open a café, a decision his distiller father rejoiced at when he heard the news.

Salis' ambitions at first were modest. What he probably had in mind was a small drinking place that would attract customers primarily because of its décor, something along the lines of the popular artists' watering-hole, the Cabaret de la Grande Pinte, on the Avenue Trudaine. The location on which he finally settled was a tiny shop at 84 Boulevard Rochechouart which had been used as a post office but was now vacant and up for rental at a price of 1,400 francs a year. The principal attraction of the vest-pocket former post office seems to have been the fact that it just happened to be very near the Grande Pinte. Competition, it seems, was much on Salis' mind. While pondering what to call his establishment, Salis happened upon a short-haired black cat perched atop a street lamp. He took the cat home with him and then hit on the idea of naming his café after it. Thus was the Chat Noir born. A picture of the cat painted by the artist Adolphe Willette, whom Salis had met in Montmartre and was on friendly terms with, was hung in the café's window.[3]

Once a name for his establishment had been settled, Salis next addressed the matter of décor. He wanted something unusual, something that would appeal especially to the artists he hoped would become "regulars" at the Chat Noir. What he eventually decided upon was what he liked to call "Louis XIII style." The walls were hung with time-worn tapestries; covers from old chests were used to fashion a kind of cashier's box above which hung a huge golden sun with shining rays, which might have been acquired from the demolition of some church; huge nails served as coat hooks. On the right side of the room stood an enormous fireplace with a mantelpiece full of copper objects, pewter mugs, and antique pitchers. The hearth contained kitchen firedogs with pothangers one of which was used as a perch for a crow named Bazouge which Willette had brought back from Trouville.[4] As legend has it, the crow lasted only a few months, dying from excess consumption of absinthe and bitter Picon. Further description of the interior of the Chat Noir comes from the pen of the poet Émile Goudeau (1872–1943) whose role in the establishment and success of the cabaret was, in its own way, even greater than that of Salis:

On a corner of the counter stood a bust, the "Unknown Woman" of the Louvre, and above it an enormous cat's head surrounded by golden rays such as one sees in churches around the symbolic triangle. In back, a second smaller room three steps higher had its own belt, equal to a man's height, of diamantine panels highlighting the tapestries above which the famous nails of the "Passion" supported old flintlocks and obsolete swords; the high fireplace—which fortunately bore little resemblance to the other one—replaced the antique knickknacks with a cheerful and quite modern stoker at which aim was taken by a semicircle of the feet of the painters and sculptors who sought out the place first as well as by those also of the poets and musicians who lost no time in arriving—following in the footsteps of us "Hydropathes."[5]

The Hydropathes

The "Hydropathes" mentioned by Goudeau were a loose circle of artists (mostly poets), headed by Goudeau himself and formally called the "Club des Hydropathes.[6] It was they who first brought fame to the Chat Noir and attracted other artists to follow them there. Goudeau had come to Paris from his native Périgueux in 1879 and settled in the Latin Quarter, which was then the center of the Parisian literary and academic *Bohème*. While employed as a supernumerary at the Ministry of Finance he pursued an active career as a poet, scoring a success with his first book of poems, *Les Fleurs de bitume* (Flowers of Asphalt), for which Anatole France, among others, had high praise. What distinguished Goudeau from many of the other young poets who made their home in or frequented the Latin Quarter in the 1870s and '80s was a certain organizational talent and drive. Dissatisfied with the itinerant life style of Latin Quarter poets who moved restlessly from one café to another, Goudeau had the idea of forming a literary circle that would come together more or less regularly in some places where they could declaim their poetry in a freedom and privacy unavailable in the cafés. The first "home" of the as yet unnamed circle was the first floor premises of the Café de la Rive-Gauche located at the corner of the Rue Cujas and the Boulevard Saint-Michel. Arrangements were worked out with the owner of the café permitting Goudeau and company to have exclusive use of the premises one evening a week in exchange for a guarantee of a minimum of twenty persons; the proprietor wanted to be sure, after all, that the privacy he was making available would not entail too much of a financial sacrifice. The first gathering of the group with not the minimum twenty but sixty people in attendance took place on Friday, October 11, 1878. It was on this occasion that the circle formally adopted the name Le Club des Hydropathes, which was suggested by Goudeau, and nominated Goudeau himself its first president.

As to what the Club des Hydropathes represented and the origin of the name "Hydropathes" Goudeau provided explanations in a retrospective article in the paper *Le Matin* on December 13, 1899:

> It was a noisy and merry association of young men from the Latin Quarter: poets, musicians, painters, actors, and students. They were twenty years old; it was twenty years ago. . . .
>
> This association with its bizarre name had an original idea for that time: to bring together around poets declaiming their verse, around musicians performing their songs, a numerous group of free auditors. . . . The founders of the "Hydropathes" appealed to the crowd, and the crowd came. . . .
>
> One evening in October 1878 . . . some musicians and poets came together to chat about art and sing songs alongside a piano in the small room of a large café, until a group of schoolboys who were on their way to regain the school invaded the place and demolished three quarters of the unfortunate harpsichord.
>
> After they left, we resolved, my friends and I, to insist that the proprietor grant us the place entirely to ourselves. Seeing that there were only five of us, the fellow told us that he was unable to do us such a favor except on the condition that there were at least about twenty of us . . . "for the sake of consumption," he added.
>
> The next day, there were sixty young people and the day after, one hundred and fifty. O glory! It was an impossible meeting. Naturally, we set up an office. I had the honor of being named president.
>
> And then when the question arose as to what name to give this association that came into being so vigorously, various ones were proposed. But, exercising my presidential prerogative, I caused the perhaps incomprehensible but resounding name of "Hydropathe" to emerge victorious in the final vote.
>
> And now, if you would like to know what "hydropathe" means, here is the answer. In the ministry where I was attached—badly attached at that—I had acquired the nickname of "hydropathe," because of the fact that for several days, as loudly as possible, I had asked the meaning of the German word *Hydropathen* which was the title of a waltz by maestro [Joseph] Gung'l, *Hydropathen Waltz,* which was played often in those days.
>
> When I succeeded in giving this name to our association, I pretended to believe that it was the name of some legendary animal that is supposed to have had crystal paws: *pathen* [paws—HBS]; *hydro:* of crystallized water. It was just whimsy and I had fun with it.[7]

Perhaps with the passage of time Goudeau had become more modest about the origin of the name Hydropathes. Otherwise, it seems rather unlikely that even twenty years later, in the piece in *Le Matin,* he had forgotten that when the Hydropathes issued their own journal, called

L'Hydropathe, the first number of January 22, 1879, contained a lead article by Goudeau himself on the etymology of the name "Hydropathe." The humorous pseudoetymology, which is too long to quote here, traces the origin of his own family name from the Stone Age down to the nineteenth century in order to demonstrate that the word "hydropathe" derived from a Greek analogy (*udor patain*) to his own patronymic which early in history had been Govd-Eav but eventually was corrupted into Goud-Eau by municipal officials, finally becoming simply Goudeau. But to those to whom the drinking habits of Goudeau and his friends were well known, the true source of "hydropathe" lay in the ironic reading of the poet's name as "goût d'eau" (taste for water).

The large, heterogeneous membership of the Club des Hydropathes included musicians, painters, monologuists, déclamateurs, and literary types of one sort or another in addition to poets. Many have long since been forgotten, now just entries in French literary dictionaries; in their time, several were among the most highly regarded and popular writers and *chansonniers* (composers and singers of chansons) in the Latin Quarter; others were to enjoy their greatest fame in the era of the Chat Noir and its epigones.

The ranks of Hydropathes poets included, besides Goudeau, Albert Samain, Georges Lorin, a poet, painter, and sculptor who soon assumed editorship of the *L'Hydropathe* journal, the Greek Jean Moréas (real name, Vannis Papadiamantopolous), the prolific Jean Richepin, the still highly regarded Maurice Rollinat, Charles Cros, the inventor of a phonograph slightly before Edison and a close friend of Rimbaud and Verlaine, André Gill, Paul Marrot, Maurice Bouchor, Gaston Senéchal, and Edmond Haraucourt; the principal *chansonniers* were Jules Jouy and Maurice Mac-Nab, eventually to be acknowledged as two of the outstanding artists of the turn-of-the-century French chanson. Alphonse Allais (1854–1905), whose popularity as a writer of humorous stories lasted long after his death, was the group's leading *fumiste,* which French dictionaries generally define as a jokester, but which can also mean a teller of amusingly outlandish tales of which Allais was a recognized master.

Although the artistic output of the Hydropathes was as varied as the group's membership, certain patterns and tendencies are discernible. Most of the artists were young men (the entire group included, by the way, only a single woman, the poet and musical composer Marie-Ann, or Maria, Krysinska, who was of Polish extraction), of libertarian and egalitarian persuasion, antibourgeois, anti- and unconventional, contemptuous of the Establishment (but willing to accept employment in its institutions and offices for the sake of income), and very much a part of the spirit and style of the late nineteenth-century Latin Quarter. In their literary works and chansons they often sang of the Latin Quarter, its people, its ambience, just as they were to do of Montmartre to which many of them migrated in the era of the Black Cat. Almost to the man, they were writers of the city, not indifferent to the beauties and mysteries of nature, but strongly attuned to the sounds and sights of the city, above all of Paris, celebrators of the great capital in its parts and as the sum of its parts.

Primarily poets, the Hydropathes tended to be more daring in content than form. Their attitude to life and art was often irreverent and devil-may-care. The lightness, casualness, whimsy, and even absurdity of their poetry barely concealed an intended mockery of convention, social as well as artistic. Take, for example, Charles Cros' "Le Hareng Saur" (The Salt Herring), which became a Hydropathes classic in its own time. The poem is brief enough to quote in full:

Il était un grand mur blanc—nu, nu, nu,
Contre le mur une échelle—haute, haute, haute,
Et, par terre, un hareng saur—sec, sec, sec.

Il vient, tenant dans ses mains—sales, sales, sales,
Un marteau lourd, un grand clou—pointu, pointu, pointu,
Un peloton de ficelle—gros, gros, gros.

Alors il monte à l'échelle—haute, haute, haute,
Et plante le clou pointu—toc, toc, toc,
Tout en haut du grand mur blanc—nu, nu, nu.

Il laisse aller le marteau—qui tombe, qui tombe, qui tombe,
Attache au clou la ficelle—longue, longue, longue.
Et, au bout, le hareng saur—sec, sec, sec.

Il redescend de l'échelle—haute, haute, haute,
L'importe avec le marteau—lourd, lourd, lourd;
Et puis, il s'en va ailleurs,—loin, loin, loin.

Et depuis, le hareng saur—sec, sec, sec,
Au bout de cette ficelle—longue, longue, longue,
Très lentement se balance—toujours, toujours, toujours.

J'ai composé cette histoire,—simple, simple, simple,
Pour mettre en fureur les gens—graves, graves, graves,
Et amuser les enfants—petits, petits, petits.[8]

The poem was an instant hit with the Hydropathes who responded to its whimsical nonsensicality and for whom the last two lines—*Pour mettre en fureur les genes—graves, graves, graves, / Et amuser les enfants—petits, petits, petits*—wholly accorded with their own inclinations. The following translation into English was recited at one of the Hydropathes soirées by Alphonse Allais, who took it from the *Memoirs of my Dead Life* (1906, p. 92) of George Moore (1852–1933):

The Song of the "Salt Herring"

He came along holding in his hands dirty, dirty, dirty,
A big nail pointed, pointed, pointed,
And a hammer heavy, heavy, heavy,
He propped the ladder high, high, high,
Against the wall white, white, white,
He went up the ladder high, high, high,
Placed the nail pointed, pointed, pointed,
Against the wall—toc! toc! toc!
He tied to the nail a string long, long, long,
And at the end of it a salt herring heavy, heavy, heavy,
He got down from the ladder high, high, high,
Picked up the hammer and went away, away, away.
Since then at the end of the string long, long, long,
A salt herring dry, dry, dry,
Has swung slowly, slowly, slowly.
Now I have composed this story simple, simple, simple,
To make all serious men mad, mad, mad,
And to amuse little children tiny, tiny, tiny.[9]

Verlaine, who was also fond of the Cros poem, referred to it in his essay on Cros in *Les Hommes d'aujourd'hui* (Men of Today, 1885–1893) as "angélique enfantillage justement célèbre" (justly famous angelic childishness);[10] Coquelin cadet (Ernest Alexandre Honoré Coquelin), a well-known actor in the Comédie Française who gained additional fame for his recitations of Charles Cros' monologues, devoted a dozen pages of the book *L'Art de dire le monologue* (The Art of Reciting Monologues, Paul Ollendorff, Paris, 1884; pp. 98–109), which he co-authored with his actor-brother Coquelin ainé (Benoit Constant Coquelin), to different possible interpretations of "Le Hareng Saur."

The Hydropathes not only wrote poems in a spirit of childish play, but also made children and animals subjects of their works. At times, the outward humor of the poems contrasts with an underlying social point of view. In André Gill's "Le Levrette et le gamin" (The Greyhound and the Urchin) a street urchin from the poor Paris district of Villette finds an unusual way to revenge his being peed upon by the elegant greyhound of a marquise from the fashionable Germain neighborhood. The urchin follows the greyhound and the liveried servant walking it after the mishap in the Tuilleries Gardens, kidnaps the dog when he has a chance, takes it back to the Villette, and there mates it with a frightful poodle. The dishonored greyhound later gives birth to a half dozen ugly, foul bastards. But, says Gill, the best part of the story is that as if imitating the behavior of her greyhound, the marquise took her own coachman as a lover shortly thereafter. Concludes Gill:

Quel triomphe pour la Villette!
Quel deuil pour le faubourg Germain![11]

(What a triumph for Villette! / What grief for the Germain district!)

In one of his more imaginative poems, "La Revanche des Bêtes et la Revanche des Fleurs" (The Revenge of Animals and the Revenge of Flowers), Émile Goudeau took as his unusual subject the cruelty and abuse man inflicts on animals and his depopulation of the forests and seas. In the nature of an indictment, the poem opens with a recitation of horrors:

Tu tapes sur ton chien, tu tapes sur ton âne;
  Tu mets un mors à ton cheval,
Férocement tu fais un spectre de ta canne,
  Homme, roi de Règne animal;
Quand tu trouves un veau tu lui rotis la foie;
  Et bourres son nez de persil;
Tu tailles dans le boeuf, vieux laboureur qui ploie,
  Des biftecks saignant, sur le gril . . .[12]

(You strike at your dog, you strike at your donkey; / You fasten a bit on your horse; / You savagely make a specter of your walking-stick, / Man, King of the Animal Kingdom. / When you find a calf, you roast its liver, / And stuff its nose with parsley. / From the steer, old plowman bent from toil, / You carve bloody beefsteaks on the grill . . .)

But a day of reckoning will come when man will be nailed to planks by Eternity and *le mangeur será mangé* (the eater will be eaten).[13] With child-like delight, Goudeau then graphically describes the way the animals will take their revenge, tearing man piece by piece. In a lyrical finale, Goudeau finds an ultimate reprieve for man in his kindness to flowers. Their roots will descend to retrieve the torn pieces of man and to veil their decay beneath a shroud of gold and azure. Ambassador butterflies dispatched by Mother Nature will fly above the tomb of man ready to bestow the kiss of pardon sent by the animals when man himself will at last have become a flower.

Poems about drinking, a subject close to the Hydropathes' hearts, were immensely popular. Besides Maurice Bouchor's "Beuverie flamande" (A Flemish Drinking Party) and "La Gloire des nez" (The Glory of Noses)[14] and Gaston Senéchal's "Chanson à boire" (Drinking Song),[15] one of the most popular of all was Émile Goudeau's unfinished epic-like "Les Polonais" (The Poles). The merry poem, about a punitive Polish campaign against the French who have spurned Alcohol, the God of Drink, and have turned to water and withheld all their wine and cognac from him, begins this way:

En ce temps-là, le duc Jean Soulografieski,
Prince des Polonais et Ruthènes, à qui
Sa soif de Danaîde avait donné la gloire,
Descendit longuement de son trône, et, sans boire,
Dit aux ivrognes vieux qui formaient son conseil:
"L'heure est enfin sonnée au cadran du soleil,
"L'heure où sur les Gaulois, ces buveurs à vergogne,
"Devra prédominer l'étendard de Pologne
"L'étendard rouge, et jaune, et blanc, drapeau divin
"Dont la forme est bouteille, et dont le fond est vin."[16]

(At that time, Duke Jan Soulografieski,/Prince of the Poles and Ruthenians, whose/Bottomless thirst of the Danaids was the source of his glory,/At length descended his throne, and, without drinking,/Said to the old drunkards who formed his council:/"The hour has finally struck at the sun dial,/The hour when the flag of Poland,/The red, yellow, and white flag, divine banner,/Whose shape is that of a bottle against a background of wine,/Must predominate over the Gauls, those modest drinkers.)

Maurice Mac-Nab, whose fame was to rest principally on his contributions to the genre of the Parisian chanson, splendidly upheld the libertine tradition of the Hydropathes in his own poems. One of his most celebrated is a ballad lamenting women's cold behinds, "Ballade des derrièrs froids" (Ballad of Cold Behinds). The source of the poet's chagrin is established in the first stanza:

Aux baisers caressants de vos lèves calines,
O femmes, j'ai parfois ranimé mes ardeurs,
En votre chair rosée enfonçant mes canines
J'a dejeuné d'amour et diné d'impudeurs
Au fond de vos boudoirs pleins d'exquises odeurs.
Et pourtant, c'est en vain que ma main promenée
Sur vas reins, a cherché la chaleur incarnée:
Séjour incombustible ainsi qu'un coffre-fort,
Ou j'ai trouvé toujours (Etrange destinée),
La froideur du derrière, image de la mort.[17]

(With the caressing kisses of your coaxing lips,/O women, I've sometimes revived my ardor,/And plunging my teeth into your pink flesh/I've lunched on love and dined on immodesties/Against the background of your bedrooms full of exquisite scents./Yet nevertheless, 'tis in vain that my hand, passing/Over your loins, sought heat incarnate./Incombustible abode as well as strongbox,/ Where I've always found (Strange Destiny)/The cold of the behind, image of death.)

Characteristically, perhaps, it was also Mac-Nab who found material for poetry in the human fetus. The point of the poem "Les Foetus" (Fetuses) is that the unborn baby really does not have such a bad life. In fact, it can even be envied:

Gentils foetus, ah! que vous êtes
Heureux d'avoir rangé vos têtes
Loin de nos humaines tempêtes!

Heureux, sans vice ni vertu;
D'indifférence revêtu,
Votre coeur n'a jamais battu.

Et vous seuls vous savez, peut-être,
Si c'est le suprême bien-être
Que d'être mort avant de naitre![18]

(Dear fetuses! Ah! How fortunate you are/For having placed your heads/Far from our human tempests!/Fortunate, with neither vice nor virtue;/Cloaked in indifference,/Your hearts have never known strife./And you alone, perhaps,/ Know if it is the supreme well-being/To be dead before being born!)

Since drinking was never long out of the Hydropathes' thoughts, Mac-Nab also finds a way of introducing this theme into his reflections on the good life of the fetus:

Foetus, au fond de vos bocaux,
Dans les cabinets médicaux,
Nagez toujours entre deux eaux,

Démontrant que tout corps solide
Plongé dans l'élément humide
Déplace son—poids de liquide!

C'est ainsi que, tranquillement,
Sans changer de gouvernement,
Vous attendrez le Jugement![19]

(Fetuses, at the bottom of your jars,/Inside medicine chests,/Swim always under water,/Demonstrating that every solid body,/Submerged in a watery element,/Displaces its weight in liquid!/And thus, quietly,/Without changing course,/You will soften Judgment!)

If his poem has to have a moral, which he supposes it does, Mac-Nab concludes that

C'est qu'en dépit des prospectus
De tous nos savants, les foetus
Ne sont pas les gens mal f . . .[20]

(In spite of the views/Of all our scientists, fetuses/Are not at all a f. . . . d up lot!)

That not all of the poetry of the Hydropathes was amusing, whimsical, offbeat, or erotic is amply attested by the work of two serious poets who enjoyed a close relationship with the Parisian cabaret of the late nineteenth century, Maurice Rollinat (1846–1903) and Jean Richepin (1849–1926). Although Rollinat's first collection of verse, *Dans les brands* (In the Heather, 1877), met with little success, his second volume, *Les Névroses* (Neurotics, 1883), established his reputation, although even then he never became a popular poet. The ability of the Hydropathes to accommodate a broad range of poetic creativity is nowhere better exemplified than in the case of Rollinat. His feeling for music and his skill at playing accompaniment to his own songs on the piano made him a prominent figure at Hydropathes soirées. Indeed, so fond of Rollinat's songs was the great chanteuse of turn-of-the-century Paris, Yvette Guilbert (1865–1944), that she incorporated a number of them into her own repertoire. But Rollinat's deeply pessimistic outlook on life, his taste for the morbid and macabre were atypical of the poetry of the Hydropathes and were only partially offset by his poems in an amorous vein. "Le

Chambre," which was dedicated to Charles Cros, typifies the bleakness Rollinat perceived both around and inside himself:

Ma chambre est pareille à mon âme,
Comme la mort l'est au sommeil:
Au fond de l'âtre, pas de flammes!
À la vitre, pas de soleil!

Les murailles sont recouvertes
D'un lamentable papier gris
Où l'ombre des persiennes vertes
Met des taches de vert-de-gris. . . .

Compagnon de ma destinée,
Un crâne brisé, lisse et roux,
Du haut de l'humble cheminée
Me regarde avec ses deux trous.

Meubles, tableaux, fleurs, livres, même,
Tout sent l'enfer et le poison,
Et, comme un drap, l'horreur, qui m'aime
Enveloppe cette prison.

Triste chambre où l'ennui qui raille
Veille à mes côtes nuit et jour,
J'écris ces vers sur ta muraille,
Et je benis ton noir séjour;

Car le torrent aime le gouffre,
Et le hibou, l'obscurité;
Car tu plais à mon coeur qui souffre
Par ton affreuse identité![21]

(My room is like my soul, / Like death it is asleep. / In the back of the hearth, there are no flames! / In the window, there is no sun! / The walls are covered / With a lamentable gray paper / On which the shadow of green shutters / Deposits stains of verdigris. / Companion of my destiny, / A broken skull, smooth and reddish, / Observes me through its two holes / From the top of a modest fireplace. /

Furniture, pictures, flowers, books, I myself / Reek of hell and poison, / And, like a sheet, the horror that loves me / Envelops this prison. / Sad chamber in which the boredom that watches over me / Sits by my side day and night, / I write this verse on your wall, / And I bless your black abode; / Since the torrent loves the abyss, / And the owl the darkness; / Since you please my heart which suffers from your frightful likeness.)

Even when writing about love, as in the poem "L'Amour," which was set to music, Rollinat yielded none of his bleakness and despair, none of his fondness for images of the corrosive and murderous:

L'Amour est un ange malsain
Qui frémit, sanglote et soupire,
Il est plus moelleux q'un coussin,
Plus subtil que l'air qu'on respire,
Plus provocant qu'un spadassin.

Chacun cède au mauvais dessein
Que vous chuchote et vous inspire
Le Dieu du meurtre et du larcin,
L'Amour.

Il voltige comme un essaim.
C'est le prestigieux vampire
Qui nous saigne et qui nous aspire,

Et nul n'arrache de son sein
Ce perfide et cet assassin,
L'Amour.[22]

(Love is an unhealthy angel / Who shudders, sobs, and sighs. / He is softer than a cushion, / More delicate than the air you breathe, / More provocative than a hired thug! / Everyone yields to the evil design / That you whisper and inspire, / God of crime and larceny, Love. / He flits about like a swarm, / He is the marvelous vampire / Who bleeds us and sucks us, / And no one can uproot from his breast / This treacherous person and murderer, Love.)

Jean Richepin (1849–1926) was hardly more cheerful a poet than Rollinat. Among the Hydropathes and the devotees of the turn-of-the-century Parisian cabaret he was most admired for the poems contained in such volumes as *La Chanson des gueux* (The Beggars' Song, 1876) and *Les Blasphèmes* (Blasphemies, 1884).[23] In their time, both collections were considered scandalous in different ways, a fact that merely raised Richepin in the esteem of the bohemian literary community of the Latin Quarter and Montmartre. *La Chanson des gueux* introduced not only the Paris of the slums and back alleys, of the poor and the homeless, of prostitutes and pimps, of drifters, thieves, and petty criminals of every hue and stamp, but also the idiom, the argot of this other Paris. Underlying Richepin's choice of subject was no mere fascination with the darker and seamier sides of Parisian life, with the indigent and criminal as a source of literary novelty, but a keen social consciousness. Richepin was an enemy of privilege and injustice, a stern critic of the existing social and economic system at whose doorstep he laid responsibility for poverty and crime. The poem "Noël Misérable," which Jules Lévy included in his anthology of Hydropathe prose and poetry, typifies the mood of the *Chanson des gueux* as a whole

Noël! Noël! A l'indigent
Il faudrait bien un peu d'argent,
Pour acheter du pain, des nippes.
Petits enfants, petits Jésus,
Des argents que vous avez eus
Il aurait bourré bien des pipes. . . .

Et le misérable là-bas
Voit la crèche comme un cabas
Bondé de viande et de ripaille,
Et dans lequel surtout lui plaît
Un beau petit cochon de lait . . .
C'est l'enfant Jésus sur la paille.

Noël! Noël! Le prêtre dit
Que Dieu parmi nous descendit
Pour consoler le pauvre hère.
Celui-ci voudrait bien un peu
Boire à la santè de bon Dieu;
Mais Dieu n'a rien mis dans son verre. . . .

Noël! Noël! Les malheureux
N'ont rien pour eux qu'un ventre creux
Qui tout bas grogne comme un fauve,
Si bien que le bourgeois, voyant
Leur oeil dans l'ombre flamboyant,
Au lieu de leur donner, se sauve.[24]

(Christmas! Christmas! The poor man / Needs a little money / To get some bread, some old rags to wear. / Little children, little Jesuses, / From the money you've gotten, / He'd have plenty to stuff his pipes with. / And the wretch over there / Sees the crèche as a basket / Crammed full of meat and goodies / And in which he especially likes / A nice little suckling pig . . . / It's the infant Jesus on the straw. / Christmas! Christmas! The preacher declares / That God descended among us / For the purpose of bringing consolation / To the poor wretch. / He, the wretch, would indeed be quite happy / To drink to the health of the good Lord; / But God put nothing in his glass. . . . / Christmas! Christmas! The unfortunate / Have nothing for themselves except an empty stomach / That growls deeply like a wild beast, / So that the bourgeois, When he sees their faces in the burning shadows, / Instead of giving them anything, runs away.)

The irreverence and cynicism in a poem on the greatest holiday in the Christian calendar serves as a kind of introduction to the repudiation of Christian belief and doctrine of *Les Blasphèmes,* which brought Richepin still greater scandal and controversy than the *Chanson des gueux.* In this later collection of poems Richepin carried his indignation and outrage at social injustice to its logical extreme: there is no God, there is no life after death, organized religion and especially Christianity are a mockery, the world itself is but chaos, life a dreary monotony meaning nothing, leading nowhere, governed only by chance. Man's only response to the world around him should be laughter, *le consolateur des hommes* (the consoler of men), as he puts it in the poem "Diagnostic."[25]

The importance of the Hydropathes to the subsequent development of cabaret in Paris explains the length to which they have been treated here. Before a fatal schism erupted in their ranks, mostly over the matter of a preference of some for outlandish practical jokes that others in the group became increasingly less patient with, the Hydropathes represented the first major step in the evolution of the *fin-de-siècle* Parisian cabaret. Their numbers became too large, their places of meeting too characterless and subject to change, their soirées perhaps too eclectic and impromptu, too unstructured, for the loose association of artists to become more than what we may regard as a proto-cabaret. But for all their diversity and eclecticism, the Hydropathes did share common points of view. They were largely younger people, iconoclastic, irreverent, rebellious, defiant of conventions, passionately antibourgeois, and by and large indifferent to public opinion. Their purpose in coming together as they did reflected awareness of similarities that created a bond among them and an obvious desire to be mutually supportive. They were the bohemian artists of the Latin Quarter and they were proud of it.

After the "official" inauguration of the group on October 17, 1878, at the Café de Rive-Gauche, it was only a matter of time, and not much at that, before other artists of the Latin Quarter came to share their soirées and drinking parties. As their ranks swelled, the premises of the Café de Rive-Gauche became too cramped and otherwise inhospitable and a new, larger location was found after the tenth evening at the *hôtel* Boileau, situated at number 19 on the same Rue Cujas. The success of the "club" led to the launching in 1879 of an ancillary enterprise, a journal or magazine called appropriately *L'Hydropathe*. Émile Goudeau became the editor-in-chief, Paul Vivien, a well-to-do law student with a sense of business, its director, or chief administrator, and Jules Jouy, its secretary. Like the later *Le Chat Noir* (and other cabaret journals), which it undoubtedly inspired, *L'Hydropathe* served as both self-advertising for the parent club or cabaret and as an outlet for smaller literary works (mainly poems and prose pieces) as well as drawings by member artists. The first issue of the journal, a weekly, appeared on January 22, 1879. *L'Hydropathe* ran for a little over a year with twenty-four numbers being published its first year. In an attempt to broaden its readership, and with the promise of outside financial assistance, the staff of the journal made revisions in format and then introduced a change of name: from number 9 of the second year of publication (1880), *L'Hydropathe* appeared under the title of *Tout-Paris,* but owing to the failure principally of the anticipated support to materialize its life was destined to be very short—only five numbers appeared in all.

Before the Hydropathes dissolved toward the end of 1881, the group went through another change of scene in its quest for an ever larger and more stable location. At the end of 1878, after moving from the Café de la Rive-Gauche to the *hôtel* Boileau, the group repaired to the Colson property at 29 Rue Jussieu, on the edge of the Latin Quarter.[26] But a practical joke involving firecrackers by some of the members, especially Alphonse Allais and Sapeck, resulted in an ultimately vain attempt by Goudeau, as president, to impose discipline on the group. Other incidents on the part of the pranksters, or *fumistes,* among the Hydropathes finally brought on the rupture that was to spell the club's doom. Frustrated by his efforts to keep his unruly flock in line, Goudeau stormed out in September 1881 swearing never to return again. Sharing his point of view, several of the Hydropathes joined him in the walkout. The remaining members under the leadership mainly of Léo Trezenick (real name, Léon Épinette) sought to reconstitute the group under the new name of the Hirsutes (The Hairy Ones). Goudeau was again invited to become the head of it, but when he refused the offer was extended to, and accepted by, the composer Maurice Petit, the former organist of the Church of Saint-Louis-des-Invalides. The new association of former Hydropathes had no easier time in finding suitable premises than the original group. After being expelled from one location because the proprietor objected to the noise they made, they finally made camp in the basement of the Café de l'Avenir, at the corner where Saint-Michel square and the quay, or embankment, of the same name meet.

The defection of Goudeau and others, the reconstitution of the former Hydropathes as Hirsutes, and the move to the Café de l'Avenir in late 1881 signaled the final dissolution of the Hydropathes. The Hirsutes hung on until May 1883, by which time the Café de l'Avenir had been renamed the Café du Soleil d'or, but then they too went the way of the Hydropathes. Their place was soon taken by other groups of similar or yet more striking ephemerality, among them the Incohérents, an association mostly of painters, led by Jules Lévy, and the Zutistes (from the French exclamation *zut,* meaning, roughly, "the hell with it"), whose principal leader was Charles Cros. Each successor group seemed to be not only of shorter life span than the original Hydropathes, but of a more tenuous relationship with cabaret.

If the Hydropathes lost their own identity as a separate group in late 1881, many of them, including members of the breakaway Hirsutes, were able to come together again under the banner of the Chat Noir. In fact, without the entry of former Hydropathes into the new Chat Noir one can only wonder if this most famous of Parisian cabarets could ever have become more than the modest café Rodolphe Salis first had in mind when he decided to abandon art for commerce.

The Chat Noir

How did the fusion of Hydropathes and Chat Noir come about? One evening, after his break with the Hydropathes, Émile Goudeau stopped in at the Grande Pinte, the popular painters' hangout on the Avenue Trudaine. Not long afterward, a small band of revelers entered, among them Rodolphe Salis and the painter René Gilbert. When he saw Goudeau, Gilbert introduced him to the tall, robust, red-haired Salis who was only too happy to talk about his plan to establish a *cabaret artistique* with the former president of the Hydropathes. Sensing Goudeau's interest, Salis asked him if he would consider joining him in his new venture.[27] The Hydropathes episode of his life behind him and anxious to reestablish himself in the public eye together with those members of the old group who remained loyal to him, Goudeau seized the opportunity. Salis' new Chat Noir thus became the new home of many former Hydropathes who became the core of the Chat Noir's programs in the early years of its history and whose migration from the Latin Quarter to Montmartre assumed a symbolic significance. Other Latin Quarter artists, ex-Hydropathes and Hirsutes among them, soon followed them to Montmartre, becoming part of the entourage of the Chat Noir and bringing to Montmartre some of the mystique previously enjoyed by the Latin Quarter.

Recalling his decision to collaborate with Salis in the Chat Noir in his later memoirs, *Dix Ans de Bohème* (Ten Years of the Bohemian Life), Goudeau drew this important distinction between what Salis intended with the Chat Noir and other cabaret-like ventures which were just beginning to become fashionable.

> At that time, medieval, Renaissance, or Louis XIII cabarets were just beginning to be opened. The "Grand' Pinte" was typical of them. But the painters met there without any fanfare, just as they might have done on the boulevard. Salis, on the other hand, dreamt of reintroducing the hubbub, the antic madness, and the ironplated chanson into our watered-down customs. Moreover, understanding well that all the arts are brothers, he asks himself why literary people do not join together with painters in order to lend them a few fleeting syllables, perhaps adorned with sonorous rhymes.
>
> I shall be a gentleman-cabaretier, says Salis, still a painter, but also a man of letters and *chansonnier*. The future belongs to me.
>
> And thus was the "Chat Noir" founded.[28]

Underlying Salis' plans for the Chat Noir was the Wagnerian concept of the *Gesamtkunstwerk,* or the total work of art, which sought a breakdown of traditional barriers between the arts for the sake of their mutual enrichment and the creation of the "new" art that would combine the verbal, visual, musical, and choreographical. The *Gesamtkunstwerk* idea was very much in the air at the time and efforts were being made to achieve a meaningful merging of the arts that would enable them to break out of the narrow confines of the conventional and traditional. As an experiment in *Gesamtkunst* in miniature, the cabaret ideally was to be an environment hospitable to all the arts by virtue of its casualness and the impromptu nature of its programs. Artists were encouraged to regard the cabaret as their own, a place where they could come together, exchange ideas, discuss art, and perform as the mood struck them. Once the collaboration of Goudeau and other ex-Hydropathes was assured, Salis' dream of establishing a real *cabaret artistique* had a good chance of reaching fruition. And it was Salis' dream, or rather ambition, that distinguished what the Chat Noir soon became from a group such as the Hydropathes which lacked the same kind of informing vision and existed primarily as a loose association of artists who recognized a basic similarity of outlook and just wanted premises where they could enjoy their own company or perform for whomever they chose.

As other artists followed the ex-Hydropathes to Montmartre and the

Chat Noir the fame of the new cabaret spread far and wide. Before long it became the most sought-out Montmartre establishment, not only by artists but by an ever growing public that included statesmen, foreign dignitaries, the fashionable, and even the bourgeois who was often the butt of Chat Noir humor and who considered himself lucky to get in.

Salis was by no means indifferent to the public at large, but he thought first and foremost of the contemporary Parisian artistic community. These were the people for whom he wanted the Chat Noir to exist, for whom he wanted his cabaret to provide a place of rendezvous. The public could be admitted as space allowed but were regarded as a species of privileged onlookers. The physical layout of the Chat Noir actually reenforced the division between artists and public. The long, narrow former post office was divided into two rooms. The first was decorated as previously described, in the style thought of by Salis as that of Louis XIII, with its wood panels, wrought iron, heavy walnut tables and highbacked chairs, lanterns hung from the ceiling, paintings and sketches of artists who frequented the place, and huge fireplaces topped with all sorts of antique and pseudo-antique bric-a-brac. This is where the public and non-regulars were seated, shown to their tables by waiters attired in the costumes of members of the ultraprestigious French Academy—green brocaded coats with gold thread, two-cornered hats, and swords, all picked up by Salis and his associates in junk shops, antique stores, and flea markets of which Paris has always had an abundance. The second or inner room, which was separated from the first by a counter and a heavy curtain that was never completely closed, was reserved for the cabaret's regulars, its habitués. This inner room, or sanctum sanctorum, soon became known as L'Institut.

The Chat Noir not only had the distinction of being the first cabaret, of inspiring the cabaret mania that swept across turn-of-the-century Europe as well as Paris itself, but of enjoying the greatest longevity of any of the great cabarets of the period. It opened its doors in November 1881 and closed them for all time sixteen years later, in 1897, the year of Rodolphe Salis' death. Actually, from 1895 until the expiration of his lease in 1897, Salis had relinquished the cabaret and its famous *théâtre d'ombres,* or shadow (silhouette) theater, to an organization that proved unequal to the task. Dismayed at what had become of his now legendary establishment, he gave serious thought to returning to Paris from his native Châtellerault and reopening the Chat Noir. He also had plans to

Façade of the Chat Noir in its second home on the Rue de Laval (now Rue Victor-Massé). Drawing by Paul Merwart, ca. 1887. (Musée Carnavalet, Paris).

take the shadow theater on a tour of the French provinces and then abroad. At least the latter intention was partially realized. Salis did accompany the shadow theater on a tour of France, but in Chateaudun, in March 1897, he fell gravely ill. He was taken to nearby Naintré for treatment, but died two days later on March 19, 1897. The Chat Noir, like Salis, was at an end.

During its relatively long history, the Chat Noir changed location only once. From 1881 until 1895, it was situated at 84 Boulevard Rouchechouart. French sources usually distinguish this fourteen-year period as that of the first Chat Noir. Several reasons prompted the change of premises. To begin with, there was the obvious need for more space in view of the great popularity of the cabaret. Then, the Chat Noir was also situated very near the Elysée Montmartre dance hall, which Salis regarded as an inconvenience both in terms of competition and the type of clientele it attracted. Finally, there was the notoriety triggered by a violent quarrel that occurred in December 1884 between Salis and some local Montmartre pimps who were becoming a problem. The fracas resulted in the death of a waiter who came to Salis' defense when the confrontation with the pimps took an ugly turn. After giving up his lease to the premises on the Boulevard Rouchechouart, Salis and his entourage moved, with considerable fanfare, to a nearby location at 12 Rue de Laval (now Rue Victor-Massé) on the night of June 10, 1885, between 11 P.M. and midnight. The Chat Noir that took up new residence on the Rue Laval (in a building previously occupied by the Belgian painter Alfred Stevens) remained there until its closing in 1897 and is spoken of as the second Chat Noir.

This thumbnail sketch of the Chat Noir, above all its relocation in 1885, enables us to better appreciate distinctions between the first and second Chat Noir, not only in terms of its physical setting, but also, more importantly, in terms of artistic character.

Although many of the artists who flocked to the Chat Noir from the Latin Quarter and elsewhere in its early days remained part of the cabaret scene through much of its history, some obviously came and went. From its opening in 1881 at least until 1895, the Chat Noir was a magnet for artists from Paris and beyond. As some left to move on to other locales and to other stages in their careers, there were always others eager to take their places and to identify with the cabaret whose fame was spreading ever wider.

Comparing the artistic makeup of the Chat Noir in its first and second periods, some differences stand out clearly. In view of Salis' own unrealized ambitions as an artist on canvas and his many associations with painters particularly in Montmartre even before he opened the Chat Noir, it stands to reason that painters would be welcome at the cabaret and would figure prominently in its activities. This indeed was the case, and of the painters who frequented the Chat Noir the most visible were Adolphe Willette (1857–1926), whom Salis had made the acquaintance of some time before, the Swiss Théophile Steinlen (1859–1923), an indefatigable book illustrator and contributor of drawings to the *Chat Noir* journal, Henri Rivière, one of the originators of the cabaret's famous shadow theater, Henri Pille, and Caran d'Ache, whose name also became closely linked to the Chat Noir's later shadow theater. When the Hydropathes quit the Left Bank and the Latin Quarter to join forces with Salis at the Chat Noir, they brought with them the literary talent Salis was so anxious to incorporate as an integral part of the cabaret's entourage. Former Hydropathes such as Maurice Rollinat. Georges Lorin, Sapeck, Jules Jouy, Aphonse Allait, Charles Cros, Maurice Mac-Nab, Marie Krysinska, Edmond Haraucourt, Marcel Legay, and others all followed Émile Goudeau's lead into the new enterprise. Salis could not have been happier and seemed to take a special pride in playing host to writers who in many cases were already well known. Among the *chansonniers* and musicians who were active during the period of the first Chat Noir were Mac-Nab, Jouy, Victor Meusy, who composed and sang his own chansons, Albert Tinchant and Charles Sivry, both pianists, and Georges Fragerolle, a former Hydropathe, who wrote the music for a number of poems by Chat Noir writers and was to play an important role in the period of the second Chat Noir once the cabaret's shadow theater became active.

The habitués of the Chat Noir found outlets for their talents in different ways. Mostly on Goudeau's initiative, literary Fridays and Saturdays were organized at which writers read from their works and poets declaimed verse. Literary Absinthes, held every now and then on a Wednesday, also became popular for obvious reasons. Since the Chat Noir had no kitchen and served only drinks, Jules Jouy thought that it might be a good idea to organize a monthly dinner, La Soupe et le Boeuf (Soup and Beef), in some neighborhood restaurant. The idea caught on; after all, as good Frenchmen the cabaret's regulars enjoyed eating as much as drinking and the monthly Soup and Beef gave them an opportunity to get together as a group over a meal much the same as they shared tables to drink at the cabaret.

It was at the literary Fridays and Saturdays as well as at the Wednesday Absinthes that the Chat Noir writers, almost all of whom were former Hydropathes, did most of their public recitation. Charles Cros' by now classic "The Salt Herring"—recited either by Cros himself or by the actor Coquelin cadet—proved as popular on the Butte, as Montmartre was commonly called, as it had been in the Latin Quarter in the days of the Hydropathes. So, too, were Cros' "La Vie idéale," which the Hydropathe and now Chat Noir poet and composer Marie Krysinska later set to music, and his "Chanson des Hydropathes," which first appeared in a comic letter to Salis published in the *Chat Noir* journal on June 30, 1883.[29] A typical Hydropathe drinking song, the "Chanson des Hydropathes" beautifully fit into the ambience of the first Chat Noir. The song begins:

Hydropathes, chantons en choeurs,
La noble chanson des liqueurs.

Le Vin est une liquide rouge
—Sauf le matin quand il est blanc.
On en boit dix, vingt coups, et v'lan!
Quand on en a trop bu, tout bouge,
Buvons donc le vin rigolo.
Blanc le matin, rouge à la brune
Qu'il fasse (nous souffrons de l'eau)
Clair de soleil ou clair de lune . . .[30]

(Hydropathes, let us sing in chorus / The noble song of drinks. / Wine is a red liquid, / Except in the morning when it's white. / You drink ten or twenty glasses, then bang! / When you've had too much of it, and you feel like you're ready to burst, / Then let's drink funny wine [*vin rigolo*], / White in the morning, red at twilight / Which makes (we suffer from the effects of water) sunshine or moonshine . . .

The poem then goes on to describe the joys of beer, apéritifs, and liqueurs.

Émile Goudeau also found no fewer admirers at the Chat Noir for his "Revenge of the Beasts," "The Poles," or for other poems from his *Flowers of Asphalt* or *Poèmes ironiques* (Ironical Poems). Of the latter collection, especially popular was the "Lamentation de la Lumière" (Lament of Light) in which the poet relates the plight of light cast down from the sky into the dark world of men to that of poets and dreamers immured in the great city. Lines such as the following struck a responsive chord among Goudeau's audience, reaffirming his position as a leading poet of the turn-of-the-century Parisian counterculture:

Mais qu' importe que le destin
Nous ait sevrés de l'ambroisie?
Nous savons porter le matin

Dans la royaume de la suie!
C'est dans le cercle du sommeil
Comme un crépuscule vermeil,
Et c'est encore le soleil,
Et c'est toujours la Poésie.

Qu' importe que ton clair Rayon
Sorte d'un piédestal de boue?
Qu' importe que sous son haillon,
En chantant, Homère s'enroue?
Le poète est un fils de dieu:
S'il a souillé son manteau bleu,
Il n'a qu' à de brosser un peau,
Et c'est de l'azur qu' il secoue.[31]

(But what does it matter that destiny / Has weaned us away from ambrosia? / We know how to carry the morning / Into the realm of soot! / In the circle of sleep, / Like a rosy twilight, / There is again the sun / And there is always poetry. / Does it matter that your bright ray / Has just a pedestal of mud? / Does it matter that beneath his tatters / Homer grew hoarse singing? / The poet is a son of God. / If he has dirtied his blue mantle / He has but to brush himself off a bit / And it is azure that he shakes off.)

Since for writers the first Chat Noir was something like an alumni association of the Hydropathes, it hardly comes as a surprise that among those performing at Chat Noir literary soirées were not only Charles Cros, Émile Goudeau, and Marie Krysinska, but also Alphone Allais, André Gill, Edmond Haraucourt, Georges Lorin, Paul Marrot, Jean Richepin, Léo Trezenick, the Greek Jean Moréas, whom Goudeau brought into the Black Cat in 1882, Fernand Icres (real name, Fernand Crésy), Paul Bilhaud, Laurent Tailhade, Louis Marsolleau, Gaston Sénéchal, Maurice Bouchor, Léon Valade, and Armand Masson whose sonnet "L'Oeil" (The Eye) was one of the poetic successes of the time:

L'oeil était dans le vase. Un caprice d'artiste
L'avait agrémenté d'un sourcil violet
Et sa prunelle peinte en rouge vif semblait
Vous regarder d'un air ineffablement triste.

C'est à la Foire aux pains d'épices qu'un beau soir,
Nous gagnâmes ce vase au Tourniquet. Fifine
Affirma qu'il était en porcelaine fine,
Et voulu l'étrenner toute de suite, pour voir.

Mais il était si neuf, le soir, à la lumière,
Qu'elle n'osa ternir sa pureté première,
Et le remit en place avec recueillement.

Elle fut très longtemps à s'y faire. C'est bête:
Cet oeil qui la fixait inexorablement
Semblait l'intimider de son regard honnête.[32]

(The eye was inside the vase. An artist's whim / Had adorned it with a violet eyebrow / And its pupil, painted in bright red, seemed / To look at you with an ineffably sad expression. / It was at the Gingerbread Fair that one fine evening / We came upon this vase at a stand. Fifine / Affirmed that it was made of fine porcelain, / And she wanted to try it out right away, to see. / But it was so new, this evening, in the light, / That she did not dare to tarnish its virginal purity / And put it back in place pensively. / She was troubled about this for a very long time. It's foolish. / This eye that stared at her inexorably / Seemed to intimidate her with its honest look.)

Apart from their public readings at the Chat Noir the writers (and visual artists) had an additional outlet for their compositions in the form of the journal published by the cabaret under the name of *Le Chat Noir.* The practice of a cabaret publishing its own journal had already been established by the Club des Hydropathes and would continue after the Chat Noir. What was different in the case of *Le Chat Noir* compared to other cabaret journals and magazines was its longevity. The first issue of the new journal came out on January 14, 1882, the last (No. 688) on March 30, 1895. For a turn-of-the-century cabaret to remain in continuous operation for sixteen years was unusual; for a cabaret journal to continue publication over a thirteen-year period, extraordinary.

In size, format, price, frequency of appearance, and overall character, *Le Chat Noir* closely resembled its immediate predecessor, *L'Hydropathe.* It was a weekly (appearing every Saturday), four pages in length, large format, and sold for 15 centimes. As the proprietor of the Chat Noir, Rodolphe Salis, appropriately, became the director of the journal, a post he relinquished to Émile Boucher in June 1893. But despite Salis' active participation in it as *Directeur* (or *Fondeur,* which he titled himself after turning over the management of the journal to Boucher), *Le Chat Noir* was run, for the most part, by Goudeau as editor-in-chief, a hardly surprising fact in view of his role in the publication of *L'Hydropathe.* Goudeau remained as editor-in-chief until 1884; the last issue to appear under his editorship was No. 111 of February 23, 1884. Although a falling out with Salis prompted his departure, Goudeau gave no hint of this in the letter of resignation addressed to *Mon cher directeur* which he published in the following issue, March 1, 1884 (No. 112):

My work prevents me from giving myself seriously and effectively to the editorship of the *Chat Noir*. Much to my regret, I am compelled to hand in my resignation as Editor-in-Chief.

Regaining thus my independence, I will have no further responsibility to bear and so remain,

Cordially yours,
Émile Goudeau

That the journal became popular is evident from the increase in the number of copies printed per edition. In its first year, 12,000 copies of each number of *Le Chat Noir* were printed. By 1889, that is seven years later, demand for it had so risen that the edition was increased from 12,000 to 20,000. The popularity of *Le Chat Noir* was based on several factors. There was, first of all, the matter of its association with the cabaret of the same name. By the time the journal made its first appearance, the Black Cat had already become a Parisian landmark and its success was bound to rub off on a journal put out by it and bearing its name. Initially, the journal also had the character not only of a "house organ" of the cabaret, but of Montmartre itself. Its original subtitle was, in fact, "Organe des intérêts de Montmartre" (Organ of the Interests of Montmartre). But lest the journal appear too parochial in scope, this subtitle was dropped after the seventh issue.

The layout of *Le Chat Noir* remained almost unchanged throughout its history. For a long time the front page was dominated by a type of editorial column which was written by Paul Dolfuss and appeared under the title "Le Boulevard." Other more or less regular features included a chronicle of Montmartre happenings ("Echoes Montmartrais"), news items about the cabaret itself ("Echoes du Chat Noir"), a "Bibliographie" featuring short reviews of poetry and prose fiction, theatrical announcements ("Théâtres"), news about the railroads ("Chemin de fer d'Orléans," "Chemin de fer du Nord," and so on), financial information ("Fantaisies financières"), and sports pieces, primarily for bicycling enthusiasts ("Chronique Vélocipédique," "Bulletins Cyclistes"); some letters to the editor were also carried in a section called "Petite Correspondence." As a rule, all the smaller items were grouped together on the last, or fourth, page of the journal.

The second page of *Le Chat Noir* was the domain of writers and it was here that virtually every literary figure in some way associated with the parent cabaret published something. Goudeau's "Les Polonais," for example, appeared in the January 14, 1882 issue, as did excerpts from his *Flowers of Asphalt.* A number of Charles Cros' works appeared on the pages of *Le Chat Noir,* among them his "Chanson des Hydropathes," which was published in the June 30, 1881 issue (No. 77) under the title "Udadushkhînan-Çruti" and offered as a hymn "discovered" by Cros in the Sanskrit *Rig Veda.* On October 6, 1883 (No. 91), Jules Jouy published one of his few outspokenly political chansons, "Les Prussiens. Sont toujours en France" (The Prussians. They Are Always in France):

Des malheurs de soixante-dix,
Aurions-nous oublié l'histoire?
Les Allemands, comme jadis,
Encombrent notre territoire
Des vils espions d'outre-Rhin,
Dans nos cités, grouille l'engeance.
Patriotes, veillons au grain:
Les Prussiens sont toujours en France.

(Can it be that we've already forgotten the history / Of the misfortunes of 1870? / The Germans, as ever, / Are overcrowding our territory / With contemptible spies from the other side of the Rhine; / Our cities are swarming with the breed. / Patriots, keep a weather-eye out: / The Prussians are always in France.)

While *Le Chat Noir* did not commonly involve itself in current political issues, Franco-Prussian tensions after the war of 1870–71 and French anxiety over Bismarck's policies prompted a spate of pieces on politics, among them the Jouy poem cited above, political articles of an anti-Bismarck, anti-Prussian character, and a special issue (No. 42, October 28, 1882) on the "Coup d'État de 2 November 1882" satirizing the unpopular Jules Grévy (1807–1891), a lawyer who at the age of seventy-one became President of the Republic in January 1879 following the resignation of Marshal Macmahon. The anti-Grévy sentiments of the issue of October 1882, in which, among other things, the "execution" of the fiercely patriotic statesman Léon Gambetta (1838–1882) is announced, were echoed a few months later in the January 6, 1883, issue (No. 52) which contains a mock obituary of Gambetta under the title "Germany Triumphant?" This was not the first time, incidentally, that *Le Chat Noir* carried a mock obituary. One for Salis himself, entitled "Un Deuil" (A Bereavement) and written presumably by Goudeau using his pseudonym A'Kempis (or A'K, for short), was carried in the April 22 issue of that same year (1882). It read:

This journal, usually so cheerful and welcomed by the public as a burst of laughter, is obliged to don mourning garb. Rodolphe Salis, our founder, our artistic director, our collaborator at times, is dead. The funeral cortège and service will take place on Monday. Mourners will assemble at two o'clock at 84 Boulevard Rochechouart, at the cabaret "Chat Noir." Poets as well as musicians have been engaged to recite and sing the funeral psalms.

Besides Salis himself, who contributed pseudo-medieval fiction over the title of "Seigneur de Chatnoirville-en-Vexin," Charles Cros, and Émile Goudeau, who apart from poetry also published an occasional "Bulletin Politique" and "Voyages de Découvertes" under his pseudonym of A'Kempis (or A'K), other writers who contributed to *Le Chat Noir* were Gaston Dumestre, a poet and *chansonnier,* Jean Richepin, Jean Lorrain, Paul Marrot, Georges Lorin, Gaston Sénéchal, Armand Masson, Edmond Haraucourt, Jean Moréas, Fernand Icres, Henry Somm, a visual artist who besides short stories for *Le Chat Noir* devised several shows for the cabaret's shadow theater, Maurice Bouchor, George Auriol, who followed Jules Jouy as secretary of *Le Chat Noir*'s editorial board, Albert Samain, Laurent Tailhade, Marie Krysinska, and Pierre Trimouillat. The well-known critic Léon Bloy occasionally contributed literary pieces to the journal such as those on the poet Maurice Rollinat in 1882 and one on Salis, "Le Gentilhomme Cabaretier," on November 24, 1883 (No. 98). Aristide Bruant, the great singer of chansons and later proprietor of his own cabaret, Le Mirliton (The Reed-Pipe), who was immortalized by the posters of Henri Toulouse-Lautrec, began his career as a cabaret *chansonnier* at the Chat Noir. His "Ballade du Chat Noir" for which he wrote the words and music was first published in *Le Chat Noir* journal on August 9, 1884 (No. 135). Dedicated to Salis and illustrated by Steinlen, the ballad contains the famous lines

Je cherche fortune,
Autour du Chat Noir,
Au clair de la lune,
A Montmartre, le soir!

(I seek my fortune / Around the Chat Noir, / By the light of the moon, / In Montmartre, at night.)

Two of the Chat Noir's more illustrious literary visitors, Charles Baudelaire and Paul Verlaine, also published in *Le Chat Noir.* Baudelaire's

"Chanson de Scieur de Long" (Song of the Pit-Sawyer) appeared in the July 31, 1886 issue (No. 238); Verlaine, who spent more time at the cabaret, was a more frequent contributor: his "Vers a la Manière de Plusieurs" (Verse in the Manner of Many) was published in the August 18, 1883 issue (No. 84); "Crimen Amoris" (Crime of Love) appeared on November 28, 1885, in issue No. 203; "A Villiers de L'Isle Adam," in the September 7, 1889, issue; "Noël," which Verlaine dedicated to Rodolphe Salis, came out on December 21, 1883; "Mes Prisons," a prose piece, was published on January 23, 1890, in No. 523, while the poem "Contre une fausse amie" (Against a False Mistress), was in the next issue, No. 524, January 30, 1892.

When *ombres chinoises,* or shadow shows, became the predominant attraction of the Chat Noir in its second period, information about performances and excerpts from texts as well as drawings of individual scenes appeared regularly in *Le Chat Noir.* An illustration by Uzès of the miniature theater used for Chat Noir puppet and shadow shows appeared on February 27, 1886 (No. 216) over the title "Le Guignol du Chat Noir." The July 17, 1886 issue (No. 236) carried announcements of two shadow performances: Caran d'Ache's *L'Enterrement d'un grand homme* (The Funeral of a Great Man) and Henri Rivière's *La Rue à Paris* (The Streets of Paris). Four of the cabaret's best-known shadow shows—Rivière's *La Tentation de Saint-Antoine* (The Temptation of Saint Anthony), Henry Somm's *Le Fils de l'eunuque* (The Eunuch's Son), Willette's *L'Age d'or* (The Golden Age), and Sahib's *Une Partie de Whist* (A Game of Whist)—were featured in the issue of January 7, 1888.

Art work was as prominent as literary in *Le Chat Noir,* which was as it should have been in view of the high visibility of visual artists in the activities of the cabaret. At first, *Le Chat Noir* tended to concentrate on political caricature, as reflected in a number of works of Caran d'Ache and Uzès, but this soon gave way to drawings of manners and other kinds of pictures. From the outset, the journal carried some type of art work each week and featured it on the third page. Contributing artists included, of course, such prominent members of the Chat Noir family as Willette, Steinlen, Henry Somm, Caran d'Ache, and Henri Rivière. Willette was represented, for example, by a series of drawings on the then fashionable Pierrot theme ("Pierrot Fumiste," "Pierrot Amoureux," and so on). Since the cat motif figured in almost everything involving the Chat Noir, the *Chat Noir* journal expectedly carried its share of cat drawings. The most prominent were those of Steinlen, but other artists made contributions in this area as well, among them, for example, André Gill.

The roster of artists frequently represented on the third page of *Le Chat Noir* included, in addition to those already mentioned, G. Amoretti, George Auriol, Maurice Barrès, Cabriol, Does (whose real name was Sabbatier), Fernand Fau, Forain, Luc Gaër, Godefroy, Alfred Guillaume, Carl Hap, Lamouche, O'Galop, Henri Pille, M. Radiguet, Albert Robida, Tiret-Bognet (also known as Ti-Bec, or Tébé), Uzès, and Verbeck.

The contributing artists often drew their inspiration from the setting and personalities of the Chat Noir cabaret itself or used their talent to illustrate literary texts carried by the journal. One of the Rivière's most famous drawings, for example, *84, boulevard Rochechouart,* depicts, in a collage effect, indoor and outdoor scenes at the Chat Noir; it appeared in the June 13, 1885 issue (No. 179) of the journal. Steinlen illustrated the text of Aristide Bruant's "The Ballad of the 'Chat Noir' " (No. 135, August 9, 1884) and contributed a well-known drawing of Salis in action as a *conférencier,* or master of ceremonies, *Salis bonimentant* (Salis Smooth-Talking), to the October 30, 1886 issue of the journal. Cabriol did the drawings for the poet Lorin's "Les Masques" which appeared in issue No. 113 of March 6, 1884. And finally, Henri Pille was the artist responsible for the illustrated heading of *Le Chat Noir* itself with its Montmartre windmills in the background and a large black cat with uplifted tail and quizically cocked head in the foreground.

Of all the people who collaborated with the *Chat Noir* journal, perhaps none became so closely identified with it as the humorist and former Hydropathe Alphonse Allais. The format of the journal, its felicitous accommodation of shorter literary pieces, and its light spirit seemed tailormade for Allais' style and type of humor, so much so, in fact, that Allais served as *Le Chat Noir*'s editor-in-chief for several years. He wrote so extensively for the journal throughout its history that his contributions to it—in the form of comic prose pieces of anywhere from a few lines to a few pages in length—comprise most of two of the three volumes of posthumous writings in the 1966 collected edition of his works.[33]

Prior to his association with *Le Chat Noir* Allais had contributed to a variety of, for the most part, short-lived journals of satirical and humorous character, among them *Le Tintamarre* (1875–1884), *Les Écoles*

1877–1878), *La Revue Moderne et Naturaliste* (1879), *L'Hydropathe* (1879), and *Le Tout-Paris* (1880).

When the *Chat Noir* journal began publication on January 14, 1882, Allais was not yet among its contributors. Indeed, no work bearing his signature appeared before March 17, 1883. The evidence suggests, however, that Allais began writing for *Le Chat Noir* as early as February 1882, but that for whatever reason (including an undeniable fondness for mystification), he chose not to use his own name until later.[34] Yet even when he did begin signing his works, his enthusiasm for literary game playing made it impossible for him to part company completely with pseudonymousness. His favorite nom de plume was, in fact, not a pseudonym at all but the name of a living person, the celebrated literary critic of *Temps* and, like Allais, former Hydropathe Francisque Sarcey. Allais began using the name Francisque Sarcey in November 1886 and then chiefly for a series of "chronicles" (especially the "Chronique du bon sens") that he wrote and that became a regular feature of *Le Chat Noir.* Allais had apparently been toying with the idea of using Francisque Sarcey as a pseudonym for a few years before 1886; in the February 18, 1882 issue of *Le Chat Noir* a "chronique théâtrale" of his appeared over the name Félicien Sarcet, while for a feuilleton in the October 14, 1882 issue, the name Le Petit Sarcey was used.[35]

Allais' contributions to *Le Chat Noir* are so numerous and touch upon so many subjects that one fairly short piece in its entirety may provide a better view of his style—and that of *Le Chat Noir* in general—than any attempt at a broad general characterization. The following selection, in translation only for the sake of space, is devoted to the artist Caran d'Ache. Allais writes:

> In connection with my article on the sketch artist Mars, whic attracted so much attention, I received an incredible number of letters urging me to continue the series on artists.
>
> You have no idea of the letters that I receive each day, from all corners of France and even from foreign countries.
>
> This correspondence is not always grammatically correct, but in general it expresses good sense and a rationalized thirst for progress.
>
> A large part of it comes from the petit bourgeois, this enlightened petit bourgeois among whom I count almost all my clientele and which is the heart and head of France.
>
> Poor petit bourgeois! Oh well! I have followed the advice of my readers and since this pleases them, I am going to review our principal artists.

If you have no objection, I shall begin with M. Caran d'Ache.

It's not that I'm so fond of his kind of talent, but he is in fashion now, and you know fashion!

Physically, M.Caran d'Ache is a big fellow, of good build, blond, attired very properly, and well groomed.

In short, he reminds me a bit of what I was like at twenty-five.

After all, I have not always been the big shortwinded Sarcey that you know.

I, too, was twenty, and likewise eighteen. And I assure you that at that age, I did not take a back seat to anyone.

I recall especially a romance that I had with the mother of one of my students when I was a teacher of rhetoric.

Imagine, this woman, who was no longer in the first blush of youth, was infatuated with me. But at that age it was all the same to me; the taste for young girls came to me later.

Every day, on the pretense of informing me of her son's progress, she came to see me, and what teasing, flirting, and titillation there was.

Oh! I'm not bored, away with you!

In order to be alone with her on Thursdays, which was my only free day, I cooked up a scheme.

On Wednesday, I kept that big booby of a son of hers after school an extra period on the most trifling pretext, and so on Thursday, we were quite undisturbed.

Splendid! The system was good, for the lad as well.

The extra work for Thursday considerably strengthened his classical studies which are the foundation of learning.

But I'm chatting idly and have strayed far from Caran d'Ache.

I was telling you that I was never terribly fond of his kind of talent. That's true, and here are my reasons.

To begin with, why doesn't he use shades in his drawings?

With outlines, he's fine, but in the final analysis, his work is nothing but outlines. I happen to be fond of shades in drawings.

And then his hair! And those funny positions!

I'm not used to seeing hair in such positions!

You can argue that all his movements are exact, and that what he does is all right as is.

Well, you know what you can do with your exactness!

The only truth in art, M. Caran d'Ache, is to do what the public thinks is true.

Otherwise, there's no safety.

You don't trample on tradition with impunity.

Up until now, painters and illustrators do hair like this. Fine! One should continue this way since that is the custom.

You're going to tell me stories of snapshots that give the exact movement of a horse at such and such a second; well, too bad about them! They're wrong, since they astonish.

The public doesn't like to be disconcerted, and they are quite right, the public! Originality, M. Caran d'Ache, is certainly useful for an artist, but one must know how to combine it wisely with tradition and respect for works that have come before.[36]

The Chansonniers

As popular as the Chat Noir's poets, humorists, and painters might have been, in the cabaret itself or on the pages of *Le Chat Noir,* there is no doubt that performances at the cabaret were dominated, above all, by its *chansonniers.* Again, if one were to draw distinctions between the first and second Chat Noir, between the establishment on the Boulevard Rochechouart and that on the Rue Victor-Massé, it could be argued that while the singers of chansons remained prominent throughout the long history of the cabaret, a formidable rival to them arose in the time of the second Chat Noir in the form of the cabaret's *théâtre d'ombres,* or shadow theater. Considering the impressive artistic and technical sophistication of the shadow shows and their immense popularity, it probably would be fair to say that just as the *chansonnier* contributed most to the fame of the Chat Noir in its first period, it was the shadow theater that assumed this role in the second.

The prominence of the *chansonnier* at the Chat Noir, particularly in the first period, was hardly a coincidence. Indeed, the emergence of cabaret in Paris in the early 1880s, exemplified, above all, by the establishment of the Chat Noir, happened to coincide with the revival of the chanson, or traditional French song, whose history goes back to the Middle Ages.[37] Closely related to public events, often an expression of social and political attitudes, the chanson was a commonplace of French life. The period between the end of the Second Empire and the decade of the '80s was, however, a time of noticeable decline for the genre; banalization and trivialization had produced an overabundance of chansons characterized by vulgarity, sentimentality, and simple-minded patriotism. Before the appearance of the Chat Noir and other Parisian cabarets, the natural habitat of the chanson was the *café-concert* (or *caf-conc',* as it was popularly known) and the *variétés,* variety halls much like the English music halls of the period.[38] The generally larger *variétés* offered a mixed fare of entertainment consisting usually of chansons, dances, dramatic skits, comic monologues, or recitations of one sort or another; the *café concert,* on the other hand, was, as its name indicates, a café where for the price of a modest consumption of alcohol one could hear a popular singer. Like the *variétés,* the *café-concerts* were to be found mostly along the city's grand boulevards; some were in working class districts such as Pigalle. Although it was the *café-concerts* and *variétés* that spawned talents of the magnitude of Aristide Bruant, Yvette Guilbert, and Edith Piaf, whose careers were launched in such establishments, they were essentially middle- and lower-class places of entertainment with no pretensions to serious art.

The great revival of the chanson that began to be felt in the early 1880s—another symptom of a renewed interest in popular culture during the turn-of-the-century period—brought to the fore a new generation of singers who succeeded in raising the level of the French chanson to heights it had not enjoyed for some time. The new *chansonniers* were also a breed apart from their predecessors. Denizens of the Latin Quarter and Montmartre, for the most part, they spurned a traditional repertoire in favor of songs of deep social concern, often anti-authoritarian and antibourgeois in character. With a few exceptions, the new *chansonniers,* who were frequently musicians as well as poets who played their own accompaniment, were also distinctly urban in orientation. Their subjects were drawn from the great city around them and as if carrying forward the banners of a Zolaesque naturalism, they concentrated on the darker, uglier, and more tragic aspects of contemporary Parisian life; poverty, homelessness, social injustice, maltreatment of the young and old, prostitution, and crime.

Once the Chat Noir was open and thriving, it became a principal locus of the new Parisian chanson. In collaborating with the new cabaret, singers such as Jules Jouy (1855–1897) and Maurice Mac-Nab (1856–1889), who had already won many admirers from the days of the Hydropathes, became the best advertisements for the cabaret, attracting other singers and the public alike. Before long, the Chat Noir became the acknowledged center of the new chanson, so much so that Maurice Donnay, a popular writer and dramatist who became one of the stars of the second Chat Noir, once characterized it "en effet une école chansonnière." He also pointed out that this "school of the chanson" of the Chat Noir was "particularly scoffing and irreverent in continual reaction against stupidity, injustice, and knavery."[39]

The chansons of Jouy and Mac-Nab were typical of the variety of styles with which similar concerns were expressed by the singers of the 1880s and 1890s who made the Chat Noir that "école chansonnière" of which Donnay spoke.

A former apprentice butcher, of small stature, blind in one eye and with a huge forehead, Jouy had already made a considerable name for himself with chansons sung at *café-concerts* and at gatherings of the Hydropathes before he became one of the Chat Noir regulars. Following a common practice among the *chansonniers* of the time, Jouy seldom composed his own music but instead wrote lyrics to the melodies of well-known songs. One of his best known chansons, "Le Temps des crises," is an example of this. Borrowing the melody of a popular song of the same name for which J.-B. Clément wrote the text and A. Renard the music, Jouy created a chanson of characteristically bitter social protest:

Vous regretterez le beau temps des crises,
Quand, pauvres sans pain et riches graves,
  Nous serons aux prises.
Les drapeaux de Mars flotterant aux brises,
Les drapeaux vermeils sur qui vous bavez.
Vous regretterez le beau temps des crises,
Quand viendra le Peuple en haut des pavés.

Quand vous pleurerez le beau temps des crises,
Le vil renégat et l'accapareur
  En verront de grises.
Les politiciens auront des suprises.
Les Judas, au ventre, auront la terreur.
Quand vous pleurerez le beau temps des crises,
Grondera partout la Rue en fureur.

Profitez-en bien du beau temps des crises,
Où le peuple jeûne et passe, en rêvant
  Aux terres promises.
Quand donc viendras-tu fondre les banquises,
O grand soleil rouge, ô soleil levant?
Profiterez-en bien, du beau temps des crises,
Où le Peuple veille et s'en va rêvant.[40]

(You will regret the good time of crises / When we, the poor without bread, and the engorged rich / Will join in conflict. / The banners of Mars will flutter in the breeze, / The ruddy banners over which you drool. / You shall regret the good time of crises, / When the People will take to the streets. / When you will weep over the good time of crises, / The vile renegade and the monopolist / Will have a bad time of it. / The politicians will also have their share of surprises. / The

Judases will feel terror in the pits of their stomachs. / When you will weep over the good time of crises, / the Street will growl in fury on all sides. / Take good advantage of the time of crises / In which the people fast and pass away dreaming of promised lands. / When will you come to melt the ice-packs, / O great red sun, O rising sun? / Take good advantage of the good time of crises / In which the People keep watch and then go away dreaming.)

Jouy strikes a yet more menacing pose in the chanson "Le Réveillon des Gueux" (The Christmas Eve Revel of Beggars) in which contrast is again drawn between the haves and have-nots, now all the more poignant because of the Christmas setting. The chanson follows the melody of a popular air about ringing bells beginning "Digue, digue, digue, digue-diguedon:"

Dans Paris glacé, les cloches des églises
Sonnent, à minuit, la chanson de Noël,
Et les vagabonds, sans pain et sans chemises,
S'en vont, grelottant et maudissant le ciel.
Blême et muselant l'appétit qui l'assiège
Le rôdeur se dit qu'il n'ira plus bien loin,
Et, loin des sergots, s'etendant sur la neige,
Comme un chien galeux va créver dans un coin. (bis)
    Digue, digue, digue, diguediguedon,
    Sonne, sonne, sonne, joyeux carillon!
    Digue, digue, digue, diguediguedon,
    Sonne l'heure du Réveillon!
    Digue, digue, digue, digue,
        etc., etc.
Les fils des famille et les filles de joie,
Les maigres viveurs et les bourgeois tout rondes,
Près d'un clair foyer s'en vont manger
Le Peuple, pour eux, a tiré les marrons.
L'on boit, l'on s'empiffre, et l'on bat la campagne,
Les catins en rut dépouillant les michés,
Répond en sourdine à l'hymne des clochers. (bis) . . .
Gros bourgeois repus, nocez, faites ripaille!
Nous, les meurt-de-faim, nous nous rêveillerons!
Près d'un clair foyer, rôdeurs sans sou ni maille,
Nous viendrons un jour pour manger les marrons!
Oui, les vagabonds sans pain et sans chemises,
Viendront démolir vos Noëls et vos dieux!
Et vous entendrez les cloches des églises
Sonner, à minuit, le réveillon des gueux! (bis) . . .[41]

(In icy Paris the church bells / Ring, at the stroke of midnight, the song of Christmas, / And the vagabonds, without bread and without coats, / Pass by shivering and cursing the heavens. / Pale and muzzling the hunger besieging him / The vagrant tells himself that he will not go any farther, / And, far from the cops, stretching out on the snow, / He'll kick the bucket in a corner like a mangy dog. / . . . Young men of good family and young girls of the night, / Lean pleasure-seekers and bourgeois nice and plump, / Are all getting ready to eat goose alongside a bright hearth. / The people have plucked the chestnuts for them. / How they drink, stuff themselves, and lose their senses! / The rutting harlots skin their johns, / And the clink of champagne glasses / Slyly responds to the hymn from the belfries. . . . / Fat bourgeois, fill yourself up, have a good time, kick up your heels! / We, the paupers, are going to rouse ourselves! / Alongside a bright hearth, vagrants without a sou or a stitch, / We shall come one day to eat those chestnuts! / Yes, the vagabonds without bread and without coats / Will come to destroy your Christmases and your gods! / And at the stroke of midnight you will hear / The church bells sound the Christmas revel of beggars! . . .)

Jouy's chansons conjure up an image of the wretchedness of urban poverty, at once universal yet distinctly Parisian, that was virtually unparalleled among the French *chansonniers* of the *fin-de-siècle*. As bleak as this image is, however, it is not one of passive, fatalistic hopelessness. The poor and the homeless, with whom Jouy identifies, whose collective voice his chansons become, seethe with resentment toward state and society and harbor a desire for vengeance impossible to deny. Jouy's chansons are full of foreboding about the inevitable day of reckoning, but until that day comes his nameless vagrants and street urchins accept their lot with defiance and even bravado. Spurning self-pity, the poor worker of the "Chansons d'hiver" (Songs of Winter) declares with a tough cynicism characteristic of Jouy's anti-heroes:

Bah! pourquoi m'plaindrais-j'? Mon log'ment,
Tas d'richards! a tout comm' les vôtres,
Des portes et des f'nêtr's, seul'ment,
C'est les port's et les f'nêtr's des autres.
Et puis, après tout, quand j'suis las,
Prenant mon chapeau comme' toiture,
Le pavé me sert de mat'las
Et l'vent qui souffl', de couverture . . .[42]

(Bah! Why should I pity myself! My lodgings / Are full of riches! Everything's just like yours, / With doors and windows, only / It so happens that the doors and windows are those of other people. / And later, after everything, when I'm weary, / Donning my hat like a roof, / The pavement serves me as a mattress / And the blowing wind as a blanket.)

Mac-Nab's world was essentially the same as that of Jouy, but his chansons often have a sparkle of wry humor generally absent in Jouy's more serious poems. Burdened with a hoarse out-of-tune voice that was compared to that of a seal with a cold and frequently drove his favorite accompanist, Albert Tinchant, to despair, Mac-Nab proved to be a highly popular singer. One of his greatest successes was the chanson "L'Expulsion" which embodies an obvious underlying sympathy for the political left but at the same time reveals an uncanny ability to find humor in almost any situation:

On n'en finira donc jamais
Avec tous ces N. de D. d'princes!
Faudrait qu'on les expulserait
Et l'sang du peuple il cri' vingince!
Porquoi qu'ils ont des trains royaux,
Qu'ils éclabouss' avec leur lusque
Les conseillers ménicipaux
Que peut pas s'payer des bell' frusques?

D'abord les d'Orléans, pourquoi
Qu'ils marie pas ses fill' en France,
Avec un bon vieux zig comm' moi
Au lieur du citoyen Bragance?
C'est-il ça d'la fraternité,
C'est-il ça d'la délicatesse?
On leur donn' l'hospitalité,
Qu'ils nous f . . . au moins leurs gonzesses!

Bragance, on l'connait c't' oiseau-là.
Faut-il qu' son orgueil soy' profonde
Pour s'êt' f . . . un nom comm' ça!
Peut donc pas s'app'ler comm' tout l'monde?
Pourquoi qu'il nag' dans les millions
Quand nous aut' nous sons dans la dèche?
Faut qu'on l'expulse aussi . . . mais non,
Il est en Espagn', y a pas mèche!

Ensuit' y a les Napoléons,
Des muff' qu'a toujours la colique
Et qui fait dans ses pantalons
Pour embêter la République!
Plonplon, si tu réclam' encor,
On va t'fair' passer la frontière.
Faut pas non plus rater Victor,
Il est plus canaill' que son père!

Moi j'vas vous dir' la vérité:
Les princ' il est capitalisse

Et l'traivailleur est exploité,
C'est ça la mort du socialisse.
Ah! si l'on écoutait Basly,
On confisquerait leur galette,
Avec quoi qu' l'anarchisse aussi
Il pourrait s'flanquer des noc' chouettes!

Les princ' c'est pas tout: Plus d'curés,
Plus d'gendarmes, plus d'mélétaires,
Plus d'richards à lambris dorés
Qui boit la sueur du prolétaire.
Qu'on expulse aussi Léon Say,
Pour que l'mineur il s'affranchisse.
Enfin, qu' tout l'mond' soye expulsé:
Il rest'ra plus qu' les anarchisses![43]

(We'll never be through / With all these princes and their fancy titles! / They ought to be expelled / And the blood of the people will cry vengeance! / Because they're of royal line, / And because they splash with that luxury of theirs / The municipal authorities / Who aren't able to afford pretty clothes! / Let's start with those of the House of Orléans. Why / Didn't they marry off their daughters in France / To a nice guy like me / Instead of to citizen Bragança?[44] / Is that what you call fraternity? / Is that what you call refinement? / In return for our hospitality / Their high-and-mightys could at least f . . . us! / Bragança, you know that bird! / His conceit must really be profound / For him to be f . . . d with a name like that! / Why couldn't he have a name like everyone else? / Why should he be swimming in millions / While the rest of us don't have a pot to piss in? / He ought to be tossed out too, but wait . . . / He's in Spain now, so it's no go! / Then there are the Napoleons, / Of the drunkards who always have colic / And who do it in their pants / In order to embarrass the Republic! / Plon-Plon,[45] if you dare complain again / You'll find yourself packed on your way in a hurry. / Victor[46] shouldn't be missed any more; / He's a worse scoundrel than his old man! / As for me, I'm going to tell you the truth. / The princes are capitalists / And the workers are exploited. / It's the death of socialism. / Ah, if you had just listened to Basly[47] / We'd have confiscated their dough / And with it the anarchist, too, / Would be able to live it up with the swells! / It's all over with the princes. No more priests, / No more gendarmes, no more soldiers, / No more moneybags with their palatial homes, / No more drinking the blood of the proletariat. / Let's also get rid of Léon Say,[48] / So that the miners can be emancipated. / And finally, let everybody be expelled; / that way, just anarchists will remain.)

The populist, antibourgeois, left-wing or anarchist sympathies of Jouy and Mac-Nab were echoed in the chansons of other Chat Noir regulars. Besides a collection of romantic *Chansons d'amour,* for which the poet Verlaine wrote a preface, Maurice Boukay (real name, Couyba), for example, was also the author of the *Chansons rouges,* so called because of their composer's social and political views. The collection includes such a typical song as "Les Ventres" (Bellies):

Chantons de ventre des bourgeois
Plus gros que le ventre des rois,
Ventre-un, ventre-deux, ventre-trois,
Chantons le ventre et son empire!
Chantons les désirs apaisés
Des ventres des bourgeois aisés
Qui font comme un bruit de baisers.
Chantons le ventre qui soupire! . . .

Pitié pour les ventres honteux!
Reposoirs des calamiteux,
Ventres, berceaux des marmiteux,
Ventres lourds de progéniturs!
Vous vous heurtez à tous les chocs,
Vous vous scandalisez tous les frocs,
Mais vous portez comme des rocs
L'espoir des justices futures![49]

(Let's sing of the bourgeois's belly / Bigger than the bellies of kings, / Belly-one, belly-two, belly-three.[50] / Let's sing of the belly and its empire! / Let's sing of the appeased desires / Of the bellies of well-to-do bourgeois / Which sound like the noise of kisses. / Let's sing of the belly that sighs. / . . . Pity the ashamed bellies! / Repositories of calamities, / Bellies, cradles of streetwalkers, / Bellies heavy with offspring! / You come up against all the shocks, / You scandalize all the frocks [of priests—HBS], / But you bear, like rocks, / the hope of future justice!)

While chansons of social and political protest were numerous and enjoyed considerable popularity at the Chat Noir, another type of chanson held a special place of affection among the habitués of the turn-of-the-century Parisian cabaret. This was the chanson whose inspiration derived from an intimate knowledge and keen observation of contemporary Parisian life, the chanson of the ordinary, unglamorous Parisian, of localities and neighborhoods, of the myriad of everyday events and people that make up the heartbeat of the great city. Since the world of these chansons is the socially insignificant and marginal, they would appear outwardly to share the same populist bias as the chansons of Jouy, MacNab, Boukay, and other singers whose energies were directed by and large to the redressing of social injustice. But appearance is deceptive in this case, since in this other immensely popular category of chanson the emphasis shifts from the poor and oppressed as objects of social concern to the familiar and everyday now observed not in moral terms but as elements in a beloved urban landscape deserving of more than the usual disinterested passing glance.

Until the very gifted and extraordinarily successful Aristide Bruant, who became surely the most popular singer ever to perform at the Chat Noir, this chanson of everyday Paris was nowhere more deftly handled than in the work of Léon Xanrof (1867–1953). A native son of Montmartre and hence well able to excel at the genre of the chanson whose subject is Paris herself, Xanrof was the son of a respected doctor whose comfortable bourgeois life gave rise to a certain prudishness easily offended by his son's enthusiasm for a career as a *chansonnier*. In order, therefore, to appease his family, Xanrof pursued the study of law, receiving his degree at the age of twenty and serving thereafter as an apprentice attorney at the Paris Court of Appeals. He eventually held a post at the Ministry of Agriculture and virtually ceased practicing law. In a further concession to his family's sensitivities, Xanrof also used a pseudonym throughout his career as a *chansonnier*. He was born Léon Fourneau and the name Xanrof was derived from the spelling backward of the Latin translation (*fornax*) of the name Fourneau, which in French means "furnace."

Xanrof's public attire squared more with his family's status than with his nocturnal activities as one of the outstanding Parisian cabaret *chansonniers*. Attired in an impeccable frockcoat and wearing a monocle, Xanrof appeared at the Chat Noir and other cabarets singing generally lighthearted songs in colloquial style of his own composition about the "little people" of the capital and about the foibles of society. In "Les Trottins" (Errand Girls), for example, the *trottins*, who regard themselves as the "pride of Batignolles"—one of the poor working class districts of Paris—are hardly indifferent to love but dream more of becoming rich and care little about the way they reach their goal.

L'amour? Oh la la! . . .
C'que nous voulons, c'est dev'nir riche,
Et peu nous importe l'moyen.
Tout se transformant sur la terre
Le trottin devient un beau jour
Fleur de lit pour célibataire,
Ou papillon de nuit d'amour.[51]

(Love? Oh la la! . . . / What we want, though, is to become rich / And the means matters little to us. / Everything on earth changes; / One fine day the errand girl becomes / A bed flower for a bachelor / Or a moth of love.)

"Les Bohèmes" offers Xanrof's personal view of the contemporary phenomenon of the song's title:

Dans des cafés au style étrange,
Les ratés et les insoumis
Drapés de paletots à frange
Disent du mal de leurs amis;
Ou, faisent des vers de bohèmes,
De leur bock ils fixent le fond . . .
La fumée et les anathémes
Montent lourdement au plafond.
"—Zola! Daudet!—En v'là des scies!
"Quand j'pens'que voil'a des feignants
"Qui produis'nt des tas d'inepties,
"Et qu'ça plaît aux bourgeois gnagnans!"
Tiens, les éditeurs, ça m'fait rire:
"Pas un viendra m'chercher seul'ment! . . .
"J'veux leur montrer c'que c'est qu' d'écrire,
"Attends qu'je m'mette à mon roman! (pp. 65–66)
Et, dans la nuit enfin venue,
Sans que nul mette le holà,
Le clan des ratés continue,
Crachant ici, bavant par là;
"Mort aux repus! place aux prophètes!"
Et tous ces braves, l'oeil ardent,
Font des projets d'oeuvres parfaites . . .
Et des dettes,—en attendant. (pp. 67–68)

(In cafés decorated in strange style, / The dropouts and unruly / Draped in fringe topcoats / Speak ill of their friends; / Or, composing bohemian verses / Stare at the bottom of their beer mugs . . . / The smoke and curses / Climb slowly to the ceiling. / "Zola! Daudet!—What bores! / When I think of such phonies / Turning out such a pile of ineptitude, / And that that's what the dimwitted bourgeois like! / Heavens, when I think of the publishers, it just makes me laugh; / Not one of them would even come looking for me! . . . / I'd like to show them what writing is really all about. / Just wait till I get working on my novel!" / . . . And during the night that comes at last, / Without anyone putting an end to it, / The clique of dropouts continues, / Spitting here, drooling there: / "Death to the satiated! Make way for the prophets!" / And all these worthy people, burning the midnight oil, / Concoct plans for perfect works . . . / While their debts pile up.)

The streets of Paris as a source of inspiration for *chansonniers* were themselves celebrated in Xanrof's "La Rue," which was set to the music of Jules Jouy's "La Terre:"

Ce que l'on chante aujourd'hui,
  C'est la rue;
Notre muse, c'est le bruit
  de la rue;
Tristesse ou gaîté nous vient
  Dans la rue;
Le mal condoyant le bien;
  v'là la rue! . . .
Et quand s'amortit le bruit
  Dans la rue,
Le public joyeux s'enfuit
  De la rue.
Gans prudents rasez le mur,
  Par la rue,
Passé minuit, c'est peu sûr
  Dans la rue. (p. 71)

(What we sing about today / Is the street; our muse is the clamor of the street. / Sadness or gaiety awaits us / On the street; / The bad rubbing shoulders with the good. / That's the street for you! / . . . And when the noise of the street / Dies down, / The happy public escapes / The street. / Wise people hug the walls / When they make their way through the street, / And when midnight falls, it is less safe / On the street.)

As a native of Montmartre Xanrof was most at home, of course, with the streets of his own neighborhood and the night life to which it owed so much of its vibrancy in the turn-of-the-century period. This familiarity, and certainly love, were reflected in several of his chansons devoted to popular entertainers in the well-known cafés, cabarets, and dance halls of contemporary Paris. Typical of these is the chanson "Le Poète aux Olives" (The Poet of the Olives) about the poet Jehan Sarrazin of the famous "Divan Japonais" who was known for his custom of passing out olives together with poems among the public:

Au milieu des "kaké-mono,"
Sarrazin surveillant sa boîte,
D'un pas vif qui jamais ne boite,
Va de l'entrée au piano.

Grassouillet comme une marmotte,
On dirait un petit Budha,
Qui, pour rire, se hasardá
A porter une redingote.

Et dans son lorgnon, à travers
Les cris et la fumée intense
Calme, il surveille la dépense,
En ciselant tout bas des vers

Car, avec des allures vives,
C'est lui qui donnait pour cinq sous
Quatre fruit,—et des vers dessous:
Jehan, le poète aux olives. (pp. 211–212)

(In the midst of gay kimonos, / *Sarrazin,* surveying his joint, / With a lively step that never falters, / Makes his way from the entrance to the piano. / Plump as a woodchuck, / One would say he looks like a little Buddha, / Who, for the sake of a laugh, takes the risk / Of wearing a frockcoat. / And through his pince-nez, through / All the shouting and heavy smoke, / Calm, he inspects the pantry / While unobtrusively cutting out verses, / Since, with quick steps, / It is he who passes out four pieces of fruit / For five sous—and some poems signed / *Jehan, the poet of olives*!)

Witty, incisive, lighthearted, Xanrof's chansons enjoyed great popularity among the devotees of the cabaret in *fin-de-siècle* Paris, so much so, in fact, that it might indeed seem risky to single out any one particular chanson as the public favorite among his many works. Were a consensus to have been reached about this, then that favorite would clearly have been "Le Fiacre" (The Horse Drawn Cab) for which Xanrof himself wrote the music and which was published for the first time in 1890 in his collection *Chansons sans-gêne.* Although its subject is, after all, marital infidelity, Xanrof strikes an almost Schnitzlerian note in his colloquial gaiety and reluctance to moralize:

Une fiacre allait trottinant,
Cahin caha,
Hu' dia! Hop là!
Une fiacre allait trottinant
Jaune avec un cocher blanc

Derrièr' les stores blaissés,
Cahin, caha
Hu' dia! Hop là!
Derrièr' les stores baissés
On entendit des baisers.

Puis un' voix disant: "Léon
Cahin, caha
Hu' dia! Hop là!
Puis un' voix disant: "Léon,
Tu m'fais mal, 'ot' ton lorgnon!"

Un vieux Monsieur qui passait,
Cahin, caha,
Hu', dia! Hop là!
Un vieux Monsieur qui passait,
S'écri: "Mais on dirait qu'c'est

Ma femm' dont j'entends la voix!"
Cahin, caha,
Hu' dia! Hop là!
Ma femm' dont j'entends la voix!"
I' s'lanc' su' l'pavé en bois.

Mais i' gliss' su' l'sol mouillé,
Cahin, caha,
Hu' dia! Hop là!
Mais i' gliss' su' l' sol mouillé;
Crac, il est escrabouillé!

Du fiacre un' dam' sort et dix:
Cahin, caha,
Hu' dia! Hop là!
Du fiacre un' dam' sort et dit:
"Chouett', Léon, c'est mon mari!

Y a plus besoin d'nous cacher!
Cahin, caha,
Hu' dia! Hop là;
Y a plus besoin d'nous cacher! . . .
Donn' donc cent sous au cocher!"[52]

(A horse drawn coach was making its way down the street at a trot . . . / It was yellow in color and its coachman was white. / Behind the lowered blinds . . . / Kisses could be heard. / And afterwards a voice saying, "Léon . . . / You're hurting me; take off your pince-nez!" / An old man who happened to pass by at the time . . . / Exclaimed: "Why I could swear that it's / My wife's voice I hear!" / . . . And he banged his walking stick down on the pavement. / But he slipped on the wet ground . . . / And smack, went down on his butt! / A woman then got out of the coach and said . . . / "Oh oh, Léon, it's my husband! / We'd best hide! / . . . Give the coachman a hundred sous!")

Xanrof's chansons had such a large following that they continued to be sung at the Chat Noir by other singers after he himself had ceased performing there. When it came to Xanrof's attention that the singer Horace Valbel was singing his songs at the cabaret without Salis bothering to inform the audience who their author was he lost little time in registering a firm protest. Anxious to avoid a possible law suit, Salis thereafter made a point of announcing when any of Xanrof's songs were sung that the chansons were the work of "Monsieur Léon Fourneau, avocat à la Cour'd Appel" (Mr. Léon Fourneau, an attorney at the Court of Appeals).[53]

Although he never lost his interest in the chanson, Xanrof also proved an able playwright. He published several dialogues in *Le Petit Journal,* presented *revues intimes* in salons, wrote a very successful operetta, *Madame Putiphar,* with Ernest Depré (to the music of Diet), and, with Jules Chancel, a *Rêve de Valse* (Waltz Dream), which was set to music of Strauss. In recognition of his contributions to French culture, he was made a member of the Legion of Honor and elected Vice-President of the *Société des Auteurs, Compositeurs et Éditeurs de Musique.*

Aristide Bruant and Le Mirliton

Whatever the popularity of such singers as Jouy, Mac-Nab, Xanrof, and others, none ever achieved the towering fame of the chansonnier whose name became virtually synonymous with the Parisian *fin-de-siècle* cabaret, Aristide Bruant (1851–1925).[54] Called the "modern François Villon" in his own time, praised by the literary likes of Anatole France, Marcel Schwob, and Maurice Barrès, painted by Toulouse-Lautrec, lionized by the small and great alike, Bruant was hardly indifferent to his fame but never forswore the common people and petty criminals whose hardships he made the subject of so many of his most memorable chansons.

Bruant's understanding of and compassion for society's outcasts and rebels was no fashionable Montmartre literary pose. Long before he became the darling of the Parisian cabaret, he acquired a firsthand knowledge of the world he was later to sing of with such verve and conviction.

Born into a landowning family that had once known better days in the town of Courtenay, on the Yonne River, about 200 kilometers southeast of Paris, he was still in his teens when his parents resettled in the French capital in the slum district around the Gare de Lyon railroad station, on the Boulevard Mazas. The nearby Mazas prison eventually came to fascinate Bruant and his frequent visits there on pass brought him the intimate familiarity with criminals, their attitudes, their way of life, and their argot which in time shaped the world of his chansons. Another regular port of criminal call for Bruant—later also to figure in his chansons—was the prison of La Roquette which was notorious for its guillotine located in the square in front of the prison.

Bruant earned a living in his early years in Paris in a variety of jobs—working in a lawyer's office, for a jeweler, and then finally becoming an employee of the French railway company Compagnie du Nord. Long interested in singing, he decided to try his luck as a *chansonnier,* singing conventional light and patriotic songs in a conventional manner. He had demonstrated a certain skill at marching songs during military service in the Franco-Prussian war of 1870–71 and was convinced that he could make a go of a career as a singer. His early appearances in the *cafés-concerts* were often in the company of a singer and prostitute named Nimi whom he had befriended and who committed suicide in 1879. Before a second, brief stint in the army in 1880, Bruant was appearing in the popular Robinson's Tavern near the Place de la Nation. By now he was attracting a growing number of admirers and won an approving nod from Paulus, then the singing sensation of Paris. Following his twenty-eight-day period of military service, he added such other popular cafés as the Époque, Horloge, and Scala to his places of employment as a singer. It was at the Scala that Bruant made his first appearance in the costume that was to become his trademark and was immortalized in the famous poster Toulouse-Lautrec painted of him in the period when Bruant was the proprietor of his own cabaret, Le Mirliton (The Reed-Pipe). A tall, robust man with red hair, Bruant accentuated his stature and complexion with an outfit consisting of a black corduroy jacket with matching pants, a red flannel shirt, black leather boots, a black sombrero-like hat, a scarlet scarf around his neck, and a flowing black cape draped around his shoulders. He also dispensed with the small moustache that previously adorned his face and now made a point of flattening his abundant mane and combing it straight back on his head.

Bruant's entry into the Chat Noir circle occurred in early January 1884. He was taken there by Jules Jouy with whom he had become good friends and who shared his enthusiasm for the rougher neighborhoods of Paris. Despite his great success at the Chat Noir Bruant chose not to follow the cabaret to its new location on the Rue Victor-Massé in 1885. Instead, he raised enough money to rent the original premises of the Chat

Aristide Bruant. Poster by Toulouse-Lautrec.

Noir and opened his own cabaret there under the name of Le Mirliton. Forsaking the antique clutter of the Chat Noir for reasons of cost as well as personal taste, he kept furnishings to a minimum at Le Mirliton. Apart from a piano, counter, and benches and chairs for customers, the décor consisted in the main of a haphazard assortment of randomly mounted pictures, posters, carvings, swords, and similar objects. The spare setting was an almost perfect foil, however, for Bruant's towering, flamboyant presence, the more so in view of the fact that the great singer ran the new cabaret virtually as a one-man show. There was, of course, an accompanist at the piano and when Bruant himself was not singing his place was taken by two singers named Chopinette and Alexandre who were hardly competition for the master.

From the moment a visitor entered Le Mirliton, attention was riveted on Bruant and would not easily have been diverted the rest of the night. Entry into the cabaret had to be first gained by knocking at the door and then waiting for Bruant's personal approval. As soon as visitors were admitted they were almost immediately subjected to a torrent of abuse from none other than the proprietor and star attraction himself. Arms akimbo, a contemptuous look on his face, Bruant would mock their appearance, often calling the men "pigs," "pimps," and "scoundrels," and regaling the women with only slightly less offensive epithets. It was, more or less, in good fun and meant to set the tone of the cabaret. Once newcomers overcame their initial shock they threw themselves into the spirit of the place with gusto, joining with Bruant and other guests in greeting newer arrivals the same way they themselves had been greeted.

With Bruant as its centerpiece, Le Mirliton was an enormous success. Its fame spread far and wide, it became a "must" on any traveler's visit to Paris, just as the original Chat Noir had been and the new establishment of Salis on the Rue Victor-Massé continued to be. It made no difference that Le Mirliton was far less lavishly appointed than the Chat Noir or that beer was the only alcoholic drink served on the premises. Unlike the Chat Noir, which offered a variety of talents in both its first and second periods and succeeded to a great extent because of the sizeable band of artists who were its habitués as well as performers, Le Mirliton had only Bruant and his songs to offer. The appeal of both, however, was more than enough to fill the cabaret night in and night out for a good ten years.

Bruant's departure from Le Mirliton began in 1895. Beseiged with requests for guest appearances throughout France, he decided to go on tour. Performing through much of the week from ten or eleven at night until usually two in the morning for a ten-year period of time obviously placed great demands on Bruant's stamina, despite his hardy constitution, and he felt ready for a change, at least from the routine of nightly performance. Having resolved, then, to make a tour of France, he

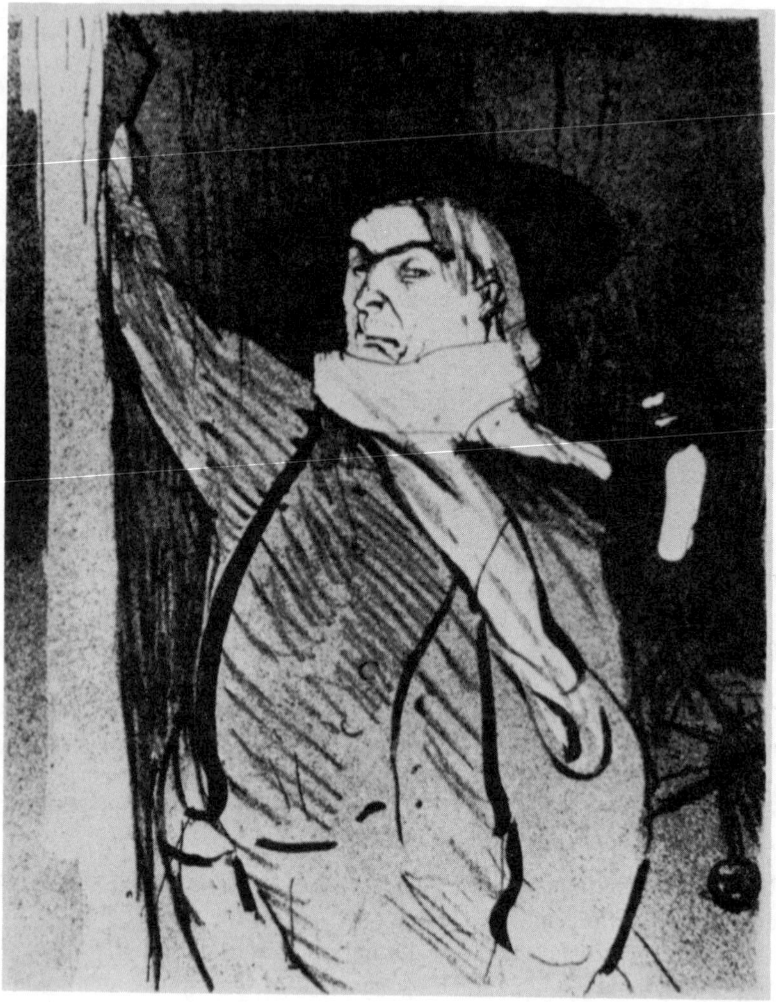

Aristide Bruant. Lithograph by Toulouse-Lautrec. (Bibliothèque historque de la ville de Paris).

turned over the direction of the cabaret to his pianist at the time, Marius Hervochon, who after Bruant's departure renamed the establishment the Cabaret Aristide Bruant.[55] If the master himself was absent, at least the cabaret he founded bearing his name would continue to attract visitors. Although at best a pale imitation of Le Mirliton, the magnetic appeal of Bruant's name was such that even without him the Cabaret

Aristide Bruant managed to survive the great artist for whom it was named, who died in 1925, by forty years.

Once he left La Mirliton Bruant never really returned to it. Following his tour of France, he came back to Paris, but not to again assume direction of Le Mirliton; instead, he accepted the offer of a co-directorship of the *café-concert* Époque where he had once sung. Although Bruant's appearances there filled the house to overflowing, he grew tired of it and sold it after the Paris World's Fair of 1900. By now, he had also sold his remaining interest in Le Mirliton and had also disposed of his old apartment on the Rue Cortot. Bruant's last major public appearances came in 1898 and in 1924. In the wake of the Dreyfus affair, the singer took a fling at politics by standing as a radical candidate for the Belleville Saint-Fargeau district in the general elections. Despite his immense popularity as a *chansonnier,* Bruant nevertheless did so badly in the elections, coming in last with a mere 502 votes, that whatever taste he had for politics was quickly spoiled. Some time after the elections and before the sale of Époque, Bruant decided to quit Paris for good and return to his native Courtenay together with Mathilde Tarquiné d'Or, the opera singer with whom he lived for forty years. His last appearance in Paris came in late November 1924 when he was persuaded to perform once again before a Paris audience in a kind of public farewell to the city and its people who had made his career the phenomenal success that it had been. His two-week appearance at the Empire music hall was nothing short of sensational, demonstrating that Bruant had lost none of his appeal or popularity. He died just a few months later, on February 11, 1925, in an apartment on the Rue Christiani and was buried in a vault at Subligny, a town near his beloved Courtenay.

In addition to his career as a *chansonnier,* Bruant was also an author. Not long after opening Le Mirliton he founded a journal of the same name on the model of *Le Chat Noir.* With Camille de Sainte-Croix as editor-in-chief and Georges Courteline as secretary, it appeared irregularly twelve times a year between 1885 and 1894. Toulouse-Lautrec, long a devoted admirer of Bruant and a frequent visitor to Le Mirliton, made his first appearance (under his assumed name of Tréclau) on the pages of the new journal in December 1886 with a two-page reproduction of his painting *Le Quadrille de la chaise Louis XIII à l'Élysée-Montmartre,* on the subject of the Louis XIII chair which Rodolphe Salis had left behind when he moved the Chat Noir to its second home on the Rue Victor-Massé and which eventually wound up as part of the décor of Le Mirliton.[56] Toulouse-Lautrec's second canvas on the same subject, *Le Refrain de la chaise Louis XIII chez Bruant,* also was reproduced on the pages of *Le Mirliton.*

At the height of his fame Bruant published his first book in 1889, *Dans la Rue,* a two-volume collection of his songs for which the artist Steinlen did the illustrations; a second edition appeared in 1895. In 1896, Bruant published the first volume of a three-volume collection of his chansons and monologues under the title *Chansons et monologues;* volumes two and three appeared in 1897. Bruant's other publications include a novel, *Les Bas-Fonds* (The Lower Depths), a dictionary of French slang which was the culmination of a long-standing interest in varieties of popular speech, especially that of the Parisian underworld, and a twenty-four-page weekly newspaper known as *La Lanterne de Bruant,* the first issue of which appeared in December 1897 and which usually contained, in addition to a song or two by Bruant, some short stories, articles on a variety of subjects, and illustrations; the journal ran for two years. In recognition of Bruant's accomplishments as a singer and a writer he was elected to the *Société des Gens de Lettres,* of which Émile Zola was then president, on April 21, 1891; Bruant was forty at the time. After he retired to the country, Bruant published a final volume of songs, *Sur la Route* (1899), notable for the country settings of a number of the songs and the appearance of a character previously unmarked in Bruant's works, that of the tramp or vagabond.

As a singer, Bruant was in the mainstream of such turn-of-the-century *chansonniers* as Jules Jouy, Jehan Rictus, and others whose songs were inspired by the poverty, wretchedness, and social injustice they saw around them in contemporary Paris. Truly "poets of the pavement" they sang of that other Paris so many in their audiences at the Chat Noir and Le Mirliton preferred to ignore or to encounter only in song in the cabarets of Montmartre. Bruant was as grim, caustic, and roughhewn as any singer of his time. But what he brought to his chansons that was different from those of his fellow *chansonniers* was an intimate knowledge of the mores and speech of petty criminals with whom so many of his songs deal, an even more striking realism of setting, character, and idiom, a somewhat greater feeling for the macabre, a distinct, indeed memorable, voice that was at once cutting and metallic, and a physical presence and personal style that lent still greater authenticity to his songs and played no small part in the aura that grew up around him.

Illustration for Aristide Bruant's *Dans la Rue* by Théophile Steinlen. (Holyoke Library, Harvard University).

Some of Bruant's most characteristic and successful chansons are set in the poorer and rougher districts of Paris that he knew so well and whose troubadour he became. These include such "classics" as "A Batignolles," "A la Villette," "A Montpernesse," "Belleville-Ménilmontant," "A Saint-Ouen," "A St. Lazare," "and "A la Roquette," the last set against the background of the grim prison where all public executions took place at the time in Paris.

Much of the appeal, and vigor, of Bruant's street songs comes from their first person stylization. Instead of singing *about* the wretched and the criminal, Bruant assumes the personae of the whores, pimps, apaches, petty criminals, murderers, unemployed laborers, and other social outcasts who crowd the stark canvas of this other Paris. In "A Batignolles," for example, the persona is that of the lover of a whore of the Batignolles neighborhood, Flora, who grew up without a father and at an early age was sent to school in Batignolles, the "school," of course, being the streets of the district. Flora had nice manners, wore her hair the color of fire in bangs, and loved to sing. And when Flora sang in the street it was as if a halo appeared above Batignolles. She had all her teeth, a round little nose, and not too large breasts, but as she used to say: *Quand on est dos, / On peut nager avec eun' sole, / A Batignolles* (When you've got a pimp working for you, / You can make your way around Batignolles / With even one).[57] Love sold cheaply in Batignolles, *pour eune obole* (for a widow's mite) (p. 13), and Flora never earned enough money, but then the narrator of the song says that he was never too demanding. Everything between him and Flora was all right, he loved her as much as he could, but then their relationship fell apart when he learned that she was deceiving him with Anatole. He is philosophical about it, however, convincing himself that the day had to come sooner or later since Anatole is a *mouchard* (stool pigeon) and, after all, *La marmite aim' ben la cass'role* (the pot loves the saucepan) (p. 14). Anyway, not long after she gave him his leave, the good Lord avenged him—Flora died of smallpox. In a cynical closing note, the narrator declares that the moral of his "prayer" is that "young girls without a father should never go to school in Batignolles" (*La moral' de c'tte oraison-là, / C'est qu'les p'tit's fill's qu'a pas d'papa, / Doiv'nt jamais aller à l'école, / A Batignolles*) (p. 15).

The relationship between whore and pimp turns uglier in "A Montpernesse." Slovenly and fat, the "heroine" of the chanson—which is sung by her male companion—consumes more and more wine as she gets older and often sneaks off to drink behind her lover's back. When he discovers that she has been pilfering money from her "take" in order to drink more (*pour boire a m'trichait su' l'gâteau*) (p. 25), he decides to do her in:

C'est pour ça qu' j'y cardais la peau
Et que j'yai crevé la paillasse,
A Montpernesse. (p. 25)

(That's why I skinned her hide, / And split the old bag open, / In Montpernesse.)

At the end of the chanson, he is in prison awaiting the guillotine, unburdened by any sense of guilt or remorse.

Since crime and violence were a way of life for the sleazy inhabitants of the Paris of Bruant's chansons, prison and the guillotine expectedly form an integral part of the picture he conjures up in his songs. The narrator of "A la Villette," one of Bruant's most popular chansons, is now a young girl who recounts the sad lot of her boyfriend, an apache named Toto Laripette, barely twenty years old, the handsomest lad in the district of La Villette, who never knew his parents and wound up in the notorious prison of La Roquette. Like Flora in "A Batignolles," the heroine of "A la Villette" also earned her living in the streets and she recalls that at night when she "retired her bottom" (*quand je re'tirais mon bas*) (p. 20) and was ready to go to bed, her lover, Toto, counted the money that she had made that day. Sometimes, when she was working the boulevards, Toto used to knock down drunks in order to rob them. But their idyll ended when the police picked him up one night along with other toughs and packed them all off to La Roquette. The last time she saw him, his chest was stripped bare and his neck was held fast in the *lunette* [the box where the victim's head was placed beneath the blade of the guillotine—HBS] of La Roquette:

La dernièr' fois que je l'ai vu,
Il avait l'torse a' moitie nu,
Et le cou pris dans la lunette,
A la Roquette. (p. 22)

In "A la Roquette," which is now set within the prison walls, the chanson itself represents the thoughts of a condemned man on the eve of his execution. Like Bruant's hoodlums and criminals in general, he is stoical, fatalistic, and concerned above all that he be seen going to his death fearlessly. Although he knows that the President of the Republic has the power to commute his sentence, he is certain that he will not, reasoning that

Si l'on graciait a' chaqu' coup
Ça s'rait trop chouette.
D'temps en temps faut qu'on coupé un cou,
A la Roquette. (p. 78)

(If he were to reprieve everyone, / That would be too good to be true. / From time to time you have to cut someone's neck, / At La Roquette.)

In thinking of the tipsy crowd that is soon to gather for the spectacle he declares that none of it bothers him. His one concern, however, is that when the collar of his shirt is torn to expose his neck for the blade of the guillotine, he will feel cold. This in turn will make him think of the cold of the blade, and he submits to the traditional wash, afraid that from the cold in his bones he is liable to shudder:

C'qui m'paralyse
C'est qu'i' faut qu'on coupé, avant l'mien,
L'col de ma ch'mise;
En pensant au froid des ciseaux,
A la toilette,
J'ai peur d'avoir froid dans les os . . . (p. 79)

(What bothers me, though, / Is that before they cut my own neck, / They have to first cut the collar of my shirt. / Thinking of the cold of the scissors, / And the washup, / I'm afraid of feeling cold in my bones.)

Since shuddering might be taken as a sign of weakness on his part, he resolves to hold himself as rigid as possible so as not to move before the blade of the guillotine falls. At this point his one wish is

J'veux pas qu'on dis'que j'ai eu l'trac
De la lunette,
Avant d'éternuer dans l'sac,
A la Roquette. (p. 79)

(I don't want it said that I lost my nerve, / Just when I had to put my head in the *lunette,* / Before sneezing in the sack, / At La Roquette.)

Prison is viewed from a different angle, that of a woman, in "A Saint-Lazare." Again, Bruant casts the chanson in the form of a letter from an inmate in prison to a beloved on the outside. This time, however, the inmate is a prostitute who has been taken into the prison of Saint-Lazare for a period of three months for the medical checkup then required of prostitutes. In her letter to her *pauv' Polyte* (poor Polyte), the prostitute bemoans the fact that while she is in prison she cannot send him anything. The awful thing about her present situation, she declares, is that "Ici, tout l'monde est décavé, / La braise est rare" (Here everyone is fleeced, / And there's hardly a chance for profit) (p. 74). She expresses concern that he will not fare well on his own while she is incarcerated and she urges him especially not to drink too much since he knows how easily he can get into trouble when he has one too many ("Et pis, mon p'tit loup, bois pas trop, / Tu sais qu't'es teigne, / Et qu'quand t'as un p'tit coup d'sirop / Tu fous la beigne") (p. 75). In closing she pleads with him not to land in a *bagarre* (brawl) because if he too is put behind bars ("si tu t'faisais coffrer") (p. 75) she would have no one to visit her, and she tells him that she adores him the way she adored the good Lord or her papa when she was a small girl and went for communion to Saint'-Marguerite.

Prostitution, and such related evils as pimping, mugging, alcoholism, and murder loom especially large in Bruant's chansons. Here, above all, is that Paris of back street tawdriness, exploitation, violence, and misery from which polite society preferred to avert its gaze. But by portraying the Paris of cheap whores and murderous pimps as graphically as possible, without any moralizing, Bruant was defiantly wrenching the head of polite society around in order to force it to confront what it abhorred and pretended did not exist. This defiance comes through very clearly in a chanson such as "Marche des Dos" (The March of the Pimps) in which the other Paris militantly claims its own rights of citizenship and mocks the virtues of the bourgeois:

A bas la romance et l'idylle,
Les oiseaux, la forêt, le buisson,
Des marlous, de la grande ville,
Nous allons chanter la chanson! . . .

Marlous, nos marmites sont belles.
Le bourgeois les adore, à genoux.
Et Paris, qui compte avec elles,
Est forcé d'compter avec nous. . . .

Le riche a ses titres en caisse,
Nous avons nos valeurs en jupon,
Et maigré la hausse ou la baisse,
Chaque jour on touche un coupon. (p. 60)

(Down with the romance and idyll, / With birds, and forests, and bushes. / We're going to sing instead / Of the pimps of the big city. / . . . Pimps, our whores are pretty. / The bourgeois adore them, on their knees. / And Paris, which reckons with them, / Is forced to reckon with us as well. / . . . The rich keep their securities in a vault, / While we have our assets in petticoats, / And whether the market is up or down, / Each night you can touch the goods.)

Even though the police ("la rousse," a slang term for "cops") cast a wide net for them,

> Nous savons, grâce à nos écailles,
> Glisser entre ses doigts crochus. (p. 62)

(We know how, thanks to our scales, / To slip between their crooked fingers.)

And when one of the pimps stands before the guillotine, his fellows turn out en masse to bid him farewell:

> Pourtant, les jours de guillotine,
> Quand la loi raccourcit un marlou,
> Nous allons lui chanter matine,
> Pendant qu 'on lui coup le cou. (p. 62)

(However, on days of public executions, / When the law is about to shorten a pimp, / We all go to sing matins, / While they cut off his head.)

The theme of the disintegration of family life among the wretched of the big city occurs frequently in Bruant's songs as, for example, in "Belleville-Ménilmontant," the name of one of Paris' poorest (and roughest) neighborhoods which Bruant hoped to represent when he stood for the general elections in 1888. Here children often do not know their own father and brothers often become their sisters' pimps. As the narrator of the chanson recalls, after the death of their father

> . . . c'est moi qu'est l'sout'neur
> Naturel à ma p'tit' soeur,
> Qu'est l'ami' d'la p'tit' Cecile,
>   A Bell'ville.
>
> Qu'est sout'neur par son grand frère,
> Qui s'appelle Éloi Constant
> Qu'a jamais connu son père,
>   A Ménilmontant.
>
> Ma soeur est avec Éloi,
> Dont la soeur est avec moi.
> L'soir, su' l'boul'vard, e j' la r'file,
>   A Bell'ville.
>
> Comm' ça j'gagn' pas mal de braise,
> Mon beau frère en gagne autant,
> Pisqu'l r'fil' ma soeur Thérèse,
>   A Ménilmontant. (pp. 28–29)

(It's me who's the natural pimp, / Of my little sister, / Who's the friend of little Cecile, / In Belleville, / Who's "looked after" by her big brother, / Who's called Éloi Constant, / Who never knew his old man, / In Ménilmontant. / My sister's with Éloi, / Whose sister's with me. / In the evening, along the boulevard, / I palm her off on somebody, / In Belleville. / This way I don't make out too bad at all, / And my dear brother does as well, / Since he peddles my sister Thérèse, / In Ménilmontant.)

Sunday being a day of rest, the narrator of "Belleville-Ménilmontant" refrains from work and climbs up to the peanut gallery of a theater to watch a play or vaudeville. All in all, he concludes at the end of the chanson, on a note of mocking cynicism typical of Bruant, that his life is not bad and could even be considered exemplary:

C'est comm' ça qu'c'est l'vrai moyen
D'dev'nir un bon citoyen:
On grandit, sans s'fair' de bile,
    A Bell'ville.

On cri': "Viv' l'Independence!"
On a l'coeur bath et content.
Et l'on nag', dans l'abondance,
    A Ménilmontant. (p. 30)

(This is the real way, you know, / To become a good citizen: / You grow up without worrying about anything, / In Belleville. / You shout: "Long live independence!" / Deep down, you feel O.K. and happy, / And you get by, in spades, / In Ménilmontant.)

Bruant's particular concern for the plight of children in an environment of poverty and crime is manifest in "Belleville-Ménilmontant" and in a number of other songs. "A Saint-Ouen," dedicated to another downtrodden neighborhood of Paris, is typical of this group. For the persona of the singer of the chanson Bruant this time has chosen a street urchin. Left by his mother to play with broken bottles and shards along the old fortifications around Paris near the River Seine, the urchin is already wise to the darker side of life around him. He observes that in Paris there are districts where young children who have no skills ("qu'ont pas de' métiers") become part of the underground ("l's s'font pégre") (p. 217). In order not to die of hunger, an eight-year-old, for example, teams up with a ragpicker and expects his share of trouble just to stay alive ("pour vivre, on a du tintoin") (p. 217). Tramping and begging are

Illustration for Aristide Bruant's *Dans la Rue* by Théophile Steinlen. (Holyoke Library, Harvard University).

the common lot and if love should come along while one is dragging around all night then it is embraced and

> . . . sous les yeux
> Du bon Dieu qu'est dans les cieux . . .
> Comme un bête,
> On r'produit dans un recoin,
> A Saint-Ouen. (p. 218)

(. . . beneath the eyes / Of the good Lord who is in heaven . . . / Then, like an animal, / You reproduce somewhere in a corner, / In Saint-Ouen.)

The chanson closes on a grim, macabre note. The urchin concedes at the end that he does not know how anyone can live honestly. It all seems like a dream, but there is one compensation anyway:

Car comme on est harassé,
    Quand on créve . . .
Et l'cim'tière est pas ben loin,
    A Saint-Ouen.   (p. 219)

(When you're so worn out / You can't go on, / And you croak . . . / The cemetery ain't too far, / In Saint-Ouen.)

In his book *Colour Studies in Paris,* Arthur Symons, that keen English observer of *fin-de-siècle* Paris, remarked about the chansons of Aristide Bruant, whom he had seen perform on several occasions, that

> these songs are for the most part ugly enough, they have no charm or surprise of sentiment, they appeal to one by no imported elegances, by none of the conventionalities of pathos or pity. They take the real life of poor and miserable and vicious people, their real sentiments, their typical moments of emotion or experience . . . and they say straight out, in the fewest words, just what such people would really say, with a wonderful art in the reproduction of the actual vulgar accent. . . .
>
> Bruant's taste lies in the direction of a somewhat *macabre* humour; he gives us, by preference, the darker side of these dark and shadowed lines; but if there is much that he leaves out of the picture, at all events he introduces nothing into it which is not to be found in the reality which it professes to copy.[58]

Much of this realism with which Bruant succeeded in infusing his songs of the "poor and miserable and vicious people" (to quote Symons) of Paris came from his use of language. Bruant, in short, was a master of the spoken French of the milieux in which he chose to set many of his chansons and it was not by chance that his publications include a dictionary of French argot of the early twentieth century. Almost any of his songs could serve to illustrate the point. Let us look at just one, as an example—the chanson entitled "Crâneuse" (The Braggart). The song is narrated presumably by a Parisian streetwalker who rails against a newcomer, Pierre's girl, who seems to put on airs and looks down her nose at her "sisters." She is, in other words, the "crâneuse" of the chanson's title. After venting her wrath at the newcomer, the narrator concludes with the threat that one of these days she is going to do her in. The song, like most of Bruant's, abounds in the elisions typical of colloquial French: *j'viens* (= *je viens*), d'recontrer (= *de recontrer*), *c'qu'a* (= *ce qu'a*), *nom de d'la* (=*nom de dela*), *un' marmit'* (= *une marmite*), *en v'la'* (= *en voilà*), *l'boul'vard* (=*le boulevard*), *faut-i' qu'nous* (= faut-il que nous), *qu'a m'f'ra* (= *qu'a me fera*), and so on. The slang *ben* for *bien,* as in *ben merde* (what shit, what crap), appears frequently as do such substandard corruptions as *dedpuis* for *depuis* (afterward, later). Since "Crâneuse," as so many of Bruant's songs, treats of prostitutes and pimps, the chanson is full of colloquial expressions drawn from the Paris gutter. Hence, such terms as *flaquant* (shitting, crapping), *salope* (slut), *putain* (whore), *charogne* (swine, bitch), *vache d'métier* (bitch of the trade, or "slut of a whore" perhaps in the context of the song), *febosse* (old bag, hag), *gonzesse* (floosy, tart). *Marmite,* literally "pot" in French, also has the colloquial meaning of "whore" and appears in this sense in many of Bruant's songs. In "Crâneuse," we meet it in the line "Un' marmit' qui fait sa soupière," which means, literally, "a saucepan, or pot, that acts as if it were a soup tureen" and is here used colloquially to describe a whore who puts on airs (or *fait du chichi,* as Bruant has elsewhere in the same song, in another colloquial usage). The envious and resentful narrator of "Crâneuse" complains in the song not only about the airs the new girl on the block puts on, but also about the fuss she makes with her showing off, bragging, complaining, and gossiping. The vocabulary for all this has a decidedly colloquial flavor, including such terms as *c'est du schpromme* (a big fuss), *jactance* (bragging), *chambard* (row), *potin* (uproar, gossip). Various forms of the popular verb *foutre* (not give a damn) appear as the narrator voices her reaction to the "crâneuse's" behavior, as for example *J'yen foutrai, moi, d'la rouspetance* (You won't catch me giving a hoot in hell about all her belly-aching). Berating herself and her friends for even letting the newcomer into the Batignolles district, the whore says that they all must have been *gnolles,* a colloquial expression meaning "silly" or "foolish." The chanson takes a sinister twist toward the end. Boasting that she is a butcher's girlfriend (*gonzesse d'loucherbéme*), meaning that presumably she knows how to use a knife, the narrator threatens to kill the newcomer. The phrasing here is typical street French of the period:

Moi j'suis gonzesse d'loucherbéme.
Un soir qu'a m'f'ra trop lierchéme
J'y fous mon vingt-deux dans la peau.[59]

(Me, I'm a butcher's girl. / One night, when I've just had her up to here, / I'll stick my you-know-what in her hide.)

Illustration for Aristide Bruant's "Crâneuse" by Théophile Steinlen. (Holyoke Library, Harvard University).

Vingt-deux (literally, twenty-two) in colloquial French usually appears as an exclamation meaning "Watch out!," "Watch it!." *Foutre,* apart from its frequent use in expressions of not caring, not giving a damn, can also mean "to strike," "to deliver a blow," as in the above instance. *Peau,* the normal French term for "skin" or "hide" can also mean "whore" in colloquial usage, so "J'y fous mon vingt-deux dans la peau" can either mean "I'll stick my you-know-what [read here blade, shiv—HBS] in her hide" or "I'll stick it to the old whore."

Bruant sang his down-to-earth, unflinching songs of a Paris of poverty, prostitution, and crime in an idiom born of the streets. His strong appearance accentuated by a costume of black and red, his contemptuous, defiant manner, and his cold, metallic singing style, sharp as the cutting edge of a knife, gave his chansons an undeniably affective power. Song, idiom, and personal style fused to produce memorable if disturbing performances and justifiably created around Bruant the mystique of

France's greatest turn-of-the-century cabaret *chansonnier,* indeed the very embodiment of the genre in the peak period of its development.

The Shadow Show

If the chanson reigned supreme in the period of the original, or first, Chat Noir its supremacy was rivaled and perhaps even overtaken by the entertainment known as shadow shows, or, as they are called in French, *ombres chinoises* (Chinese shadows). As their name indicates, shadow shows consist, in essence, of the silhouettes, or shadows, of figures projected by means of a light source on to a screen made of some material. The shadows originally may have been the silhouettes of people performing in a type of dumb show related to pantomime; eventually the most popular form of shadow show involved the use of cutouts—from paper, cardboard, or metal—which were animated by a person or persons who remained unseen—in the manner of a puppeteer—so as to act out a story. That the origin of shadow shows goes back to ancient times seems obvious from the French name for them. The belief is widespread that the form arose in the East, first among the Chinese, and then spread to the West, perhaps from Turkey where the shadow show is known as *Karagöz* (black eye) from the name of the figure who appears most prominently in it.

Western interest in the shadow show developed in the seventeenth century, but this form of entertainment came to enjoy real popularity for the first time only in the eighteenth century when so-called magic lanterns were employed for the projection both of human shadows and the silhouettes of cutout figures. The Swiss Johann Kaspar Lavater (1741–1801) invented a machine for the projection of silhouettes which might also have been black and white drawings, while the Frenchman François-Dominique Séraphin (1747–1800) in 1772 established at the Hôtel Lannion in Versailles what was to become an immensely popular theater combining marionettes and silhouettes. The form continued to be cultivated well into the nineteenth century, particularly in France where its most able practitioner was Louis Lemercier de Neuville (1830–1918).[60]

The renewed interest in shadow shows during the *fin-de-siècle* can be best understood if seen within the context of the enthusiasm of the avant-garde for minor, or marginal, theatrical forms associated with popular culture. Among these were puppet and marionette plays, pantomime, and the shadow show. Another attraction of the shadow shows, particularly for the cabaret, which provided an especially hospitable environment for their cultivation, was the fact that because puppet and shadow shows represented a kind of miniature theater they could easily be adapted to the usually small stage of the average cabaret.

The inauguration of shadow shows at the Chat Noir—which was the first cabaret to feature them—came as an outgrowth of the opening of a puppet theater in the cabaret. The idea of adding puppet performances to the program of the Chat Noir seems to have originated with the musician Charles de Sivry who encountered little resistance when he suggested it to Rodolphe Salis. The first puppet show to be presented was a little piece by the caricaturist Henry (or Henri) Somm entitled *Madame Garde-Tout.*[61] Henri Rivière, then a twenty-year-old painter and by now one of the regulars of the second Chat Noir, was asked by Salis to take charge of the production which meant, in effect, that it was his responsibility to design the puppets' costumes as well as the sets, to direct the puppeteers, who were all amateurs, in their roles, to correct the movements of the puppets, and to regulate the lights of the tiny puppet theater.

In the course of his work with the Chat Noir's new puppet stage, Rivière had the idea of trying to revive the tradition of shadow shows of his eighteenth-century predecessor Séraphin. He put his idea into practice for the first time one night during a performance by Jules Jouy of a well-known chanson ("Sergots," Cops) that begins

Quand les sergots s'en vont par un,
C'est qu'ils n'sont pas avec quelqu'un;
Pour mieux inspecter, pour mieux voir,
A la mêm' place jusqu'au soir
Ils restent plantés su' l'trottoir . . .

Rivière first extinguished all the lights in the auditorium and then from behind a napkin suspended across the opening of the miniature stage used for the puppet shows mimed Jouy's songs with silhouettes cut out of cardboard.[62]

The innovation proved so successful that Rivière was encouraged to go ahead with more elaborate shadow show productions. These not only came to represent a major new direction for the Chat Noir in its second period, but were so brilliantly designed and ingeniously executed that they were justifiably regarded as a distinct art form in themselves. Rivière's genius, as well as that of other artists who eventually joined him in shadow show productions, manifested itself in several areas. There was, first of all, the matter of the figures themselves. In the immensely talented hands of Rivière and his co-workers, they quickly evolved from simple card cutouts into highly elaborate, indeed sophisticated designs. Rivière was also not content to use only cardboard, but experimented as well with zinc cutouts and, more impressive yet, with glass panels on which he painted figures with paints designed specifically for application on glass. Rivière's experiments extended also to the mechanics of animation and lighting. On the whole, Rivière sought to achieve his effects less through the animation of figures than through the cleverness of their individual design and the method of presentation of scenes. As productions became more ambitious and the number of figures, or characters, greatly increased, Rivière discovered that he could achieve more dynamic effects, especially with crowd scenes, not by following the old practice of moving his figures along the base of the screen one at a time, but by attaching the figures to each other so that a large number of them could be paraded across the screen in a broad band. The result, of course, was a marked enhancement of the overall pictorial value of the production.

With respect to light, Rivière experimented with the placement of his figures relative to the screen. Flush against this background, the figures illuminated from the back would appear black to the spectators, the true silhouettes, in other words, of the classical shadow play. But placed in grooves at certain distances behind the screen, they would appear not black, but gray. Positioning the figures at different distances from the screen, therefore, Rivière discovered that the conventional alternation of black and white in the shadow show could be made to yield a broader range of shades from solid black to a variety of grays. Rivière's most imaginative work was with glass panels on which entire scenes were painted. When projected, the color scenes created the visual effect of motion pictures in color and, in a sense, anticipated the color film. As for sound, both music and the human voice were used in Chat Noir shadow shows. The music, generally improvised, was provided by an accompanist at the cabaret's piano. Rodolphe Salis, as the Chat Noir's proprietor, reserved for himself the right to introduce the shadow shows and to comment on them while they were being performed. The arrangement, in fact, proved more than satisfactory. Apart from a good speaking voice, Salis also demonstrated a considerable ability for improvisation that won him many admirers. Recalling his own role as the author of shadow plays for the Chat Noir in his book of memoirs, *Mes Débuts à Paris,* the prolific writer Maurice Donnay has high praise for Salis' gifts as a commentator:

> It was wonderful to hear Salis' commentaries to the little shadow plays such as *L'Age d'or,* by Willette, or *Berline de l'Émigré.* Sometimes he'd embark on a sentence and we'd think, "He'll never get out of it." But he'd always find a way out by means of a pirouette, a somersault, an unexpected twist, some impertinence or other.[63]

The first full program of shadow plays to be presented by the Chat Noir consisted of three pieces: Henry Somm's *L'Éléphant,* Lunel's *Un Crime en chemin de fer,* and the popular caricaturist Caran d'Ache's Napoleonic "epic" *L'Épopée,* which, in an earlier, more modest form bore the title *1808!.* Two of these shadow plays—Somm's *The Elephant* and Caran d'Ache's *Épopée*—proved so successful that they went on to become acknowledged "classics" of the Chat Noir's shadow theater; *The Elephant,* in fact, because of its immediate appeal and lack of need for accompanying commentary, was frequently used at the cabaret as a curtain raiser. Short and humorous, *The Elephant* exemplifies the kind of wit possible in a shadow play. When the curtain opens, the only figure that appears on the screen is a black man, bent over, holding the end of a cord behind his back. Shortly thereafter, the figure begins to move forward and as he does so, the cord continues to lengthen. Soon, the figure of the man disappears entirely leaving just the cord, stretched the length of the screen, in view. Next, a knot appears in the cord and begins to move slowly along its entire length. The cord seems to go on endlessly until at last an elephant appears at the end of it. After moving to the center, the elephant pauses long enough to deposit, according to Salis' expression, "une perle odoriférante" (an odoriferous pearl). As the elephant trudges off, and the shadow show comes to an end, a rosebush appears growing out of the heap left behind by the great beast. The popularity of *The Elephant* was not limited to French audiences. It was presented at the Chicago World's Fair Exposition in 1893 as part of the program of a visiting French company which included some of the Chat Noir regulars.

Drawing by Paul Merwart of audience at Chat Noir viewing a shadow play, 1886. (Musée de Montmartre, Paris).

Caran d'Ache's *1808!* (or *L'Épopée*) was beyond any doubt the most spectacular and famous of the Chat Noir's shadow plays. Conceived on a grand scale, the work was an attempt to demonstrate the full potential of the tiny shadow theater by presenting some of the greatest episodes of Napoleon's campaigns. Divided into two acts and fifty tableaux, the "epic" covered such events as the Battle of Austerlitz, the retreat of the Grande Armée from Moscow, and the return of Napoleon's battered army to Paris. For a change of pace and mood, Caran d'Ache made a point of alternating the larger historical scenes with short ones of a lighter, more human, more amusing character. Like the vernacular *intermedia* or *interludia* in the Latin-language medieval mystery plays, these scenes were interpolated for the sake of comic relief.

Maurice Donnay, who was present at the inaugural performance of *Épopée,* regarded it as so sensational as to be "un événement parisien" (a Parisian event). What follows is his description of the performance itself:

The epopée consisted of the Italian, Egyptian, and Prussian campaigns; it was Marengo, Austerlitz, Wagram, and Jena; it was the reckless charges, the magnificent marches which, in the darkness of the auditorium, the gentle poet and pianist Albert Tinchant accompanied with appropriate music, stirring marches, patriotic songs, and bravura airs. Carried away by all these tableaux dedicated to French valor, stirred by the martial music, and electrified by the gab of Rodolphe Salis, the audience applauded and stamped its feet. When the silhouette of the Emperor appeared surrounded by his generals and the gentleman cabaretier [Salis—HBS] shouted, "The Emperor!," the audience, impassioned, roared back, "Long live the Emperor!" The windows of the room trembled. The shouts could be heard outside on the street. One could imagine that a Bonapartist movement was ushering forth from the "Chat Noir."[64]

Another member of that same inaugural audience was the outstanding French critic Jules Lemaître (1853–1914). That he shared the general enthusiasm for Caran d'Ache's Napoleonic shadow play is obvious from the remarks about it in his *Impressions de Théâtre:*

But what one could have foreseen less was that the silhouettes of men cut out of zinc and illuminated from behind a white cloth a meter wide could communicate to us the thrill of combat and the feeling of grandeur. . . . this type of drawing, which can interpret only the life of the body, is, by the same token, very suitable to render the life of multitudes, the collective life wherein the particular expression of faces becomes obliterated and gets lost. . . .

His silent poem [Caran d'Ache's—HBS], in gliding shadows, is, I believe, the sole epopée that we have in our literature.[65]

After seeing other shadow shows at the Chat Noir including Sahib's *La Partie de Whist,* Willette's *L'Age d'or,* Somm's *Le Fils de l'eunuque,* and Rivière's *La Tentation de Saint Antoine*—all of which he wrote reviews of—Lemaître was so enthusiastic about shadow theater and the work, in particular, of Rivière and Caran d'Ache, that he saw the miniature theater of silhouettes capable of an extraordinary range of expression:

Above all, by means of a bold and unerring simplification of the contours of the body, they [Caran d'Ache's and Rivière's silhouettes—HBS] were able to express with intensity souls, characters, and also epochs, countries, stages of civilization. They have made of the "Chinese shadows" the generalizing and philosophical art par excellence, an art that gives pleasure to children by its simplicity and supreme clarity, and to thoughtful mature minds by its power of synthesis, by everything that its black or colored blots convey. The shadows of Rivière or Caran d'Ache are truly the shadows of Plato's cave. That is because the outlines and appearances of things are the things themselves. All reality is nothing but a reflection. (p. 332)

An enthusiast of the turn-of-the-century Symbolist efforts to create a new poetical drama based on religious and mystical themes, Lemaître found much to admire in Chat Noir shadow theater shows along the same lines. The earliest production in this vein seems to have been a version of the *Temptation of Saint Anthony* for which Flaubert's well-known work on the same subject may have served as the model. In the Chat Noir version, the tale has been updated: the temptations are now visited upon the saint in the modern setting of Paris. This modernization notwithstanding, Lemaître saw in the production confirmation of his view that

> the shadow plays excel in rendering myths and legends, the most general and the most simple of ideas, in bringing before our eyes ideal figures and abundantly human, grandiose spectacles, the life of crowds, the recapitulated images of civilizations, and great historical events. (p. 338)

Lemaître also called attention to what was undoubtedly the production's most outstanding feature—Henri Rivière's extraordinary use of color. Working for the first time extensively with color in a shadow play, Rivière succeeded in combining color and transparent paper in such a way as to achieve something of the effect of stained glass. Of this facet of the Chat Noir's *Temptation of Saint Anthony,* Lemaitre writes:

> There is the brilliance of a stained glass window ablaze with light. And the comparison is absolutely just since the tableaux are in effect composed like those of the stained glass windows of a church, with the sole difference that the outlines have been determined not by ribs of lead but by cutouts of zinc, and that the glass has been replaced by colored paper through which oxyhydrogen light passes. (pp. 341–342)

The pianist-poet Albert Tinchant provided the musical accompaniment for the production—accompaniment that Lemaître praised as "ingeniously appropriate to the various tableaux" (p. 343)—while Rodolphe Salis narrated the shadow show.

The most celebrated of all Chat Noir shadow plays—*La Marche à l'Étoile* (The Procession to the Star)—was, like *The Temptation of Saint Anthony,* another religiously inspired work. First performed in 1890 and repeated several times thereafter, *The Procession to the Star,* about the Nativity, was a "mystery play" in one act and ten scenes with words and music by Georges Fragerolle and drawings by Henri Rivière. The text, in verse (as was usually the case with Symbolist neo-mysteries on religious themes), was set to music and assumed the form of an oratorio which was performed by its composer and author, Georges Fragerolle.

The great success of *The Procession to the Star,* which ran for only about ten minutes, can be attributed to two facets of the production, apart from the appeal of Fragerolle's text and music: first, Rivière's skill at creating tableaux depicting groups of shepherds, soldiers, women, slaves, and other groups of different people symbolizing the whole of humanity on its way to the manger, and second, his ability to conjure up the image of a star-studded dark-blue sky by means of a piece of blue paper that had been varnished, then pricked with a needle, and placed in front of the source of light.

Relating *The Procession to the Star* to the renewed interest in mysticism of the period, Lemaître, in an extensive review of the show, expressed the opinion that no surprise should attach to the fact the Chat Noir was host to such a production. "The 'Chat Noir,' " he declared, was a "sanctuary in which foolery and mysticism always get on well together" (p. 350). Moreover, the small theater of the Chat Noir was, in Lemaître's words, "a skylight opened on a supernatural world" (p. 350). This was because of the element of the mystical and supernatural which the critic believed was evident in Caran d'Ache's *Épopée* and in Rivière's *Temptation of Saint Anthony.* In fact, Lemaître does not hesitate to call both *Épopée* and *The Temptation of Saint Anthony* "mysteries" (p. 351). Embracing a simple yet great idea, *The Procession to the Star* belonged in the same category, as Lemaître writes in an account that conveys much of the spirit of the shadow show:

> First of all, infinity, heaven, on a starry night. A new star rises in the East. All those to whom Christ brings deliverance or hope make their way toward the star. The first to cross the plain are the shepherds followed by their long flocks. It was as if a painting by Millet were moving by. Afterward, the army of the wretched, of lepers, and of cripples, their incomplete silhouettes, bizarre and tormented, standing out against the clear sky, their bodies deformed, their outlines sharp, the intersection of their crutches and the jagged edges of their tatters. Later on, a crowd of slaves appears dragging their worn chains behind them. After them, a plaintive procession of women, in long hair, clothed in long folds and stretching their lovely supplicant arms toward the star. They are followed by the Magi, as luxurious as Byzantine bishops, with a train of multicolored servants and elephants laden with the earth's riches. Then, as if the entire universe had trembled on that night, and as if the flux of the ocean turned in the direction of the star, behold, there upon the calm sea, ships and fishermen, themselves pointed toward the invisible manger, bear people kneeling on their bows, while the nocturnal light traverses the links of suspended netting . . .
>
> And then, the divine stable, the infant encircled with a halo, asleep in the man-

ger, Mary and Joseph, the ox and the donkey, cut out like figures of stained glass and shining with the brilliance of precious stones; and all around, on all levels as far as the farthest horizons, an immense multitude in prayer . . . And finally, Golgotha; the hill, at the foot of which swarm innumerable heads, its somber ridge where the solitary cross is erected jutting out against a sky the color of blood . . .

Never has M. Henri Rivière done anything more moving or more profoundly expressive (pp. 351–352)

Maurice Donnay, himself the author of two shadow plays performed at the Chat Noir, also witnessed the premiere production of *The Procession of the Star* and has left this account which adds further detail to that of Lemaître:

With *The Procession to the Star,* with words and music by Georges Fragerolle, the theater of the Chat Noir, this time in the biblical and religious genre, has again had a resounding success. Guided by the star, one beheld marching across the lighted screen the Magi, Roman soldiers, shepherds, fishermen, slaves, children, and women, all headed for the plains of Judaea, for the village where the Savior was born.

They passed beneath colored skies, in evocative settings. More than one spectator asked how these effects were obtained, having no idea of the complicated machinery. For these landscapes, no fewer than a hundred colored papers were used. And this star that shone up above? A piece of blue varnished paper, pricked by a needle and through which the oxyhydrogen light passed. And when the picture appeared representing the manger radiating light where the infant Jesus was sleeping, and around which the Magi and the fishermen and the children were singing:

We come all full of hope
To greet with reverence
the infant born in this humble place.
Noël! Noël for the infant god!,

you felt that all the spectators were ready to cry out, "Noël! Noël!" just as they had cried out "Long live the Emperor" on the evenings when *Epopée* was performed.[66]

Donnay's own shadow plays for the Chat Noir—*Phryné* and *Ailleurs* (Elsewhere), both first performed in 1891—were among the cabaret's most popular. *Phryné,* subtitled Greek Scenes (Scènes Grecques), was premiered at the Chat Noir on January 9, 1891. Its figures and sets were designed by Henri Rivière and the music for it was composed by the pianist Charles de Sivry.

Phryné is a light entertainment, as most of the nonreligious, non-"mystical" shadow shows tended to be. Set in ancient Athens, the work recounts in seven tableaux the trial and eventual acquittal of the voluptuous courtesan Phryné (nicknamed "The Sieve," le Crible) who has had the audacity to disrupt at a crucial point the performance of a play about Leda, the wife of King Tyndare, who has grown weary of the love of humans and dreams of the love of the gods, in particular that of Jupiter. The rest of *Phryné* is taken up with the titular character's eventually successful efforts to use her womanly charms to win a verdict of acquittal from the court before which the case against her "blasphemy" is brought.

Setting the humorous tone of *Phryné* is the fact that the play about Leda and Jupiter, which Phryné mischievously interrupts, is presented as a play-within-a-play performed in the small theater of the Ombres Athéniennes (The Athenian Shadow Theater) within the Chat Noir of Athens. This "famous" ancient Greek cabaret, located in the Acropolis quarter of the city, is presided over by one Lissas (read, of course, Salis)—"un homme d'une grande audace et d'un langage abondant" (a man of considerable audacity and abundance of speech).[67] With its mixture, therefore, of allusions to the actual Parisian Chat Noir where *Phryné* was produced, its erotic subject, and its entertaining combination of prose and verse (in the latter of which the characters of the play speak, as opposed to the prose of the *récitant* or narrator of the piece), Donnay's first contribution to the cabaret's *ombres chinoises* had much to assure its success.

Encouraged by the favorable reception of *Phryné,* Donnay, on Salis' urging, composed another shadow show for the Chat Noir soon afterward. This was *Ailleurs* (Elsewhere), a "revue symbolique" in twenty tableaux on which Rivière and Sivry again collaborated and which Donnay dedicated to the great poet Paul Verlaine, who was not only a personal friend but a frequent visitor to the Chat Noir. *Elsewhere* had its premiere on November 11, 1891, and as a measure of Salis' esteem for the popularity of his shadow shows the proprietor of the Chat Noir upped Donnay's salary from the one louis per show that he had paid for *Phryné* to thirty louis per show for *Elsewhere.*[68]

A "Parisian midsummer night's dream" (songe parisien d'une nuit d'automne), as Jules Lemaître called it, *Elsewhere* was conceived not as a cabaret in-joke, as was *Phryné,* but as an expression of Donnay's personal displeasure with contemporary literary symbolism in France.

Donnay makes this genesis of *Elsewhere* quite clear in *Mes Débuts à Paris* where he recalls:

In September, when Henri Rivière returned from Brittany, from where he brought back some wonderful studies, I began a new piece of work. This time, it took the form of a symbolic review entitled *Elsewhere.* This was the time when the Symbolists were taking many liberties with rhyme and metrics. These novelties troubled me; I had been trained on Parnasssian disciplines and found *vers libre* too simple. In view of these revolutionary efforts, I asked myself if I was on the right road and if it was not, in fact, the innovators who were right. And, with respect to fugitive and already antiquated fashions, this word "anguish" [*angoisse*] could only make one laugh. But as long as one writes verse, everything that touches art and the craft of poetry assumes an importance of the first order, even if one has the right to be "the poet died young whom the man outlives."

Between free verse and Parnassian verse, I was like Hercules between a rock and a hard place. Some Symbolists were among the purist of artists; but to free oneself from every rule and from every constraint, more than one disciple gave the impression that he wrote in verse simply because he did not have the time to write in prose.[69]

Donnay's exposure of the inadequacies of symbolism in *Elsewhere* is revealed through a Jules Verne-like fantastic journey to Elsewhere which Voltaire, accompanied by the poet Terminus, takes, beginning in the depths of the River Seine. Along the way (to be exact, in the Fifth Tableau), they meet Adolphe, "the sad young man" (le jeune homme triste). Adolphe, who has read the works of Schopenhauer, Renan, and Nietzsche, does nothing and spends all his time seated upon a lonely rock in a pensive and doleful attitude his eyes "constantly fixed on a pond whose stagnant desolation reflects all discredited and faded images in such a way that he sees the universe topsy-turvy" (p. 150). To dispel Voltaire's curiosity, Terminus relates, in verse, the story of Adolphe who no matter what he undertook was forever sad:

Et quelque chose qu'il tentât,
Dans l'Art, dans l'Amour, dans l'État,
Il était quelque chose en iste
De triste, triste, triste, triste. (p. 152)

(And whatever he tried, / In Art, in Love, in Politics, / He was something ending in "-ist," / And always, sad, sad, sad.)

When he died, of eczema, continues Terminus, he was cremated according to his own wishes and on the urn containing his ashes a Symbolist wrote the words: "He was sad!"

The rest of the shadow play is taken up with Voltaire's search, with the help of Terminus, for the causes of Adolphe's sadness. Their journey takes them through a forest filled with poets, a pagan temple, a field of orchids peopled with voluptuous naked women, a gallery fringed with statues of classical deities, the ruins of a temple where a black mass is celebrated, the banks of the Nile, the ruins of the Paris Stock Exchange, a battlefield, a huge construction site, and, finally, the Notre Dame cathedral. Along the way Voltaire learns that the roots of Adolphe's sadness lay in a) his being ill-conceived and in aesthetically blameworthy conditions—even before he was born his mother moved among people in a milieu of repugnant statues; b) his learning of poetry through "Schools, Vanity, and Publicity in place of Art and Enthusiasm" (p. 160); c) the influence of the god Eros, now an effete deity who presides over Sapphic loves and whose currency is sterility and circumspection; he is now, in fact, the god of neurotics; d) his desire to love being thwarted by his finding not women, but Lesbians; e) his failure at the practical life—business and the stock market—after his inability to live the ideal and sentimental life; f) his failure, next, to pursue a meditative and intellectual life because of the clamor of false patriotism and militarism that kept invading his study where he had hoped to pursue his study of science, philosophy, and civilization; and g) his failure to learn the value of labor represented by workers and socialism. When Voltaire and Terminus reach the end of their journey at the Cathedral of Notre Dame in the early light of morning, Terminus closes the shadow play with a poem of faith which includes the refrain:

Et dans des Cycles de l'Ailleurs
J'ai vu l'Au-delà salutaire,
Et je pressens des temps meilleurs.
Non dans le ciel, mais sur la terre,
Pour ceux de bonne volunté. (pp. 191–192)

(And in the Cycles of Elsewhere/I have seen the salutary Next World,/And I feel the coming of better times/Not in heaven, but on earth,/For those of good will.)

Donnay's putdown of literary symbolism in *Elsewhere* is a commentary as well on a contemporary French culture whose decadence has made possible the emergence of a type such as Adolphe, a true hero of his age. After Voltaire's acceptance of the idea of redemption through toil, it is left to Terminus, himself enlightened by all that he has seen, to vow to serve others as a guide in order

Raviver la Foi qui se meurt
Et la Charité souveraine,
Et je serai le bon semeur
Qui va semant la bonne graine. (p. 191)

(To revive the Faith that is dying / And the supreme Charity, / And I will be the good sower / Who goes about sowing the good seed.)

For the typical Chat Noir audience the topicality of the journey of Voltaire and Terminus to seek out the roots of Adolphe's sadness could not have missed striking sympathetic chords. But it would be doing Henri Rivière considerable injustice not to recognize the importance of his great talent to the success of the production. Donnay himself had high praise for Rivière's settings for *Elsewhere,* as he writes in *Mes Débuts à Paris:*

Parisian landscapes or dream landscapes, twilight or nocturnal scenes; living and changing skies, where clouds race above the moon; green, rose, pearl-gray skies; skies mixed with thunderstorms; delightful or terrible skies mirrored in transparent waters; and standing out in relief against backgrounds of luminous or dark mother-of-pearl, the silhouettes of buildings, of trees, of rocks, and of shores, of a nobility of harmonious and singular grace.

Henri Rivière invented effects of rare ingenuity! At one moment, in the woeful forest, the trees were suddenly deprived of their foliage; at another moment, the stage represented a field covered with heather; the wind grazed the plain and the *heather moved.*

The spectators were astonished. (p. 225)

All told, some forty shadow shows were produced at the Chat Noir during the life span of the cabaret's *ombres chinoises.* Apart from the most celebrated—Henry Somm's *The Elephant,* Caran d'Ache's *Épopée,* Rivière's and Fragerolle's *The Temptation of Saint Anthony* and *The Procession to the Star,* and Maurice Donnay's *Phryné* and *Elsewhere*—several others enjoyed considerable popularity. These included Somm's *Berlin de l'Émigré* and *Fils de l'eunuque,* Willette's *L'Age d'or,* on the Pierrot theme, Sahib's *Une Partie de Whist,* about a group of Englishmen who play a game of whist aboard a ship through a storm, a pirate attack, and other disasters until they and the ship go to their doom, Jacques Ferney's *Le Secret du manifestant,* for which Fernand Fau did the illustrations, Jules Jouy's *Une Affaire d'honneur,* also illustrated by

Fau, Maurice Vaucaire's *Le Carnaval de Venise,* with art work by Louis Morin, Rivière's and Fragerolle's *Clair de lune* and *L'Enfant Prodigue,* Fragerolle's and Vignola's *Sphinx,* Louis Bombled's *La Conquête de l'Algérie,* and Léopold Dauphin's and Claudius Blanc's *Sainte Geneviève de Paris,* another shadow theater "mystery play" along the same lines as *The Temptation of Saint Anthony;* Henri Rivière was in charge of the production which employed ten singers, four choirboys from the Paris opera, an organist, a pianist, and a violinist. It was, in Michel Herbert's words, Rivière's "most prodigious success."[70]

The popularity of shadow shows, like that of the cabaret itself, survived the closing of the Chat Noir. Even before the demise of the greatest of all Parisian cabarets, shadow shows and *théâtre d'ombres* of one sort or another had already sprung up elsewhere. The *chansonnier* Vincent Hyspa, who in 1895 became one of the organizers of a Chat Noir-inspired cabaret called the Chien Noir (Black Dog), presented a *Noël* shadow play in 1890 with music by Eric Satie and the "shadows" and stage décor designed by the Catalonian artist Miquel Utrillo, the father of the painter Maurice Utrillo, and a member at the time of a small circle of Catalonian artists who had come to Paris, mostly from Barcelona, to study the new trends in art and easily blended into the fabric of Montmartre Bohème. In 1892, the Théâtre des Ombres lyriques du Lyon d'Or, devoted wholly to shadow play performances, was established. Between 1898 and 1900, shadow shows were regularly presented at the Théâtre d'Application (later the Théâtre de la Bodinière), located at 18 Rue St.-Lazare. Another *théâtre d'ombres,* La Boîte à musique, opened on the Boulevard Clichy in the Pigalles area in 1898. Sometimes already established theaters acknowledged the current enthusiasm over shadow shows by mounting their own productions. Thus, the theater of Antoine staged *Le Juif errant* by Henri Rivière and Georges Fragerolle shortly after the turn of the century. The Théâtre des Mathurius followed suit with a program of shadow shows, among them the popular *Aladin* in fifteen tableaux by Lucien Métivier, with music by Janvieu.

Several of the successor cabarets of the Chat Noir also attempted to keep alive the tradition of cabaret-based shadow shows, but none with greater sense of dedication than the Cabaret des Quat'z' Arts (Cabaret of the Four Arts). Here, in 1900, Dominique Bonnaud mounted some of the most famous Chat Noir shows as well as a few of his own. After leaving the Quat'z' Arts, Bonnaud installed himself in 1904 in the Cabaret de la Lune Rousse (Red Moon) first located on the Boulevard de Clichy and later on the Rue Pigalle. Under Bonnaud's direction, virtually all the programs of the Lune Rousse were made up of shadow performances. When the Lune Rousse changed locations, its premises on the Clichy were taken over by the Cabaret de la Chaumière (The Thatched Cottage) which also continued the presentation of shadow shows.

In view of the enormous popularity of shadow theater in the period of the "second" Chat Noir, perhaps it was fitting that it was with this aspect of the cabaret, above all, that Rodolphe Salis chose to be identified toward the end both of his life and that of the cabaret he founded. Disappointed in the fortunes of the Chat Noir after he relinquished control of it in 1895, Salis planned to return to Paris from his country retirement with the aim of attempting a revival. He was especially enthusiastic about the prospect of a domestic and foreign tour of the cabaret's shadow theater, under his personal direction. But time had run out on him. His beloved cabaret had slipped irretrievably from his grasp. The shadow theater tour, once launched, had to be halted abruptly in Chateaudun on March 17, 1897, when illness overtook Salis and he was unable to continue. Treatment in nearby Naintré proved to no avail and two days later the master cabaretier was dead.

Long before the end of Rodolphe Salis and the Chat Noir, the cabaret itself had begun to celebrate its legendary status by sponsoring several publications about itself apart from the *Chat Noir* journal. As early as 1885 a special Chat Noir album, *L'Album du Chat Noir,* began to be published. Each issue of the album was to consist of a single fascicle containing six drawings by such artists as Willette, Caran d'Ache, Uzès, Somm, and Lunel, and six poems by various Chat Noir literary regulars. All told, six fascicles appeared before the undertaking came to an end. A few years later, in 1887–1888, to be exact, the cabaret arranged publication of a *Chat Noir Guide* containing detailed information about all its interior furnishings, *objets d'art,* bric-a-brac, and so on. A projected four-part fictional series, to be called *Les Contes du Chat Noir,* written by Salis himself, was half realized. The first volume, subtitled *L'Hiver,* was published in Paris in 1888 by the Libraire Dentu; the second volume, *Le Printemps,* was issued by the same house in 1891. Both volumes bore covers designed by the artist George Auriol who was long active in the *Chat Noir* journal.

A literature about the Chat Noir also began springing up before the cabaret's demise. As early as 1888 a collection of Chat Noir chansons (*Chansons du Chat Noir*), by Maurice Mac-Nab, was published by Au Ménestral in Paris. The singer Victor Meusy's *Chansons d'Hier et d'Aujourd'hui,* mostly on Chat Noir themes, was issued by Ferreyrol in 1899. A collection of Chat Noir stories entitled *Les Gaietés du Chat Noir* appeared in 1894 over the imprint of Ollendorf of Paris. And in 1897, the well-known Parisian publisher Flammarion came out with the *chansonnier* Gabriel de Montoya's *Le Roman Comique du Chat Noir.*

The importance of this Chat Noir popular literature to a reconstruction of the history of the cabaret cannot be overestimated especially in view of the dispersal of the cabaret's artifacts following Salis' death. On April 28, 1897, less than a month and a half after Salis' passing, the first of several public auctions of Chat Noir properties was held. The first disposed of material related to the cabaret's shadow theater. Subsequent auctions on May 16, 17, 18, and 19, in 1898, and on March 22, 1904, resulted in the dispersal of Chat Noir drawings and paintings belonging to Salis among a number of private and public bidders.

Even these auctions became part of Chat Noir literature. In a personal farewell to the cabaret, Alphonse Allais wrote a short bittersweet piece entitled *Finis Chat Noir!,* which he dedicated to Salis' widow Gabrielle and published in the *Chat Noir* journal on May 17, 1898, after a few of the public auctions had already been held. Despite the obvious avoidance of sentimentality and the overall lighthearted tone of the work, Allais nonetheless strikes a clear note of regret in the opening farewell invocation, the more poignant for its allusion to the dispersal of Chat Noir artifacts:

> The "Chat Noir" is dead! The cabaret closed; the theater, annihilated! The Chinese shadows, vanished! The poets and singers, scattered! The journal, abolished!
>
> Something considerable is leaving us, and when I heard of the sale today of the last pictures, drawings, and other *objets d'art* that are going to be dispersed
>
> *To the four winds, Sir, of public auctions,*
>
> something like a tear quivered on my old eyelashes.
>
> Ah! The "Chat Noir," the first "Chat Noir," the one on the Boulevard Rochechouart!
>
> You are too young, my lads, to have known this marvelous dive![71]

For the one hundredth anniversary of the founding of the Chat Noir, in 1981, the Musée de Montmartre in Paris was able to collect many of

Cover of brochure of Chat Noir centenary exhibition published by the Musée de Montmartre. The cover is based on a Chat Noir poster designed by Théophile Steinlen. (Musée de Montmartre, Paris).

the long scattered properties of the cabaret from private and public sources in order to mount a commemorative exhibition on their premises at 17, Rue Saint-Vincent in Montmartre. In his preface to the illustrated brochure published by the Musée in conjuction with the exhibition, M. Claude Charpentier, the curator of the museum, declares that "It is not excessive to say that for seventeen years the Cabaret du Chat Noir launched one of the most important movements of the end of the nineteenth century."[72]

That movement was cabaret. It began with the Chat Noir, whose extraordinary, truly legendary success initiated the cabaret epidemic that swept across Europe in the late nineteenth and early twentieth centuries. In the chapters that follow, we will see how that fever affected other parts of Europe, as far east as Moscow and St. Petersburg.

CHAPTER TWO
BARCELONA: FOUR MORE CATS

That we move south to Barcelona at this point may come as something of a surprise to anyone unprepared to imagine (for whatever reason) that a vigorous cabaret might have appeared in the Catalonian capital before the end of the nineteenth century, hence before the very emergence of cabaret in central and eastern Europe. The surprise is quite unjustified, however, in view of the fact that Barcelona was the center of a dynamic turn-of-the-century Catalonian cultural revival known as the *Renaixença* (Renascence) which lasted until the suppression of Catalan regional privileges in 1925 by the Spanish dictator Primo de Rivera (1870–1930).[1] But the flame of Catalonian nationalism, once kindled, could not be permanently extinguished, neither by Primo de Rivera nor by Generalissimo Francisco Franco (1892–1975) after the downfall of the Spanish Republic and a still harsher crackdown on manifestations of Catalonian cultural as well as political autonomy. The death of Franco and the subsequent reaffirmation (in 1977) of Catalonian privileges under King Carlos I solidified and, indeed, handsomely extended the gains of the *Renaixença,* at last removing a long-standing source of deep resentment among the Catalonian people.

The rebirth of the Catalan language and Catalan literature, which has a rich heritage going back to the early Middle Ages, was made possible, to a great extent, in the time of the *Renaixença* by a new generation of Catalonian political leadership that emphasized cultural nationalism as a fundamental aspect of political autonomy. One of the most eloquent advocates of such linkage was Enric Prat de la Riba (1870–1917), who in 1914 became the president of the *Mancomunitat,* which then functioned as a form of Catalonian local government.[2] Prat de la Riba's own manifesto of 1906, *La Nacionalitat Catalana* (The Catalonian Nationality), was a well-reasoned argument for the necessity of promoting the indigenous language and culture of the province within the context of the campaign for recognition of Catalonian political rights.[3] The convening of the first International Congress on the Catalan Language in 1906, and the creation the following year of the *Institut d'Estudis Catalans* (Institute for Catalan Studies) were two of the more significant institutional achievements of the new Catalonian leadership.

As important, if not more so, to the success of a vibrant Catalan-based regional culture as a supportive political ideology was the symbiotic relationship between the turn-of-the-century cultural revival and the emergence of an exceptionally impressive modernist movement in the arts. The *Renaixença* of the period 1890 to 1915, that era of rebirth of the Catalan language and literature, coincided with the advent of modernism. The result was the crystallization of an internationally esteemed Catalonian modernist art—represented by such artists as the painters Pablo Picasso, Miquel Utrillo, and Ramon Casas, the architect Antoni Gaudí, the writer and painter Santiago Rusiñol, and the poet Joan Maragall—that epitomized the fulfilment of the Catalan potential and at the same time assumed the role of a vigorous champion of Catalonian cultural nationalism.[4]

Barcelona, with a population at the time in excess of half a million, was the logical center of Catalonian modernism. Then, as now, a great seaport and Spain's most cosmopolitan city, Barcelona was also close to France both geographically and spiritually. Because of this greater sense of kinship with France and French culture than with Madrid or the rest of Spain, and because of the relative closeness of the Catalan language to French compared to Castilian, Catalonian artists, most first trained in Barcelona, had already made themselves part of the Parisian art scene in the 1890s. For cultural and linguistic reasons, therefore, the migration was well motivated and, to the artists themselves, wholly natural. Paris was a powerful magnet for any artist attracted to the new in the turn-of-the-century period; but for a Catalonian artist in particular, this reason, together with an inclination to look to Paris for inspiration rather than to Madrid, made a stay in the French capital a virtual necessity. As Jaime (Jaume, in Catalan) Sabartés, Picasso's lifelong friend and chronicler, put it in *Picasso: An Intimate Portrait:*

We breathed an air infested with northern modernism. Nothing counted except the fashion from Paris. All our intellectuals had been to France. If, perchance, one among them became famous without the benefit of the trip, it was either because time had proved his worth or because he wrote in Catalan and knew French. But sculptors and artists—like dressmakers—had no alternative but to cross the frontier.[5]

Chronologically, the first important Catalonian artist to set up shop in Paris was the father of a much better known son, Miquel Utrillo, also known as "Morlius" (1862–1934). The fame of his illegitimate son Maurice, the issue of his liaison with the Parisian model Suzanne Valadon (ca. 1865–1938), has so overshadowed the career of Miquel Utrillo that very little has been written about him.[6] He began his career in science and engineering, served in 1879–1880 as a member of the staff of the Spanish scientific journal *Revista Internacional de Ciencia,* and in 1880 came to Paris to pursue further studies in mathematics and metereology at the Institut National Agronomique. Once in the French captial, Utrillo the elder's scientific interests soon became secondary to his fascination with the cabaret life of Montmartre. Having discovered a new world with which he had undeniably stronger affinities, Utrillo threw himself into it with unconcealed enthusiasm.

He took up quarters at the Moulin de la Galette and lost little time in making himself a member of the Chat Noir circle. It was the cabaret's shadow theater that seemed to attract him the most, so much so in fact that he learned enough about the art of *ombres chinoises* to operate his own shadow theater for a while at the Auberge de Clou (Hock-Shop Inn) on the Avenue Trudaine. The resident musician here was Erik Satie and the close friendship that developed between Utrillo and Satie dates from this period. When the World's Columbian Exposition in Chicago in 1893 included performances by the Parisian shadow theater Les Ombres Parisiennes of Lêon-Charles Marot in its program, Utrillo, an indefatigable traveler, went along as a member of the troupe. He returned to Barcelona in 1895 where not long afterward he entered into close collaboration with the artist Santiago Rusiñol, one of the foremost figures in turn-of-the-century Catalonian modernism, whom he had known from his earlier stay in Paris. Out of this collaboration came Utrillo's participation in the founding of the most famous cabaret in the history of Barcelona (and Spain in general)—Els Quatre Gats (The Four Cats)—in 1897.[7]

Whatever fame Utrillo has, outside the context of his place in the development of Catalonian modernism, owes much to his romantic relationship with Suzanne Valadon, who had also posed for Puvis de Chavannes, Renoir, Toulouse-Lautrec, Zandomeneghi, and Degas.[8] It is, however, his less famliar role in the activities of the Barcelona Quatre Gats that interests us here. By the early 1890s, Paris had a small but closely knit and lively circle of Catalonian artists who, like Utrillo, had come to France either to study the new trends in art or to play some part in the modernist movement. Besides Utrillo, the group included three men who were to add the establishment of the Quatre Gats to their other accomplishments as artists: Santiago Rusiñol (1861–1931), Pere Romeu (ca. 1862–1908), and Ramon Casas (1866–1932).

Beginning in 1892 and owing much to Rusiñol's initiative, modernist *festes* began to be held in the Costa Brava town of Sitges, not far south of Barcelona along the coast.[9] At the second *festa* in 1893, Rusiñol, who was also a dramatist with a strong interest in theater, staged a Catalan version of Maurice Maeterlinck's exemplary Symbolist play *L'Intruse* (The Intruder; *L'Intrusa,* in Catalan). The third *festa,* in 1894, became the occasion for the "official" inauguration of the Sitges modernist center of Cau Ferrat, which Rusiñol named after the small musuem that he had opened in Barcelona in 1885 to house his personal collection of medieval ironwork and other *objets d'art.*[10] The afternoon literary session was preceded by a lyric discourse by Rusiñol in which he exalted the modernist movement and which was followed by Rusiñol's own production of Ibsen's *Ghosts.*

Rusiñol's literary activity was almost as varied as his painting. Apart from a number of plays, he also followed in Utrillo's footsteps by covering Paris for the leading Barcelona newspaper *La Vanguardia,* which then, as now, is published in Castilian and not Catalan. It was in *La Vanguardia,* beginning in the early 1890s, that Rusiñol's account of *fin-de-siècle* artistic Paris and the Catalonian circle there began appearing under the title "Desde el molino" (From the Mill), a reference to Rusiñol's apartment above the famous Montmartre landmark, the Moulin de la Galette. Utrillo moved there in 1890 and the apartment became the favorite gathering place of Catalonian artists in Paris at the time.

Published in book form in 1894, *Desde el molino,* which was subtitled *Impressions of a Trip to Paris in 1894* and was illustrated by another key member of the Catalonian artists' circle in Paris, Ramon Casas, offers a lively picture of contemporary Montmartre as seen through the eyes of a visiting Catalonian artist who is also informing the reader back home of the comings and goings in Paris of fellow Catalonian artists. The book is essentially a diary of artistic-literary impressions covering the period 1890 through 1892; it became, in fact, Rusiñol's first literary work.

For the student of late nineteenth-century Montmartre, *Desde el molino* is a valuable complement to better known accounts and offers interesting vignettes of, among others, Toulouse-Lautrec's favorite Divon Japonais, of course the Chat Noir, the Parisian chanson, and the popularity at the time of shadow shows. The book is divided into thirteen small chapters, the first of which, "Artistas catalanes en Paris" (Catalonian Artists in Paris), is devoted to the Catalonian artists' colony in the French capital. Like Utrillo, Rusiñol took a keen interest in shadow shows and puppetry and as if anticipating the prominence of this type of entertainment at the Barcelona Quatre Gats offers detailed descriptions in *From the Mill* of the *théâtre d'ombres* of the Chat Noir and other Parisian cabarets. He also notes that as enthusiasm for shadow theaters grew "el cielo del arte parece obscurerse de tal modo que, si el viento de otra moda no despija el horizonte, pronto Paris, el gran Paris de la luz, se vera convertido en el reino tenebroso de las ombras" (the heaven of art appears to have become so dark that unless a wind from another direction clears the horizon, then Paris, the great Paris of light, will soon be transformed into the dark kingdom of shadows).[11]

The illustrations for the *La Vanguardia* edition of *From the Mill,* as mentioned before, were supplied by perhaps the most outstanding turn-of-the-century Catalonian painter who was also an active participant in the activities of the Quatre Gats, Ramon Casas (Carbo). Casas' collaboration on the *From the Mill* illustrations as well as other projects began in 1890 when Casas joined Rusiñol in his quarters above the Moulin de la Galette. This was eight years after Casas had come to Paris from his native Barcelona in order to study painting. Casas was a talented and industrious artist who came to exhibit regularly in Paris as well as in Barcelona. Once the Quatre Gats was established not only did he join other Catalonian artists in exhibiting there, but he also supplied it with paintings for decorations and was the principal artist of its posters.

Utrillo's fascination with shadow shows as well as puppetry was shared by another Catalonian artist, Pere Romeu, who is remembered above all as the moving spirit of the Quatre Gats from its opening in 1897 until its closing in 1903. It was also for the purpose of studying painting that Romeu came to Paris in the mid-'80s, and like Utrillo before him he soon found himself enamored of the ambience of Montmartre and became a familiar face at the Chat Noir. It was some time in the early 1890s that Romeu and Utrillo met for the first time. Whether Utrillo's enthusiasm for shadow and puppet theater was infectious or Romeu had developed a similar interest before even meeting Utrillo remains problematic. But however he came to the art of shadows, Romeu, like Utrillo, traveled with Marot's theater Les Ombres Parisiennes to the World's Columbian Exposition in Chicago in 1893. After his visit to the United States as a member of the troupe, he returned to Catalonia, participating in the modernist festivals in Sitges and then virtually running the Quatre Gats between 1897 and 1903. Although he obviously patterned himself on Rodolphe Salis as a *cabaretier,* Romeu lacked the Frenchman's entrepreneurial talents, a factor of no small importance in the ultimate demise of the Barcelona cabaret.

When the Quatre Gats opened in 1897 to become the first cabaret in Barcelona and the most illustrious in turn-of-the-century Spain, the way was well prepared, as the preceding sketch of Catalonian artists in Paris should clearly demonstrate. Once the Catalonians had assimilated the new currents in art it was only natural for them to return to their homeland and attempt to create there a Catalonian modernism capable of functioning as the centerpiece, so to speak, of a much desired Catalonian nationalist cultural revival. It was also no less natural for them to carry back to Catalonia a fervent desire to create a Catalonian cabaret which would assume in the life of Barcelona a role similar to that of the Parisian cabaret. For all its ambitions, however, Barcelona was not Paris. It was hoped, therefore, that the existence of an outstanding cabaret in the Catalonian capital on the order of the Chat Noir would not only prove its worth by being a meeting place of the new wave of Catalonian artists, but that it would serve the very important function of drawing attention to the new Catalonian art by making itself available as an exhibition center.

That the Parisian Chat Noir was the immediate model for the Catalonians is apparent in the very name of the Barcelona cabaret, Els Quatre Gats (The Four Cats), the cat motif borrowed from the Parisians

Exterior view of the Casa Martí in which Els Quatre Gats was located. (Arxiu Mas, Barcelona).

and the Four Cats referring to the cabaret's four founders—Pere Romeu, Santiago Rusiñol, Ramon Casas, and Miquel Utrillo. Picasso, who was born in 1881 and was thus much younger than the "four cats," began to participate in the activities of the cabaret a few years after his family had moved to Barcelona in 1895. He was, therefore, not one of the cabaret's founding fathers, but he was quickly drawn into the Quatre Gats circle once he had settled in Barcelona and made contact with fellow artists there. His first Barcelona exhibition was held, in fact, at the cabaret in 1900 and it was on that occasion that he made his acquaintance with the man who was to become his most loyal life's companion, the artist and writer Jaime Sabartés.

When the Quatre Gats opened its doors on June 12, 1897, it was billed as a *cerveseria-taverna-hostal* (beerhall-tavern-inn) and was housed in a splendid example of contemporary Catalonian neomedieval architecture, the Casa Martí, which was designed by a leading architect and Catalonian cultural nationalist of the period named José Puig i Cadafalch (1867–1956). The building is still standing at the corner of the Carrer Montesion (no. 3-bis) and the Passatge del Patriarca, although the cabaret that made it famous is little more than a memory today. The cabaret's logo, a metal sign in the shape of two cats with their backs arched, black on one side and gray on the other, hung above the imposing entrance made up of a pair of oversized Gothic arches. The main room of the Quatre Gats, the so-called *sala gran,* and the focal point of the cabaret's activities as a cabaret, was filled with a variety of *objets d'art* the most prominent of which were native Catalonian ceramics hung all over the walls and reaching right up to the establishment's beamed ceiling. In the style of most of the other early cabarets of Europe, the walls of the Quatre Gats were also adorned with paintings and drawings by the artists who became regulars there. These regulars clustered, for the most part, at a long table designed by Puig i Cadafalch and located in a kind of alcove alongside a wall opposite the windows. In 1897, much of the wall above the table was adorned with a huge canvas painted by Ramon Casas depicting Casas himself and Pere Romeu riding a tandem bicycle. In 1900, the painting was replaced by another one by Casas of both himself and Romeu now no longer astride a bicycle but in their newest craze, an automobile. A charcoal on paper drawing from around 1900 by one of the Quatre Gats artists, Richardo Opisso, shows a group of cabaret habitués seated at their *Stammtisch,* Picasso now among

Interior view of Els Quatre Gats showing painting by Ramon Casas of Pere Romeu and himself riding a tandem bicycle. (Arxiu Mas, Barcelona).

them, directly beneath the huge painting of fur-clad Casas and Romeu driving in their open car with a dog perched atop its dashboard.

For the puppet performances that were to become a highlight of Four Cats performances, a small stage was built topped by a ceramic painting and bearing the legend in Catalan *L'home que be vulge viure, bons aliments y molt riure* (The man who leads a good simple life, [needs] good food and much laughter). The subject of the painting is a woman appearing to drift through a field of irises. Floating toward her in the sky are figures in caricature including a skeleton, a member of the Spanish *Guardia Civil,* the devil, and a few portraits, one of which is clearly that of Pere Romeu wearing a nightgown. Below the painting, Casas' emblem for the café, Romeu's head next to four cats, was executed in ceramic tiles. The same design was also duplicated on ceramic beer mugs and on printed invitations and handouts.

Unlike the Parisian Chat Noir and cabarets elsewhere in the late nineteenth and early twentieth centuries, the Quatre Gats of Barcelona openly sought the presence of the public among whom it hoped to gain favor for the new Catalonian modernist painting represented by its participants. For much of its nearly seven year history, the Quatre Gats operated much like a salon exhibiting the works of native Catalonian artists and others. Many exhibitions were held on its premises, the first of which opened one month after the cabaret's inauguration.[12] The names of artists who participated in Quatre Gats exhibitions reads like a roster

The puppet stage of Els Quatre Gats. (Arxiu Mas, Barcelona).

ward might provide just the right kind of balance. Whatever the circumstances, however, Wolzogen was in high spirits, expecting nothing short of a triumph for the opening of the Überbrettl. A private dress rehearsal for critics, artists, theater directors, and "other knowledgeable people"—all in all, over sixty men and women—had already been held in Wolzogen's residence.[17] The event was covered by the press, which the Baron was doubly happy over since he was sure his guests would serve the useful purpose not only of publicizing the opening of the Überbrettl but also of disseminanting positive information about the new art of "small forms."[18]

When the fateful night of January 17 came it was almost a disaster. The whole Goethe program was, in Wolzogen's words, "a real orgy of tastelessness" which, in his opinion, just confirmed "the Berliners' innate lack of talent for festivals and celebration."[19] So overloaded was the Goethe program that the Überbrettl was unable to make its appearance until after midnight. The crowd was of overflow proportions and so badly managed that when it began proceeding from the main auditorium where the Goethe festivities were held to an upper hall for the cabaret program, the entrance quickly became jammed and fistfights erupted. Women joined in the fracas and very soon hairdos were pulled apart and clothes torn to shreds.[20] When the electric lights failed, the program that had begun to get underway despite the din and tumult had to be called off. The next performance of the Überbrettl was scheduled for four in the morning for those who were unable to get into the first, but by now the performers' nerves were frayed so badly they walked out with Wolzogen himself following right behind.

The entire Überbrettl program was due to be repeated the next night, that of the 18th, on the stage of the Sezession (Secession) Theater on the Alexanderplatz. The dress rehearsal scheduled for the morning of the 18th, that is just a few hours after the fracas of the early hours of the same morning, was a waste of time. The performers were so exhausted and out of sorts because of the events of the opening night that nothing went right. Wolzogen ordered them to go home and sleep until five in the afternoon and then return to the theater. When the evening of the 18th arrived and Wolzogen set out for the Alexanderplatz it felt, he writes, as if he were riding out "to his own execution."[21] Adding to his anxieties in the light of everything that had already happened was the fact that on the same evening a highly competitive affair was also scheduled to take place: a commemoration of the two hundredth anniversary of the establishment of the Kingdom of Prussia together with a celebration of the Order of the Knights of the Black Eagles, with both fêtes being held amidst much pomp and glitter in Berlin's Royal Castle. With this other event—which he heard of only on his way to the theater—now much on his mind, Wolzogen promised himself that in presenting the "baptismal celebration" of his own Überbrettl he had to find some way or ways of making a spiritual connection between this event and the important jubilee being celebrated the same night.

Wolzogen's anxieties and concerns proved in vain. Unplagued by the bedlam of the preceding night's opening at the Berlin Philharmonic, the debut of the Überbrettl at the Secession Theater was a huge success. Wolzogen's later description is ecstatic:

> The battle was won, the victory was complete. The beaming cashier could confirm the enterprise's booking straight through to Easter Week since the little theater was sold out every evening for weeks in advance. After only ten performances I was already able to repay my backers their small capital with a ten percent profit. And the entire, still considerable excess flowed straight into my own pocket.[22]

What the audience viewed on this first successful opening of Wolzogen's Überbrettl has been described in some detail by Rudolf Presber in his book of memoirs, *Ich gehe durch mein Haus:*

> When the curtains of the unfortunately ill-suited Secession Theater stage parted at the beginning of the performance, the audience beheld a simple room decorated in Biedermeier style. A Bechstein grand piano to the right. Next to it, a small bright yellow leather sofa. Through the middle door the master of the house, Ernst von Wolzogen, enters in brown dress coat with golden buttons and pigeon gray "unmentionables." He then presents the first conductor of the "Überbrettl," Oscar Straus, a still young, excessively thin man with short black hair who was soon to become for a while the most popular man in Berlin.[23]

The program[24] was initiated by a recitation of the humorous but coarse poem "Der Mistkafer" (The Dung-Beetle) by Hanns Heinz Ewers (who later published a book about the German cabaret, *Das Cabaret,* in Berlin in 1904) whom Wolzogen personally introduced to the public in these words:

> Esteemed Ladies and Gentlemen, I have the satisfaction of presenting a poet who will share something from his own work with you. It appears, moreover,

that the aversion of poets to mounting the boards of the "Brettl" already seems to have diminished . . .[25]

With Wolzogen directing the proceedings in the capacity of cabaret *conférencier,* the first part of the program was made up of poems by Wolzogen himself, Bierbaum, Hugo Salus, Robert Eysler, and others which had been set to music by James Rothstein, Victor Hollaender, and Bogumil Zepler. The acting out of poems and dance numbers was executed by other members of Wolzogen's cast: Olga L'Estrée, Olga Wohlbrück (the aunt of the actor Adolf Wohlbrück and herself a writer), and the singing and dancing team of Bozena Bradsky and Robert Koppel.

During the intermission, Wolzogen stepped forward again to amuse the audience, which included some of Berlin's most prominent theater critics, by reading imaginary reviews, which he himself had written, of the Überbrettl's program.

The second part of the program employed the technique of theater-within-theater (or here, more appropriately, cabaret-within-cabaret) to stage a parody of the Italian writer Gabriele D'Annunzio under the title *Das Mittagsmahl* (*Il Pranzo*) (The Noonday Meal) which had been written by the poet Christian Morgenstern (1871–1914), known best in the English-speaking world for his "gallows humor" poems collected under the title of *Galgenlieder* (Gallows Songs). Without anyone quite realizing it at the time, perhaps, Morgenstern's parody of D'Annunzio was not only to set a precedent for what was eventually to become one of the early German cabaret's most outstanding and characteristic entertainments, but was soon to crystallize as a commentary by the cabaret on the leading contemporary artistic "schools." Opposed to the solemnity and ethereality of symbolism, on one hand, and to the social determinism of naturalism, on the other, cabaret artists took particular delight in lampooning both, and all in the spirit of play which the cabaret, after all, dedicated itself to advancing. Since no better tool for literary mockery exists than parody, cabaret poets and playwrights embraced the form with a vengeance, making it one of the most popular and typical literary activities of the time with more meaning as a reflection of changing literary sensibility than may be apparent at first glance. Furthermore, for a theater of "small forms" into which the cabaret was in part evolving, parody offered almost limitless possibilities.

In the course of a life terminated prematurely by illness, Morgenstern wrote some thirteen dramatic sketches typologically classified as "grotesques" and parodies and published as a collection under the title *Die Schallmülle* (The Sound Mill).[26] Of those performed at the Überbrettl and elsewhere, none achieved the popularity of *Der Mittagsmahl,* the D'Annunzio parody, or *Egon und Emilie* (Egon and Emilie), subtitled "Kein Familiendrama" (No Family Drama) and a parody of the popular nineteenth-century type of bourgeois family drama.

The point of departure for the D'Annunzio parody is the Italian's neoromantically aestheticized classical epicureanism and paganism. A meal presumably fit for the gods is prepared for members of his family by the Sicilian landowner and amateur artist Degno. All recall the superb fish dinner that Uncle Degno had served once before on his estate in Girgenti, the classical Agrigentum. Olio's rhapsodic recollection of it encapsulates the style and tenor of Morgenstern's parody:

> Do you recall, Melissa, how once in Grigenti, the ancient Agrigentum, in your uncle's house we ate for the first time that indescribable fish [which Degno later painted from memory] in whose taste there seemed to us to be consumated a mystic marriage of Antiquity, the Renaissance, and the Modern, which we ourselves try so often in vain to achieve in Art and Life? I say "in vain" because we are so distant from those deep conditions of nature whose mysterious interrelations give birth to the dreams of the gods in ever new incarnations.[27]

The Melissa to whom Olio's words are directed is Degno's niece and a fit subject for Morgenstern's parody of the goddess-like D'Annunzian heroine:

> Her teeth are as white as Diana's breast and as sharp as a sonnet by Stechetti. Her hair has the luster and color of the southern slopes of the Alban Mountains when covered with the endless yearning of August. Her eyes are like the Lago di Como and Lago Bellagio. Her eyebrows are curved like a declaration of love of the immortal Gabriele. Her nose is that of the Venus de Milo, while her mouth is that of the Medici Venus. The movements of her limbs have the grace of those dancers of Benozzo Gozzoli [1420–1497. Florentine painter—HBS] in the wedding of Jacob and Rachel.[28]

Much of the humor of the parody resides in the contrast Morgenstern draws between the mystical and aesthetic raptures to which Degno's food gives rise and the plain down-to-earth hunger of the young boy Ghiotto to whom food is just food and who keeps interrupting the seemingly endless talk of the adults by an increasingly shrill clamor to be fed. The little play ends as all the principals fall unconscious—or dead (poisoned by the food?)—and Degno's servants, whose patience has already been worn thin by the excessive demands of the aesthetes, appear with carafes of water and towels to try to revive them.

In its extreme brevity (about two and a half pages of printed text), *Egon and Emilie* typifies the cabaret preference for "small forms." Pulling Egon into the room by the hand, Emilie declares how happy she is with him, how happy they both are, but when she asks him to agree with her he remains silent. No matter what Emilie says, until the end of the play, Egon keeps his silence. In despair, Emilie berates Egon for denying her her role, for forcing her now to leave the boards without having played her part, without having lived. She then calls for the curtain to fall and for the audience to go home as there will not be a family drama this night; Egon, instead, wants his peace. At this point, Egon arises and speaks his only lines in the play, declaring that he wants his peace, that indeed he wants no family drama, and asking the spectators the question must he be at the mercy of this waterfall of a wife for the sake of their eyes, must he become hopelessly entangled in endless idle chatter? As he too dismisses them from the theater, he tells them that for the first time in their lives they have seen on stage a truly reasonable man who not only calls to mind the saying "Speech is silver, but silence is golden," but fearlessly follows the axiom in life as well.

Wolzogen was duly appreciative of the popularity of Morgenstern's sketches,[29] but it was because of their popularity that Morgenstern began getting letters from Friedrich Kayssler urging him to send his parodies and other dramatic pieces to him, promising him that they would be more favorably presented at the Schall und Rauch (Sound and Smoke)—another cabaret that opened in Berlin not long after Wolzogen's—than at Wolzogen's Überbrettl where "the people there haven't the slightest idea what theater is and want to do everything with literature."[30]

After the D'Annunzio parody, the remainder of the Überbrettl's program followed predictable patterns: a one-acter from Schnizler's *Anatol* cycle, a shadow play in the style of the Parisian Chat Noir's "Chinese shadows" based on a ballad (*König Ragnar Lodbrog*) by Detlev von Lilliencron, another alumnus of Otto Julius Bierbaum's *Deutsche Chansons,* and the pantomime *Pierrots Tücke, Traum und Tod* (Pierrot's

Spite, Dream and Death) by Rudolph Schanzer, with music by Oscar Straus; the role of Colombine was played by Olga Wohlbrück, and Pierrot by Luigi Spontelli.

The strict Prussian censorship then in force in Berlin virtually ruled out the possibility of any of the political satire for which the German cabaret was to become famous in the Weimar period. Yet one surprise of the Überbrettl program of January 17–18, 1901, was a recitation of the popular writer Ludwig Thoma's poem "Wiegenlied" (Lullaby), which had first appeared in the eminent Munich satirical journal *Simplicissimus* over his pen name Peter Schlemihl. An attack on the docility and submissiveness of the Prussian populace, Thoma's verse includes such lines as the following which managed to slip past the censors' usually attentive eyes and ears:

> Untertanen sind wie Kinder,
> Brauchen eine starke Hand,
> Manchmal strenger! Manchmal lender,
> So gedeiht das Vaterland . . .[31]

(Subjects are like little children, / Always needing some strong hand, / Sometimes sterner, sometimes gentler. / Thus the Fatherland does thrive.)

The final item on the program, which was to prove the evening's greatest success, was the duet "Der lustige Ehemann" (The Merry Husband). Based on verse by Otto Julius Bierbaum and with music by Oscar Straus, the duet was sung and danced by the dancer Bozena Bradsky and the musician Robert Koppel. In its lightheartedness and *joi de vivre,* its playful attitude toward life, the "Merry Husband" was something new and seemed to embody the very spirit of the cabaret. This undoubtedly explains the number's great success. Although it loses most of its appeal in translation and in the absence of the music and dance that accompanied its performance, the "Merry Husband" became so legendary a number in the history of the German cabaret repertoire that, if more for the record than anything else, the original German text and English prose translation are given here:

> Ringelringelrosenkranz,
> Ich tanz mit meiner Frau,
> Wir tanzen um den Rosenbusch,
> Klingklanggloribusch,
> Ich dreh mich wie ein Pfau.

Zwar hab ich kein so schönes Rad,
Doch bin ich sehr verliebt
Und springe wie ein Firlefink,
Dieweil es gar kein lieber Ding
Als wie die Meine gibt.

Die Welt, die ist da draussen wo,
Mag auf den Kopf sie stehn!
Sie interessiert uns gar nicht sehr,
Und wenn sie nicht vorhanden wär;
Würd's auch noch weiter gehn.
Ringelringelrosenkranz,
Ich tanz mit meiner Frau,
Wir tanzen um den Rosenbusch,
Klingklanggloribusch,
Ich dreh mich wie ein Pfau.[32]

(Ringelringelrosary, I'm dancing with my wife./We dance around the rosebush,/Clingclangglorybush,/I strut just like a peacock./Indeed, I haven't such a lovely tail,/But I'm very much in love/And jump like a jack-in-the-box,/Since there's no thing dearer than my wife./The world, it's out there somewhere,/Can go stand on its head./It doesn't interest us very much,/And if it didn't exist at all,/Then so much the better./Ringelringelrosary,/I'm dancing with my wife./We dance around the rosebush,/Clingclangglorybush,/I strut just like a peacock.)

Pleased with the undeniable success of the Überbrettl in the very first season, Wolzogen decided to take it on tour over the summer of 1901.[33] The premises of the Theater am Alexanderplatz, where performances were then being given, were turned over to a rival entrepreneur named Victor Bausenwein who lost little time in trading on Wolzogen's success by opening a new cabaret misleadingly named Buntes Brettl (Variety Stage, which sounds very much like the official name of Wolzogen's enterprise—Buntes Theater). On its staff were performers who in fact had either begun their careers with Wolzogen or first won fame at the Überbrettl—the previously mentioned Hanns Heinz Ewers, the *conférencier* Arthur Pserhofer, and Oscar Straus who went over completely to Bausenwein's Buntes Brettl after a blowup with Wolzogen which for a while threatened to land in the courts. So anxious was Bausenwein to steal Wolzogen's thunder that he spared no effort or expense to attract as many of Wolzogen's stars as he could. No better example of this was the proposal to the poet Detlev von Liliencron that for a thousand marks a month he permit his name to be used for the artistic direction of the Buntes Brettl without having to trouble himself ever by putting in any personal appearances. But the cabaret fever had so caught on now among the Germans that Bausenwein's zeal seems pardonable under the circumstances. Even Otto Julius Bierbaum (who was later to deny any great enthusiasm for cabaret when the phenomenon appeared to be entering a decline), together with Franz Blei as *Oberregisseur* (Chief Director), established his own Trianon Theater during this period; but it proved a dismal failure and lasted only a few weeks.[34]

Once back in Berlin again, and undaunted by the emergence of rival cabaret ventures, Wolzogen was so confident of even greater success that he gave up any idea of returning to the theater on the Alexanderplatz and instead commissioned the architect August Endell to design a new 800-seat theater in the then progressive *Jugendstil* style to be erected on the premises of number 68 Köpenicker Strasse in the northern (and, not unimportantly—as time was soon to make abundantly clear—poorer) section of Berlin.

Wolzogen's hopes for his new theater could not have been higher. In an interview in the *Berliner Tageblatt* on November 27, 1901, he spoke of the Köpenicker Strasse theater as a virtual temple of the art of "small forms" (*Kleinkunst*):

> "In my new home I intend to pursue *Kleinkunst,* but not small art, however, in the sense of art that is small only in its forms . . . I would like to present one-act plays, parodies, and satires." In answer to the question, "Will your [new] Variety Theater also offer political satire?," he replied: "Indeed, though not in the style of the French cabaret. The satires of the times and customs which you will be able to hear in my establishment will be those, so to speak, of a well-educated man of the world with no political party proclivity. A well-wishing smile, gentle but expressive, should sweep over the stage . . . The foremost principle of the variety theater [*Buntes Theater*] must be its cheerfulness [*Buntheit*]"

The official opening took place on November 28, 1901, and the excitement was almost palpable. Would Wolzogen be able to top his original Überbrettl? Would the new theater make a go of it in a poor district like Berlin North which was unused to theater? The interest and curiosity were so great that the well-dressed, perhaps sensation-seeking audience that turned out included such cabaret oldtimers as Bierbaum and the poet Richard Dehmel. All in all, it was, as Ludwig Thoma later recalled it, "the first and last big evening in Berlin North."[35]

Although not much time was to elapse before he broke with Wolzogen on distinctly unfriendly terms, Thoma had been impressed by the original Überbrettl. Already a member of the editorial board of the well-known Munich satirical journal *Simplicissimus* (founded by Albert Langen in April 1896) when Wolzogen invited him to join his Überbrettl, Thoma had reported on the January 18 opening of the cabaret in a letter to Langen dated February 12, 1901.[36] He characterized it as a great success and singled out his own satirical poem "Zur Dichtkunst abkommandiert" (Detailed to Poetry Writing), which was performed that evening, as having made the strongest impression. The butt of the satire was the artillery major-versifier Josef Lauff whose special claim to fame was the popularity of his poetry with the Emperor. Elevated to the nobility in 1913 (and thereafter known as Josef von Lauff), Lauff enjoyed the distinction of being the "poet of the Hohenzollerns" and as such was commissioned to write a special work honoring the same Prussian state holiday on which Wolzogen's Überbrettl made its public debut. As the Lauff work was similarly scheduled to be performed in the Berlin Opera House the same day that the Überbrettl was to make its bow, the coincidence was one a keen satirist like Thoma was constitutionally unable to let pass without notice.

Despite what appeared to be an auspicious beginning, the Überbrettl had an uncertain future, in Thoma's opinion, though at the time of his writing to Albert Langen in February 1901 he gave no specific reasons for his feelings.

Whatever his misgivings about Wolzogen and the cabaret, Thoma was willing to go along with it, submitting works to the original Überbrettl, then agreeing to join it as a writer, and finally accepting the position of *dramaturg* at the new Köpenicker Strasse establishment. Within a couple of months of the enthusiastic letter to Langen previously mentioned, Thoma was contacted by Wolzogen's secretary who had come from Berlin to see him about his joining the Überbrettl company as a writer. The rumor of Thoma's joining Wolzogen was also reported by Berlin newspapers which Thoma sought to reassure Langen (who was afraid of losing his services for *Simplicissimus*) was just nonsense. But about two weeks after denying any intention of leaving Munich to work with Wolzogen in Berlin, Thoma was already speaking of his continued cooperation with *Simplicissimus* from *Berlin* to where he repaired via Vienna on October 27, 1901.[37]

Once active as the *dramaturg* of the Köpenicker Strasse establishment, Thoma tried to realize Wolzogen's desire to bring distinction to the new Überbrettl especially through an augmented program of dramatic fare featuring one-act and slightly longer plays. Besides Thoma, who contributed his own highly regarded one-act comedies *Die Medaille* (The Medal) and *Die Protestversammlung* (The Protest Meeting), other dramatists who stood out in the relatively short period of time that the new Überbrettl was to remain in business on Köpenicker Strasse were Hanns von Gumppenberg, who under his own name or that of his alias "Jodok" was to become one of the most prolific providers of plays to the early German cabaret, and Frank Wedekind, whose major cabaret involvement lay ahead in Munich at the Elf Scharfrichter (Eleven Executioners).

Within a short period of time, however, Thoma was on the point of breaking with Wolzogen and the new enterprise on Köpenicker Strasse itself was on the verge of collapse. Writing to Karl Rothmaier on December 1, 1901, Thoma speaks of joining Rothmaier's recently opened Überbrettl which he says should be merrier than Wolzogen's "eccentric trash shed" (*verstiegene Kitschbude*). And, more strongly, in a letter to Dr. Reinhold Geheeb (Berlin, December 5, 1901), Thoma expresses himself as follows: "Wolzogen can kiss my arse with his Tingel-Tangel. I let them pay me my salary monthly and don't trouble myself about anything any more."[38]

The immediate source of consternation was Thoma's bitterness over what he regarded as the dismal failure of the premiere of his play *The Medal.*[39] Although noting in a letter to Konrad Dreher on December 28, 1901, that the play itself did not "fall through," Thoma left no doubt that, in his opinion, the premiere was a shambles because the play either did not suit the new stage on Köpenicker Strasse or the other way around. In any case, the experience left Thoma with a sour taste about Wolzogen that he never quite got over.[40]

Whatever Wolzogen's high hopes for the Köpenicker address, the flap over Thoma's *The Medal* only served to offer additional evidence that a cabaret, even one with the Überbrettl's visibility, could not hope to survive in a poor blue-collar neighborhood. Wolzogen's ambitions for the theater had resulted, moreover, in an investment of too much time in its building, so that when it finally opened in November (1901), the Überbrettl itself was no longer a novelty and keen competition had already appeared in the interim to challenge its primacy.

Despite Wolzogen's failure to achieve his goal of a German cabaret equal to if not superior to that of the French, the *annus mirabilis* of 1901 for the history of cabaret in Germany was not to end without others taking up the challenge with far greater achievement. On January 23, 1901, in fact, just five days after the official opening of Wolzogen's theater on Köpenicker Strasse, the first German cabaret of real distinction celebrated its inaugural evening as a private affair in the Künstlerhaus (Artists' House) on Bellevuestrasse in another part of Berlin. The cabaret was called Schall und Rauch (Sound and Smoke) and it was the brainchild of the writers Christian Morgenstern, Friedrich Kayssler, Richard Vallentin, Martin Zickel, and, above all, the future great director of the German theater, Max Reinhardt (1873–1943).

In a pattern somewhat reminiscent of the origins of the Paris Chat Noir, Schall und Rauch was the outgrowth of a lighthearted bohemian artists' society known as Die Brille (The Spectacles) which used to meet in a beer cellar and restaurant on the Lessingstrassse. Die Brille in turn had evolved out of a looser association of actors, painters, and writers (mainly poets) among whom Reinhardt had made his first friends upon undertaking his work with the Deutsches Theater in Berlin, then under the direction of Dr. Otto Brahm, on September 1, 1894. When the Café Metropol at the Friedrichstrasse railroad station (Reinhardt was living at the time at Friedrichstrasse 134, together with his friend and co-explorer of the Berlin Bohème, Max Marx) lost its appeal as a meeting place because of the crowds and noise, the decision was taken to move to other quarters and to put the group on a formal footing. Satisfactory arrangements for space in a dining hall on the Lessingstrasse were worked out and before long a quasi-mystical initiation rite was devised according to which new members would have their eyes covered and would be outfitted with glasses through which they would be able to "see" for the first time.[41] See, that is, in the sense of the new aesthetic insight and perception their endeavors in Die Brille would, presumably, make possible.

For the most part, these endeavors consisted of parodies directed mainly by Reinhardt and reflective of both the growing compatibility of cabaret and dramatic parody and Reinhardt's personal enthusiasm at the beginning of his career for "small" theatrical forms that considerably reduced or eliminated the barriers separating players from audience.[42] Die Brille went public for the first time before an audience of invited guests on New Year's Eve 1900. So successful was the affair that the group decided to mount another such program, this time before a larger invited audience. The date chosen was January 23, 1901—just five days after the establishment of Wolzogen's Überbrettl. As plans began to be made, there was also a sense that the name Die Brille had outlived its usefulness and that the time was ripe to find a new one better suited to the group's more self-confident and professional image. It fell to Reinhardt to make the final choice. Recalling a saying by Goethe, the future director suggested Schall und Rauch (Sound and Smoke). The name was accepted and it was as Schall und Rauch, then, that the first successful German cabaret came to be known.

The performance on January 23, which was presented as a benefit for the ailing and impecunious Morgenstern and was held in the rented Künstlerhaus on the Bellevuestrasse, was nothing short of a triumph. The highlight of the evening was a three-part parodic variation based on Schiller's *Don Carlos.* The first part consisted of a parody of Schiller ("Don Carlos auf der Schmiere," Don Carlos in Greasepaint) performed in the style of a troupe of strolling players; the second, a parody of Gerhart Hauptmann's naturalism ("Karle: Eine Diebskomödie," Carl; A Thieves' Comedy); and the third, a parody of Maeterlinck's *Pelléas et Mélisande* ("Carleas und Elisande," Carleas and Elisande, subtitled "A Globinesque in Five Veilings [*Verschleierungen*] by Ydisore Mysterlinck"). The last part must have had a special appeal of Reinhardt as an auto- or self-parody in view of his playing the role of the old king in the first German production of *Pelléas et Mélisande* on February 12, 1899, by the Berlin Akademisch-Literarischer Verein. Yielding to calls for a repetition of the program of January 23, Reinhardt and company held two additional performances of it, also in the Künstlerhaus, on February 6 and March 3, 1901.

Although the premiere public performance of the "new" cabaret on its own premises took place almost nine months later, Schall und Rauch—as represented by Reinhardt, Kayssler, and Zickel—did make a debut of sorts on May 22, 1901, at a special matinee at Otto Brahm's Deutsches Theater. Both the name of the new cabaret and the spirit that guided it were announced when the trio stepped forward to present itself with the following verse:

Wir kommen ins Deutschen Theater
Und machen Schall und Rauch
Und wenn sie sich dabei amüsieren
Amüsieren wir uns auch.

(We come to the Deutsches Theater / And kick up both sound and smoke. / If this should make you happy, / Then we are happy too.)

True to its commitment to the genre of parody, the Schall und Rauch group presented a parody of Karl Weber that was so enthusiastically received the *Berliner Illustrierte Zeitung* reported on it in a two-column article in its June 2 issue (1901).

Impressed by the critical acclaim accorded Schall und Rauch as well as by the financial support that began to be offered, beginning with 50,000 marks from the well-known actress Louise Dumont, Reinhardt determined to establish a more cohesive company of performers made up of old Die Brille members and newcomers like Dumont herself and Berthold Held. Encouraged by his financial success, he was also anxious to establish the new cabaret in a proper home of its own in place of the borrowed premises the group had lived with since the Friederichstrasse railroad station days. In July, an appropriate location was found in the rebuilt former Hotel Arnim at number 44 Unter den Linden and Reinhardt and company, assisted by the artists Edmund Edel and Emil Orlik, plunged with glee and expectation into the business of renovation.[43] Work on the hall and the program for the first public performance went on through the rest of the summer and into early fall and finally when both were in good enough shape an opening date of October 9 was decided.

When guests arrived for the inaugural public performance of Schall und Rauch in its new home on the evening of Wednesday, October, 9, 1901, they were greeted by the new hallmark of Schall und Rauch performances: members of the company serving as attendants garbed in white Pierrot costumes and wearing black pompoms on their heads. The program itself, which proved a smashing success, was a typical mixed bag cabaret evening of literary recitations, songs, poetry readings, dialogues, caricatures of various products of culture and civilization, grotesque dances, and pantomime. The opening number, or "Prologue," was a recitation from Shakespeare's *Hamlet* by Friedrich Kayssler in his own translation. This was followed by a "Narrenlied," or Fool's Song, sung by Alice Berend to the music of Hugo Koppel. Next came the high point of the first half of the program and the dramatic centerpiece of the entire evening—three "culture caricatures" consisting of "Die Dekadenten" (The Decadents), based on G. K. Hardenberg's novel *Die Jugend* (Youth); "Der deutsche Jüngling" (The German Lad) by Robert Eysler, with music by

Gustav Lazarus; and "Die Dichterschule" (The School of Poets) by Victor Ottman but based also on Hardenberg's *Die Jugend.*

Making up the second half of the program, after a five-minute intermission, was a dialogue by O. G. Friedrich ("Die Gefangene," The Prisoner), a cabaret song ("La Jongleuse," with music by Bogumil Zepler) by Christian Morgenstern, a gavotte ("La Dernière") by Fénicienne Verques with music by Lucienne Delormes, Gustav Falke's poem "Hinterm Deich" (Behind the Dike), which had been set to music by Kurt Schindler, a "comic-tragic duet" by R. Geneé ("Zahnweh," Toothache) with Ernst Grinzenberger playing both roles of Doctor and Patient, and, finally, a pantomime called *Rex* ("An Old Tale without Words") by Richard Vallentin.

While successive Schall und Rauch evenings adhered, for the most part, to the same general format, each program had a high point which consisted most of the time of a dramatic parody. On October 12, 1901, for example, the parody was based on Maeterlinck and took the form of a "Traumdichtung" (Dream Poem) by Max Reinhardt called the "Brettlleiters Höllenfahrt" (The Cabaret Director's Journey to Hell). Along with Maeterlinck, Schiller and Hauptmann were the favorite targets of German cabaret parody. So it was then that the Schall und Rauch program of November 6, 1901, featured a Schiller parody entitled *Don Carlos oder der Infant von Spanien oder der unnatürliche Sohn* (Don Carlos, or The Infanta of Spain, or The Unnatural Son), and the program of January 1, 1902, a parody of Hauptmann's famous Naturalist play *Die Weber* (The Weavers) under the title *Die Weber, sociales Drama als Sondervorstellung vor Serenissimus, bearbeitet von Freiherrn von Kindermann* (The Weavers, A Social Drama Presented as a Special Performance before Serenissimus, Composed by Baron von Childman). More pointedly social in their satire than the purely literary parodies mounted by Schall und Rauch, the so-called Serenissimus parodies, dialogues, or skits soon came to the fore as the Schall und Rauch's most popular entertainments—and a source of consternation for Berlin police officials ever mindful that a thin line divided social lampooning from punishable political satire.

What made for the great success of the Schall und Rauch in its first few programs also contained the seeds of its demise. With time—and repetition—the wit and humor of songs, dances, and one-act social satires lost their bloom while the "big number" on each program, which was usually a dramatic parody, became a too familiar and predictable item. When the doormat of hospitality wore thin for Maeterlinck, Schiller, and Hauptmann as the favorite targets of Schall und Rauch parodies, fresh welcomes were prepared for such outstanding turn-of-the-century German-language writers as Stefan George and Hugo von Hofmannsthal, but not much time elapsed before they too enjoyed the contempt of familiarity.

Around the end of November 1901, guest Schall und Rauch performances by the French *chansonette* Anne Judie were seized upon as a way of breathing new life into the cabaret by infusing it with the spirit of the original Parisian cabaret. But it was too late for the transfusion to be of much help. Something more radical was needed and when that was applied the Schall und Rauch ceased to exist with an entirely new enterprise, no longer a cabaret, standing in its place.

Reinhardt's outlook at this time was also a determining factor. As his involvement first in Die Brille and then in Schall und Rauch programs deepened, Reinhardt became not only the prime mover of the cabaret, but in effect the director of a small theater. It was Reinhardt who planned the programs, Reinhardt who invited the participation of other stage personalities, including such then lesser-known actors as Gertrud Eysoldt, Emanuel Reicher, and Rosa Bertens, and Reinhardt who expanded the dramatic repertoire of the cabaret by writing especially one-acters such as *Das Regie-Kollegium* (The School of Directing) and *Die Parkettreihe* (The Orchestra Stalls).

The success of his own acting, directing, and writing at the Schall und Rauch[44] and a maturing sense of purpose left no doubt in Reinhardt's mind that his future was in the theater and that his mark would be made as a director. As the sound and fury of Schall und Rauch evenings began fading in its second season of 1902, which began on September 25 of that year, Reinhardt now perceived the cabaret period of his life, represented by the Die Brille and Schall und Rauch, as a stepping-stone to a full-fledged career in the theater. Accordingly, starting in February (1903), he began adding more and more one-acters, by such writers as Strindberg and the Austrians Arthur Schnitzler and Felix Salten—besides his own—to the programs as if thereby to hone his skill at directing dramatic pieces rather than cabaret numbers.

With the cabaret's de facto partial transformation into a little theater not much time was to elapse before the name Schall und Rauch was dropped in favor of the obvious Kleines Theater (Little Theater) and its metamorphosis into a legitimate theater made complete and formal. The process was complete, in fact, before the end of the 1902 Schall und Rauch season. But change is not necessarily a guarantee of success. Reinhardt's first favorable notice as the director of the Kleines Theater came with a production of Strindberg's *Frenzy* starring Gertrud Eysoldt. A *succès de scandal* was achieved next with a production of Oscar Wilde's *Salomé,* again with Eysoldt in the leading role. After the censors banned the production, Reinhardt made a point of staging a private performance before an elite audience consisting of the poet Stefan George and his circle, the composer Richard Strauss, Eugen (or Eugène) d'Albert, a musician who had collaborated on several works with Ferdinand Lion, among them the opera *Revolutionshochzeit* (The Revolution's Wedding) and a musical version of the *Golem,* and a goodly mix of prominent writers, actors, and representatives of the press. As one might imagine, sufficient influential pressure was brought to bear to have the censorial ban lifted.

Reinhardt still needed a big hit, a "smash," to make the name for himself and his theater that he felt he had to have at this juncture. When he heard of the response to the Moscow Art Theater's production in December 1901 of Gorky's *The Lower Depths,* he sent August Scholz to Moscow to scout the property. Scholz returned to Berlin with the play which Reinhardt staged with enormous success in 1903 under the German title *Nachtasyl.* Reinhardt was now on his way. Emboldened by the acclaim accorded his production of *The Lower Depths,* he shopped around for a second theater and soon opened the Neue Theater am Schiffbauerdam, for which the cooperation of such prominent artists as Corinth, Orlik, Walser, Roller, and Slevolgt was enlisted. The premiere production of the new theater was the often parodied *Pelléas and Mélisande* by Maurice Maeterlinck, with Reinhardt himself playing the role of the King and Louise Dumont that of the Queen. Reinhardt had turned his corner and one success followed another. With the great controversy aroused by the technical advances (a revolving stage, for example) of his *Minna von Barnhelm* and the thunderous reception that greeted his production of *Midsummer Night's Dream,* Reinhardt's position as the foremost *regisseur* of Germany was beyond dispute. The fledgling flights of Die Brille and Schall und Rauch—stepping-stones whose importance cannot be minimized—now belonged to the past.

Munich: Die Elf Scharfrichter

Cabaret also functioned as a sort of artistic laboratory in the case of another prominent figure in turn-of-the-century German theater, Frank Wedekind. The undisputed *enfant terrible* of contemporary German literature on the basis of such thought- and scandal-provoking plays on the subject of human sexuality as *Spring's Awakening* (written 1891, first produced 1906) and *Earth Spirit* (first produced 1898), Wedekind also exhibited no mean talent as a performer by acting in productions of his own plays and by entertaining in the early Munich cabaret.

The hub of German bohemian culture at the time with its Montmartre-like Schwabing district, Munich was a natural habitat for cabaret.[45] And indeed when it demonstrated an undeniable receptivity to cabaret in 1901 (the *annus mirabilis* again), the chemistry was immediate. Munich soon became the locus of the most successful and thriving cabaret life in pre-World War I Germany.

As had been the case in Berlin, the idea of establishing a Parisian-type cabaret in Munich was articulated some time before the cabaret itself came into existence. It was, in a sense, symptomatic of the affinities with contemporary French culture felt in Munich during this period and the strong gravitational pull of Paris. When Albert Langen founded in April 1896 what was to become the most famous (and outrageous) satirical magazine in all Germany, *Simplicissimus* (to which, by the way, Wedekind at one time was an important contributor)—he had before him the example of the Parisian *Gil Blas*. Langen's enthusiasm for Paris and its Bohème went beyond the imitation of a French satirical paper. He had translated chansons of Aristide Bruant and gave serious thought to the establishment in Munich of a Parisian-style *Literatur-Variété*. Whatever his enthusiasm, however, Langen himself never succeeded in making the transition from thought to deed.

In view of the common perception in Munich that the Bavarian and French capitals were kindred spirits, that Munich was a German Paris in its own right, it may have been entirely proper and fitting that the first real initiative in founding a cabaret in Munich was undertaken by an itinerant Parisian who occupies a definite place in the history of the cabaret for his pioneer work not only in Munich, but also later on in Vienna. The Frenchman's real name was Achille Georges d'Ailly-Vaucheret, but he preferred the pseudonym for which he became best known, Marc

Henry. Besides earning a small living by offering private lessons in French language and literature to Munich's aristocracy, Henry (as he shall be known here) was also the moving spirit behind a Franco-German literary and sociological review known as the *Revue Franco-Allemande.* The *Revue* (in German, *Deutsch-französische Rundschau*) was founded in 1898 both by Marc Henry and his friend, the French musicographer J.-G. Prodhomme, who had recently come to Munich. The *Revue,* which actually got underway "toward 1900" as Henry mentions in his book *Trois Villes: Vienne-Munich-Berlin* (p. 152), lasted some four years. Its main purpose—apart from entertaining and bringing in additional money—was to narrow the cultural gap between the French and German peoples.[46]

Because of his French background and, more important, his experience with the *Revue Franco-Allemande,* Henry was regarded—with some justification—as an authority on cabaret. And when local Munich artists, principally the young writer Otto Falckenberg and the writer and lyricist Leo Greiner, were persuaded that the time was ripe to establish a cabaret in the Bavarian capital, it was understood that no more knowledgeable a person to consult on the project than Marc Henry was to be found. The Frenchman, to be sure, had already gained entry into Munich's artistic and intellectual circles. Both because of his *Revue* and the *conférences* he had begun giving on French language and culture he was personally familiar with most of the figures who were soon to become prominent in the Munich cabaret. Writing about the ferment from which arose the first cabaret in the Bavarian capital in his books *Au Pays des Maîtres-Chanteurs* (In the Land of the Meistersingers) and *Trois Villes: Vienne-Munich-Berlin,* Henry notes especially the strong interest in *theatrical* reform among Munich's younger artists and intellectuals. "I understood," he notes in *Trois Villes,* for example, "that they would enthusiastically greet the creation of an experimental stage where they would be able to have contact with the public, realize their program, and, finally, acquire a technical skill and a routine which were indispensable to their evolution."[47]

With that goal in mind, Henry invited such literary lights of contemporary Munich as Max Halbe, Frank Wedekind, Count Eduard von Keyserling, Hanns von Gumppenberg, and Otto Julius Bierbaum, as well as a few musicians and artists from the staff of *Simplicissimus,* to a Schwabing brasserie to discuss the matter. The purpose was to create "a sort of artistic-literary republic with a clearly defined program." "We wanted to establish a stage," Henry recalls, "endowed with the most up-to-date technical innovations, an invisible orchestra, an auditorium of original design, and everything in miniature since the public to whom we were addressing ourselves was limited."[48]

How serious, and yet at the same time enterprising, Henry himself was concerning the new project is manifest in the idea he hit upon to provide financial support for it:

> I proposed printing an illustrated proclamation in which we would explain our aims. We would put together a subscription list and we would request that the patricians of Munich be willing to facilitate our debuts by purchasing tickets for a hundred marks which would grant their owners the right of assisting each month—throughout our entire existence—in the first production of our new program. This performance, behind closed doors and strictly private, would be reserved for the press and our backers, who would be flattered by this exclusivity.[49]

With respect to the commercial aspect of the venture, Marc Henry may, in fact, have had Ernst von Wolzogen's Überbrettl in mind. In *Au Pays des Maîtres-Chanteurs,* he recalls Wolzogen's desire, after becoming familiar with the cabaret life of Montmartre, to establish a German artistic and literary theater along the lines of the Chat Noir in order to combat "the dullness" (*l'abêtissement*) of the music hall.[50] So successful was he at the outset that tickets to performances were much sought after and went at times for as high as 250 marks. *En passant,* Marc Henry notes that Wolzogen's Überbrettl was especially popular with the well-to-do Jewish population of West Berlin. What made a particular impression on the Frenchman was the considerable *commercial* success of the Überbrettl's principal performers and the success of phonograph records and printed editions of their songs. As an example of the kind of monetary success possible in the cabaret for a performer, he mentions Oscar Straus' piece "Die Musik kommt" (The Band is Coming) which was based on poems in a volume by Detlev von Liliencron.

Responding then to "une tentative de réforme théâtrale" (an attempt at theatrical reform) which was developing in Germany at the time, "the young writers and artists (of Munich) sought the opportunity to perform their new ideas before a public"; they turned to Marc Henry and, as he himself observes, "I placed myself at the head of the movement in Munich and founded an avant-garde theater, 'Die Elf Scharfrichter' (The Eleven Eexecutioners)."[51] The new cabaret to be born on German soil was called the Eleven Executioners both because of its satirical tendencies and the number of its charter members. By the time the preparatory work was finished and the name for the cabaret agreed upon, a location had also been found: a back room in the Inn of the Golden Hare (Zum Goldene Hirsch) on Türkenstrasse (Street of the Turks) number 28 in Schwabing which formerly had seen service as a student hangout and fencing arena.

The roster of the charter members of the cabaret, that is the "eleven executioners" themselves, consisted of: 1) Robert Kothe, an attorney, who performed under the name of Frigidus Strang; 2) Marc Henry, the *directeur* and *regisseur,* whose stage name was Balthasar Starr. Apart from his direction of the cabaret, it should also be noted that Henry functioned as a *conférencier* as well in the spirit of Rodolphe Salis and Aristide Bruant. Moreover, like Wedekind and Brecht after him in the German cabaret tradition, he composed songs—mostly along old French peasant and folk lines—and accompanied himself on the guitar. He mentions in *Au Pays des Maîtres-Chanteurs* how important a role music came to play in Elf Scharfrichter programs and the prominence he himself gave to the popular French chanson, taking great pains to achieve as authentic a setting as possible for their performance with respect especially to costumes and musical instruments ("I completely renovated the concept of a concert by adding to it an unknown pictorial note, a new concern for line and color");[52] 3) Otto Falckenberg, who later became director of the renowned Munich Kammerspiele (Chamber Theater) and performed in the cabaret as the full-bearded Peter Luft; 4) Hanns Richard Weinhöppel, a long-maned bohemian musician and composer who took the name of Hannes Ruch; 5) Willi Rath, a politically oriented critic and author of sketches whose cabaret name was Willibaldus Rost. Three months after the opening of the Elf Scharfrichter he left it in order to establish his own theater, the Lyrische Theater, on Munich's Sonnenstrasse; 6) and 7) Wilhelm Hüsgen and Willi Oertel, two local painters, who made their way on stage as Till Blut and Serapion Grab, respectively; 8) Max Langheimrich, an architect and stage designer who took the name of Max Knack; 9) Viktor Freisch, a sketch artist, metamorphosed in the cabaret into Gottfried Still; 10) Leo Greiner, the writer and lyricist, now known as Dionysus Tod; 11) Ernst Neumann, a graphic artist, who as Kaspar Beil was responsible for the stage pictures and silhouettes in the cabaret's shadow shows.

As the above roster reveals, Frank Wedekind was not one of the charter members of the Elf Scharfrichter, although Marc Henry's reminiscences make clear that he certainly did belong to the original group among whom the idea of establishing a cabaret in Munich was raised. Once he became a performer at the Executioners, however, Wedekind, despite misgivings about cabaret, threw himself into it with gusto and won recognition as one of its stars.

Capable of accommodating about a hundred people, the Türkenstrasse locale—in the best tradition of the early European cabaret—was soon adorned with a splendidly eclectic conglomeration of every manner of art work including paintings, drawings, etchings, lithographs, Japanese woodcuts, illustrations from *Simplicissimus* and the only slightly less celebrated Munich publication *Jugendstil.* Among the contributing artists were Rudolf Wilke, Ernst Neumann, Olaf Gulbransson, Julius Diez, Arpad Schmidhammer, Vrieslander, and such popular French artists of the time as Léandre, Steinlen, and Rops. The masks which the Executioners wore when decked out in their full regalia of blood-red robes were the creation of the highly esteemed Munich artist Wilhelm Hüsgen.

The executionary artifacts and motifs with which the Türkenstrasse cabaret was liberally, and menacingly, adorned—above all a pillory with a Philistine's skull bedecked with a judge's wig and a huge ax conspicuously displayed alongside it—were less whim than intent. The executioner's block so prominently displayed on the premises was the symbolic deathplace of all the Executioners' foes, including Prussian authoritarianism, censorship, conservative bourgeois mores, and the artistic fashions of naturalism and symbolism. The song with which each program began was appropriate. Dancing and singing grotesquely, flinging their blood-red robes around with abandon, a chorus of Executioners would intone the first two stanzas:

Erbauet ragt der schwarze Block.
Wir richten scharf und herrlich
Blutrotes Herz, blutroter Rock,
All unsere Lust ist schmerzlich.

Wer mit dem Tag verfeindet ist,
Wird blutig exequieret,
Wer mit dem Tod befreundet ist,
Mit Sant und Kranz gezieret.[53]

(The black block towers high, / We pass sentence sharply and masterfully. / Blood-red heart, blood-red cloak, / All our pleasures are painful. / Who is an enemy of day, / Will be bloodily executed; / Who is a friend of death, / Will be decorated with song and wreath.)

Elf Scharfrichter program cover by Arpad Schmidhammer depicting the "Executioners" in their opening dance. (Münchner Stadtmuseum, Munich).

In a tone now of pseudo-pathos, the following verses were sung solo:

Wie Rausch verrinnt der bunte Sand
Der Zeit, die uns mit Nacht umwand,
Doch unsre Fackeln stehn im Land,
Hoch ihrem Flug zu lodern.
Wir leuchten dem, was rasch verfällt,
Was kaum ein Tag im Licht erhält.
Mag uns der tolle Gott der Welt
Vor seinen Richtstuhl fordern.

(The bright sand of time that has turned us 'round/With night, passes like ecstasy,/Although our torches stand in the ground/To blaze high with their flight./We light the way to that which decays swiftly,/To that which lasts but a day in light./May the mad god of the world/Summon us before his tribunal.)

After this, the chorus resumed with:

Ein Schattentanz, ein Puppenspott!
Ihr Glücklichen und Glatten,
Im Himmel lenkt der alte Gott
Die Puppen und die Schatten.
Er lenkt zu Leid, er lenkt zu Glück
Hoch dampfen die Gebete,
Doch just im schönsten Augenblick
Zerschneiden wir die Drähte!

(A dance of shadows, a puppets' joke!/You fortunate and polished people,/ The old god in heaven rules/The puppets and the shadows./He rules for sorrow, rules for good;/Prayers soar up high./But just at the loveliest moment,/ We cut the puppets' wires!)

Heightening the tone of the opening night on April 13, 1901, was the performance especially of the *femme fatale* of the Elf Scharfrichter, Marya Delvard (1874–1965). The daughter of a professor in Paris, Delvard was born in Réchicourt-le-Château near Nancy (in Lothringen) and was brought up in a covent there. She came to Munich in 1896 originally to study music at the Akademie für Tonkunst. There she met her fellow Frenchman, Marc Henry, whom she had seen in Paris at the popular artists' hangout Le Lapin agile (The Nimble Rabbit).[54] Before long, the two were traveling throughout Europe as a cabaret team.

Tall, thin as a reed, exceptionally pale, Marya Delvard chose as her stage attire a long black day dress which she wore tightly. In order to accentuate her funereal aspect, Marc Henry had her draw the dress still

Elf Scharfrichter program cover with caricature silhouette of Marya Delvard by Thomas Theodor Heine. (Münchner Stadtmuseum, Munich).

tighter and then bathed her entirely in a violet light for the length of time that she was on stage. Contrasting with her flaming red hair, wide mouth, and ghostly pallor, the effect was startling. The audience's response was overwhelming and Delvard and her outfit became permanent fixtures for the lifetime of the cabaret, captured to perfection in the famous caricature silhouette of her by the artist T. T. Heine. Contemporary accounts attest to her electrifying presence on stage. In his *Der Tag des jungen Arztes* (The Day of the Young Doctor, 1955), the well-known writer Hans Carossa offers this description of her:

All at once, the tiny theater was suspended in magical lilac light, and as if arisen from her coffin, Marya Delvard stood in front of the pale curtain. It grew as quiet as in a church, not a plate rattled any more. She did not perform as dead still as she appears in illustrations; nevertheless, an unexpected encounter with her in solitude might have really frightened someone. She was frightfully pale; one thought involuntarily of sin, vampirically parasitical cruelty, and death. . . . She sang everything with a languid monotony which she only occasionally interrupted with a wild outcry of greedy passion. The high point of the evening, however, was Lautensack's poem "Der Tod singt" [Death Sings]; she spoke and hummed the words which Emanuel Franz then sang as one of a circle of watchmen walking around the deeply darkened stage.[55]

Franz Kafka's diary entry for 1911 of a Delvard-Henry performance strikes, however, an infrequently heard critical note, although some allowance for the time gap perhaps ought to be made:

Marc Henry—Delvard. The tragic feeling bred in the audience by the empty hall increases the effect of the serious songs, detracts from that of the merry ones. Henry does the prologue, while Delvard, behind a curtain that she doesn't know is translucent, fixes her hair. At poorly attended performances, W., the producer, seems to wear his Assyrian beard—which is otherwise deep black—streaked with gray. . . . Much display of costumes, Breton costumes, the undermost petticoat is the longest, so that one can count the wealth from a distance—Because they want to save an accompanist, Delvard does the accompaniment first, in a very low-cut green dress, and freezes.—Parisian street cries. Newsboys are omitted. . . . Delvard is ridiculous, she has the smile of an old maid, an old maid of the German cabaret. With a red shawl that she fetches from behind the curtain, she plays revolution. Poems by Dauthenday in the same tough, unbreakable voice. She was charming only at the start, when she sat in a feminine way at the piano. At the song "A Batignolles" I felt Paris in my throat. Batignolles is supposed to live on its annuities, even its Apaches. Bruant wrote a song for every section of the city.[56]

If Delvard's special charm had worn somewhat thin by the time Kafka had a chance to observe her on stage in 1911, the early years of her cabaret performances at the Elf Scharfrichter earned her the reputation of a legend. Although the songs in her repertoire came from a variety of sources, none seemed more tailor-made for her particular talent and haunting appearance than those of Wedekind, several of which were set to music by Executioner Hannes Ruch. Probably the most famous was "Ilse," on the theme of unrepentant awakened passion touched on in several of his poems and plays:

Ich war ein Kind von fünfzen Jahren,
ein reines, unschuldvolles Kind,
als ich zum ersten Mal erfahren
wie süss der Liebe Freuden sind . . .

Er nahm mich um den Leib und lachte
und flüsterte: O, welch ein Glück!
Und dabei bog er sachte, sachte
den Kopf mir auf das Pfühl zurück.
Seit jenem Tag lieb' ich sie alle
des Lebens schönster Lenz its mein.
Und wenn ich keinem mehr gefalle
dann will ich gern begraben sein.[57]

(I was a child of fifteen, / A pure, innocent child, / When I first experienced / How sweet the joys of love are. / He took me in an embrace / And laughed / And whispered, "Oh, what joy! / And then gently, gently / He bent my head onto the pillow. / Since that day I love them all, / Life's most beautiful spring is mine. / And when I no longer please anyone, / Gladly will I be buried.)

Her special way of transmitting the chill of Wedekind's songs of crime and passion proved equally effective in her rendition of "Die Pfarrerstochter von Taubenheim" (The Parson's Daughter of Taubenheim, set to music by Hannes Ruch) from the famed collection of German folk songs, *Des Knaben Wunderhorn* (1806–1808), by Achim von Arnim and Clemens Brentano:

Da drunten auf der Wiesen,
Da ist ein kleiner Platz,
Da thät ein Wasser fliessen,
Da wächst kein grünes Gras.

Da wachsen keine Rosen
Und auch kein Rosmarein,
Hab ich mein Kind erstochen
Mit einem Messerlein.

Im kühlen Wasser fliessert
Sein rosenrothes Blut,
Das Bächlein sich ergiesset
Wohl in die Meersfluth.

Von hohen Himmel sehen
Zwei kleine Aeugelein,
Seh ich mein Englein stehen
In einem Sternelein.

Dort droben auf dem Berge,
Da steht das hohe Rad,
Will ich mich drunter legen
Und trauern früh und spat.

Hast du mich denn verlassen,
Der mich betrogen hat,
Will ich die Welt verlassen,
Bekennen meine That.

Der Leib der wird begraben,
Der Kopf steht auf dem Rad,
Es fressen den die Raben,
Der mich verführet hat![58]

(Down below there in the meadow, / There is a little place, / Where a rivulet trickles, / Where no green grass grows, / Where no roses bloom, / Nor any rosemary. / There I stabbed my child / With a little knife. / His rose-red blood / Flows in the cool water, / The brooklet carrying it / Right into the waters of the sea. / From heaven up above, / Two little eyes peer down; / I see my little angel standing / In a little star. / There up on the mountain, / Stands the high [executioner's] wheel. / I want to lie down beneath it / And grieve both night and day. / As you have forsaken me / Who deceived me, / I want to forsake the world / And confess my deed. / His body will be buried; / His head stands upon the wheel. / The ravens eat him / Who seduced me!)

With particular reference to this song, the respected literary historian, bibliophile, editor (E. T. A. Hoffmann's works) and collector, Carl Georg von Maassen (1880–1940), a prominent figure on the early twentieth-century Schwabing scene, recalls the kind of impact Delvard was capable of making on an audience:

When Marya Delvard, with her unique sharply contoured silhouette, standing in the narrow frame of the stage, against the tinted background, bathed in ghostly bluish light, sang "Die Pfarrerstochter von Taubenheim" from the *Knaben Wunderhorn* collection, to the unspeakably effective melody of Hannes Ruch, the sounds of an invisible organ flowing in all the while, a ghostly hand seized the audience's heart and twisted it twice around. Seldom have I seen people so gripped and shaken as then in the little cabaret on the Türkenstrasse.[59]

Delvard's appearance and style were also well suited to the morbid, haunting, death-fixated poetry of the youngest member of the Elf Scharfrichter, Heinrich Lautensack (1881–1919). The "factotum" of the group, as the writer Franz Blei calls him in his book of memoirs, *Erzählung eines Lebens,*[60] probably because of his age and a provincial naiveté that never quite left him despite his time in Munich, Lautensack was much admired as a poet among devotees of the Munich cabaret and had some success also as a dramatist.[61] Lautensack's best-known poem, from his "Cabaret" cycle, which seems tailor-made for Delvard's style, was "Der Tod singt" (Death Sings):

Löscht aus—
  zuviel des Lichts und Weins—
  und traümt von Sinn und Ziel des Seins!
  Und einer traümt sich kalt und bleich
  und ist am Morgen im Himmelreich . . .
                Löscht aus.

Löscht aus—
  und faltet die armen Händ
  und betet—just wie ihr beten könnt!
  Und morgen steigt ein Licht herab
  und morgen legen wir ihn ins Grab . . .
                Löscht aus.

Löscht aus—
  gerade Mitternacht—
  da wird ihm ein Kind zur Welt gebracht—
  wie er so recht im Sterben ist.
  Und das Kind hat die Augen Herrn Jesu Christ . . .
                Löscht aus.

Löscht aus—
  und ich muss wachen und gehn—
  muss sterben und gebären sehn!
  Löscht aus—zuviel des Lichts und Weins—
  und traümt von Sinn und Ziel des Seins . . .
                Löscht aus![62]

(Dies out—/too much light and wine—/and he dreams of the sense and aim of existence!/And another dreams himself cold and pale/and in the morning is in the kingdom of heaven . . ./Dies out./Dies out—/and clasps his poor hands/and prays—just as you can pray!/And tomorrow a light will descend/and tomorrow we shall lay him in the grave. / Dies out. / Dies out—/ just at midnight—/ a child is then brought into the world unto him—/ as he is so right in dying. / And the child has the eyes of the Lord Jesus Christ . . . / Dies out. / Dies out—/ and I must wake and go—/ must die and be born! / Dies out—too much light and wine—/ and he dreams of the sense and aim of existence . . . / Dies out!)

Wedekind, whom Lautensack fanatically admired and patterned himself after, was also an effective interpreter of his own poems and ballads, above all with the songs of lust, depravity, and crime for which he was known best as a cabaret performer. What induced Wedekind to take the stage of the Elf Scharfrichter, as well as to write specifically for the cabaret, were his psychological and financial needs at the time.[63] The first of his plays, on which he pinned his hopes as a dramatist—*Spring's Awakening* and *Earth Spirit*—met with open hostility on the part of theatrical producers and seemed to be without hope of staging. When *Earth Spirit* finally was accepted for production in Munich—a performance in which Wedekind himself played the major role of Dr. Schön—the public's reaction to the play turned the premiere into a shambles, and a scandal. In a mood of bitter frustration and resentment, Wedekind turned to the Elf Scharfrichter whose irreverent anti-Philistine ambience seemed to offer him an outlet for pentup emotion and, at the same time, the close contact with an audience that the performing artist in him craved. A letter to Martin Zickel from Munich on April 27, 1901, indicates not only that Wedekind had already become a performer at the Executioners, but that a previous attempt to reach an agreement with Wolzogen's Überbrettl in Berlin had proved unsuccessful. Referring to the melodies he had composed for poems in his *Fürstin Russalka* (Princess Russalka) collection, Wedekind informs Zickel that

At present, I am performing the things (with guitar) evening after evening here in Munich at4the "Executioners." I had also proposed them to Wolzogen; but Wolzogen had no faith in the effectiveness of my performance before a larger audience. On the other hand, he would gladly have taken me on lock, stock, and barrel as a jokester [*Witzmacher*] and that was something I simply could not permit.[64]

Wedekind again alludes to his new status as a cabaret entertainer in a letter of May 21, 1901, to Beate Heine, the wife of Carl Heine (1861–1927), the director of the Ibsen Theater in Leipzig (which was the first to stage Wedekind's *Earth Spirit*), in which he also speaks of the *Überbrettl* fad in Berlin, the artistic superiority of the Elf Scharfrichter over Wolzogen's Überbrettl, and the eventual collapse of the cabaret mania:

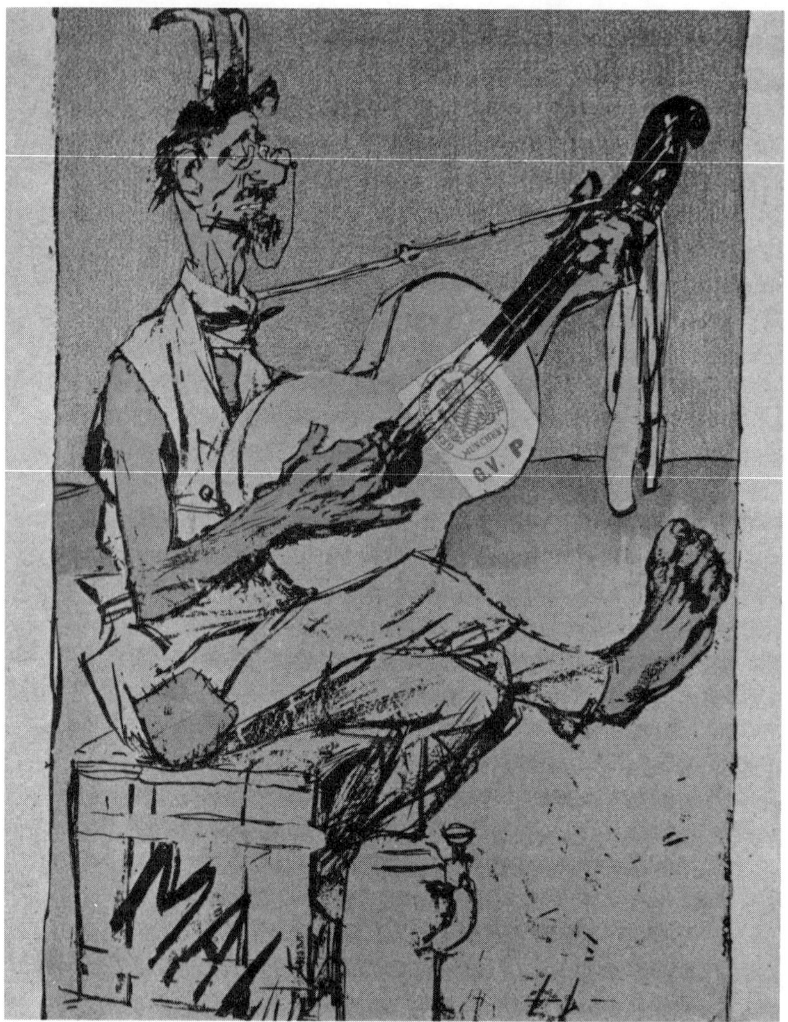

Elf Scharfrichter program cover with caricature of Ernst von Wolzogen as a cabaret performer. (Münchner Stadtmuseum, Munich).

Today I am singing my poems and compositions and also playing the guitar in the local "Überbrettl." *O quae mutatio rerum!* [Oh, how things have changed—HBS.] The general opinion is that the cabaret here is much more tasteful and artistic than Wolzogen's in Berlin. In Berlin these institutions have shot up now like mushrooms after a rain. Complete numbers and productions of the "Executioners" have already been won for Berlin for the coming winter; and every day new offers and publicity come in from there. I believe that sooner or later a serious crisis will befall all this junk.[65]

Wedekind's fears about the inevitable bursting of the cabaret bubble seemed confirmed by his experience as a guest performer at Wolzogen's establishment in Berlin. Writing to Beate Heine again from Munich on August 5, 1902, he mentions that

a smashing success before the kind of an audience that Wolzogen brought in was from the outset impossible.—Poor Wolzogen. To add to the misfortune, I happened to come just at the time when he was renounced by his own undertaking. The sight of this spectacle was as unpleasant as it was sympathy provoking. The whole cabaret mania [*Überbrettelei*] has turned out pretty much as I foresaw and feared from the beginning. Whether or not our "Elf Scharfrichter" can still hold on next winter is a question that will be resolved only by experiment.[66]

Whatever his misgivings and doubts about cabaret, Wedekind nevertheless clung to it in this period of his life as much for the living he earned from it as for the emotional outlet it provided him in the wake of his disappointments in the theater. That money was no small part of the appeal of the cabaret to him at this time is obvious from his remark in the above-quoted letter to Beate Heine that "still they [the Elf Scharfrichter—HBS] offer me an easy possibility of earning my daily subsistence without my having to compromise myself too much."[67] Wedekind's financial situation was anything but salutary at the time and the five, later ten marks that he received for an evening's performance did make a difference.[68]

Of the songs Wedekind performed at the Elf Scharfrichter not only as a singer but as a poet who composed the music for his own poems and accompanied himself on the guitar, those written specifically for the cabaret include "Brigitte B.," "Das arme Mädchen" (The Poor Girl), "Der Tantenmörder" (The Auntie Murderer). "Franziskas Abendlied" (Franziska's Evening Song), "Der Taler" (The Robe), "Die sieben Rappen" (The Seven Black Horses), "Mein Lieschen" (My Lieschen), "Galathea," "Die Symbolisten" (The Symbolists), "Als ich in Hamburg war . . ." (When I was in Hamburg), "Die Heilsarmee" (The Salvation Army), "Der Zoologe von Berlin" (The Zoologist from Berlin), "Hundeballade" (Dog Ballads), "Lied des Knaben" (Song of a Boy), and, of course, the previously mentioned "Ilse," with music composed by Hannes Ruch, which Marya Delvard made famous.

Typical of Wedekind's songs calculated to shock and thrill, and one he took a particular delight in performing, is "Der Tantenmörder" (The Auntie Murderer), the full text and English translation of which follow. The poem is presented in the form of a murder's confession which begins with the well-known line "Ich hab' meine Tante geschlachtet. . . ." (I murdered my dear old auntie). The work then continues:

Meine Tante war alt und schwach;
Ich hatte bei ihr übernachtet
Und grub in den Kisten-Kasten nach.

Da fand ich goldene Haufen,
Fand auch an Papieren gar viel,
Und hörte die alte Tante schnaufen
Ohne Mittleid und Zartgefühl.

Was nutzt es, dass sie sich noch härme!—
Nacht war es rings um mich her—
Ich steiss ihr den Dolch in die Därme,
Die Tant schnaufte nicht mehr.

Das Geld war schwer zu tragen,
Viel schwerer die Tante noch.
Ich fasste sie bebend am Kragen
Und stiess sie ins tiefe Kellerloch.—

Ich hab' meine Tante geschlachtet,
Meine Tante war alt und schwach;
Ihr aber, o Richter, ihr trachtet
Meiner blühenden Jugend-Jugend nach.[69]

(My auntie was so old and so weak. / I happened to stay overnight there / And went looking for what I could take. / I came across gold by the heaps, / And papers I'm sure worth a lot. / I heard how dear auntie was snoring / But I didn't feel a thing in the least. / What difference if harm should befall her— / How false the sound of my words! / I just shoved the knife in her guts / And auntie was snoring no longer. / The gold wasn't easy to carry, / And auntie was heavier still— / I grasped her, my body a-trembling, / And heaved her in the cellar below. / I murdered my dear old auntie, / The poor thing was so old and so weak. / But judging me harshly, Your Honor, / You begrudge me my life in full bloom.)

Bertolt Brecht, who was one of Wedekind's greatest admirers, and imitators, captured the essentials of Wedekind's personal stage magnetism in the obituary he wrote for him for the March 9, 1918 edition of the *Augsburger Neueste Nachtrichten:*

> His vitality was his finest characteristic. He had only to enter a lecture hall full of hundreds of noisy students, or a room, or a stage, with his special walk, his sharply cut bronze skull, slightly tilted and thrust forward, and there was silence . . . There he stood, ugly, brutal, dangerous, with close-cropped red hair, his hands in his trouser pockets, and one felt that the devil himself couldn't shift him . . . A few weeks ago at the Bonbonnière he sang his songs to a guitar accompaniment in a brittle voice, slightly monotonous, and quite untrained. No singer ever gave me such a shock, such a thrill. It was the man's intense aliveness, the energy which allowed him to defy sniggering ridicule and proclaim his brazen hymn to humanity, that also gave him this personal magic . . .[70]

In his "Recollections of Frank Wedekind," Heinrich Mann recalled the mesmerizing qualities of Wedekind's cabaret style in similar terms:

> Little steps, "I'm coming; you can't escape me." Thick-set, sharply cut head with the profile of Caesar, forehead promising mischief set off by close-cropped hair. But the eyes which darted with a tinge of malice were somehow strange. They also flashed with irritation and immediately afterward fell silent, full of melancholy.
>
> Strumming, as if annoyed, then the performance. Nasal, sharp, ringing. In pregnant pauses the singer turned and twisted in response to his own private motives. He took only himself seriously and almost entirely forgot his public. Suddenly, his mimicry provoked shamelessly. Too impudent and agile the mouth for one whose eyes betrayed such depths. Who grasped the sense of his songs, of his eyes? One smiled. He opposed the idea of a politely brought up epoch. One followed the new fashion of the cabaret and its depraved geniuses, unconfused by puzzles which some of these wished to pose, by thrills which could not always be resisted.[71]

Another great admirer of Wedekind, Heinrich Lautensack, who in a fit of madness at his funeral, according to Franz Blei, wanted to throw himself into his open grave "screaming after his Master,"[72] composed a requiem on the occasion of Wedekind's funeral in Waldfriedhof, Munich, on Sunday, March 12, 1918, which includes this poetic description of Wedekind in performance:

> Auf Deinen Saiten reglos Deine Hand.
> Dein Pierrot-Antlitz weiss wie Alabaster.
> Im Wind des Vorhangs wallt vom Silber-Kapodaster
> Ein Rosa und ein grün und schwarzes Band
> Mit weissem Trauerrand.
>   —Laute, ganz kurz—
> Du beugst Dich vor dem hasenden Publikum.
> Die Leute streckend weit von Deinem Leib.

Caricature of Frank Wedekind performing at the Elf Scharfrichter by Ernst Stern. (Deutsches Kabarettarchiv, Mainz).

Dich wie vor Lulu weg vom Auditorium,
Das hierher kam aus lauter prassendem Zeitvertrieb
Faul gähnend ohne Bleib.
—Laute, ganz kurz—
Was hebst Du an mit Deiner runden Stimme?
Was steigt als Erstes Deinem Kehlkopf auf?
Der Zoologe von Berlin. Der kurze Lebenslauf
Brigitte B.'s. Ilse! Und einer Blinden grimme Mädchenstimme . . .
—Blende—[73]

(Your hand motionless on your strings. / Your Pierrot countenance white as alabaster. / A rose and a green and black ribbon / With white mourning borders / Flutter from the silver bridge of the guitar in the wind of the curtain. / —Sounds, very clipped— / You bow before the hating public. / People stretching far from your person. / Making a path for you, as for Lulu, before the audience / That came here out of purely carousing time passing, / Idle yawning without a place to stay. / —Sounds, very clipped— / What are you raising up with your round voice? / What is the first thing that rises from your larynx? / The Zoologist from Berlin. The short life history of / Brigitte B. Ilse! And the frantic girl's voice of blind children . . . / —Stop—)

Dramatic productions were no less prominent a part of the programs of the Elf Scharfrichter and while typologically they followed established cabaret patterns, there were still some surprises.

Puppet shows began to be presented as early as the cabaret's first program on April 12, 1901. *Die feine Familie* (The Fine Family), a "European Drama in 3 Sensations and One Prologue" (Ein europaisches

Drama in 3 Sensationen und einem Prologo), by Willi Rath (Willibaldus Rost) commanded as much attention for its political subject—a sharp satire on Germany's growing imperialist ambitions set in the time of the Boer War in South Africa and the Boxer Rebellion in China—as for the puppet figures designed by the Munich sculptor Waldemar Heckler whose name looms large in the history of German puppetry.

The artistic climate in contemporary Munich favored the kind of theatrical heterogeneity typical of Elf Scharfrichter programs. Puppetry, for example, was raised to a high artistic level by the eventually and justifiably famous Marionetten Theater Münchener Künstler (The Munich Artists' Marionette Theater) with which Waldemar Hecker and, among others, the artist Kandinsky's friend Alexander von Salzmann were associated.

Although Willi Rath's *The Fine Family* was the most popular puppet show staged by the Elf Scharfrichter, Peter Luft got a good response with his fairytale-like puppet play *Prinzessin Pim und Laridah, Ihr Sänger* (Princess Pim and Laridah, Her Singer), subtitled a "Grosse Kartoffel-, Rettig-, Rüben- und Apfeltragödie, Insceniert und mit eigenem Obst und Gemüse aufgeführt von Paul Larsen" (A Great Potato-, Radish-, Beet-, and Apple-Tragedy. Staged and Performed with His Own Fruit by Paul Larsen). *Princess Pim* made her debut at the Executioners on the March–April program of 1902.

The shadow show (*Schattenspiel,* in German) was also crystallizing as a serious interest among turn-of-the-century Munich artists, a fact reflected in the establishment in the city's Schwabing district of the Schwabinger Schattenspiele by Alexander von Bernus (1880–1965) in 1907.[74] The first shadow show presented at the Elf Scharfrichter beginning with the May program of 1901 gave further evidence of a French lead in the field. It was the well-known Parisian shadow epic in fifteen scenes, *The Sphinx* (background and shadow figures designed by Vignola, with original music by Fragerolle), in which are portrayed the dreams of the Sphinx from the time of the ancient Assyrians to Napoleon's Egyptian campaign. For the Elf Scharfrichter's production, the German text was written by Willi Rath. November 1901 saw the appearance of an original German shadow play called *Truppen-Einzug in Berlin* (The Entry of Troops into Berlin). The text was written by the prolific early German cabaret dramatist Hanns von Gumppenberg (who often wrote under the name of Jodok) and was based on a work by the German Romantic writer Theodor Fontane. The shadows were the creation of Executioner Kaspar Beil, while the performance itself was conducted by Peter Luft. A high point of the Elf Scharfrichter involvement in shadow theater was reached in October 1903 when guest performances of the nine-scene shadow play *Moisson* (Harvest; *Ernte,* in the German version) were given by Clément-Georges (real name: Abel Georges Clément Moulin) of the Chat Noir of Paris.

Whatever the popularity of the puppet and shadow shows presented at the Elf Scharfrichter, they were soon overshadowed by the most important theatrical works staged by the cabaret in the few years of its existence, the so-called *Überdramen* (Superdramas) of Hanns von Gumppenberg (1866–1928) and some of Wedekind's early pieces for the stage.

Gumppenberg had already appeared as a cabaret dramatist in Berlin, at Wolzogen's Überbrettl, but the Elf Scharfrichter in Munich became the principal showcase of his talent. At least seven of Jodok's *Überdramen* were staged by the Executioners: *Der Nachbar* (The Neighbor), *Monna Nirwana, Lucrezia, Die Kokette* (The Coquette), *Die Verlobung* (The Engagement), *Das Geständnis* (The Confession), and *Das Spitzhütlin* (The Pointed Hat). The most famous of these was, beyond doubt, *The Neighbor,* followed closely by *Monna Nirwana* and *The Engagement.*

A parody of Gerhart Hauptmann's classic naturalistic drama *Vor Sonnenaufgang* (Before the Sunrise, 1889)—whose premiere on October 20, 1889, at the Berlin Freie Bühne scandalized the audience and initiated the stage history of German naturalism—*The Neighbor* is distinguished above all by its absence of dialogue. The place of dialogue is taken by a monologue of Franz Eberspacher (the "neighbor" of the play) which runs virtually the length of the work and consists of a single sentence of about five hundred words. In the printed text of the play, after the stage directions, Eberspacher's unbroken monologue appears on one side of a two-columned page with the other side devoted to directions governing the (exclusively) physical responses of the play's "silent people" (Schweigende Menschen)—the pharmacist Gottfried Schwalbe and his morally decayed family. In a sense, *The Neighbor* is two little plays in one, comprising Franz Eberspacher's parodic monologue and a pantomime acted out by members of the Schwalbe family who wind up killing each other and themselves as Eberspacher's revelations about adultery, fraud, and incest in the family mount in horror.

In the area of literary parody Gumppenberg's jibes at neoromanticism and symbolism outdistanced his caricatures of the Naturalists. Maeterlinck, expectedly, was an obvious target. In *Monna Nirwana* Gumppenberg based his (in this instance) rather witless parody directly on the Belgian writer's play *Monna Vanna. Der Veterinärarzt* (The Veterinarian), a "mystodrama" in one act and one of Gumppenberg's most popular cabaret plays, is a more successful exercise in parody not based on a single work of Maeterlinck, as in the case of *Monna Nirwana,* but on the style generally of Maeterlinck's early paradigmatic plays such as *L'Intérieur* and *Les Aveugles.* There are also motifs alluding to Ibsen's more symbolic plays, especially *Ghosts* and *The Lady from the Sea.*

As in Maeterlinck (and Ibsen's *The Lady from the Sea,* for example) the atmosphere in *The Veterinarian* is tense with expectation and foreboding concerning the arrival of a mysterious stranger. Here the stranger is a veterinarian and those awaiting him the family of Benedikt Rummel, consisting of his wife Adele and his three daughters, Tilli, Cilli, and Lilli. Who the veterinarian is, why he is coming, and why the expected stranger in this case happens to be a veterinarian remain mysteries. The appearance of Freind (the veterinarian) is eagerly anticipated as he is believed to hold the answers to everyone's questions. But when he comes on stage, he is unable to provide any enlightenment and so the mystery deepens. At the end of the play, the veterinarian is shot to death off stage, presumably by Rummel's wife Adele who has been brandishing a revolver through much of the play. The veterinarian's death is announced by the Man in Gray, another mysterious presence who has been hovering throughout the play and has been invisible to all except the daughter Lilli. That Gumppenberg clearly intended the work as a parody of a particular facet of the dramatic art of both Ibsen and Maeterlinck is suggested by the following statement by him about *The Veterinarian* in his memoirs: "I composed the 'mystodrama' *The Veterinarian* in order to make fun of the completely unintelligible but very pompous mystery-mongering that has come into full swing with the Ibsenites and Maeterlinckians."[75]

In *Der Wartesaal* (The Waiting Room), subtitled an "Onomatopapyrodrama," two "neo-Romantic lyric poets" Heydeck-Ubbelohe (modeled on Otto Julius Bierbaum) and Von Vilmar (alluding probably to Rainer Maria Rilke) appear in the first-class waiting room of a train station in anticipation of the arrival of Heydeck-Ubbelohe's publisher, Gabbler, and a young writer named Muck to whom they intend to introduce him. The publisher, it appears, has ruined himself financially publishing

Heydeck-Ubbelohe's poems and has now broken a contract to do the poet's collected works because of his inability to satisfy his demands that the new edition of his poems be printed on a certain type and color paper which the publisher has been unable to find. The appearance of Muck and then Gabbler and the absurdity of introductions involving long strings of given names reduces the eagerly awaited meeting to a shambles and ends with the publisher racing for a train.

Bourgeois affectations were another target of Gumppenberg's satire and parody, especially in *Die Verlobung* (The Engagement), "Ein Etepetetodrama in 74 Umschreibungen" (An Etepetetodrama in 74 Paraphrases) in which a periphrastic "Philistine language" of the pious and prudish bourgeoisie is taken to task. If elsewhere the verbal ethereality of neo-Romantic mysticism and supernaturalism was held up to ridicule, the source of the parody on this occasion is the grotesque circumlocutions to which the straitlaced bourgeois will go to avoid the everyday vocabulary of the body and physical functions. The effort to prettify the lexicon of the physical results in such absurdities as *Vorbau* (front, or forward, construction) for *Brust* (bosom, chest) and *Fortbewegungsgelenk* (forward movement joint) for *Knie* (knee). The main practitioners of this kind of periphrasis in the play are Bruno Gottgetreu, a book seller, and his fiancée Cäcilia Schwarz, the daughter of a member of parliament. The romantic scenes between the two generate the greatest humor. As their excitement mounts each tries to avoid what for them would be the embarrassment of any ordinary, direct verbalization of physical sensation. Bursting out in a sweat at one point Gottgetreu exclaims: "Ich schwitz' wie ein Schwein . . ." (I'm sweating like a pig), but suddenly aware of his "lapse" into crudity, excuses himself and then goes on to express the same physical phenomenon in a manner acceptable to his intended: "Meine Poren geben ihren ganzen Feuchtigkeitsgehalt an die Atmosphäre ab" (My pores give off their entire capacity for moisture to the atmosphere). Contact with Gottgetreu's moustache during a kiss produces this reaction from Cäcilia: "Oh—wie dein Oberlippenschmuck mich zu nervöser Heiterkeit erregt!" (Oh, how your upper lip ornament excites me to nervous gaiety). When her fiancé grasps the nape of her neck too exuberantly during an embrace, Cäcilia exclaims in pain: "Und hier rückwärts am Krageninhalt haben mich deine langen Fingerblumen verwundet. . . ." (Here on the back of the contents of my collar your long finger flowers [meaning, of course,

Gottgetreu's fingernails—HBS] wounded me). Stunned, Gottgetreu's answer can only be the promise, "Ich will mir von heute die Fingerblumen ganz kurz halten." (From tomorrow on I will keep my finger flowers quite short). Probably the wildest circumlocution occurs after a second ardent kiss is exchanged between the lovers. In ecstasy, Cäcilia declares: "Ach, wie pocht mein Seelenwerkzeug gegen den Vorbau!" (Oh, how my soul instrument [heart, in other words—HBS] beats against my front construction [chest, bosom—HBS]).[76]

A serious writer and philosopher whose major philosophical works appeared in 1892 and 1903,[77] Gumppenberg's obvious pleasure in writing little satiric and parodic plays specifically for cabaret performance was based on two factors: his desire to spoof what he, like so many other contemporary artists, regarded as the excesses of such reigning literary fashions as naturalism and neoromanticism, and his need, again shared by many of his contemporaries, to enjoy the psychic release of being able to create in an atmosphere of uninhibited freedom. He speaks of this motivation for his collaboration with the cabaret and the writing of *Überdramen* in his memoirs:

> The need of the "Executioners" for small grotesque plays [Grotesk-Stücken—HBS] presented me welcome possibilities to let go the reins of my inclination for merry satire. The opportunity for the fastest realization of dramatic jests of this sort was tempting enough, but it also provided me with an outlet for my eagerness to poke fun at the newest stupidities of literary fashion. My light and exuberant production in this field was thus able to afford me a not too despised side income, quite apart from the cheerful spiritual satisfaction it gave me. So I became, under the pseudonym Jodok, a collaborator of the enterprise.[78]

Although the physical dimensions of the Elf Scharfrichter were small, the cabaret's ability to stage dramatic productions was considerably enhanced by its stage, perhaps the most advanced of any among the European cabarets of the time. Besides a sunken orchestra pit and the lighting facilities of the most modern stages of the period, the Executioners also employed an unusual innovative curtain which ran along two semicircular rails and proved highly suitable to the cabaret's very limited playing area. The Eleven Executioners took no small pride in their stage and Otto Falckenberg, for one, placed the cabaret, at least in this respect, in the same privileged category of such sanctuaries of the contermporary German theater as the Prinzregenten Theater in Munich and the Bayreuth Festspielhaus.[79]

The superior production capability of the Elf Scharfrichter acted as an inducement to dramatists to write especially for the cabaret. This was certainly the case with Hanns von Gumppenberg, the most productive dramatist associated with the Executioners, and must no doubt have figured in Wedekind's willingness to have certain of his own dramatic works performed at the establishment on Türkenstrasse. Wedekind's debut as a dramatist at the Executioners took place in November 1901 with the performance of a dialogue based on his story about sensual fulfillment, *Rabbi Esra.* As enthusiastic about acting in plays as writing them, Wedekind assumed the role of Rabbi Esra and the well-known actress Olly Bernhardi played that of his son Moses.[80] Wedekind's next appearance as an actor in one of his own plays at the Executioners came about a year later when the first act of *Earth Spirit,* the first of his famous "Lulu" plays, was staged with Wedekind performing as the painter Schwarz. Otto Falckenberg also participated in the production in the important role of Lulu's ill-fated patron, Dr. Schön. The cabaret performance of the first act of *Earth Spirit* was not, however, a premiere. The play was first presented in its entirety on February 25, 1898, in the auditorium of the Leipzig Kristallpalast; this was, in fact, the first stage production of any dramatic work by Wedekind. The dramatist also appeared in the production, under the pseudonym Heinrich Kammerer, as Dr. Schön. A Munich premiere, on October 24, 1895, also preceded the production by the Executioners.

Certainly Wedekind's most distinct theatrical contribution to the repertoire of the Elf Scharfrichter was his pantomime *Die Kaiserin von Neufundland* (The Empress of Newfoundland), which he may have written as early as his Paris-London period (1891–1895). All told, Wedekind wrote four pantomime plays: *The Empress of Newfoundland, Die Flöhe oder Der Schmerzenstanz* (The Fleas, or The Dance of Sorrow, 1892, first printed 1897), "Der Mückenprinz" (The Prince of Mosquitoes, written before 1895, printed 1897), which was incorporated as a dance drill or exercise in the novel *Mine Haha,* and the "circus-grotesque" *Bethel,* which was written in 1893–1894 and first printed in 1921.[81]

Wedekind's cultivation of pantomime, like his incorporation of circus elements in his plays, owed much to the impact of his experiences in Paris and London. For the sake of chronological accuracy, it should be pointed out, however, that his interest in circus in particular antedated his stay in Paris by a few years. In 1887 and 1888, in fact, Wedekind wrote two articles on the circus, based on performances of the Zirkus Herzog in Zurich, for the *Neue Zürcher Zeitung.*[82] Furthermore, among the new friends Wedekind made in Munich after moving there from Zurich in 1889 was the well-known circus clown, singer, and painter Willi Morgenstern (real name, Rudinoff) who not only added another dimension to Wedekind's interest in circus but for a time accompanied him, as if a guide, on his travels through the world of Parisian popular entertainments in the 1890s. The importance of Wedekind's stay in Paris (and for a few months in London) for his dramatic writing lay in the fact that it came at a time of heightened receptivity to the artistic possibilities of circus, pantomime, variety theater, and music hall, a receptivity reflected in such essays of the period as "Pariser Tagebuch" (Parisian Diary) and "Middlesex Musikhall. Ein Fragment aus meinem Londoner Tagebuch" (Middlesex Music Hall. A Fragment from My London Diary).[83]

Underlying Wedekind's enthusiasm for circus, pantomime, and variety theater acts was an interest in physicality common among artists in turn-of-the-century Europe who were moving in various ways toward an exploration of nonverbal communication. In Wedekind's case in particular it arose, to quote Fritz Strich, from his "urge for elemental nature" which "found here [in the circus and pantomime—HBS] its unliterary form. The confidence in the body's power of expression, which had been ignored for too long, the pleasure of rhythm awakened in him and displaced the necessity for words."[84]

Intent on depicting the power of the flesh, of the physically erotic in human life, Wedekind now began embodying his ideas in dramatic form as early as the three-act comedy *Der Liebestrank* (The Love Potion, also known as *Fritz Schwigerling* after the play's male protagonist), which was finished in 1892 but published for the first time only in 1899. A circus performer named Schwigerling, for whom Willi Rudinoff served as the prototype, becomes Wedekind's quintessential physical man as hero. Such better-known plays as *Earth Spirit* and *Die Büchse der Pandora* (Pandora's Box), which together comprise the so-called Lulu tragedy, are major vehicles for Wedekind's philosophy of the corporeal and significantly make extensive use of circus motifs.

Symptomatic of the *fin-de-siècle* retreat from the verbal and literary was a renascence of the ancient art of pantomime. Nowhere was this more evident than Paris where a veritable temple of mime, the Cercle Funambulesque, was founded in 1888 on the pattern of the earlier nineteenth-century Théâtre des Funambules and where in 1892 an entire issue of the periodical *La Plume* was devoted to mime in its many aspects.[85] Since Germany lacked a significant pantomime tradition, Wedekind, once his interest was aroused, would have been all the more receptive to what was happening in France; writing his own pantomime drama could appear a more original and experimental departure for him as a German artist. The move to pantomime also had its own logic in terms of Wedekind's development as a dramatist. Now, instead of depicting characters who embody the physical principle or using circus settings and performers as symbolic motifs, Wedekind could carry physicality on stage further by completely eliminating spoken dialogue and reducing the drama entirely to physical action.

Nietzsche's important views on dance and tragedy, which enjoyed much currency throughout Europe in the late nineteenth and early twentieth centuries, lent additional support to Wedekind's own feelings about physicality and the transformation of contemporary dramatic art by enhancing the physical dimension of performance at the expense of the verbal. Significantly, dance became an important ingredient of Wedekind's dramatic writing, especially in his pantomimes, a fact reflected in their designation in German as *Tanzpantomime* (dance pantomimes).

The Empress of Newfoundland, the most impressive of Wedekind's pantomimes, probably arose in the author's Paris and London period.[86] Wedekind himself claimed that the work was written in January and February 1897, but there is some reason to doubt this. In any case, it was first printed in the theater section of Wedekind's collection *Die Fürstin Russalka* (The Princess Russalka), along with his other pantomime *The Fleas,* in 1897. *The Empress of Newfoundland* enjoys the distinction of being the only pantomime by Wedekind to have been performed in a cabaret. Its premiere at the Eleven Executioners took place, with great success, on March 12, 1902.[87] Subsequent performances at the Überbrettl in Berlin in 1903, the Munich Kammerspiele in 1923, the Vienna Raimundtheater in 1924, and the Leipzig Stadttheater in 1929 were equally successful. Because of the spatial limitations of the Executioners stage, the version of *The Empress of Newfoundland* presented there was necessarily an abridgement. But the originality of the conception together with Richard Weinhöppel's music woven together of Wagnerian motifs and popular dances and marches and with Wedekind himself reciting the brief introductions to the acts in his highly personal style assured the pantomime's favorable reception.

The fairytale character of *The Empress of Newfoundland* as well as its colorful settings and costumes and the physical humor of many of its scenes momentarily divert attention from the work's underlying seriousness. Here, as elsewhere, Wedekind takes as his subject the power of physical desire. After a medical checkup by her court physician, Prof. Dr. Didi Zeudus, the Empress Filissa is advised that the best thing would be for her to get married. The prime candidates are the poet Heinrich Tarquinius Pustekohl, whose recitation of his own poetry only reduces all to laughter, "the great Napoleon" (der grosse Napoleon), whose military prowess fails to impress the Empress and who soon quits the court in disgust, and the inventor and magician Alwa Adison (referring, of course, to Thomas Alva Edison) whose feats astonish the public but only induce slumber in the Empress. When the weightlifter Eugen Holthoff (also based on a real personage) appears and begins lifting weights, the Empress rivets her attention on him. His magnificent physique, the rippling muscles, the great display of energy and endurance magnetizes Filissa who showers Holthoff with sumptuous presents as an expression of her admiration. Head over heels in love with her weightlifter, she is in ecstasy and cannot do enough for him, including ordering sacks of money brought in and deposited at his feet. Efforts by the poet Pustekohl and Dr. Didi Zeudus to warn her of the danger of her infatuation get nowhere. When Holthoff, drunk with champagne, cannot lift a 2,000 kilo set of weights as the greatest challenge yet faced by him, the Empress is distraught and Pustekohl revives his campaign for her affection. At a nod from her, Holthoff moves to eject the poet, but Pustekohl pulls out a dagger, plunges it into his own heart, and dies, his blood flowing onto the Empress's feet. His energy renewed following this episode, Holthoff proceeds to lift the 2,000 kilo weights. The Empress falls into such a state of ecstasy at the feat that she goes into a wild demonic dance all around him until finally restrained and straitjacketed by Holthoff and Dr. Didi Zeudus and then put in a cage. The Empress' dance, during which she brandishes a sword and which is accompanied by appropriate music, is the high point of the pantomime as an exemplification of the possessive power of erotic desire.

The third and last act is set in a tawdry honky-tonk filled with drunken sailors, prostitutes, and rowdies. Holthoff is in his true element, gambling with money him given by the Empress and already equipped with a new girlfriend. There is dancing also in this act, extending the choreographical aspect of the preceding, but now instead of the ecstatic frenzied solo dance of the Empress Filissa, couples dance in a style appropriate to the honky-tonk setting. The pantomime moves toward its finale when a distraught and disheveled Filissa enters and attempts to win back the affection of a disinterested and even abusive Holtoff. As if to reawaken the old magic between them she entreats him to lift a small 50 pound weight that she finds on the premises, but dissipation has cost him his energy and he is unable. Realizing finally that Holthoff is beyond hope and dismayed at discovering jewelry she gave him adorning the neck of one of his girlfriends, Filissa decides that honor leaves her no choice but death. She indicates that she wants Holthoff to bash in her head with one of the weights, but he fails to understand the intention of her actions. However, just before leaving the tavern, Holthoff bows to the crowd's wish that he lift the weight and succeeds in doing so. With Filissa at his feet imploring him with her eyes that he bring one end of the weight down on her head and thereby end her misery, it appears for a moment that he will. But the weight slips from his hands and crashes on his own feet sending him rushing away in pain. With no recourse left her but to take her own life, Filissa parts her loose hair into two strands, draws them around her neck, and strangles herself.

While reiterating a theme common to Wedekind—the possessive and potentially destructive power of sensuality—the fairytale and humorous aspects of *The Empress of Newfoundland* together with its pantomime form invest the work with the character of a grotesque. It is as if Wedekind had succeeded in stepping away from himself for a moment, achieving a new perspective on his own obsessions in which the playful and morbid combine in an act of self-mockery. By eliminating spoken dialogue from the work and relying only on the language of the body, Wedekind hit upon an exaggerated but appropriate stage idiom for a drama wholly motivated by consideration of the power of the purely physical. How relatively advanced Wedekind's stagecraft was can be gauged by comparing *The Empress of Newfoundland* with Strindberg's *Miss Julie* which deals in essence with the same theme. Strindberg also infused his play with a pervasive physicality in which dance is a factor. But Wedekind went Strindberg two better, first by conceiving a dramatic work about physicality and sensuality as a speechless pantomime, and second, by introducing elements of the grotesque into the pantomime, thereby anticipating the new vision of a grotesque theatrical art of the early twentieth century.

The great success of *The Empress of Newfoundland* on the cabaret stage of the Elf Scharfrichter is understandable. The revival of interest in pantomime in the turn-of-the-century enhanced its appeal to the avant-garde, particularly in terms of its emphasis on the physical, its elimination of spoken speech, and its close relationship to dance and music. Like the shadow show and the puppet performance, the pantomime was also thought of as chiefly a physical activity which in its integration of the visual, choreographical, and musical placed it solidly among the "small arts" then in the vanguard of the artistic transformation.

The Empress of Newfoundland was Wedekind's last major contribution to the Elf Scharfrichter. Never very happy about the harsh realities of life that made his appearance on a cabaret stage a virtual necessity and concerned, above all, with the furtherance of his career as a dramatist, Wedekind used disagreements with Marc Henry during a tour to Nuremberg as the pretext for severing his ties with the Executioners in early 1903.[88] When nearly a year later his financial state of affairs drove him back to the cabaret, it was not to the Elf Scharfrichter that he returned but to the so-called Münchener Künstler-Kabarett Intimes Theater organized by a sometime stage performer named Josef Vallé (real name, Hunkele). In September 1901, this same Vallé had opened what he billed as an "original Munich cabaret" in Berlin under the plagarized name of Die Zwölf Scharfrichterinnen (The Twelve Lady Executioners). Unable to make a go of it in Berlin, Vallé returned to Munich with his troupe and performed for a time in the city's vaudeville halls. After the closing of the Elf Scharfrichter in December 1903, he moved to fill the vacuum by starting a new cabaret called Die Sieben Tantenmörder (The Seven Auntie Killers), also on Türkenstrasse, in an obvious borrowing from Wedekind's ballad "Die Tantenmörder" (The Auntie Killer). Despite his promotion of the participation of former members of the Elf Scharfrichter in his cabaret, Vallé was able to deliver only a few. Unable to live up to its advanced billing and a pale imitation of the original Elf Scharfrichter at best, the Seven Auntie Killers fell into virtual oblivion when Vallé went with it on tour in the summer of 1904. When he returned to Munich in October that same year, he launched yet another enterprise, the Münchener Künstler-Kabarett Intimes Theater.

At this point, Vallé's and Wedekind's needs coincided. Vallé needed a star of Wedekind's reputation to make his newest cabaret viable and Wedekind, needing money, was willing to swallow his pride once again and return to the small stage. Wedekind vented his thoughts on the matter of his resumption of cabaret stage performance in a letter to Beate Heine from Munich on July 28, 1904:

> There are official successes, but nevertheless I continue to sit as ingrown as dry rot and without the freedom of movement which any traveling salesman has available to him. It reaches the point that through the Munich beer life one distances oneself as far as possible from the rich interesting world. After I again lived through a really gloomy time this spring, I finally said to myself that such a state of affairs is unworthy of me, and so I accepted an engagement in a Tingel-Tangel. Others followed the first, so that in all likelihood I will be strumming the strings before an audience for the whole of next winter. But in return I am lifted over petty disagreements and, of greatest importance to me, I will finally once again come into contact with the world and its inhabitants . . . I am finished with literature. Even in the next ten years, through the hottest battles, I would hardly stand a chance of overcoming the public's stubborn rejection of me, and what will I then have had from my entire life! Every day I experience a feeling of relief that from now on literature can slide off my back . . . Now I believe that I have found the way out: the grating opens and I climb up to the light. Freedom, your name is Tingel-Tangel![89]

With Wedekind performing regularly up until 1906 (and earning far more than at the Elf Scharfrichter), Vallé was able to attract sizable audiences. When Wedekind left the Intimes Theater, Vallé managed to keep it going until mid-May 1909 largely on the basis of appearances by the comic Josef Schäffer and the popular *chansonette* Mary Irber (whom Klaus Budzinski characterizes as "the first vamp in German cabaret"),[90] and increasingly tasteless programs having more in common with "girlie" shows than cabaret. As performances became more revealing and more pronounced in their sexual content, the Intimes Theater found itself on the defensive against mounting pressure on the police to close it on grounds of indecency. Vallé successfully countered this pressure until a run-in with the Munich *Allgemeine Rundschau* proved his undoing. A libel trial over the newspaper's charge of obscenity escalated into a full-scale legal battle which left Vallé without a leg to stand on. A court decision in favor of the newspaper resulted in the official closing of the Intimes Theater on May 15, 1909.[91]

Wedekind's "defection" from the Elf Scharfrichter in early 1903 was hardly the only reason for the demise of the cabaret later that same year. The very popularity of the cabaret was also a contributing factor in its downfall. As the Executioners became a Munich landmark—without, however, acquiring the legendary mystique of the Chat Noir of Paris—people came from all over to visit its small premises, putting pressure on the cabaret for more frequent performances. Instead of mounting shows three days a week, it now increased them to daily performances and in the fall of 1902 even Sunday matinees were introduced. The additional performances imposed a strain on the capacity of the Elf Scharfrichter that could be relieved only by the hiring of professional actors and entertainers to augment the cabaret's regular troupe. Once this occurred, the integrity of the original Executioners cooperative concept was undermined and the intimate working relationship of its regulars dissipated. Although Wedekind's departure from the cabaret was motivated by strong personal reasons, it could also be viewed as symptomatic of the weakening of ties that held the cabaret together. Before long, Weinhöppel, Falckenberg, and Gumppenberg also manifested signs of restlessness and a desire to pursue more "serious" artistic goals.

Besides being burdened financially by the need to hire additional performers, which imposed severe strain on its generally meager resources, the Elf Scharfrichter also chafed under a tightening noose of censorship. Political as well as some forms of social satire had become all but impossible after the cabaret lost its "private" ("members" and "invited guests" only) status in October 1901 as the result of a performance in the fifth program of a little play by Otto Falckenberg entitled *Das Geständnis* (The Confession). Subtitled "Ein Dialog nach einem unveröffentlichen Manuskript des Kardinals Bibbiena (1470–1520) frei ins Deutsche übertragen vom Scharfrichter Peter Luft" (A Dialogue Based on an Unpublished Manuscript of Cardinal Bibbiena . . . Freely Translated into German by Executioner Peter Luft [i.e., Otto Falckenberg—HBS]), *The Confession* dramatizes the anything but pious thoughts of a priest as he hears a confession of Lucrezia Borgia. The work was enough to bring down the wrath of Munich's conservative Catholic establishment on the Executioners' heads. In the wake of complaints to the Bavarian authorities about the moral offensiveness of its programs, the cabaret lost its relative independence and was hereafter required to submit all works to be presented on stage to the censors for prior approval. The Elf Scharfrichter was also officially demoted to the level of a vaudeville, which meant that its license to operate could be revoked at any time, thus hanging a Damocles sword above it.

As time went on, the cabaret's programs reflected its narrower range of operation. Lieder, which had figured prominently in Executioners' programs from the beginning, were now given an even greater role. Sung by such regulars as Marya Delvard, Olly Bernhardi, Friederika Gutmann-Umlauft, Hannes Ruch (Hans Richard Weinhöppel), Frigidus Strang (Robert Kothe), and Heinrich Retting, lieder had a twofold appeal. They were, to begin with, further evidence of the cabaret's commitment to the merging of popular and high cultures manifest also in the interest in puppet and shadow shows, folk and other dances, and pantomime. Then, lieder tended generally to be innocuous (from the political and social point of view) and often carried sentimental as well as patriotic associations. While a number of the lieder sung at the Elf Scharfrichter were of contemporary composition, the work of such writers as Bierbaum, Dehmel, Gumppenberg, and Liliencron, others were drawn from a classical German repertoire which included songs by the medieval Minnesinger Walther von der Vogelweide and the Romantics Joseph von Eichendorff and Heinrich Heine. There were also *Soldatenlieder,* such as those by Peter Schlemihl [Ludwig Thoma—HBS], and modern versions of traditional German *Narrenlieder,* or "fools songs," written by Bierbaum, Gumppenberg, and Liliencron. Augmenting the folkish lieder of Executioners' programs were modern *Pierrotlieder* inspired by the turn-of-the-century fascination with the Pierrot figure, and French cabaret and folk songs written or performed by Marc Henry in keeping with his "mission" of promoting French culture in Germany.

Programs of the Elf Scharfrichter from May 1902, June–July 1902, the "Carnival" program of 1903, and October 1903 clearly demonstrate the impact of censorship—a sharp diminution of works, especially poems and dramatic sketches, of social or political satire, the predominance of songs, the appearance of such patently innocuous items as translations of comic playlets by the French writer Georges Courteline (1860–1929), guest performances of Parisian Chat Noir shadow shows by Clément-Georges, who also sang *Chansons Montmartroises*—some of which he had himself composed—a *Fastnachtspiel* (Shrovetide comedy) by the late medieval German dramatist Hans Sachs, and a three-part ballet suite from Rameau's *Achante et Cephise* (1751).

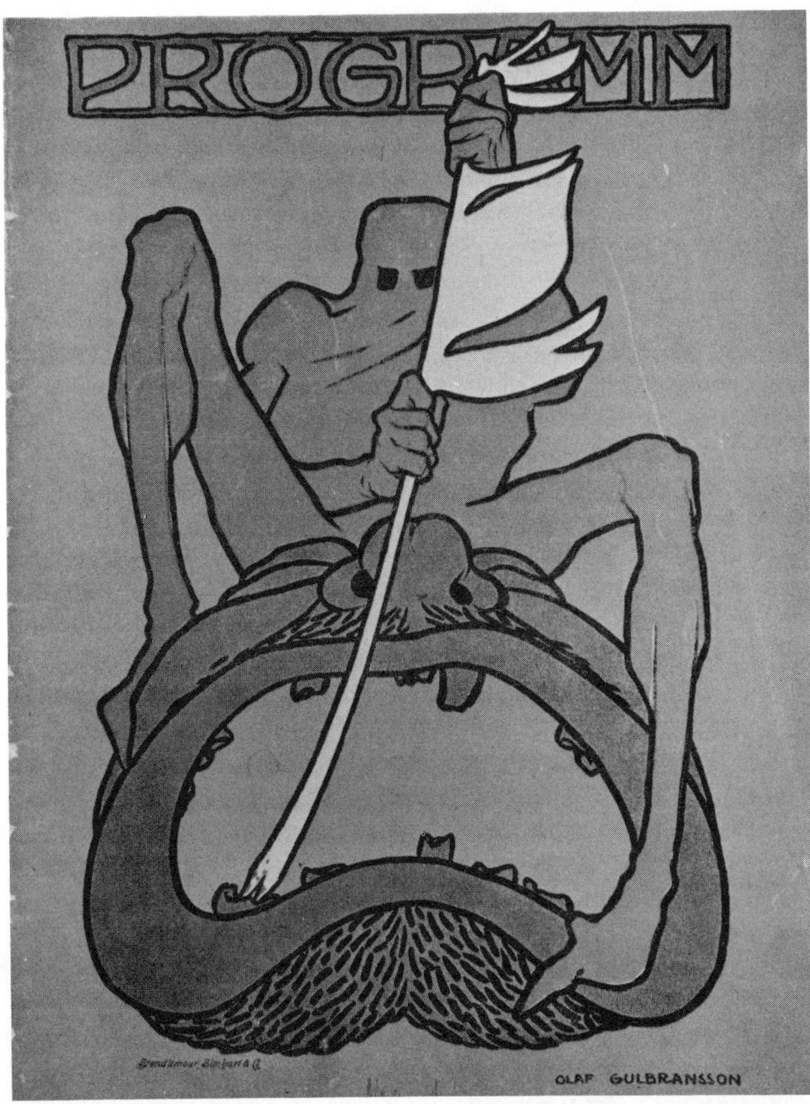

Elf Scharfrichter program cover by Olaf Gulbranson. (Münchner Stadtmuseum, Munich).

Writing of the demise of the Elf Scharfrichter in his memoirs, Hanns von Gumppenberg took due note of the element of fatigue and the trivialization of programs, but also laid at least some of the responsibility at the doorstep of Marc Henry, which lends further support to the belief that friction with the Frenchman, not only on the part of Wedekind, served to undermine the unity of the Executioners:

Among [the cabaret's—HBS] literary mainstays a serious overtiredness showed up. Their nerves could not long endure such universal demands as playwrights, song writers, performers, *conférenciers,* producers, and financial managers. They finally saw themselves compelled to return again to their literary activity and leave everything else to average and less than average talents who then more and more vulgarized and trivialized the entire undertaking. Furthermore, the business management fell in this way for a year's time to the agile and industrious Frenchman Henry. He was well versed in producing even more opulent hangman's fodder with the help of tours, but he conducted the enterprise as a whole all the faster to its demise. He also disregarded all the more unscrupulously the rights of the original leading founders, participants, and collaborators until he finally misused their names—mine among them—only for purposes of publicity. The success and prestige of the "Executioners" in its first period was soon to be attested to by the fact that later all kinds of banal vaudeville endeavored as convulsively as unjustifiedly to refer somehow or other to their pedigree or at least to recall it by means of a similar grotesque claim.[92]

By November 1903, most of the original Executioners had gone their separate ways. The spirit of the cabaret had clearly evaporated. That it was incapable of sustaining further blows was demonstrated by the police crackdown on certain items of a sexual and political-satirical nature announced for its new program. After publicly complaining before the audience about censorship on November 7 (1903), Marc Henry was summoned by the police for interrogation—and a stern warning—for the following day.[93] This was the last straw. With its original membership fragmented, its original purpose undermined by censorship and an ever growing commercialism beholden to public taste, the Eleven Executioners closed its doors by mid-December 1903. The most successful and artistically significant German cabaret of the *fin-de-siècle* had reached its end.

Recalling his days as an Executioner in his book of memoirs, *Mein Leben—Mein Theater* (1944), Otto Falckenberg captured the essence of the cabaret's significance:

It will always remain the glory of the "Elf Scharfrichter" that this stage for the art of small forms—in contrast to so many later unliterary or supposedly literary cabarets as well as to the countless Berlin *Überbrettlen* of the time—truly arose and created only from a genuine artistic and artistic-political passion and enthusiasm. The "Elf Scharfrichter" did not keep one eye cocked on any authorities, nor on the cash box, and least of all on the public. They could never be accused of doing anything just to please anyone, or of a capitalistic fear of literature or real art, or of crowd-pleasing obscenity. It is indeed no accident but a laurel wreath honorably earned through decency, bravery, unselfishness, and skill that knowledge of the "Elf Scharfrichter," almost like the myth of the literary cabaret itself, has penetrated to our very time and that commemorative pieces can appear even today.[94]

Like the cabarets of Paris and Barcelona that had preceded it and far more than other German cabarets of its own time, the Elf Scharfrichter exemplified the possibility of synthesis of popular and high cultures. Although inspired by the revival of the chanson at the Chat Noir and Le Mirliton, the Elf Scharfrichter quickly moved beyond imitation to a renewed interest in such indigenous forms as the lied and especially the *Bänkelsang* and *Moritat.*

If Wedekind's ballads for the Elf Scharfrichter recall the socially defiant and grim chansons of several of the French singers, they owe more to the street minstrel tradition of the German *Bänkelsänger* whose stage was usually just a bench (*Bänkel,* in German, hence the name *Bänkelsänger,* "bench singers") set up in public places, often fairs and markets, and whose songs, mostly about sensational happenings from near and far, were also accompanied by an illustrated signboard. To turn-of-the-century artists such as Bierbaum, Liliencron, Mühsam, Thoma, Wedekind, and Wolzogen, much of the appeal of the *Bänkelsänger* tradition derived not only from its popular fair and marketplace associations, but from its primitive synthesis of text, music, picture, and performance (the singer vocally dramatized the text of the picture signboard, to which he often referred with a pointer, and usually accompanied himself or was accompanied on the guitar, accordian, or fiddle). Frequently, the *Bänkelsänger* were war veterans or invalids licensed by the state to practice their craft and were often assisted by their wives and children. The *Bänkelsänger* tradition was, therefore, a kind of popular *Gesamtkunstwerk* capable of being easily assimilated by the cabaret which on a more sophisticated level both represented and sought a similar synthesis of the arts. Many of the songs sung by the *Bänkelsänger* were *Moritaten,* that is songs about crime, above all murder.[95] The emphasis was on the sensational, the lurid, and the grotesque, and the aim of the singer was to inform, frighten, and move.

The appeal of *Moritaten* and the *Bänkelsänger* tradition to German cabaret artists and other enthusiasts of a synthesis of popular and high cultures endured well into the years of the Weimar Republic. The prominence of cabaret in Weimar culture, for which the Elf Scharfrichter had paved the way, and the now largely unobstructed functioning of cabaret as a vehicle of satire, indeed as a genre of satire, enhanced the appeal of the *Bänkelsang-Moritat* style and gave rise to newer adaptations of it, above all by such luminaries of the interwar German cabaret as the leftwing revolutionary poet Erich Mühsam, the popular fiction writer Erich Kästner, and the cabaret performer Joachim Ringelnatz.

Bertolt Brecht, who not only admired but learned from Wedekind, carried the *Bänkelsang-Moritat* into the theater in his world-famous *Dreigroschenoper* (Threepenny Opera) of 1928. A "Moritat singer" (*Moritatensänger*) sings a *Moritat* in the Soho scene while "The Ballad of Mack the Knife" is actually a *Moritat,* as the original German title "Moritat vom Mackie Messer" clearly indicates. The anticapitalist opera parody's underworld setting, peopled with a variety of criminals and prostitutes, was an appropriate setting for a new adaptation of the *Bänkelsang-Moritat* tradition. Brecht's use of it extended not only to modern versions of *Moritaten,* but to the pictorially related epic element in which the singer narrates a series of events depicted in pictures. So cognizant was Brecht of the potential of the *Moritat* for his own work that he wrote several *Moritaten,* among them "Von der Kindesmörderin Marie Farrar" (About the Child Murderess Marie Farrar), "Apfelböck, oder Die Lilie auf dem Felde" (Apfelböck, or The Lily in the Field), the previously mentioned "Moritat vom Mackie Messer," and, also from *The Threepenny Opera,* "Ein Paar neue Verser einer soeben veralteten Moritat" (A Pair of New Verses of a Now Obsolete *Moritat*).[96]

The influence of the performers and programs of the Elf Scharfrichter cast a wide net. Besides the successor cabaret of the Weimar period, which, now free of the stifling prohibition of police censorship, could freely vent its satirical spleen, and the latterday adapters of the *Bänkelsang-Moritat* tradition such as Brecht, the pre- and postwar German theater also came under its sway. Without the Executioners' example of the fusion of dramatic art and popular theatrical small forms such as puppet show, shadow play, pantomime, circus and music hall routines—the fusion, that is, of high dramatic art and *variété*—it is doubtful that innovative stage works such as Brecht's antiwar comedy *Mann ist Mann* (A Man's a Man, 1926), with its cabaret, music hall, and circus elements, and, of course, *The Threepenny Opera* (1928) would have appeared when they did.

The intimacy of cabaret performance, the close actor-audience relationship, clearly affected Max Reinhardt's thinking about theater long after the days of Die Brille and Schall und Rauch. Despite his eventual fame as a master of great spectacle drama, Reinhardt applied lessons assimilated from the cabaret to his small theater experiments at the Kleines Theater and exemplary Kammerspiele and never wholly distanced himself from the special properties of cabaret performance, as any close analysis of the structure of his major Shakespearean and classical Greek and German productions easily bears witness. The successful reshaping of pantomime by a dramatist of the talents of Wedekind must surely have aroused Reinhardt's interest in the possibilities of the wordless drama to which he gave full expression in his outstanding production of *Sumurûn* at the Kammerspiele in 1910 and the phenomenally successful *Das Mirakel* (The Miracle) in 1911.

The important twentieth-century German theatrical theorist Georg Fuchs (1868–1949), who together with the designer Fritz Erler (1868–1940) founded the initially exciting but eventually unsuccessful Munich Künstlertheater in 1907, drew not only on ideas of Adolphe Appia and Gordon Craig in the conceptualization of an antinaturalistic "retheatricalized" theater (which Vsevolod Meyerhold and Nikolai Evreinov in Russia would carry still further, and with greater success), but on the experience of popular theater and cabarets such as the Elf Scharfrichter. Intent on creating a new theatrical culture that would weld audiences, whatever their social backgrounds, into a single cohesive community, above all through the inducement of a state of ecstatic intoxication, Fuchs placed great emphasis on the physical dimension of performance, on dance and the visual and rhythmic aspects of popular theatrics. He openly acknowledged his admiration for the Elf Scharfrichter, principally because of its success in integrating such popular nonverbal theatrical forms as dance and pantomime in contrast to the (in his judgment) excessive text-oriented literariness of other cabarets. To read Fuchs' major writings on theater, such as *Die Schaubühne der Zukunft* (The Stage of the Future, 1905) and *Die Revolution des Theaters* (The Revolution of the Theater, 1909)—which were of enormous impact on the development of European (and Russian) avant-garde theatrical theory and practice in the twentieth century—without considering the extent to which cabaret shaped his thinking about the role of popular theater in the creation of a newly theatricalized theater, is to miss one of the most important elements in the development of his artistic program.

The great painter Vassily Kandinsky (1866–1944), who attempted a theatrical reform of his own with such experimental works, essentially scenarios, as *Der gelbe Klang* (The Yellow Sound), *Violett* (Violet), *Grüner Klang* (Green Sound), and *Schwarz und Weiss* (Black and White)—all composed between 1909 and 1914 (only *The Yellow Sound* and *Violet* have ever appeared in print)—was even more enthusiastic about popular theater and cabaret. Also commited to the *Gesamtkunstwerk* concept of a synthesis of the arts, but convinced he could overcome Wagner's weaknesses in achieving this goal, Kandinsky attempted to develop a type of theatrical performance that would bring together the principal elements of stage works (drama, opera, ballet). He identifies these, in his article "Über Bühnenkomposition" (On Stage Composition), which was originally intended as a preface to *The Yellow Sound,* as: 1) musical sound and its movement, 2) bodily spiritual sound and its movement, expressed by people and objects; 3) color-tones and their movement (a special resource of the stage). "All three elements," wrote Kandinsky, "play an equally significant role, remain externally self-sufficient, and are treated in a similar way, i.e. subordinated to the inner purpose." That inner purpose was understood by Kandinsky to be the achievement of the "cosmic element," the "spiritual life of man" which nineteenth-century drama lacked due to its emphasis on external action. To Kandinsky, the drama of realism and naturalism is "in general the more or less refined and profound narration of happenings of a more or less personal character. It is really the description of external life, where the spiritual life of man is involved only insofar as it has to do with his external life." In his own highly abstract, largely enigmatic stage compositions, Kandinsky sought to overcome the inadequate spiritual dimension of nineteenth-century drama by eliminating narration and plot-related external action concentrating instead on the interplay of colors, dance-inspired individual and group movement capable of producing an abstract effect and the "inner sound" (*Klang*) the evocation of which in the viewer's soul was the ultimate goal of art, and words alone or combined into sentences and used to create a particular "mood," "which prepares the ground of the soul and makes it receptive."[97]

Kandinsky always expressed admiration for and interest in folk and popular culture and recognized the vibrancy and dynamism of popular theater compared to such formalized traditional genres as drama, opera, and ballet. In the madcap clown routines of the circus, in such *Variété* entertainments as puppet shows and pantomime, he found that feeling for the purity of artistic expression (color and movement as spectacle, words as sound often unrelated to meaning) that became the basis of his own experimental theater writing. Linearity, logicality, narration, plot in any traditional sense meant nothing and had virtually no place in Kandinsky's stage compositions. What mattered most was the artist's ability to reach the innermost being of the spectator and this could be brought out only by configurations of the purest, most abstract elements of physical movement, color, and musical and human sound.

Kandinsky's experiments may have been too abstract and enigmatic, too technically demanding, either to be produced on stage in his lifetime[98] or have any but a historical role in the development of twentieth-century avant-garde theater. But they arose out of a rejection of traditional forms of drama and theatrical expression that found new sources of creative energy in the subculture of popular theatrics and in cabaret as an example of the effective synthesis of popular and high culture as an alternative to outmoded forms. If Kandinsky was inspired, in part, by the cabaret in his quest for the truly successful and spiritually affective total work of art (*Gesamtkunstwerk*), his theoretical ideas and concepts, above all with respect to sound, were soon to have their own impact on cabaret when the most radical movement of the early twentieth-century avant-garde, Dada, was spawned in the Cabaret Voltaire in Zurich in the years 1916 and 1917.

Summing up the achievements of the early German cabaret, as he saw them, in his book *Jahrhundertwende: Erinnerungen an eine Epoche* (The Turn of the Century: Recollections of an Epoch), the writer Max Halbe emphasized, with greater understanding than many, the revolution in taste and outlook that they represented. He wrote:

> The objection could be raised that it does these beginnings too much honor if they are related to or perhaps equated with similar currents in high literature. But whoever lived through this period can have no doubt that the real revolution at first came less from above, from high literature, than from below, from the art of small forms, from vaudeville, from cabaret. It was the subsequent loosening, indeed disintegration of all hithertofore valid literary and aesthetic norms that

then first created the atmosphere for the revolution also in high literature. Was it not indicative of this that from Max Reinhardt's motley vaudeville "Schall und Rauch" with its shortwinded sketches and grotesques there arose within a few years that triumphant new Reinhardt stage and its renowned directorial feat, *Midsummer Night's Dream?* The connections for each insight lie clear at hand. Not everywhere, however, did the developments take place so tangibly and effectively. But the Berlin and Munich examples were, in the final analysis, so influential that just a few years later the subversive transformation in the spiritual and artistic customs of the Germans of the time was complete. People were tired of seeing the world only in the miniature format of bourgeois or proletarian rooms and longed for color, irregularity, the unleashing of all the arts of the theater. Who was worried at the time that this way led necessarily one day to universal deterioration, that it had to end in a literary and ethical jungle from which only a resolute return to the healthy foundation of formbound reality and nature could save us![99]

CHAPTER FOUR

VIENNA: NIGHTLIGHTS AND BATS

The brilliance of *fin-de-siècle* Viennese art and culture should have made the capital of the Hapsburg Empire a thoroughly hospitable environment for the cabaret.[1] But the first attempt to establish one proved an even less auspicious beginning than Wolzogen's early Überbrettl enterprise in Berlin. The attempt was undertaken by Felix Salten (real name: Siegmund Salzmann, 1869–1947), the literary and dramatic critic at the time of the influential *Neue Freie Presse* of Vienna, the putative author of an erotic classic named *Josefine Mutzenbacher, oder Die Geschichte einer Wienerischen Dirne, von ihr Selbst erzählt* (Josephine Mutzenbacher, or The Story of a Viennese Whore, Told by Herself, published anonymously in 1906), and best known in the English-speaking world as the author of the famous children's story *Bambi* (1923) which was made into a full-length feature cartoon film by Walt Disney.

Salten was a member of the prominent *Jung-Wien* (Young Vienna) literary circle whose membership included Peter Altenberg (1859–1919), Leopold von Andrian (1875–1951), Hermann Bahr (1863–1934), Richard Beer-Hofmann (1866–1945), Hugo von Hofmannsthal (1874–1929), and Arthur Schnitzler (1862–1931), and which came together frequently in one of the great Vienna coffee houses of the period, the Café Griensteidl.[2] It was almost certainly in this urbane milieu of men of letters that the idea first arose of establishing a cabaret that would be patterned after those that had opened recently in Berlin and Munich but would have an authentic, indigenous Viennese character.

Out of deference to his literary circle, Salten dubbed his new cabaret the Jung-Wiener Theater zum lieben Augustin (Young Vienna Theater in the Name of Dear Augustin). Despite its name, the cabaret was no theater and indeed lacked its own premises. Salten's idea was to incorporate performances of his cabaret group into the program of an existing theater. He chose for this purpose the Theater an der Wien, which then had no regular program, repertoire, or even personnel and was used for performances mostly by visiting Austrian and foreign troupes.

Opening night of the Viennese cabaret took place on November 16 of that inaugural year in the history of German-language cabaret, 1901. The first program, comprising, among other things, dramatized ballads by the German Swabian School Romantic poet Ludwig Uhland, Wedekind's poetry, and appearances by the popular Viennese entertainer Hansi Niese, failed miserably. All told, seven performances of the first program of the Jung-Wiener Theater took place, from November 16 through November 22, and then the cabaret folded. There was no second program.

Although Salten intended to infuse the Jung-Wiener Theater with a distinctly Viennese flavor, nothing of any real distinction was achieved in this respect. What resulted had less the appearance of something indigenous than a repetition of the weaknesses of Wolzogen's Überbrettl. The opening night was nothing short of a disaster and when it was obvious after the next several performances that the situation was hopeless, Salten bowed to the inevitable and rang down the curtain for good. If the Viennese public was unable to appreciate what Salten was attempting to do with his cabaret, his intentions were also thwarted by the absence from the opening program of the literary talents whose circle inspired the name of the cabaret and whose contributions might have redeemed at least some part of that first evening. How unresponsive the public was is manifest in its behavior during a production in the opening program of a shadow show by Georges Fragerolle and Henri Rivière called *Ahasuerus.* The outstanding feature of the production was the optical projection of cleverly designed dioramas which were accompanied by music and recitation. Fragerolle, who had come to Vienna for the performance, sang the text while accompanying himself on the piano. But the audience, totally misunderstanding the work, laughed or shouted incredulously. Salten needed no further proof that his cabaret venture had misfired.

The collapse of the Jung-Wiener Theater zum lieben Augustin was followed by no new serious effort to transplant cabaret in Viennese soil for nearly another five years. Then, Munich's loss when the lights went out forever at the Elf Scharfrichter became Vienna's good fortune, at least relatively speaking. Like restless gypsies on the move to a new encampment, some of the hardiest of the Munich troupers struck out for Vienna. In the lead were the ubiquitous *Kulturträger* Marc Henry and his favorite partner, the "soul" of the Elf Scharfrichter, Marya Delvard. Before long, a suitable location was found at number 6 Ballgasse and the Nachtlicht (Nightlight) cabaret was born, its logo a burning candle in the middle of which a bat appeared with wings extended on both sides.

Marc Henry assumed responsibility for the artistic direction of the Nachtlicht, Marya Delvard was the principal female performer whose Munich repertoire required little adjustment to the new surroundings, and Hans Richard Weinhöppel (whom we met previously as the Executioner Hannes Ruch) took charge of the cabaret's musical direction. A local artist with a particular penchant for caricature portraits, Carl Hollitzer, soon was installed as the resident artist in charge of the layout of programs and costume design. But Hollitzer had another skill for which he was pressed into service on stage as well: his singing of farmhands' songs in appropriate dialect and a booming voice for which there was no dearth of admirers.

Other local talents soon joined the itinerant Munichers attracted like moths to the flame of the Nachtlicht: the writers Hermann Bahr, Franz Blei, Alexander Rosenfeld (1872–1945), who made his greatest reputation as a raconteur and humorist under the assumed name of Roda Roda, Felix Dörmann (1870–1928), the librettist of the *Waltzertraum,* and the actor, playwright, essayist, and later, historian of culture Egon Friedell (born Friedman, 1878–1938). A few guest appearances by Erich Mühsam provided rare moments of sharper social criticism.

Although the ex-Executioners and their new Vienna confrères tried hard to make a go of it, the Nachtlicht was doomed to close down within a year. That it began to attract attention is beyond doubt. Among the curious drawn to programs made up, for the most part, of much of the Munich repertoire (Marc Henry's and Marya Delvard's songs and Wedekind's ballads) and one-acters and prose sketches by Roda Roda, Friedell, and others, were two of the outstanding figures of contemporary Viennese culture: Karl Kraus (1874–1936), whose *Die Fackel* (The Torch) was the leading literary journal of the time, and Peter Altenberg (born Richard Engländer, 1859–1919), a writer and storyteller but, above all, the acknowledged personification of the contemporary Viennese coffee house Bohème and its foremost chronicler whom Felix Salten once characterized this way:

> In today's Vienna, he is one of the most interesting, subtle, and touching personalities. For those in the know in Europe, he is a beloved and admired poet, an instrument in the great spiritual orchestra whose particular sound remains penetrating and recognizable from among a thousand voices . . . And for the entertainment-seeking citizenry at Maxim's, Café Central, and Cabaret Fledermaus, he is but a curiosity, a ridiculous showpiece.[3]

Working against the success of the Nachtlicht were two factors, principally: a location less than ideally suited to cabaret, and a type of program representing something of an attempt at a symbiosis of proven Munich numbers and works by such Austrian writers as Bahr, Friedell, and Roda Roda who presumably had a firmer finger on the pulse of Viennese taste. The symbiosis never really cohered, the mix simply refused to jell, and no distinct Nachtlicht style emerged.

That it was the program that ultimately proved the crux of the problem seems attested by the most notorious incident related to the Nachtlicht's brief flicker.

Like Altenberg, who was dramatically different in all other respects, Karl Kraus relished the advent of cabaret in Vienna and doubtless sensed in it as well a potentially productive vein of material for the type of short essays on social and cultural topics at which *Die Fackel* excelled. He began to frequent the Nachtlicht regularly, often accompanied by a group of friends. Once he had made the acquaintance of the Nachtlicht performers, he wrote a few sketches for it and also appears to have directed a one-act play at least at one performance. Mercurial as well as brilliant, Kraus was known for rapid, seemingly arbitrary changes of mind that inevitably resulted in imbroglios of one sort or another. Until the early hours of April 30, 1906, these generally took the form of journalistic sallies and ripostes.

What set off the ugly fracas that April night involving Kraus and members of the Nachtlicht troupe was an interview with Marya Delvard published by the Viennese newspaper the *Fremden-Blatt.* Kraus had apparently permitted himself to be annoyed by Delvard's seemingly ungrateful and self-promoting piece which appeared in the paper on Sunday, April 15, 1906, under the title "Die guten Ratschläge" (Good Counsels).[4] Delvard began her article by condemning all the people who had insisted on giving her "good advice." She recalls especially how when she was about to make her first appearance at the Elf Scharfrichter in Munich she was advised not to appear on stage wearing her long black street dress. Spurning the advice, she appeared in the dress anyway and it proved so enormously popular she adopted it as a kind of professional trademark. Further in her article, Delvard recalls meeting the legendary Sarah Bernhardt and the great singer Yvette Guilbert. According to her, both were impressed with her talent and took an interest in her professional career, Bernhardt advising her to remain as thin as she was, and Yvette Guilbert counselling that the only place for her to go to make money was Berlin. Instead of Paris or Berlin, however, she chose to favor Vienna with her presence and was very happy with her decision because her "good friend" Peter Altenberg *never* gives her advice. Put out as much by Delvard's boastful name-dropping and a snide remark at one point about Yvette Guilbert as by her criticism of his one-time directorial stint at the Nachtlicht, Kraus published a rejoinder in the April 19 issue of *Die Fackel* (Nr. 201). Dripping with irony about Delvard's talents, the article concludes with the accusation that since Delvard has achieved no real distinction of her own, she tries to use the names of the famous (here Wedekind, the artist Lenbach, Yvette Guilbert, Sarah Bernhardt) to promote herself.

Feelings were bruised on both sides and the stage set for a confrontation. When it came it was not on the premises of the cabaret but in a popular wine cellar named the Casino de Paris. Erich Mühsam, who was then performing at the Nachtlicht and, along with Roda Roda and Egon Friedell was a witness to the affair, gives this account of it in his memoirs, *Unpolitische Erinnerungen* (Unpolitical Reminiscences):

> I was sitting in a wine cellar together with Karl Kraus when the gang from the "Nachtlicht" appeared and seated themselves at another table. Suddenly, with no warning at all, Marc Henry lunged at Kraus whom he thrashed nastily to the point of senselessness. It was extremely unpleasant and rough. In an effort to make peace, I found myself pushed aside unceremoniously and lay in a corner on the floor with a sprained finger, broken pince-nez, and my engagement agreement a shambles.
>
> Peter Altenberg, who was also a witness to the altercation, consoled himself by drinking whatever wine remained in the glasses on the tables of the combatants and onlookers.[5]

This, to be sure, was not the first time Karl Kraus had come to blows with someone over his literary assaults. In the heydey of the *Jung-Wien* circle's "residence" in the Café Griensteidl, Kraus and Felix Salten fell into an altercation over Kraus' attack on him, *inter alia* in his famous essay *Die demolirte Literatur* (The Demolished Literature, 1897). In his recollections of his youth in Vienna, *Jugend in Wien* (Youth in Vienna), in the entry for December 15, 1896, Arthur Schnitzler recalls that "Yesterday evening in a coffee house Salten gave little Kraus (who had also attacked him) a slap in the face, which was greeted joyfully on all sides."[6]

The Marc Henry-Karl Kraus fight did not end there, and indeed how could it in a city as fond of gossip as Vienna. When it finally landed in the hands of attorneys, nothing short of a miracle could have prevented it from becoming the sensation it did. Since Kraus had his enemies, especially among journalists, the opportunity to pull him down a peg or two was not lost. The *Neues Wiener Journal,* for example, carried a spiteful report directed against Kraus that soon found its own momentum and made the rounds of a number of German-language newspapers.

Kraus himself was far from mute about the matter and in an attempt to put an end to what he regarded as misinformation, if not downright lying, about the whole business, gave his own (seven-page) account of it in the 203rd number of *Die Fackel* on May 12, 1906 (pp. 17–24), under the title *Nachtlicht.* Begging his readers' pardon for discussing an event that took place in a public house, which *Die Fackel* would not normally have covered, Kraus excuses the exception this time on the grounds that because of the pending court case—court cases being within the purview of *Die Fackel*—he feels an obligation to air the matter. He begins by recounting how supportive he was of the new Viennese cabaret undertaking and how just because of his enthusiasm he withheld direct participation in it at the outset so as not to provide his journalistic antagonists with an excuse to kill it in its infancy. Despite his high hopes for the cabaret, Kraus, however, was disappointed, seeing in it, at least in its early stage, not the bastion against the Philistines that he had hoped, but a song program suited to the tastes of a champagne sipping audience. Kraus loses no time in settling scores. Were it not for the participation of the former Munich Executioner Hannes Ruch and such genuine talents as Ludwig Scharf, Erich Mühsam, Egon Friedell, and Ingrid Loris (Irma Karczewska, who appeared in Wedekind's play *Pandora's Box*), the Nachtlicht would have been a disaster; Marc Henry struck him as a "puzzling" choice for director, not only because of the fractured German he spoke, and Marya Delvard was much overrated as well as megalomaniacal.

Kraus' affection for cabaret was genuine, however, but he makes the point in his article that he regarded his involvement in it as a part of his private life, as something he wanted kept detached from his career as a publicist. And it was as a regular guest friendly to the arts ("ein kunstfreundlicher Stammgast") that he by chance agreed to direct a one-act play presented at the Nachtlicht. How scrupulous Kraus was about preserving his amateur and guest status is obvious from the fact that once the performance was over, he insisted on returning to the box office in order to re-enter the auditorium as a regular paying guest. It was this appearance of his as a director that Marya Delvard chose to criticize, thereby violating his privacy as an ordinary citizen, inviting a rejoinder from him, and thus touching off the whole unpleasant affair.

How unpleasant it actually was we can get an idea of from Kraus' contention that he had never declared that Marya Delvard was nothing compared to Yvette Guilbert, insisting only that he had quoted Delvard to the effect that Guilbert was envious of her singing, and that he had never actively sought to provoke or threaten Marc Henry with whom his previous relations had been good. Once his rejoinder to Delvard came out, however, no further relationship between them was possible and the altercation that erupted on the premises of the Casino de Paris would appear by hindsight to have been unavoidable.

As if that fracas was not nasty enough, the sensationalist rumor-mongering reporting of it in the press seems to have pained Kraus the most. And perhaps not so much by the offensive publicity, but by the fact that the fracas gave his enemies in the press the golden opportunity to have a field day at his expense. In the light of this, we can understand why the most venom of Kraus' Nachtlicht article of May 12 (1906) was reserved for Herr Jakob Lippowitz, the co-founder and longtime editor-in-chief of the *Neues Wiener Journal,* whose paper (characterized by Kraus as a *Dreckblatt,* or "shit-sheet") was, as we have already seen, the principal offender.

Kraus closes his account of the affair by quoting in its entirety a letter he received from Berlin dated May 9, 1906, from none other than Frank Wedekind in which Wedekind expresses outrage over the beastly things done to Kraus by Marc Henry and Marya Delvard. Whatever the relations between Wedekind, Henry, and Delvard in the good old days of the Munich Executioners, Wedekind is unstinting in the defamation of them in the letter to Kraus. Marc Henry is dismissed as the kind of a person who because of his lack of principle sooner or later makes impossible any situation in which he happens to find himself. Furthermore, he calls himself Monsieur Henry because he is on such bad footing with so many people under his real name of Achille Vaucheret. Wedekind is hardly any kinder to Marya Delvard. In order to rid herself of her pretty colleagues at the Elf Scharfrichter because she could not bear the competition, he asserts that she circulated sories that they were suffering from infectious venereal diseases. It was on account of such slander, reports Wedekind, that some three years previously a Munich district court sentenced her to pay a considerable fine.

As outraged as he is by what befell Karl Kraus, Wedekind is even more incensed over the fact that such disreputable people as Henry and Delvard are performing his poems and songs nightly in the Nachtlicht. Since he is powerless to do anything about it himself—his forbidding Delvard to perform his works certain of earning only the superhuman contempt with which she views anyone to whom she is indebted—he appeals now to Kraus to inform his readers and above all the Viennese public that he would prefer never to have written the works of his being performed in the Nachtlicht than to have them offered to the public by the likes of a Marc Henry or a Marya Delvard.

The matter was still far from being laid to rest. In Nr. 204 of *Die Fackel* for May 31, 1906, Kraus quotes in its entirety a letter from a Dr. Herzberg-Frankel dated Vienna, May 23, 1906, repudiating the charges made by Frank Wedekind in his letter to *Die Fackel* of April 9. He denies vehemently that Delvard ever tried to get rid of her female colleagues at the Elf Scharfrichter by spreading rumors that they were suffering from venereal diseases or that she was forced to pay a heavy fine some three years previously. Acknowledging that Delvard had once been involved in some court case on account of Wedekind, he insists that no judicial sentence was imposed and that the matter turned out well.

Armed with facts to the contrary, Kraus refuted the refutation by quoting Nr. 294 of the Munich *Neuste Nachrichten* for June 28, 1907, on the case of the actress Olga Stoe (Olly Bernhardi) brought against Achille Vaucheret (Marc Henry) and Marie Biller (Marya Delvard).

As if hell-bent on having the last word in the matter, Kraus picked it up again in the October 4, 1906, issue of *Die Fackel* (Nr. 208). In what was to be his last public statement about the case, Kraus devoted four

The Fledermaus auditorium in a postcard designed by the Wiener Werkstätte. (Österr. Museum für angewandte Kunst, Vienna).

full pages, under the heading of "Alcoholics," to a rehashing of the episode including now the previously unmentioned imputation of anti-Semitic abuse to Marc Henry (Kraus was Jewish) and the court's resolution of it. But whatever gratification he derived from the overexposure of the fracas on the pages of *Die Fackel,* Kraus was to be denied the final victory. The first court to hear the case imposed a sentence (on May 25) of a month's incarceration on Marc Henry and a fine of 300 crowns on Marya Delvard. Five months later, however, an appellate court modified the verdict, sympathetic (in Kraus' judgment) to Marc Henry's "confession" of being under the influence of drink despite the earlier testimony of witnesses to the contrary. Instead of a month in jail, Henry was now required to pay a fine of 600 crowns, while Delvard's fine was reduced from 300 to 150 crowns. With a few parting shots at the travesty of justice he experienced and the decline of the Vienna judiciary, Kraus at long last—and undoubtedly reluctantly—put the whole embarrassing matter behind him.

Whether primarily because of the Kraus affair, which had left a bad taste, or because of its location or the lack of focus in its programs, the Nachtlicht closed its doors on the Ballgasse before the year (1906) was out. But the lights of the Vienna cabaret were not to remain out too long. Most of the Nachtlicht regulars, as undaunted as ever, made a fresh start with another cabaret that proved of greater durability. They called it the Theater und Kabarett Fledermaus (The Bat Theater and Cabaret) or just Fledermaus (Bat) and located it on the Johannesgasse, near Vienna's Fifth Avenue, the Kärntnerstrasse. The location was good and from the outset there was a sense of permanence lacking in the case of the Nachtlicht. Great care went into the planning of décor and the services of such members of the then triumphant Wiener Werkstätte für angewandte Kunst (Vienna Applied Arts Workshops) as Josef Hoffmann, Berthold Löffler, and C. O. Czeschka were enlisted.

The auditorium of the cabaret itself was done in gold and white and had tiny loges with red trimmings. A small but comfortable bar was installed which Egon Friedell recalls in his short piece *Kabarett Fledermaus* as having made a hit with local journalists both for its charm and its faultless drinks[7] and the foyer was distinguished by walls of hand-painted tiles containing caricatures of well-known Viennese personalities. At a time when Vienna was still the locus of great ferment in art, architecture, and the crafts, and the works of the Secessionists were transforming contemporary sensibility, the participation of talents of the caliber of Gustav Klimt, Emil Orlik, Oskar Kokoschka, and Carl Hollitzer in the Fledermaus' decorative undertakings needed little persuasion. Designed and ornamented by artists and craftsmen at—or close to—the vortex of the Viennese artistic upheaval, the Fledermaus became in fact an extension of the Secession and a similar expression of the dislocation elsewhere in society in the imperial capital.

The more marked Viennese character of the Fledermaus compared to its predecessor, Nachtlicht, was evident as well in its programs. Overall artistic direction remained in the hands of Marc Henry, music was the principal domain still of Hannes Ruch, and the star status that clung to Marya Delvard ever since her first appearance at the Munich Elf Scharfrichter showed no signs of diminishing despite the unfortunate affair with Karl Kraus and Wedekind's denunciation of her in his letter to Kraus of May 9, 1906. If any change in Delvard's style worth commenting on took place then it was the reduction in appearances in her famous slinky black dress. Contemporary Viennese taste was ill served by the gallows humor and unrepentant criminality of Wedekind's songs. As if yielding to the neo-Byzantine opulence of the Secession, Delvard soon found her repertoire of Celtic songs and her colorful Bretonese folk cos-

The Fledermaus foyer and bar. (Osterr. Museum für angewandte Kunst, Vienna).

tumes more in the spirit of time and place and she appeared less and less frequently in her funeral black.

Henry, Delvard, and Hannes Ruch were the remaining links with the Nachtlicht and the Munich past. They were experienced cabaret-wise performers, and as the affair with Kraus makes abundantly clear, once they established themselves somewhere they were not about to be displaced in a hurry. But Viennese taste exerted its own imperative and this came to be satisfied ever more increasingly by the involvement of artists better able to take its measure.

True to now established patterns of cabaret programs, the Fledermaus continued to feature song and dance routines. Joining Delvard on stage as a singer was the versatile Carl Hollitzer who never failed to delight an audience with his provincial farmhand songs. Dances inclined more to the elegant and stylish. Gertrude Barrison, Hollitzer's steady companion and a member of the famed Barrison Sisters who after the troupe broke up went on to become one of Europe's leading exponents of modern dance, won acclaim for her dancing of Grieg's *Morgenstimmung* (Voice of Morning); the daughters of the artist Franz Wiesenthal, Berta, Elsa, and Grete, already popular Vienna performers, danced Schumann's *Karneval* (Carnival), Beethoven, and Johann Strauss and established an appropriate mood of lightness and gaiety in their original rococo costumes of unmistakable Viennese stamp.

Literary divertissement, however, was not long in establishing its primacy. The colorful, eccentric, and irrepressible Peter Altenberg provided a number of sketches as well as serving as the butt of humor of other writers' contributions. Altenberg was by now a city- (if not nation-) wide "character," the leading spirit of turn-of-the-century Vienna coffee house culture, and a seemingly inexhaustible source of stories about which Hugo von Hofmannsthal expressed himself in the following memorable way: "His stories are like very small fishbowls over which one bends in order to see goldfish and multicolored stones and suddenly beholds a human face arising indistinctly."[8] Although he was notoriously shy and incapable of getting up on a stage and performing himself, he loved writing sketches and occasional poems for others to recite for him, while stories about him, especially those told by the ever red-vested and monocled Roda Roda, whose own reputation as a storyteller rivalled Altenberg's, were always good for laughs.

Another Altenberg crony of growing reputation as a cabaret writer and wit-about-town was the ebullient, corpulent, cigar-chomping Egon Friedell.[9] The son of a prosperous silk manufacturer, Friedell met Altenberg for the first time around 1899 when the latter was forty. Threading his way through the bars and cafés between the Kohlmarkt and Kärntnerstrasse, Friedell was bound to run across the legendary Altenberg, most probably in Altenberg's favorite haunt, the Löwenbräu, a café located behind the Burgtheater and popular with actors and the theater-going public. Hollitzer, Gertrude Barrison, and the well-known Secession architect Adolf Loos, whose wife, the actress Lina

A view of the foyer and cloakroom of the Fledermaus in a postcard designed by the Wiener Werkstätte. (Österr. Museum für angewandte Kunst, Vienna).

Vetter, would also perform at the Fledermaus, were the other regulars at the Löwenbräu.

Until his suicide leap from his apartment in 1938 to avoid arrest by Austrian Nazis after the *Anschluss* with Germany, Friedell had developed a formidable reputation as an essayist, satirist, storyteller, playwright, and popular historian of antique culture. Long attracted to the stage, he had even acted for a while with Max Reinhardt's company. At the outset of his literary career, his friendship with Altenberg and the Löwenbräu regulars made his entry into the cabaret inescapable. He threw himself into his new role with such unabashed enthusiasm that in 1908, at the age of thirty, he was asked to take over the artistic direction of the Fledermaus, a position he held until the cabaret's demise in 1910.

Another addition to the Fledermaus' "literary staff" was the prolific writer of feuilletons for the *Weltbühne,* Alfred Polgar (1873–1955). The son of a Jewish composer and music teacher in Vienna, Polgar, besides his widely read and highly regarded feuilletons, also became a regular contributor of music and theater reviews. Luckily, he succeeded in leaving Austria before the Nazis caught up with him, too, and eventually settled as an émigré in the United States.

While at the Fledermaus, Friedell and Polgar, who shared a common interest in theater, developed a fruitful collaborative relationship responsible for some of the better dramatic fare offered by the Vienna cabaret. As with cabaret writers elsewhere, their preference was for the short play form within the limits of which they produced several immensely popular works, the most famous of which was a satire on prevalent teaching and examination methods in the schools. Before looking more closely at Fledermaus programs and the sketches of Altenberg, Friedell, and Polgar in particular, let us return to the matter of the Viennese acculturation of the cabaret. As the art and culture of cabaret struck roots in its triumphant march across Europe in the late nineteenth and early twentieth centuries, individuating national characteristics inevitably arose either to challenge or take their place alongside the more purely international elements of the form. The inadequate cultivation of these characteristics was the main reason for the early demise of the Nachtlicht, but whether by conscious effort or by chance the error was corrected once the Fledermaus opened its doors.

The raw street chanson of the Parisian cabaret, Wedekind's macabre poetry, the shadow shows of the Chat Noir in Paris or the Quatre Gats of Barcelona, the pantomimes and acidulous social satire of Munich found little resonance in the aristocratic elegance and bourgois liberalism of turn-of-the-century Vienna. The tensions and destabilizing forces lying just below the surface of that society have been amply examined in Carl E. Schorske's *Fin-de-Siècle Vienna.* A sense of imminent collapse, of fragmentation, of the falling away of a center had already begun seeping through society and finding expression in art and literature. Social and political change was becoming progressively harder to resist, but the ripples across the deceptively calm surface of social and political accommodation hardly gave evidence of the depths of turbulence. Outwardly, an upperclass style still set the tone. A cultivated sense of the aesthetic, proper reverence for the classical heritage of Western civilization, and a refined gaiety of courtly manner and verbal polish were the meeting ground of privilege and liberal bourgeois aspiration.

The cultural and socio-political ferment of the time ushered in a period of Austrian literary distinction represented, on one hand, by the *Jung-Wien* movement of which Hugo von Hofmannsthal and Arthur Schnitzler were the most impressive advocates, and, on the other, by a vigorous Viennese journalism splendidly exemplified by the career of Karl Kraus.

The contemporary press became the principal forum (indeed, often the battlefield) of the crosscurrents and conflicts of *fin-de-siècle* Viennese society and no feature of the press stood out with greater prominence or typicality than the feuilleton. The feuilleton, which appeared as a regular feature of the cultural section of the press, grew into a Viennese institution and attracted the talents of some of the best writers of the period. Carl E. Schorske has given the following apt description of the feuilleton as a literary genre in *Fin-de-Siècle Vienna:*

> The *feuilleton* writer, an artist in vignettes, worked with those discrete details and episodes so appealing to the nineteenth century's taste for the concrete. But he sought to endow his material with color drawn from his imagination. The subjective response of the reporter or critic to an experience, his feeling-tone, acquired clear primacy over the matter of his discourse. To render a state of feeling became the mode of formulating a judgment. Accordingly, in the *feuilleton* writer's style, the adjectives engulfed the nouns, the personal tint virtually obliterated the contours of the object of discourse. . . . The feuilletonist tended to transform objective analysis of the world into subjective cultivation of personal feelings. He conceived of the world as a random succession of stimuli to the sensibilities, not as a scene of action. The feuilletonist exemplified the cultural type to

whom he addressed his columns: his characteristics were narcissism and introversion, passive receptivity toward outer reality, and, above all, sensitivity to psychic states. This bourgeois culture of feeling conditioned the mentality of its intellectuals and artists, refined their sensibilities, and created their problems.[10]

Elsewhere, Schorske relates the Viennese feuilleton to Walter Pater's idea of the function of art in general, namely: "a corner of life screened through a temperament."[11]

The brevity, acuity of observation, topicality, wit, and superficiality of the feuilleton found an easy accommodation in the cabaret. Serving as a kind of bridge between contemporary Viennese journalism and the cabaret, the feuilleton also enhanced the receptivity of the cabaret to other generically related minor prose forms such as the sketch, the caricature, and the anecdote, and in concert with them eventually brought about the literary transformation of the early Vienna cabaret. Whatever other entertainments won favor, whether musical, choreographical, or dramatic, it was, beyond doubt, the writer and performer of small prose forms who came to the fore of the Vienna cabaret and left his mark on it.

In a feuilleton-like piece on the institution of the cabaret written on the occasion of the opening of the Fledermaus, that archetypical turn-of-the-century Viennese storyteller himself, Peter Altenberg, celebrated the essence of the cabaret as a sanctuary of small forms:

Cabaret—the theater of the art of Small Forms, the art of doing small things in the theater the way really big things are done. An art commanded by ever fewer people now. In my opinion, till now the preserve just of Yvette Guilbert, Mela Mars, Marya Delvard, at her best, Dr. Egon Friedell, Coquelin ainé, Girardi, Otto Tressler, and the Nieses. It's talents such as these that can truly make everything of nothing!

One can write a 200-page novel and have it turn out superb. But one can also say the same in just three pages and have that turn out equally superb. It's all a matter of saving time. Today there are many able people who simply lack the time to read 200 pages. To such people one gives three pages in summary!

There are many people nowadays who can't endure a ten-course dinner. So they live on snacks instead; after all, why should they exert themselves in order to digest 200 pages. Instead, one gives them 3 pages that fulfill the same purpose! This then is how the cabaret (Kabarett) stands in relation to "theater." That is to say, that's how it ought to be. . . .

The cabaret should also be, ideally speaking, a refuge of small great art! Not all birds are vultures, sea eagles, or condors who can rise 12,000 feet in the ice-clear sky from there to look down imperiously on vast stretches of earth! There are also precious and delightful little birds like the wren, the kingfisher, and the crested titmouse. Perhaps they are even more original, noteworthy, and admirable than the big birds! And so it is as well with the artists of small forms! Perhaps they don't rise 12,000 feet above the earth like Ibsen, Gerhart Hauptmann, Hamsun, Strindberg, Maeterlinck. But they flit indescribably gracefully over the earth, through meadows and bushes, and bring pleasure through their "small arts" of living life! So it was in their time with the "military music" of Detlev von Liliencron and the music of Oscar Straus. And so it was also with the splendid "Ringeltanz" of the same composers. Must one bury all the "pearls" in one-and-a-half-hour operettas and then have them fished out only by divers dispatched after them? The cabaret spares the paying public this effort! It delivers the "pearls" and lets all the mud and other worthless things run off. Just like the pearl divers![12]

Of the several outstanding purveyors of small prose forms to the Fledermaus, above all Friedell, Polgar, and Roda Roda, none achieved quite the legendary status of Altenberg himself and, if his shyness negated any possibility of appearances by him on stage, in Egon Friedell he found his perfect (if not only) interpreter. The result was that the team of Altenberg and Friedell, Altenberg supplying anecdotes or serving as the butt of them, and Friedell reciting them, became a Fledermaus institution.

Despite the failure of his own attempt to establish a cabaret, Felix Salten never lost his enthusiasm for it and long remained a faithful observer of it in its many and varied manifestations. It's to Salten that we owe the following description of the Altenberg-Friedell team in action:

Dr. Egon Friedell tells Altenberg anecdotes in the Cabaret Fledermaus. So often he begins: "It has befallen me to play the same role in the life of the poet Altenberg that Eckermann played in the life of Goethe . . ." The audience roars, believing that Altenberg is going to get the drubbing due him. They already assume that Dr. Friedell is joking when he says, "The poet Altenberg," for they think that it is really quite impossible to call him a poet. They also roar at the anecdotes and don't grasp how brilliantly they have been concocted. The tumultuous cheerfulness, which Dr. Friedell never fails to evoke with his Altenberg stories, is, to a certain extent, false, a cheerfulness based on a misunderstanding. What the people fail to understand is that the whole value of these splendid little stories consists of their illuminating and sometimes clarifying the touching and unique character of Altenberg with a clear and uncommonly psychological humor. People see him from afar. They behold his works from the distance of a middle-class standpoint constricted into lifeless truths, just as they see his person from far off when he accidentally passes them on a street or when he happens to be sitting in the auditorium while Dr. Friedell is talking about him . . .[13]

At this point, perhaps, after hearing so much about Altenberg, we ought to let him speak for himself. The two following stories have been chosen as much for their brevity as their typicality:

So wurde ich (That's How I Got to Be)

In the thirty-fourth year of my godless life—the details are impossible for a newspaper to carry—I was sitting in the Café Central, Vienna, Herrengasse, in a room with pasted English gold wallpaper. In front of me I had the *Extrablatt* with the photograph of a fifteen-year-old girl who disappeared forever on the way to a piano lesson. Her name was Johanna W. Deeply shaken by the story, I was writing my sketch "Local Chronicles," which was based on it, on quarto paper. Just then, in came Arthur Schnitzler, Hugo von Hofmannsthal, Felix Salten, Richard Beer-Hofmann, and Hermann Bahr. Arthur Schnitzler said to me: "I had no idea that you wrote! And on quarto paper at that, with a portrait in front of you; that's certainly suspicious!"

Next Sunday, Richard Beer-Hofmann organized a "literary supper" at his place and for dessert read my sketch out loud. Three days later, Hermann Bahr wrote me: "I heard your sketch about a missing fifteen-year-old girl at Richard Beer-Hofmann's. Am requesting it urgently as a contribution for my newly founded weekly *Die Zeit!*"

Later on, Karl Kraus, also known as Torch Kraus because he hurled the torch of his superbly jovial anger at the putrid world either to burn it up or at least "purify it by fire," sent a pack of my sketches to my present publisher, S. Fischer, Berlin W., Bülowstrasse 90. Along with the recommendation that I'm an original, a genius, one of those people who's different, a *nebbish.* S. Fischer published me; and that's how I got to be!

Just imagine on what chance happenings the destiny of a person's life depends! If I happened to be sitting in the Café Central at the time writing out a bill for all the coffees unpaid for for months, if Arthur Schnitzler hadn't warmed up to me, Beer-Hofmann not arranged a literary soirée, and Hermann Bahr not written me . . . Karl Kraus indeed might have sent my sketches to S. Fischer in any case since he's a "unicum" and an "uninfluenceable." But all together "made" me. And what did I become? A *schnorrer!*

So sollte es immer sein (So Should It Always Be)

A gentleman approached me in the Café and said: "I'm a fanatic admirer of yours."

"You're very kind," I answered. "Perhaps then you would stand me a fine champagne?"

"With the greatest of pleasure."

We drank three bottles of G. and H. Mumm, extra dry, sweet.

It got to be seven in the morning. I went off to the Central Baths, porcelain tubs, 27 degrees Centigrade. A young woman with aristocratically delicate hands sat in the cashier's booth. I said to her with my eyes: "Sweetest cashier . . ." And: "A shame you can't be included for the price . . ."

Peter Altenberg (on the right) with the architect Adolf Loos in a 1933 photograph. (Bildarchiv der Österr. Nationalbibliothek, Vienna).

Then I had breakfast in a charcuterie. Cold smoked sturgeon from the Volga, 12 hellers for 10 grams. Shrimps from Ostende. Big green olives from Spain, 10 pieces 60 hellers. Prague ham, 10 grams 6 hellers, 90 hellers. Two bananas, gold-yellow-black flecked, from Africa, 30 hellers apiece, 60 hellers.

Then I bought a blue phototyped picture postcard: "Route along the Sea." In a winter landscape. I though of it framed in a 5-centimeter-wide ashtree wood frame.

Carried away by such reveries I came home at 9:30 in the morning. The young janitoress who helped me to the lift said: "Mr. Altenberg must have had a good tossing around again last night."

"Yes, ma'am," I said, "the Philistine world order!

She thought: "Well, he paid 40 heller for the lift, even though it's already reckoned into the rent. . . ."[14]

If Altenberg's stories, and Friedell's about Altenberg, infused the Fledermaus with the wit and gossip of turn-of-the-century Viennese café society, those of the third great Fledermaus storyteller, Alexander Roda Roda, or just plain Roda Roda as he was best known, drew his humor from a wide range of material. He also seemed to have access to an inexhaustible supply of humorous little stories, sketches, and anecdotes ranging in length from a few lines to several pages. Particularly identified with him—and among his best—were stories about life in the imperial Hapsburg army, in which Roda Roda had served from 1892 to 1903, caricatures of familiar everyday Viennese types, and stories reflecting the multiethnic character of the Hapsburg state for which the author, as a native of a Slavic- and Hungarian-populated part of the Empire, obviously had a special feeling. Although he wrote satirical novels and comedies (in collaboration with Carl Rössler and Gustav Meyrink), Roda Roda's fame rested primarily on his stories and anecdotes.

By virtue of his growing status as a legend, as the archetypical Viennese café bohemian, and as the Viennese storyteller *par excellence,* Peter Altenberg's association with the Fledermaus as author as well as character was a foregone conclusion. Apart from his stories, which were read at the cabaret, Altenberg also wrote poetry and dramatic sketches for the Fledermaus and became something of a chronicler of the cabaret by writing review summaries of several of the programs for the 1907/08 and 1908/09 seasons.

Altenberg's presence was very much in evidence in the cabaret's opening program. As the curtain rose, Lina Vetter appeared striking a pensive mood. Her monologue, written by Altenberg, was meant to express a worldly-wise ennui, melancholy, and narcissism typical of *fin-de-siècle* Viennese society and culture and a restless desire for a kind of freedom then associated with cabaret:

Dejected, disappointed by every Nothing, the Other as yet unperceived, I sit here! Who and what am I? Is the world too empty for me? Am I too empty for the world? I am saddened by the intimate room, the perfect order of my dwelling place, and everything that whispers to me: "That's how it is today, and that's how it's going to be tomorrow, and the day after that, and forever and ever, always the same way!" And there are mountains of obligations that oppress me, that bury me beneath their weight. We are obligated by Everything, each and every one of us! What for others becomes "pleasant habit," for me becomes despicable experience. The habitual only makes me sick and tired. Concert, theater, much too heavy fare in a steamy auditorium! I'm dreaming of a not too wide room where freedom reigns. Comfort, art, and culture all at the same time, and fresh air for our poor lungs. Our light mood, after all, comes only from oxygen. In such a room, I'd like to linger with total strangers who, like me, want just to relax from some pressure. I'd like to be my own master at a small table, not a hostess or a guest, do what I feel like at the moment, eat, drink, smoke, be inspired or just stare into empty space as happens in a certain inexplicable mood, or turn eye and ear toward the various events of the tiny stage, my innermost attentiveness magnanimously given them should I be so moved. I'd like to surrender myself perhaps more, for a moment, to the smoke of a fine cigarette than to some ever so lovely song, and to the song still more perhaps than to the glance that meets me yearning from the next table. I want to be inspired by This and cold to That! Let the life of the day and of the hour be indeed full for us, the so called carefree people! But our deepest care is how we can pass the day without a care. For the specter of boredom forever menaces us. To be able to banish it means virtually: Be cultivated! So I dream of such a room where freedom, comfort, art and culture reign and all at the same time. Will it arise? In my dream, it already has![15]

Focusing again on the growing sense of a woman's ability to shape her own destiny and to dominate men, Altenberg's best known cabaret chanson, *Kabarettlied* (Cabaret Song), which was also recited by Lina Vetter as part of the opening program, reiterates themes struck in the Lina Vetter monologue and at the same time anticipates one of the theatrical sensations of the Fledermaus, the production there of Oskar Kokoschka's little play *Sphinx und Strohmann* (Sphinx and Strawman).

The speaker in *Cabaret Song* is a woman who coolly contemplates the spiritual anguish and emotional agony of her lover who out of fear and envy of her giving herself to another man comes closer to the brink of self-destruction. The more she holds herself aloof, the greater the torment not just of her man but of all men, and thus the greater her sense of power, her excitement. Seeing the pain she is capable of inflicting, which

Cabaret Fledermaus program cover. (Holyoke Library, Harvard University).

becomes, above all, a demonstration of her own power to herself, she sees herself as man's "highest good on earth."[16] A fleeting insight into the essential "evilness" of the game engenders a brief sensation of pity for her lover and even doubts as to the durability of his faithfulness. But the moment yields to the conviction that it is best for her to remain as she is, for the longer the game goes on, the longer age is kept at bay!

Altenberg's grasp of his own society and the ease with which he was able to convey, often with parodic undertones, the sense of world-weariness, the yearning for freedom from tired patterns of thinking and behaving, the not fully understood hunger for transcendent experience, and the facile quasi-philosophizing endemic to the *fin-de-siècle,* come very much to life in the very short, almost surrealistic "mask play" ("Maskenspiel") that he wrote for the opening program under the title of *Masken* (Masks). With music by Hannes Ruch, the little play features a dramatis personae of nine masked women in costume each of whom represents what Altenberg—keenly as ever interested in the feminine psyche—perceived to be a distinct female type. Hence, such designations as "The Philosophical One," "The Thirster after Knowledge," "The Coquette," "The Complicated One," "The Dancer," "The Tragedienne," "The Poetess," "The Painter," and "The Woman of the World." Played by such Fledermaus regulars as Lina Vetter-Loos, Marya Delvard, and Gertrude Barrison, among others, the "masks" step forward, one at a time, and declaim short, aphoristically "pointed" sentences characteristic of the individual "mask" and collectively meant to typify the outlook of the age. In this spirit, "The Thirster after Knowledge" declares, for example, "I ask you, what do we mean by 'grotesque'? That which life compels us to give up of our own nature." "The Philosophical One" expresses the conviction that "You see, O Neighbor, only a thousandth part of our real being, but if you could behold the whole of us, you would for certain not recognize us." And "The Complicated One" addresses herself to the meaning of mask itself: "Without masks, we are just masks! Distorted to simplicity and grossly exaggerated for the common understanding." After all the masks have spoken their lines, they join in a chorus to close the playlet with the apologia: "Do you see in us only dissolute painted little playthings? We can't help it. If anything is made with taste, it also lives without any idea."[17]

Of the dramatic fare presented at the Fledermaus, the most spectacular works came from the writing team of Egon Friedell and Alfred Polgar and from the writer-painter Oskar Kokoschka. Friedell and Polgar collaborated on several projects, but never with the extraordinary success achieved by their "Grotesque in Two Scenes" *Goethe,* a satire lambasting the artificiality and aridity of contemporary pedagogy, on the one hand, and, on the other, in the familiar style of cabaret irreverence, mocking a literary great, this time, in the German context, the greatest of all—Goethe! The "Grotesque" was an immediate success. In his review of the January program of the 1907/1908 Fledermaus season, Altenberg wrote of it that

It is, first of all, something entirely new, simple, and good: a grotesque, ingenious judgment on the Goethe-syllable-stabber. It is literary and crudely urgent at one and the same time, but above all short and intelligible to everyone. The direction of the small skit was impeccable. May the "modern cabaret" give birth to as many as possible such fine, unusual short plays.[18]

His note on the February program of the same 1907/1908 season reported that

The *Goethe* satire of Dr. Friedell and A. Polgar is increasing in popularity from one evening to the next. Friedell's performance as Goethe and Koppel's as Kohn are truly exceptional. The playlet has already been acquired by the Hoftheater in Mannheim and Dr. Friedell engaged for a guest tour as Goethe.[19]

Besides Mannheim, the play also made successful tours of other German cities such as Munich, Frankfurt, and Hamburg. *Goethe* became, in fact, one of the most frequently performed works of world drama, and Friedell himself played the lead role of Goethe over a thirty-year period, the last time being in January 1938, just a few weeks before his death.[20]

The novelty of the little play is twofold: the appearance of Goethe in old age, speaking in comic dialect, and agreeing to take an examination *on Goethe* for a student for whom Goethe's life and works are too formidable to learn, and Goethe's own difficulties in answering the school examiner's questions which become progressively more absurd.

The work opens with the poor student Züst complaining to his girlfriend Linerl how hard it is to study Goethe, and especially for an examination—he wrote so much, lived so long, was involved in so many things. And what makes matters worse by far is that according to his teacher, *everything* in Goethe is important. Or, quoting the teacher, "Goethe ist ein Heiligthum!" (Goethe is something sacred!). After Züst screams in frustration, "Der Teufel soll ihn holen! Der Teufel soll ihn hollen! (The devil take him! The devil take him!), the stage goes dark and amidst lightning and thunder, a deep voice advises, "You have to say it *three* times!" After repeating the curse a third time, old Goethe appears. Once he regains his composure, Züst tells him that if he fails his examination the next day, he'll have to take a job as a bank clerk, but what he really wants instead is "to become a Doctor of Philosophy in order to be able to appear in cabarets."[21] To help Züst, Goethe agrees to change into the student and take the examination for him.

When the examination begins the next day, Goethe starts off well giving very detailed answers—in dialect, of course—to questions about Goethe's family: where his grandparents lived, first on his father's side, then on his mother's side. But the teacher finally trips him up with a question on the month in which Goethe left Wetzlar. Whenever Goethe falters, the teacher asks the same question of the good student, Kohn, who gives very correct, precise answers. Apart from the humor of the situation itself—a dialect-speaking Goethe standing in for a student in an examination about himself—a comic contrast develops between a faltering Goethe and the smart student Kohn who can answer questions about Goethe which Goethe himself cannot. After failing the question about when he left Wetzlar, Goethe gets into further difficulty over the publication date of *Hermann und Dorothea,* arguing that the book came out in 1796 and the teacher insisting on 1797. The shouting match between the two is ended when Kohn hands the teacher a book open to a page containing proof of the teacher's date.

The examination resumes its calm interrogation concerning trivia until a still more bitter argument ensues over Goethe's last words:

TEACHER: . . . What were Goethe's last words?

GOETHE: Well, he wanted milk.

TEACHER: W-h-a-a-t? What do you mean, "wanted milk," eh?

GOETHE: Well, you see, milk, like in his coffee, since it was too dark. And then he said: Lighter!

TEACHER: (*rising from his seat in terror*): Quite apart from the fact that through the distinguished works of Düntzer, Erich Schmidt, and Minor—names which of course mean nothing to you (*Goethe nods in agreement*)—it has been shown that with the exclamation "lighter" Goethe wanted to point out new goals to man's Promethean drive, it demonstrates the utmost baseness of mind to suppose that a genius like Goethe could have been capable of choosing such a trivial subject for his last words![22]

Matters threaten to get completely out of hand when Goethe is questioned about the women in his life. Exploding in anger, and swearing like a trooper, Goethe is about to beat a hasty retreat from the examination room when the teacher commands him to stay telling him that as punishment for his insolence he must bear witness to his humiliation. After this pronouncement, the teacher orders Kohn to stand and then fires a series of short questions to which Kohn responds with equally short answers. The tempo now is very brisk, increasing a comic effect strengthened all the more by the progressively more inane and irrelevant factual questions such as when Goethe's devoted lifelong assistant Eckermann was born, the name of Goethe's sister, and ending, in a crescendo of absurdity, with almost simultaneous questions of the teacher's and Kohn's answers regarding the fate of Goethe's sister's four children.

As the assembled Collegium assigns grades, expressing their greatest satisfaction with Kohn's performance, Goethe, unable to restrain himself further, bursts out laughing. When the din of the examination subsides, the teacher turns triumphantly to the roaring Goethe and exclaims: "You see! That is education."[23] And at this point, the curtain descends rapidly.

Freidell had other successes at the Fledermaus, as author (together with Alfred Polgar) of the dramatic sketch *Soldatenleben im Frieden* (Military Life in Peacetime), in which Roda Roda appears as a character, and as actor in Max Reinhardt's old Schall und Rauch number *Die Regieprobe* (The Directorial Rehearsal) and in *Der Schatten des Lord Rahu* (The Shade of Lord Rahu), a "grotesque parody" in which, in the words of Peter Altenberg, "Dr. Egon Friedell performs Sherlock Holmes in an elegant, restrained manner."[24] But no work of Friedell, or of the Friedell-Polgar team, ever approached the phenomenal reputation of the Goethe work, which truly became a theatrical legend in its own time.

Although not well known, the outstanding Austrian Expressionist painter and dramatist Oskar Kokoschka's involvement with the Fledermaus was by no means limited to decorative work on the cabaret's premises and programs. A few of his literary efforts, in fact, made their first public appearance as program numbers. One of them was his long poem *Die träumenden Knaben* (The Dreaming Lads), which was read at the Bat toward the end of 1907. Two others were dramatic works. The first was a typical cabaret shadow play called *Das getupfte Ei* (The Spotted Egg). Although listed in the first program book among the numbers to be presented at the opening of the Fledermaus, *The Spotted Egg* was performed, in fact, a week after the opening. Based on an Indian folk tale and symptomatic of the influence of Oriental art on Kokoschka in this period, the shadow play was notable above all for its brilliant colors, reminiscent of Oriental miniatures, and for its technical construction. Kokoschka undertook the work himself, designing and painting the figures on paper and then glueing them to copper sheet cut accordingly. The figures, which were movable at the joints, were situated within a box lighted from the inside and were manipulated by means of a spring mechanism. They were then "projected" to the audience with the help of a large mirror.[25] The writer Max Mell's description of it sheds further light on the production:

In November, an Indian fable called *The Spotted Egg* by Oskar Kokoschka was presented on the small stage of the Vienna cabaret "Fledermaus." Only a few people came to see it. The projection machine, which was operated by the artist himself with trembling fingers, functioned only haltingly and the audience, who wanted to enjoy themselves, began to laugh, crack jokes, and swear. It was a flop, and a repetition of the presentation was not undertaken. But it did not demand too much good will at all to recognize the worth of the pictures. There was a compelling poetry in them. In their style and variety of colors, the figures reminded one of Oriental miniatures, just as they also brought to mind the simplicity of old wood carvings. At one point, the heroine of the tale, a dancer, was composing a tune when the stars came up and began turning about the vault of the heaven, or there was a picture of similarly sweet simplicity: the shepherd waiting on a garden wall for the dancer to come by. And then one first saw a deer, then a fox pass by before The Awaited put in her appearance. This motif of expectation was useful to enable the viewer to grasp that the fable was not Indian, but a poem by the painter Kokoschka himself, something that the entire poetic fluidum of the projected images seemed to deny.[26]

The second theater piece by Kokoschka presented at the Fledermaus was his better known play *Sphinx and Strawman.* Like other dramatic works of Kokoschka, the short (one is tempted to add "cabaret length") *Sphinx and Strawman* was subsequently revised and altered, so that in speaking of the play as staged at the Fledermaus on March 12, 1909, it is important to understand that the version presented was indeed the original as first performed in 1907 by Kokoschka's fellow students at the Vienna School of Arts and Crafts.[27] It differs in several important respects from the still better known version which Hugo Ball and Tristan Tzara were to produce at the Cabaret Voltaire in Zurich on April 14, 1917, and which has been celebrated as a "high point" of Dada theater.[28] In its final form, the short play was given a new title, *Hiob* (Job).

Despite its brevity, *Sphinx and Strawman* is thematically related to a broad current of turn-of-the-century literature devoted to the dynamics of sexual conflict, a foretaste of which the Fledermaus already had in several of Peter Altenberg's cabaret pieces.

Behind the triangle of the partially self-cuckolding Herr Firdusi, his erotic antagonist Herr Kautschukmann (Mr. Rubberman), and Firdust's sexually ravenous wife Lilly lies the theater of Strindberg and Wedekind and the new study of human sexual behavior represented, above all, by Freud and Otto Weininger (1880–1903) whose *Geschlecht und Charakter* (Sex and Character, 1903) aroused so much controversy in its day.

Exemplifications of Weininger's ideas on sexual degeneration, Lilly (the "Sphinx" of the play) and Kautschukmann (the "snakeman" with "lobster-red face") act out an erotic play of lust and passion which inevitably brings Firdusi to his ruin. If Firdusi, whose outstanding physical characteristic is an enormous revolving strawcolored head, is spiritual man incapable of physical love, Lilly and Kautschukmann, by contrast, are incapable of expressing feelings in any way but the physical. Firdusi's imbalance is thrown into bolder relief, in keeping with the play's proto-absurdist character, by his advocacy of sexual abstinence. This makes his fondest wish, to have a son—symbolized by the rubber figure of "Adam" he carries in his pocket—impossible of realization. When Kautschukmann points out that "Adam" also requires a father if he is to come to life, Firdusi replies that his "son" also needed a mother, a non sequitur typical of many in the play.

The doll figure, representing the son Firdusi yearns for but cannot have, has a relevance for Kautschukmann and appears familiar from similar metaphorical uses of doll and puppet imagery in European turn-of-the-century literature. A living correlative of the "Adam" figure, the Adonis-like Kautschukmann is a human marionette manipulated by invisible strings held by Lilly herself, the embodiment of sensuality, of lust, of man's erotic drive.

As if presaging Ionesco's later absurdist satire on modern marriage in *The Bald Soprano, Sphinx and Strawman* dramatizes the impossibility of communication and complete estrangement between Firdusi and Lilly by means of a new marriage between them in which Firdusi perceives that he is marrying his own wife only as he dies. Hardly are the wedding rings exchanged when Lilly gives herself to Kautschukmann and implacable and unrepentant to the end steps over Firdusi's dead body like a "parade horse."[29]

The impossibility of resolving the sexual conflict, of establishing unity of spirit and flesh, of man and woman, is conveyed by the play's final curtain on which nine black suits and nine top hats are painted. When the curtain closes on Firdusi's death, nine men poke their heads through nine holes in the curtain from behind it, one after the other. Snarling and hissing, the heads embodied now as pasteboard, one-dimensional figures by the suits and hats painted on the curtain represent the continuum of the conflict which in Firdusi's death has merely claimed another victim. The ninth and last head delivers the play's last line, summing up the essence of the meaning of the entire work: "By day, lust is silent, but during the night the scream of shame of the youngest girls and the oldest men shrieks at our ears."[30]

The designation of *Sphinx and Strawman* in its Fledermaus version as a "comedy for automats" places the little play within the mainstream of turn-of-the-century enthusiasm for the puppet figure both as a theatrical motif and as a philosophical metaphor. Closely related to this is the theme of the wish-fulfillment of the artist as creator to infuse life into inanimate matter, hence transforming robots and automata into living beings, creating Golems and Pinocchios. In his study on Kokoschka, *Oskar Kokoschka: Maler und Dichter,* Gerhard Lischka draws a parallel between *Sphinx and Strawman* and the Italian Futurist Filippo Iommaso Marinetti's 1910 novel *Mafarka le futuriste.*[31] In Marinetti's work, the automaton Gazurmah, the son born without a woman, was awakened to life by a kiss from his father, Mafarka; in *Sphinx and Strawman,* Kokoschka equips Firdusi with a son, Adam, whom he describes as a "figure made of rubber which one sticks on one's thumb and moves by flexing the digit, as if operating a hand puppet."

No less significant as sources for the conception of *Spinx and Strawman* as a "comedy for automats" than Marinetti or such other contemporary theatrical enthusiasts of the marionette as Gordon Craig and Alred Jarry (recall that Jarry's famous *Ubu Roi,* Ubu the King, was originally conceived as a puppet show) was the circus and variety theater in which Kokoschka (as Wedekind before him) was intensely interested at the time.[32]

In its cabaret production form *Sphinx and Strawman* incorporated a variety of clown routines and sight and verbal gags. The play came alive with acrobatic stunts and the physical dynamics of pantomime; like Craig, Marinetti, Meyerhold, and other revolutionaries of the late nineteenth- and early twentieth-century stage, Kokoschka, too, had come to believe that in the theater movement could surpass spoken language in expressiveness. Linking Kokoschka to Austrian theatrical tradition, Lischka also finds in *Sphinx and Strawman* traces of the Jewish burlesque theater as well as of the Viennese folk drama of Nestroy and Raimund with its strong parodic tradition.

Other puppet—and puppet-like—shows were also staged at the Fledermaus. The program on which Kokoschka's *Spotted Egg* appeared contained as well a puppet version of C. Schloss' *Pyramus and Thisbe* designed by Fritz Zeymer. The novelty here had much less to do with the show's content than with the fact that the puppets were made entirely out of pumpkin heads with only rudimentary facial features cut into them. The figures, and indeed the entire presentation, were conceived and executed along the lines of a typical children's amusement.

When the cabaret introduced 5 P.M. matinee performances—consisting in the main of dance numbers—in March 1908 as a way of expanding

Cabaret Fledermaus program cover. (Holyoke Library, Harvard University).

its program, one of the more popular entertainments presented within the framework of the new schedule was a program offered by the visiting Marionetten Theater Münchener Künstler (The Marionette Theater of Munich Artists) which Paul Brann had founded in 1906. Along with the rough-hewn puppet shows of Count Pocci featuring the German folk figure of Kasperl, the Munich troupe also staged Schnitzler's *Der tapfere Kassian* (The Brave Cassian), one of a small group of plays for adults written by Schnitzler for presentation either by puppet theaters or by live actors and actresses performing as puppets.

The interest of the Fledermaus in the art of the puppet derived, in this particular instance, from more than the universal enthusiasm of the late nineteenth- and early twentieth-century cabaret for puppet and marionette shows as ideally suited to the miniature stage. A manifestation of the *fin-de-siècle* fascination with the various possibilities of the puppet figure already mentioned, Schnitzler's own cycle of plays for marionettes must certainly have provided an additional stimulus. Another was the plan by the Wiener Werkstätte itself to establish a marionette theater. The level of interest in it was high, a fact reflected in the projected direction of the theater by the great German puppeteer Richard Teschner (1879–1948), and must surely have been communicated to the Fledermaus circle in view of the involvement of artists associated with the Werkstätte in the cabaret. Despite the high hopes for the Werkstätte's marionette theater, the plan never reached fruition and little information has survived to explain the failure of the enterprise to get beyond the drawing board.

Pantomime and puppetry were hardly strangers to the European cabarets by the time the Fledermaus had reached its peak in 1907 and 1908. There were, however, variations of both introduced at the Fledermaus deserving of mention. In March 1908, for example, the cabaret staged a satire on human callousness entitled *Die Wohltäter* (The Do-Gooders) based on a text by Olaf Gulbransson, a Norwegian writer and caricaturist who contributed frequently to the Munich *Simplicissimus.* It was in the *Simplicissimus,* in fact, that *The Do-Gooders* first appeared. The Fledermaus production of the piece was notable less as a dramatization of Gulbransson's text than as a conceptualization of an illustration come to life, in the form of short scenes reminiscent of the old tradition of *tableaux vivants.* Captivated by the performance, Peter Altenberg extolled it in a review in the *Wiener Allgemeine Zeitung* on March 6, 1908, as a "new departure, caricatures transformed into short meaningful scenes, a living *Simplicissimus*" (p.2).

If the Fledermaus' staging of *The Do-Gooders* had much of the character of a novelty not to be repeated, this "novelty" was destined to be one of the most characteristic, successful, and "transportable" entertainments offered by the most famous of all Russian cabarets, the obviously Vienna-influenced Moscow Letuchaya mysh (Bat) which was long associated with the name of its founder and principal *conferéncier,* Nikita Baliev.

Somewhere between the "living illustrations" of *The Do-Gooders* and pantomime but of greater visual than dramatic significance were two highlights of the winter and spring 1908 season. For the carnival (Fasching) of 1908, the Fledermaus requested the assistance of the Wiener Werkstätte in the execution of domino costumes for an arrangement of *redoutes* (or masked balls) for which the decision had been made to forego historical costumes (hence the designation of the presentation as *Moderne Redoute*).[33] The dominoes were designed principally by two Werkstätte-affiliated artists, E. J. Wimmer-Wisgrill (1882–1961), a fashion designer who was to become an important costume designer for the Fledermaus in its second season (October 1, 1908–Spring 1909), and R. Jószef Divéky (1887–1951), a student of Berthold Löffler. The Hungarian Divéky's were by far the more unusual both in design and color reflecting, despite a pronounced element of fantasy, the "purest Secessionist style as well as the very strong influence of Aubrey Beardsley."[34]

For the Fiedermaus' April program that same year Wimmer-Wisgrill, working alone, designed and directed a production called *Die weissen Schwestern* (The White Sisters) and based on sayings by Peter Altenberg. The attraction for the audience here was not in the animation of illustrations in the manner of the dominoes of the Fasching program of a few months earlier, but in the assumption by two naked actresses painted snow-white, with golden tassels hanging from their hips, of a series of visually stunning poses behind yellow-gold veils. Now, instead of "living illustrations" in the manner of *The Do-Gooders,* the Fledermaus offered, as the advertisement on the front page of the *Wiener Allgemeine Zeitung* for April 8, 1910, read, "living sculpture in black, white, and gold architecture" ("lebende Plastiken in schwarz-weiss-goldener Architektur"). A stylized exercise in the sculpture of the human body, the production reflected at one and the same time the aesthetic eroticism characteristic of the Austrian *fin-de-siècle* Jugendstil—accentuated by Wimmer-Wisgrill's choice of black, white, and gold as the color of the stage décor—and the popularity during the period of renewed interest in the human form of the dancer whose nakedness was concealed only by a veil. As if anticipating objections to this nakedness on stage, Peter Altenberg presented the matter as one of aesthetic transcendence in his review of the performance in the *Wiener Allgemeine Zeitung* of April 8, 1908 (p.3): "One is moved, touched by this nakedness idealized and enveloped in a golden mist. Everything sexual is transformed into something aesthetic, thus achieving the essential of art. . . .So long as a woman is beheld as an object of desire, she cannot be truly aesthetic. Only the cold, clear eye of the artist enables her to realize her aesthetic admiration!"

The importance that the art of the dance in general was to assume for the Viennese cabaret was signaled by the prominent appearance on the opening program of Gertrude Barrison. The fame of her previous conquest of the cabarets of Montmartre had preceded her and in part explains the care that went into the designing and costuming of Barrison's numbers at the Fledermaus, beginning with the work by Fritz Zeymer (1886–1940) on her debut in Grieg's *Morgenstimmung.* So highly were Zeymer's sketches for the dance regarded that they served double duty as the design for one of the best known of the Fledermaus posters.

Because of his romantic relationship with Gertrude Barrison, the multitalented Carl Hollitzer took a personal interest in her performances and designed some of her most exceptional numbers. These included the dance she performed during the first program in a resplendent Biedermeier costume of Hollitzer's invention as well as her eighteenth-century gavotte of November 1907 in an authentic period costume also concocted by Hollitzer. Gertrude Barrison also provided the occasion for the cabaret debut of one of the most distinguished artists and designers of the Vienna Secession, Koloman (Kolo) Moser (1868–1918). For the February 1908 program Moser undertook the design of Barrison's costume (in green) for a number billed as an "edel-groteske Tanz" (noble-grotesque dance).[35]

January 1908 (the 16th to 19th, to be exact) marked the debut at the Fledermaus of another dancing troupe of sisters—the Wiesenthals (Berta, Elsa, and Grete)[36]—whose popularity rested primarily on their often highly individualistic interpretive, as opposed to illustrative,

The Vienna cabaret dancer Gertrude Barrison, in a 1919 photograph. (Bildarchiv der Österr. Nationalbibliothek, Vienna).

dances based on, among others, Massenet's music to *Manon,* Johann Strauss' Danube waltzes, the "Valse noble" from Schumann's *Carneval,* and a joint Lanner-Schubert piece.

The noticeable extension of the dance part of the Fledermaus program when the cabaret launched its second season on October 1, 1908—the first ended on May 15, 1908—could be seen, on one hand, as the logical outgrowth of the success the cabaret had achieved with dance. But on the other hand, it also presaged the decline of the Fledermaus into a largely commercial entertainment without any further pretension to artistic distinction. The change did not come overnight, however. With stage as well as costume design in the hands of talents of the caliber of Wimmer-Wisgrill and Kolo Moser, dance numbers of the earlier part of the 1908/1909 season still bore the stamp of a creative excellence. This was apparent, for example, in Wimmer-Wisgrill's designs for the "Tanzreigen" (square dance) *Die Spieldose* (The Game Box), which the English dancers Brattie Young and Nelly Moyse presented on the inaugural program of the new season. More striking still were the black and white costumes designed by Kolo Moser for the same dancers' "grotesque" called *Die Fledermäuse* (The Bats). In her study of the reflection of the Secession in the Austrian theater, Gertrud Pott characterizes Moser's achievement here as the realization of the "ideal harmony between performing and decorative art in that he designed costumes appropriate to the whirling rhythms of the dance movements" (die ideale Harmonie zwischen darstellender und dekorativer Kunst her, indem er die dem wirbelden Rhythmus der Tanzbewegungen adäquaten Kostüme schuf).[37]

The Bats performed by Brattie Young and Nelly Moyse in Moser's designs appeared within the context of a new departure for the Fledermaus indicative of its greater commitment to dance. Beginning in January 1909, the cabaret began to offer programs of dance matinees which featured extravagances of various sorts but also, in a more serious vein, other dance numbers clearly motivated by the attempt to probe new techniques. Peter Altenberg caught the spirit of this search for new expression in the dance in a review in the *Wiener Allgemeine Zeitung* on January 26, 1909 (p.3), when he wrote: "The Fledermaus is young and full of propulsive energy! It has opened its doors to the 'evolutionary efforts' of the new dance art . . . Alone of all institutions the Fledermaus can reap the glory of placing its premises at the disposal of bold experiments with youthful eagerness."

It was also on the same matinee dance program that another English dancer, Miss George, as she was known, attempted to create dances in the style of her widely popular, influential, and often imitated countryman, Aubrey Beardsley. Moreover, clad in a brown veil, she danced a number based on a seventeenth-century "tone piece" by Francesco Cavalli after which, as Gertrud Pott informs us," wearing a black-and-white Pierrot costume, she then executed, with skillfully realized scenic-decorative effects, a dance between two huge church candles which had been set up on both the right and left sides of the stage for the performance."[38]

The dance matinees owed their genesis as much to the interest in experimentation with new forms and techniques as to the possible enhancement of the profitability factor by attracting larger audiences. But they were, however, a sign of the changing times. When the first season of the Fledermaus came to an end in May 1908, the artistic direction passed from Marc Henry to the composer Heinrich Reinhardt. Marc Henry had also acted as his own *conférencier.* When he relinquished this position as well as the artistic directorship of the Fledermaus he was succeeded by Elfriede Rossi who is chiefly remembered for the white suit he appeared in which was made for him by the Atelier Flöge and designed by Gustav Klimt.[39] Mostly for financial reasons, it was Reinhardt who set in motion the cabaret's redirection along more commercial lines. The movement from the verbal to the visual, while inexorable, did not preclude the continued production of dramatic works. The writing team of Egon Friedell and Alfred Polgar collaborated on two new works for the 1908/1909 season, *Der Freimann* (The Freeman), a "grotesque," and the highly popular *Der Petroleumkönig* (The Petrol King), a "Musteroperette," or model (exemplary) operetta, parodying the genre of the operetta itself. Another well-known novelist and playwright of the period, Gustav Meyrink, also began writing for the Fledermaus during this period. Among the leading contributors to the Munich *Simplicissimus,* Meyrink wrote a one-act play, *Der Albino* (The Albino), subtitled "Ein Nachtgesicht" (A Night Face), especially for the cabaret. With Wimmer-Wisgrill's stage design greatly heightening the play's ghostly, nightmarish character, Meyrink's *Albino* attracted good reviews and proved to be one of the Fledermaus' few dramatic successes in the second season.

Although dramatic productions such as those of Friedell-Polgar and Meyrink and the decorative art of Wimmer-Wisgrill continued to maintain the original spirit of the Fledermaus, the salad days of the most distinctive and famous Vienna cabaret were unmistakably over. The more spectacle oriented and, at the same time, shallower tendencies already apparent in the second season under the direction of Heinrich Reinhardt became the overriding pattern in the cabaret's third season which began in the autumn of 1909 under the direction now of yet another director, Leo Stein (1861–1921), an opera librettist who had collaborated especially with the opera composer and conductor Leo Ascher (1880–1942). Any pretensions of artistic distinction, to say nothing of uniqueness, were no longer entertained and the Fledermaus began a rapid descent into banality. The end came definitively in 1913 when, under the management of the brothers Schwarz, the once splendid cabaret was transformed into a "girlie" revue theater named the Femina. In its brief heyday the Fledermaus appears to have followed the main patterns of other cabarets, Wolzogen's Überbrettl in Berlin and the Elf Scharfrichter in Munich in the German-speaking world, for example. But one very special circumstance sets the rise and fall of the Fledermaus apart from other cabarets. No other European cabaret of the late nineteenth and early twentieth centuries developed, in its totality, in as intimate a relationship with contemporary indigenous artistic movements as did the Fledermaus. From its inception in 1907 to its effectual demise, in a creative sense, by the end of 1909, the Fledermaus was so closely linked with the fortunes of the Vienna Secession, the *Jugendstil* style, and the Wiener Werkstätte, that it would not be amiss to regard it as an extension in cabaret form of the resplendent Viennese *fin-de-siècle* art represented by these achievements.

CHAPTER FIVE

CRACOW: LITTLE GREEN BALLOONS

Let's start with a bit of history.

The European revolutions of 1848 and the unsuccessful January Insurrection of 1863 against Russia isolated Poland from the West to a degree greater than at any time since the country lost its independence as a state in the partitions of 1772, 1793, and 1795.[1] Disappointed in armed upheaval as a means of achieving national independence, Polish intellectuals in the era of post-Romantic positivism inclined to a program of "organic work" which had as its immediate goal a firm strengthening of Polish life throughout the occupied realm. In cultural life especially, the most significant and far-reaching accomplishments came to be realized in the province of Galicia in Austrian Poland.

In the first half of the century, Austria had been no less repressive a partitioning power than Russia or Prussia. But the defeats the Hapsburg Empire suffered in 1859, in the war against France and the Kingdom of Piedmont, and again in 1866, in the Prussian campaign, revealed serious weaknesses in the state structure. Enlightened opinion came to understand that unless Austria was to be relegated to the position of a secondary power, restrictions on the Empire's subject nationalities had to be eased and their support actively encouraged. Various attempts at the reorganization of the Empire along federal lines were undertaken, most notably by the Pole Count Agenor Gołuchowski who in 1860 was appointed Minister of State, and in 1866 Viceroy for Galicia. These proved largely unsuccessful, but a more liberal constitution was in time effected and a certain measure of autonomy obtained for Galicia. The Polish province was now permitted it's own Diet (*Sejm*) which met in Lwów, its own local administration, and a network of schools in which Polish, not German, was the language of instruction. Intellectual life began to flourish in the changed political climate of Galicia. In 1872, the Cracow Academy of Arts and Sciences was founded and the universities of Cracow and Lwów again became important centers of Polish learning—at a time, it must be remembered, when the University of Warsaw had become subject to intense Russification. Young Poles, fugitives from the policy of linguistic and cultural harassment of the Russian and Prussian governments, flocked to Galicia to breathe the freer air, to study in Polish schools, and to regain a lost sense of national dignity.

The center of the Galician cultural revival was Cracow, the ancient Polish capital.[2] Comparatively small at this time, Cracow was traditionally a conservative city. Proud of the history in which it was steeped, its citizens took pleasure in erecting monuments to its past and fought to preserve its time-weathered walls. Under the impact of Galician semi-autonomy, however, the city was compelled to undergo a transformation. A stronghold of conservatism and traditionalism, it became the seat of a dynamic renascence of Polish art. This renascence reached its culmination between the years 1890 and 1914 and is known in Polish cultural history as "Young Poland" (*Młoda Polska*), the term used to denote—just as "Young Germany" or "Young Scandinavia"—the period, above all, of turn-of-the-century modernism.[3]

Comparing the era of Young Poland with Poland's Romantic period in the first half of the nineteenth century, the writer and *cabaretier* Dr. Tadeusz Boy-Żeleński once made this incisive observation:

> The Romantics of the previous generation had been sentenced to vagabondage over the face of Europe and endless yearning for the homeland; their descendants, on the other hand, were obliged to submit to an opposite sentence: to sitting quietly at home and longing endlessly for the almost mythical Europe beyond the border.[4]

Young Poland made a feverish attempt to embrace this "mythical Europe" and in the remarkable florescence of the arts it achieved once again eloquently reaffirmed Poland's Western heritage.

Lyric poetry was handsomely represented by such talented poets as Kazimierz Przerwa-Tetmajer (1865–1940), Leopold Staff (1878–1957), and Jan Kasprowicz (1860–1926). It was a poetry that was cosmopolitan and local at one and the same time. Nourished by excellent translations from the French Symbolist writers, it took pride in its modernity and "Europeanism," yet found time to rediscover the beauty of the Tatra Mountains to the south of Cracow, the Tatra capital, Zakopane, and the people of the region, the colorful *górale* (mountaineers).

After the historical romances and disappointing social works of Poland's first Nobel Prize winner for literature, Henryk Sienkiewicz (1846–1916), the novel reached new heights in the capable hands of such major talents as Wacław Berent (1873–1940), Stefan Żeromski (1864–1925), and Władysław Reymont (1867–1925)—the latter Poland's second Nobel Prize recipient for literature on the strength of his four-volume epic about the Polish peasantry, *Chłopi* (The Peasants, 1904–1906). The great drama of the Polish Romantics—Adam Mickiewicz (1798–1855), Juliusz Słowacki (1809–1849), Zygmunt Krasiński (1812–1859)—found a worthy successor in Stanisław Wyspiański (1869–1907), the most powerful dramatic talent in twentieth-century Polish literature. It has been said that without Chekhov there would have been no Moscow Art Theater and without the Moscow Art Theater, no Chekhov. Perhaps the same could be said of Wyspiański and the Cracow Theater. For it was Wyspiański's plays, above all his most famous, *Wesele* (The Wedding, 1901), that revitalized the theater and provided it with the necessary stimulus to become one of the best in Europe at the time. When its directorship was assumed in 1893 by Tadeusz Pawlikowski (1861–1915), the Cracow Theater entered its golden age; in the five years of his administration, it reached unprecedented heights. In addition to his often brilliant productions of the plays of the Romantics—plays written in emigration and never intended for stage presentation[5]—Pawlikowski also brought to the boards the works of leading contemporary European dramatists: Ibsen, Bjornson, Hauptmann, Wilde, Maeterlinck, Curel, Becque, Courteline, Porto-Riche, and D'Annunzio.

Young Poland also witnessed a rich growth of literary and artistic journals. Zenon Przesmycki (Miriam, 1861–1944), who rescued the fine late Romantic poet Cyprian Kamil Norwid (1821–1883) from literary near-oblivion, had founded a literary paper in Warsaw in 1887. Besides publishing the works of new and older writers along with articles by leading Positivist publicists, it devoted considerable space to poetry and was international in its choice of translations. Selections from the works of such poets as Poe, Swinburne, Rossetti, Baudelaire, Verlaine, Maeterlinck, Heredia, and Leconte de Lisle, appeared on its pages. An able translator in his own right, Miriam also published translations in the Cracow paper *Świat* (World), edited at the time by Zygmunt Sarnecki. A few years later, Cracow had its first literary review, *Życie* (Life), the same name as Miriam's Warsaw publication. It was founded in 1897 by the young Cracovian poet Ludwik Szczepański, Viennese educated and an ardent supporter of the new trends in art. Publishing Tetmajer, Kasprowicz, Wyspiański, and many others, *Życie* championed the freedom of art and dedicated itself to the struggle against obscurantism in contemporary Polish life. In 1898, the directorship of the journal fell to the *enfant terrible* of Young Poland, Stanisław Przybyszewski (1868–1927), who had just returned from Germany where he had been one of the leading figures in the Berlin Bohème. The first issue of *Życie* to appear under Przybyszewski's aegis contained his "Confiteor" (I Confess), a vehement proclamation of the autonomy of art. Although *Życie* was short-lived (publication ceased in 1900), it became the chief organ of the new literature. When its end came, the spirit of Young Poland had begun to reach out from Cracow to embrace other cities of Poland, especially Warsaw and Lwów.

Like literature, Polish painting flowered during Young Poland. A dynamic, strongly French-oriented society of artists was formed, taking the name *Sztuka* (Art). Exhibitions of its members' work attracted attention even beyond Poland and claimed for Polish art an interest it had not previously enjoyed. After the death of Poland's great painter of historical canvases, Jan Matejko (1838–1893), the presidency of the recently transformed Cracow Academy of Fine Arts passed into the hands of one of the most talented exponents of Polish modernism, the watercolorist Julian Fałat (1853–1929). Under his leadership, younger Paris-trained and Paris-inspired artists such as Leon Wyczółkowski (1852–1936), Teodor Axentowicz (1859–1938), Józef Pankiewicz (1866–1940), Wójciech Weiss (1875–1950), Fryderyk Pautsch (1877–1950), and others were brought to Cracow and a new life infused in the academy. Toward the close of the century, new tendencies in decorative art were expressed by the dramatist Wyspiański, an able watercolor and pastel painter, and Józef Mehoffer (1869–1946), whose painting of the stained glass windows for the Fribourg Cathedral (in Switzerland) between 1896 and 1924 earned him an international reputation.

The era of Young Poland was not noted for the levity of its art. But just as medieval mystery dramas had their *intermedia* for comic relief, so

Young Poland had its Zielony Balonik (Green Balloon). The Balloon has been called many things: the "quintessence (the dot over the "i") of the cultural changes Cracow underwent in the first decade of the present century," the "spiritual synthesis of Cracow," an "anticipation of [Poland's] freedom," a "revindication of the right of laughter," an "outburst of gaiety that embraced all Poland," a "joyful consciousness." It was—a cabaret. The most famous cabaret in Polish history. A part of and yet apart from Cracow and Young Poland, it was an expression of and comment on both the society and period in which it arose. In an address delivered at the Sorbonne on February 19, 1927, Boy-Żeleński, its most faithful lover, summed up the importance of the Green Balloon in these terms:

> At the time, quite near the Academy of Fine Arts, a small café was located where painters, sculptors, and the whole Cracow Bohemia used to gather. Before long, the walls were covered with sketches, caricatures, and things of that sort that left no doubt that someone had the idea of establishing an artistic cabaret.
>
> That is how the "Green Balloon" came to be born, a "Chat Noir"-type cabaret that brought together the majority of those who are today directing the artistic life in Poland and who at the time were suffocating in too solid and too small Cracow. [The Green Balloon] was an outburst of mad gaiety, a boisterous laugh whose echoes reverberated throughout all of Poland; it was a "counsel of revision," sometimes cruel, of the many false grandeurs and offical falsehoods which for a very long time found shelter within the labyriths of our complicated and tormented national life.[6]

It was, perhaps symbolically, in October of the revolutionary year of 1905 that the Green Balloon opened its doors for the first time. The idea for a cabaret had originated, it seems, with the popular dramatist Jan August Kisielewski (1876–1918),[7] who had recently returned from a trip to Paris where he had spent considerable time between September 1899 and August 1903. Convinced that Poland was ripe for the introduction of "artistic cabaret," which, in his view, represented a desperately needed alternative to an ossified "official" culture, Kisielewski set forth his ideas on the subject in an essay entitled "Panmusaion" (which he hinted might even be a good name for the new enterprise). Kisielewski's original focus was on the capital, Warsaw, however, rather than on Cracow. The "artistic cabaret," or "theater of independents" (*teatr niezawisłych*), as he also refers to it, could in fact become the

> center of Warsaw artistic life, a "salon of the elite," a metropolis of everything young and new, which, removed from official seriousness and official cares and

responsibilities, and within the limits of artistic taste, would be able to cultivate, create and reveal, serve and test—and enjoy a many-colored Beauty, something that does not yet—and never will be able—to be fit into academic categories of art. That Warsaw today needs such an institution, with a considerable outlay of consistently maintained effort seriously thought out with respect to program and execution (and by serious I do not mean boring and hackneyed), would be superfluous for me to add.[8]

Kisielewski made a point of emphasizing that the new Polish "artistic cabaret" should not follow in the same footsteps of unsuccessful previous attempts to bring West European after-dark entertainment to Poland:

The efforts of *music halls,* such as last year's French *Tingel-Tangel* in the "Elizeum" [a basement establishment on Karowa Street which to Kisielewski seemed an ideal location for his new cabaret—HBS], or of cabarets modeled on Parisian café concerts or Berlin *Überbrettl,* met with no success since lacking sense and providing neither amusement nor aesthetic impressions, they do not correspond to the needs of our audience which, unlike in other European centers, is not yet "mature" enough (thank goodness!) for this type of vulgar or degenerate entertainment. (p. 166)

Kisielewski's cabaret would not, therefore, be a locus of banal *divertissement,* but would instead function as the Polish counterpart of "that which in the West represents a fundamental and lofty element of an 'independent art' blazing new trials, an art both unusual and exceptional" (p. 167). Acknowledging that the artistic material from which this new art would emerge still existed in raw form in Poland, Kisielewski was nevertheless confident that when the time came enough of it would be found among young actors, singers, musicians, and literary people. He also emphasized that the development of an authentic Polish cabaret must draw on original, native, inborn resources:

It is proper to learn from the West and to transplant in our soil that which is worthy and appropriate to our character, that which steers us to the discovery of our own sources of creativity (that is the genesis of the literature of Young Poland), but never to imitate! Hence, not Berlin *Überbrettl,* not Paris cabarets, nor London music halls—but the Stage of Independent Youth, with a repertoire embracing everything from choreography to mime drama, from song to fashionable causerie, with dignity and freedom, with humor and good spirit, with artistry and party-like amusement. (p. 169)

Despite Kisielewski's preference for Warsaw, it was in Cracow, that bastion of conservatism and traditionalism, that the first Polish cabaret opened, and then not in a basement place of amusement but in a confectionary and coffee shop known as the Cukierna Lwowska (The Lwów Confectionary). It was operated at the time by Jan Apolinary Michalik at 45 Floriánska Street, very near the Main Marketplace that is the heart of Cracow. The selection of what in time came to be known as Michalik's Cave (Jama Michalikowa) seemed logical. To begin with, the shop was a stone's throw from the Academy of Fine Arts. Second, it had been a favorite meeting place for young artists and had its own painters table (*stolik malarski*). Once the idea of a cabaret caught on, the question arose of what to call it. The answer came soon, and quite by chance. As members of the artists' group with whom Kisielewski was discussing his idea left the shop and strode out toward the marketplace, they

Interior view of the Zielony Balonik (Green Balloon).

Interior view of the Zielony Balonik (Green Balloon). The glass case to the left contains dolls used in the cabaret's puppet shows.

caught sight of a street vendor selling children's balloons, all of which happened to be green. One of the members exclaimed that here was the name for the cabaret: "The Green Balloon." And so it remained.

The opening of the Green Balloon on October 7, 1905, took place with much exuberance, the tone set by the announcement which Kisielewski himself wrote:

On Saturday the 7th there will take place the
tumultuous opening of the first
Cracow Cabaret of Artists
Baptised in noble wine with the name
The Green Balloon
In Michalik's Cave
(The Lwów Confectionary on Floriańska Street)

Beginning after 10:30 P.M.
Admission free on presentation of invitation.

Invited guests will be merry and boisterous, enthusiastically applauding everything and everyone. Dress absolutely required: the label CAPTIF [French for captive, prisoner.—HBS] on a ribbon tied to a button, and above the head at a height of 35 cm. a floating "green balloon." All other parts of the wardrobe superfluous. Nonpossession of this frivolous emblem of a "member-spectator" in the cabaret can expose an invited person even worthiest of honor to indifference and ceremonious expulsion past the gates of the cave of the "Green Balloon."

The Committee does not accept responsibility for the payment of bills for dried-up drinks.

Poets are given no advance payment.

During the "numbers" people are expected to howl and upon summons of the animal trainer-director applaud with a passion worthy of the "Green Balloon."

Before or during the evening, improvisors should make known their wishes, advising the director (J. A. Kisielewski) that a creative and humoristic madness has seized them and that they want to show people their bare soul; their immodest desires will be immediately complied with.

Death to rats and Palefaces!
The Green Balloon
Entrance through the gate of the establishment.[9]

In his humorous inaugural address—which clearly shows traces of Aristide Bruant's contemptuous and insulting style of greeting—Kisielewski welcomed the first audience with a torrent of flowery abuse aimed, above all, at "today's wretched and emaciated little flock of pseudoartists all decked out in feathers plucked from the tail of the recently deceased 'peacock.' " The "peacock" Kisielewski had in mind was the room in Turliński's *kawiarnia,* or coffee shop, opposite the Cracow Theater which Przybyszewski had dubbed Pod Paonem (Under the Sign of the Peacock, from the French *paon*) and which was the most popular artists' gathering place in Cracow before the opening of the Green Balloon. Kisielewski went on to ask:

How is it that from that dappled, rainbow-colored bird, from beneath his tail spread wide with pride, gluttony, and guzzling, that from beneath such a tail there could fall out a flock of noisy cock, sparrow, starling, and rook chicks, clumsy, dumb, arrogant, jabbering about themselves and about their sickening and boring pieces of gossip with awkward nonchalance? How this fact of lame stooping could arise will remain a mystery of your comicality, a hieroglyph of our ignorance, a symbol of your soft, flabby, impertinent micromania, a problem of your Vienna-elegant, commercial traveler-Zakopane, mawkish snobomania. My kind sirs and dear sylphids, it will remain your problem the resolution of which someone will surely attempt.

Your simian maliciousness, your dwarf's impertinence, your street sentimentality, your competitive tobacco-shop aestheticism, your unpleasantly sticky unceremoniousness, your clumsy pettiness, particularistic stupidity, parochial pretensions and small aspirations do not amuse, do not provoke, but just bore, bore . . .

And so, deeply moved, sincerely and from the bottom of my heart, with complete effusiveness and dedication, I greet you my young friends, with these words of admiration and adoration, you fanatic votaries of youth, devotees of the impertinent thrust of irony and amused flights of mad emptiness—I greet you, young asses . . . I mean, eagles! I greet you, magnificent con . . . con . . . condors!

I love the boundlessness of your idiocy, I adore the affrontery of your silliness, I esteem the cynicism of your bluffery! Oh, my dears, how repulsive you are to me! Oh, if I could gather you all together here to the bosom of my contempt and antipathy, how sweet, how irrevocably thorough would be your last breath! But no! That is a physical impossibility, that would be too lovely and too comic!

Thus, before there begins the electrically amused night of your fantastic laughs and toasts over the grave of your day, over the lid of the coffin of your stumbling about the pavement around St. Mary's [Church in Cracow's Main Marketplace—HBS], before the glow-worms gnaw away your skulls to the very shells of the brains—shout and laugh, sing and dance, pinch and bite yourselves, and loudly, boisterously, noisily! . . .

Let your amusement flow lightly and emptily, like the little green balloons above your heads, let the late Peacock deliver in this cave beneath the "green balloon" the monologue of a parrot and let the Parisian specter of the "Black Cat" meow out above you a coquettish, grateful, and most pleasant *Zutalors* [French for "What the hell!"—HBS]![10]

With Kisielewski as its first *conferëncier,* very soon followed (because of Kisielewski's poor health) by the hard-drinking "Stasinek" Sierosławski who always appeared in tuxedo and white tie, the "Balloon" began to meet regularly after theatrical premières, which at the time took place on Saturdays. The usual hour for meetings was midnight. Cabaret activities lasted until about three in the morning, but it was often considerably later that guests took their leave of Michalik's shop. The first debuts of the Balloon were strictly closed affairs. Each program was a semi-improvised premiere and was not repeated. Admission was free, but invitations issued by the Balloon committee were required and were highly prized.[11] The invitations were generally drawn by the cabaret artists themselves and were printed by a lithographer named Zenon Pruszyński, whose shop was located on Pijarska Street. A

Zielony Balonik (Green Balloon) invitation. (Biblioteka Jagiellońska, Cracow).

great patriot of the cabaret, Zenon (as he was known) later wrote a monograph on Jan Michalik, *Jama Michalika* (Michalik's Cave), which was published in 1930 on the twenty-fifth anniversary of the Balloon.

In the beginning, the Green Balloon was essentially a painters' club and this was reflected in the entertainment if offered. Although programs included singing, dancing, and recitation, it was the art exhibitions that captured the greatest interest, as had been the case with the Barcelona Quatre Gats. During the second program, for example, the painter and stage designer Karol Frycz (1877–1963) displayed his sensational cycle of caricatures dedicated to the restoration of the old royal castle in Cracow on Wawel Hill. Other fine caricatures were drawn by Kazimierz Sichulski (1879–1943), who later was commissioned to paint the Parliament in Vienna.

No curtain separated public from performer at the Green Balloon and the stage was just a small podium near the piano. The confectionary shop held between one hundred and one hundred and twenty people at the very most. For Balloon programs it was usually filled to capacity, with guests even standing in the doorways. Later, when the Balloon was well on its way to becoming a legend, the proprietor, Michalik, added a second larger room.

The audience that attended Green Balloon functions was elite. It included professors of the Academy of Fine Arts, artists and their friends, theater people, journalists, and enthusiastic visitors from Lwów, Warsaw, and even Vienna. The participants in early Balloon shows were recruited from Cracow's art colony and occasionally included such improbable personalities as Jan Starzewski, the Treasurer-Councillor of Cracow, who sang, and Roger Battaglia, a member of the Austrian parliament who came in by train from Vienna to recite both verse and prose and, if the spirit moved him, to dance.

Conservative Cracow did not take kindly to the Green Balloon and attacks on it and on the institution of cabaret in general began to be heard. How infelicitous an environment for cabaret Cracow represented at the time can be gleaned from the vitriolic denunciation of it by the prominent Young Poland critic Zenon Przesmycki (Miriam) even before the founding of the Green Balloon. In an article entitled "Nadsceny" (Superstages, the Polish equivalent of the German "Überbrettl," from which the term was obviously borrowed) and published in the journal *Chimera* in 1901, Miriam regarded the emergence of cabaret in Germany as a contagion of the worst possible taste, one to be resisted by Poles at all costs:

Warsaw newspapers, with tender and touching sympathy, have supported the transplantation in our soil of one of the most wretched, most insipid, and most speculative German products, the *Überbrettl* or superstage. . . .

After a year's experience, the Germans themselves (naturally, not those with vested interests in the "enterprise" such as Messrs. Bierbaum or Wolzogen) have affirmed the worthlessness [of cabaret—HBS], some more gently, asserting that "one should see in it not just no new evolutionary period in literature, but not even the smallest contribution to its evolution" (*Das literarische Echo,* October 1901); others, more sharply, saying that it is "ein dreister Missbrauch mit dem heiligen Namen der Kunst" [a brazen abuse with the holy name of art—HBS] and that "no German theatrical genre, no Adolf-Ernstiada,[12] no idiotic operetta is as despairingly devoid of any kind of artistic note as the *Überbrettl* of 1901 (*Die Zeit,* 1902, nr. 381).

Among us, meanwhile, this veiled bourgeois *tyngel* [as in Tingel-Tangel—HBS], this glittering proof of the disintegrative process of contemporary society, this fruit of internal dry-rot, of intellectual and emotional atrophy as well as of the greatest hypocrisy has found support, praise, and admiration as something that will renew society, animate it, free it from its fetters, and even more, as something that is art itself, today's art, modern, "corresponding to the mood of contemporary psychology (?), in a word "applied poetry."[13]

An apostle of "high" as opposed to "low" art, Miriam saw profound and irreconcilable differences between cabarets, of which he disapproved, and *théâtres d'art,* for which he had high regard, and between poetry, at whose altar he worshipped, and popular songs, which in no way could be considered art. Noting the growing interest in Poland in the Parisian chanson, Miriam took careful aim at this target as well:

> The sung song (chanson) which has proliferated so handsomely in France in the nineteenth century, as perhaps nowhere else or even before, is a hybrid genre that has almost no connection either with the art of the ancient *chansonniers* (jongleurs, trouvères, and minstrels) with which they are related by name, or—for instance—with the *chansons sans paroles* of Verlaine, or with poetry in general. It is a kind of *poesis vulgivaga* [roving poetry—HBS] directly reflecting passing daily occurrences and feelings and seeking to find a direct, immediate response among the crowd.
>
> It is obvious, in the light of the above, that the chanson renounces all deeper or more subtle things, and as to content devotes itself exclusively either to practical matters (social, political, the caricature of manners), or to entertainment, cheap sentimentality, facile heroism, more or less spicy or coarse humor, puns, and allusions. (pp. 113–114)

As opposition to the cabaret grew and rumors began circulating around Cracow that the Green Balloon was the scene of orgies, nude dancing, and all manner of dissipation, Boy-Żeleński responded with a satire written in 1906 under the title "Co mówill w kościele u kapucynów. Pieśń dziadkowa" (What They Have Been Saying in the Capuchin Church. A Beggar-Storyteller's Song). A beggar-storyteller (*dziad*) reports that

W przedostatnią niedzielę
W kapoceńskim kościele,
Mówila mi moja starka,
Straśna była tam pogwarka
  O jakimsiś baloniku.[14]

(On Sunday before last, / in the Capuchin church, / My old woman was told / A frightful thing / About some kind of balloon).

The Balloon, says the beggar-storyteller, is Sodom and Gomorrah. Things never before seen happen there. The entrance to the place is lighted by three candles and admittance is gained only after the name of Lucifer is repeated three times. Once inside the café, all the pagans undress and dance strange dances which one is embarrassed to describe, especially the *maczicza.*[15] Even pregnant women come to have a good time. A bathub filled to the brim with drink stands in the middle of the room and all quaff from it. When anyone refuses to imbibe, the others seize him and pour it into his throat. All the while bawdy songs are sung. Some accompany the singer vocally, others hammer away on his belly. The beggar-storyteller closes his tale by saying that when the orgy is over and all are satiated, they can be found lying about on and under the tables, worse than animals.

The antics of the Balloon at times startled even the proprietor of the Lwów Confectionary, Jan Michalik. Although originally from Lwów (hence the name of his shop), he had by now assimilated a fair measure of his adopted city's conservatism. Whatever reservations he may have had, however, about allowing a cabaret (of all things) to open on the premises of his café, it soon became evident to him that these popular artists' gatherings had a certain commercial advantage in that their very notoriety might increase the number of customers during the café's regular hours.

There are conflicting stories about Michalik. He is often portrayed as a true friend of art, always ready to help struggling artists, to extend them credit whenever necessary. The Michalik "myth" (as others) was exploded by Boy-Żeleński in a humorous song written in 1910: "Nowa pieśń o rydzu, czyli: Jak Jan Michalik został mecenasem sztuki, czyli: Niezbadane są drogi opatrznośći" (A New Song about a Mushroom, or How Jan Michalik Became a Patron of Art, or Inscrutable Are the Ways of Providence).[16] Michalik, relates Boy-Żeleński, was at first a mortal enemy of credit, with a heart made of stone. That is why God looked upon him with favor and saved him from bankrupcy. But it was not long before he discovered that his establishment was a veritable gold mine. And so

> W końcu Michalik na serio
> Zaczął brać swoją galerią.
> Uderzyło mu do głowy.
> Że taki sklep ma morowy.

(In the end, Michalik began / To take his cabaret seriously. / The idea had finally entered his head / That his shop had become "pestilential.").[17]

Michalik now freely extended credit and encouraged the artists:

> "Hej, panie Mączyński, panie Frycz,
> Bierzcie, co chcecie, nie szczędźcie nic,

Urządźcie pięknie mi salę.
Niech się przed światem pochwalę."

(Hey, Mr. Mączyński, Mr. Frycz / Take what you need, don't skimp. / Please make my shop as pretty as you can / So I may glory before the world.)

The artists willingly accepted Michalik's encouragement and proceeded to decorate the walls of the café with frescoes, a thing quite new in Poland at the time. Frycz, Sichulski, Mączyński, Wójtkiewicz, Kamocki, Filipkiewicz—some of the best contemporary artists—contributed their time and talent to the project.[18] On occasion, the artists' imagination ran away with them and there were misunderstandings with Michalik. Once, for example, an egg shell was glued to a wall as part of some decoration. Michalik's conservatism rebelled and the shell was removed. When the artist noticed it gone, he thought that it had just fallen off and so replaced it. Seeing a new shell on the wall, Michalik grew furious. An argument ensued, but Michalik was adamant. The shell left the wall for the second, and final, time. Despite such occasional disturbances, Michalik in his way did perform a service for Polish culture which Boy-Żeleński, equally in his own way, acknowledges in his "A New Song about a Mushroom, or How Jan Michalik Became a Patron of Art, etc."

Nie mamy w Polsce monarchy,
Same w niej golce lub parchy:
Michalik został nam jeden,
By Sztuki stworzyć w niej Eden.[19]

(In Poland no monarch have we, / Only the poor and the wretched! / Michalik remained the only one / To create an Eden of art from it.)

In the second period of the Green Balloon's activity, literary entertainment took precedence over the artistic. To a great extent this was due to the influence of the most outstanding individual connected with the cabaret in the seven years of its existence, Tadeusz Żelenski (1874–1941), known best by his pen name, Boy. A pediatrician by profession and a writer by inclination, Boy-Żelenski was a gifted and versatile personality.[20] In addition to his original writings on an astonishingly wide variety of subjects, he was a respected critic and translator of French literature. He was born the son of Władysław Żeleński, a noted composer, and Wanda Grabowska, an aunt of the poet Tetmajer. Upon receipt of his degree from the Jagiellonian University in Cracow in 1895 he went to Paris to study medicine. After his return from France, he settled in

Zielony Balonik (Green Balloon) invitation. The caricature is that of Dr. Tadeusz Boy-Żeleński. (Biblioteka Jagiellońska, Cracow).

Cracow officially earning his living as a railroad doctor, unofficially becoming a kind of Boswell to the Young Poland phenomenon. That is why he adopted a pseudonym. Since (as he himself acknowledged) it would have been awkward in staid Cracow for one and the same person to write prescriptions by day and cabaret songs by night, he concealed the identity of Dr. Tadeusz Żeleński, the pediatrician and railroad doctor, under the nom de plume of "Boy," an English word that happened to strike his fancy and seemed to epitomize the playful attitude of the cabaretist and song writer. Besides his delightful writings about the whole epoch of Young Poland and his reminiscences of its most vital personalities,[21] Boy-Żeleński took so active a part in the affairs of the Green Balloon it would not at all be inappropriate to consider him its moving spirit from 1906 on.

For Balloon entertainments Boy-Żeleński wrote mostly songs, many of which were set to music by his friend Witold Noskowski (pseudonym Taper, 1874–1939), a Cracow journalist and talented amateur musician. A serious student of French culture, Boy-Żeleński enjoyed an intimate knowledge of the French chanson and considered himself instrumental in introducing the genre to Poland. In an article written in 1907, "Kilka słów o piosence" (A Few Words about Song), he speaks with affection of an earlier trip to Paris and of his acquaintance with the chanson:

> When i was in Paris a few years ago for the first time, I fell in love from the first moment with the French chanson. I sought it everywhere, and its refrains echoed continually in my ears. A few years later, when I had the chance again to hear the old and so eternally happy classic air of the "Chat Noir"
>
> un jeune homm' venait de se pendre
> Dans la forêt de Saint Germain
>
> I felt like Sienkiewicz's lighthouse keeper[22] (if one is permitted to make the comparison), the tears filling my eyes. In all certainty, this love would have gone with me to the grave had it not been for the emergence of the Cracow "Green Balloon," which drew forth from each of us some grain of happiness that had been slumbering deep inside us in view of the unhappy conditions of our life.[23]

Some years later, in 1927, in the address he delivered at the Sorbonne, Boy-Żeleński recalled even more vividly his romance with the chanson and the meaning it came to hold for him:

> But there was something else that greatly decided my change of career. I am speaking of the chanson, of the Parisian chanson. I was vaguely enamored of this chanson from my first days in Paris. It was something exotic for me; in Poland, there was nothing at all like it. I encountered it virtually everywhere. On the street, I willingly joined groups of people who gathered around a strolling singer. Later, to my astonishment, I came across shops where chansons were sold like rolls and where a gramophone of sorely tried endurance was teaching the public the chanson of the day. I enjoyed hearing the girls sing whom I had met at the "Bal Bullier." But the true origins of the Parisian chanson were unknown to me. To be sure, the echoes of the glorious success of the "Chat Noir" had even reached Cracow, but for me, a young savage, alone, lost in this immense Paris, bewildered, it didn't even enter my mind to ask about it; besides, the "Chat Noir" no longer existed.
>
> One evening, however, a friend, an old Parisian whom I happened to meet by

chance, led me to a small street—the Rue Champollion, I believe, not far from the Sorbonne—to a nightclub called "Le Grillon," which later on changed to the "Noctambules." And it was there that, for the price of a franc, including a beer or a coffee, I heard Paul Delmet, Marcel Legay, Gabriel Montoya, Numa Blès, Vincent Hyspa, and the other fine singers of Montmartre. I was fascinated, awe-struck; I had the feeling that a veil had fallen from my eyes, that for the first time I was seeing the world the way one is supposed to see it, reflected in this chanson, which is as varied as it is charming. And even today I can still repeat almost by heart the songs that I heard that first evening. The simple and so exquisite melodies that Delmet, then so near his premature end, used to sing in the delicate manner of a consumptive; then Montoya, who every evening, for many years, used to coo his pleasant *Chanson d'antan* (Song of Yesteryear) in his falsetto voice, like some huge bird desperately calling his mate; and the others who in their lively spirit lashed out at big and small alike and gave more rhythm and more sense to life's occurrences. Oh! The wonderful Parisian chanson, it was truly she who completed my education; and it was the nostalgia that she left in my heart that later decided my life.[24]

Although he spoke warmly of Blès, Montoya, and Legay, and actually borrowed some of Paul Delmet's melodies,[25] it was the spirit of the Parisian chanson rather than the style of any one singer that captivated Boy-Żeleński and was brought back to Poland by him. Highly talented and individualistic, with a remarkable feeling for language, he developed his own technique—simple, direct, yet full of verve and gaiety.

Despite occasional pieces in which a certain perhaps surprising lyricism peeps out from behind a mask of wry humor, the majority of Boy-Żeleński's Balloon songs were in a satirical vein. His satire, like that of the Chat Noir singer Leon Xanrof's, was light and good-humored. There was none of the bitterness, defiance, or resignation met with so frequently in the songs of such Parisian singers as Jehan Rictus or Maurice Rollinat. In Boy-Żeleński's gentle but capable hands satire was forged as a weapon not against social injustice, but against the conservatism and traditionalism of the little world of contemporary Cracow, on the one hand, and against some of the modernist excesses of the writers of Young Poland, on the other.

To Boy-Żeleński, who loved to shock and whose songs are so often pervaded by a gleeful irreverence, there were few "sacred cows." Young Poland itself, Polish national dignity, the church, marriage and the family, morality, tradition—all came under his keen scrutiny. Consider the matter of the three partitions of Poland. A tragic subject a Pole could hardly be expected to treat lightly—except Boy-Żeleński. His "Pieśń o naszych stolicach i jak je Opatrzność obdzieliła" (Song of Our Capitals and How Providence Endowed Them, 1907) is a good example of his gift for irony. Beginning with the quote "Wszytko nam dałeś co dać mogłeś Panie" (Thou has given us all that Thou couldst, O Lord) from the well known "Psalm of Good Will" by the Romantic poet Zygmunt Krasiński (to whom Boy-Żeleński refers as "a certain great jester," *pewien wielki kpiarz*),[26] Boy-Żeleński examines Poland's good fortune. While other nations have only one capital, she has three: Cracow, Warsaw, and Lwów. As a matter of fact, there is even an extra "summer capital"—the "pearl" of the Tatra Mountains, Zakopane (at this time a favorite artists' retreat). God's fairness, argues Boy-Żeleński, is well known and His bountiful gifts were distributed equally among the three capitals. Cracow got Wilhelm Feldman (a literary critic who had some harsh things to say about Boy-Żeleński, the Green Balloon, and the institution of the cabaret in general); Warsaw was granted Aleksander Rajchman (the first director of the Warsaw Philharmonic);[27] and to Lwów went a painting presumably by Raphael and the principal adornment of the newly opened Lwów Museum.

Cracow's self-intoxication with its rich past expressed itself frequently in public celebrations and processions. In the period of the Green Balloon these usually began and ended at the foot of the statue of the poet Adam Mickiewicz in the old marketplace in the town's center. This is the subject of another typical Boy-Żeleński satire, "Pomnikomania krakowska" (Cracow's Monument Mania).[28] The author imagines the thoughts of the poor poet who is tired of the constant fuss about him but who must stand and bear it all, alas, because he is made of bronze.

Events of local or regional interest also attracted Boy-Żeleński's attention. On the occasion of the opening of the new Municipal Museum in Lwów in 1907, for example, he wrote a little song about the museum's prize possession, the Raphael "original" ("Song about the Raphael in the Newly Opened Lwów Museum").[29] The following year, two other events were celebrated in song: the restoration of the parish church in Szczucin ("Głos dziadkowy o restauracji kościoła parafialnego w Szczucinie," The Beggar-Storyteller's Tale of the Restoration of the Parish Church in Szczucin," which Boy-Żeleński wrote in peasant dialect), and the procession of the Cracow Brigade in Vienna on the occasion of the sixtieth anniversary of the reign of the Emperor Franz Joseph ("Pobudka banderii krakowskiej," Reveille of the Cracow Brigade).[30]

When the National Museum in Cracow held a jubilee celebration in 1909, Boy-Żeleński sent a congratulatory greeting from the Green Balloon ("The Green Balloon—to the National Museum") which closed with these words:

I cały świat
Wykrzyknie mu: wiwat!
Niech setki lat
Do grata zbiera grat.[31]

(And the whole world / Shouts: Long live! / For hundreds of years / May it add rubbish to rubbish.)

Boy-Żeleński conceived a special dislike for the "high priests" of Polish literary criticism of the time, above all Stanisław Tarnowski, professor of Polish literature at the University of Cracow, an avowed foe of Polish modernism, and, in Boy-Żeleński's opinion, a pompous and narrow-minded man. One of Boy-Żeleński's best-known Green Balloon poems is a satire of Tarnowski entitled "O bardzo niegrzecznej literaturze polskiej i jej strapionej cioce" (About the Very Naughty Polish Literature and Its Distressed Auntie). An old aunt (Tarnowski), a virgin (*panna czysta*), has reared a nephew named Józio, who is a modernist. What is a modernist, asks Boy-Żeleński in the poem?

(Modernista—znaczy chłopak,
Co wszystko robi na opak;
Każdego się głupstwa czepi,
A zawsze chce wiedzieć lepiej.)[32]

(A Modernist is a fellow / Who does everything topsy-turvy; / He clings to every stupidity, / But always wants to know better.)

Józio is naughty and refuses to follow the example of such good little boys as "Lucek" (or "Lutek," a contemporary poet, Lucjan Rydel, of whom Tarnowski approved) and "Henio" (the novelist Henryk Sienkiewicz, whose obvious conservatism offended younger writers). Józio, writes Boy-Żeleński, runs around in the nude, saying: "But Auntie, this is cabaret style!" He also depraves the younger children. Little Hanka calls herself an "erotomaniac," a term Józio taught her. Auntie decides to tell the children tales of old. When she asks them to name their favorite military hero, Józio answers "Cambronne."[33] When Auntie speaks of the "three psalms" (a reference to a cycle of religious-patriotic verse by the Romantic poet Zygmunt Krasiński), Józio tells her of the "dancing palms" of Nietzsche.[34] Auntie speaks of Apostles, Józio of spermatozoa (the rhyme in Polish helps: *Ciotka mu o apostołach, / On jej o spermatozoach*). When Auntie asks who was Gallus (the anonymous author of a twelfth-century Polish chronicle in Latin), Józio answers: "Auntie, Phallus!" Trying another approach, Auntie talks about the beginning of the world. Józio maintains that the world arose from lust (an allusion to the dictum "Am Anfang war das Geschlecht," In the beginning there was Lust, attributed to the foremost exponent of Polish literary modernism, Stanisław Przybyszewski). Before he goes to bed at night, Józio must pray to God to make him a faithful servant of traditions and church. Auntie's closing words are a warning: "Let not the nation be polluted / By the modern and erotic."[35]

There is a double edge to Boy-Żeleński's satire here. It is directed primarily against the refusal, or inability, of Tarnowski and other old guard critics and literary historians to come to grips with the literature of the younger generation, with the literature, that is, of Young Poland. At the same time, however, there is an undeniable element of parody in his playful flaunting of the eroticism that was indeed prominent in much of the fiction of Young Poland.

The "Lucek" (or "Lutek") mentioned before refers to the young lyric poet Lucjan Rydel (1870–1918), who had also earned a reputation as a dramatist with such plays as *Zaczarowane koło* (The Enchanted Circle, 1900) and *Betlejem polskie* (The Polish Bethlehem, 1905). It was indirectly through Rydel, as a matter of fact, that Boy-Żeleński first established contact with the Green Balloon. Away from Cracow engaged in medical work, he happened to read an article by Rydel published in the paper *Czas* (Time) demanding the canonization of the medieval Polish queen Jadwiga. Boy-Żeleński wrote a ballad on the subject (never published) and sent it to the Green Balloon. Later on, when Rydel's play *Bodenhain* (about German colonization in Poland) was staged by the Cracow Theater, the Balloon asked Boy-Żeleński to write a review of it. He submitted instead a short parody preserving the original title.[36] Performed with marionettes designed by the artist Karol Frycz, it inaugurated the second season of the Green Balloon in 1906.

The preface to Boy-Żeleński's *Bodenhain* is worth noting in passing. It provided the author with an opportunity to deflate the reputation of yet another contemporary literary critic and historian, this time Ferdynand Hoesick (1867–1941) who enjoyed a certain renown for his biographical studies of the Polish Romantics.[37] His best-known works were *Życie Juliusza Słowackiego* (The Life of Juliusz Słowacki, 3 vols., 1897) and *Miłość w życiu Zygmunta Krasińskego* (Love in the Life of Zygmunt Krasiński, 1899). Hoesick positively doted on Professor Stanisław Tarnowski, which in itself was more than enough to provoke Boy-Żeleński. But what made Hoesick insufferable was his publication in 1906 of a two-volume panegyrical-biographical monograph on Tarnowski while the conservative literary scholar was still alive.[38]

In the preface to his *Bodenhain,* Boy-Żeleński states that the work to follow is a fragment of a drama found in the Small Marketplace (*Mały Rynek*) of Cracow by one Ferdynand Esik (the spelling is Boy-Żeleński's), the author of a work to which the Polish Academy had granted an award: *Kobiety w życiu Lucjana Rydla* (Women in the Life of Lucjan Rydel).[39] A "history" of the manuscript follows. Esik ("that well-known investigator of Polish literature") once upon a time was buying plums in the Small Marketplace. He noticed that the fruit was wrapped in what appeared to be a manuscript whose writing looked familiar to him. Investigating his find at home, he was convinced that he had stumbled upon a fragment of the original manuscript of Rydel's play *Bodenhain.* The work was subjected to "exhaustive" research in order to determine with greatest accuracy the period in which it arose. In an "interesting article," continues Boy-Żeleński, Esik announced that it had been written in November 1905. How was this conclusion reached? By analysis of the type of ink used. This ink proved identical to that produced by a certain firm which was founded in October of 1905 and went out of business in December of the same year. Thus, the manuscript must have been written during the month of November 1905. The information obtained later from the author himself in Sauer's coffee house confirmed the quick conclusion reached by the "indefatigable researcher of our literature—Mr. Esik."

When not undermining Cracow provincialism or the Tarnowski-Hoesick literary axis, Boy-Żeleński, his own *conseil de revision,* was impishly chiding the poets of Young Poland for their neo-Romantic attitudinizing. His feet planted firmly on terra firma, he was amused by the exaggerated solemnity and the soaring mystic flights in which contemporary poetry abounded. In "Pieśń o ziemi naszej" (Song of Our Land, 1907), Boy-Żeleński wrote:

A czy znasz ty te kawiarnie
(W całym świecie takich nie ma),
Gdzie dzień cały marnie, gwarnie
Wałkoni się cud-bohema? . . .

Wszystko tylko Duchem żyje,
Wszystko tylko Pięknem dyszy;
Nigdy ucho tam niczyje
Prozy życia nie zasłyszy . . . [40]

(Do you know these cafés? / (In all the world there are none such), / Where all day long the wonder-Bohème / Senselessly, noisily idles . . . / Everything lives only with Spirit, / Everything breathes only of Beauty; / Not a single ear there ever / Hears the prose of life.)

In "Pieśń o mowie naszej" (Song of Our Speech, 1907), Boy-Żeleński had this to say on the subject of language:

Rzecz aż nazbyt oczywista,
Że jest piękną polska mowa:
Jędrna, pachnąca, soczysta,
Melodyjna, kolorowa,

Bohaterska, gromowładna,
Czysta niby błękit nieba,
Mądra, zacna, miła, ładna—
Ale czasem przyznać trzeba,

Że ten język, najobfitszy
W poetyczne różne kwiatki,
W uczuć sferze pospolitszej
Zdradza dziwne niedostatki;

Że w podniebnej wysokości
Nazbyt górnie toczy skrzydła.
A nas, ludzi z krwi i kości,
Poniewiera—gorzej bydła.[41]

(It is all too clear, / That Polish is a pretty tongue— / Virile, fragrant, succulent, / Melodious, colorful, / Heroic, powerful, / Pure as the azure of the sky, / Wise, noble, pleasant, kind— / But at times one must confess, / That this language, so abundant / In all sorts of poetic flowers, / In the common sphere of feelings / Reveals certain weaknesses; / That in its sky-high loftiness / It extends its wings too sublimely. / And neglects us—flesh and blood human beings—worse than cattle.)

At times the poets of Young Poland must have reminded Boy-Żeleński of the "medium" spirit—the young girl—in Mickiewicz's early Romantic drama *Dziady, Część druga* (Forefather's Eve, Part 2, 1823).

They too needed to touch earth and Boy-Żeleński was there to point the way:

Skończcie wasze komedyje,
Schowajcie pawie ogony.
Żyjcie—czym każdy z nas żyje,
Idźcie—kochać. . . . za miliony!

Dość "nastrojów" waszych, dranie!
Uczcie m ó w i ć waszych braci:
To jest wasze powołanie!
Od tego was naród płaci!

Język naszym skarbem świętym,
Nie igraszką obojętną;
Nie krwią, ale atramentem
Bije dzisiaj ludów tętno . . .[42]

(End your comedies, / Hide the peacocks' tails, / Live—with what each of us lives, / Go—love . . . the millions! Enough of your airs, fools! / Teach your brothers to speak; / That is your vocation! / For that the nation pays you! / Language is our holy treasure, / Not an indifferent plaything, / The pulse of men today beats / Not with blood, but with ink.)

Of contemporary literary figures, none offered Boy-Żeleński so rich a source of material as the talented yet faintly ridiculous Lucjan Rydel. When Boy-Żeleński came to know him, the young poet was already becoming a legend. His marriage to a woman of peasant stock created a sensation and provided the dramatist Wyspiański with the subject for his haunting play *Wesele* (The Wedding, 1901)—in which Rydel appears as the Bridegroom (*Pan Młody*). In class-conscious Cracow society of the late nineteenth and early twentieth centuries, marriages between peasants and members of the predominant landowning noble class (*szlachta*) were still rare, although a precedent had been established when the artist Włodzimierz Tetmajer (1862–1923, the poet's brother) took as his wife a peasant girl from the nearby village of Bronowice.[43] This tradition-shattering event heralded the begining of the "peasant mania" that became characteristic of Young Poland (consider, for example, Kazimierz Tetmajer's poems and short stories in Tatra mountaineers' dialect, Reymont's novel *The Peasants,* and the attempt, by Michał Pawlikowski, to translate Homer into the mountaineers', or *góral,* dialect).[44] Some ten years after Tetmajer's marriage, Rydel courted and wed his sister-in-law, Jadwisia.[45]

Following his marriage, which lacked the novelty of Tetmajer's, Rydel made every effort to adjust to village life. But he was thoroughly bourgeois and the task was anything but easy. He lacked any real feeling for the country and the peasantry, into whose midst he had voluntarily removed himself. In his desire to acclimatize as rapidly as possible, Rydel transgressed village etiquette on more than one occasion. When he was courting his peasant wife, for example, he made it his practice to call barefoot.[46] He carried this folksiness to such a degree that once, on a visit to the village of his aunt (the *Radczyni* in *The Wedding*), he requested permission to remove his shoes, as this was now his custom.

If Rydel's village antics were not enough to earn him a reputation, his garrulity most certainly was ("in his mouth alone he has the strength of three hundred horses," wrote Boy-Żeleński in his song "The Reveille of the Cracow Brigade," 1908). Fascinated by the comic potential of Rydel's "weakness," Boy-Żeleński returned to it in a number of works. Here, for example, is his vivid account of Rydel's talkativeness from an article on the characters in Wyspiański's *The Wedding:*

> In the children's room in Wielopole Street, as everywhere a bit, Lutek Rydel was loved and ridiculed at the same time. Chiefly on account of his garrulity, which was something unique in the world, gargantuan, something of which I have never found the like. Here is one episode from the time of his premarital adventures, when Lutek lost himself in conversation twice as much as usual. One day he arrives at Wielopole at 2:30 in the afternoon; just for a while, to get something off his chest. The lady of the house offers him some black coffee. "Thanks, but I can't, I have to fly now." "Won't you sit down, *Pan* Lutek?" "I can't, I must leave immediately." The result was that at about 1 in the morning *Pani* Liza telephoned Starzewski at *Czas,* imploring him to come fetch Rydel, because she has no more energy left; he has talked her to death!
>
> Another episode. On the occasion of the 500th anniversary of the Academy (i.e., the University of Cracow, celebrated in 1900), there arrived various well-known foreigners, invited to Cracow homes. Among others was Gabriel Sarrazin, a friend of the Poles, the author of a book about our poets [*Les grandes poètes romantiques de la Pologne,* 1906—HBS]. This Sarrazin ran across Lutek Rydel and here began a most peculiar tournament. Sarrazin, a Frenchman, after all, an elegant chap, rose to the battle; but when he stopped to gather his breath, Rydel broke in and did not let go! The Frenchman turned pale, withered, and blew away completely. The girls and their guests observed this scene through the open doors, just as divers observe a battle of monsters on the ocean floor. At a certain moment, Maryna entered the room and offered Rydel a small draught on a tray. Rydel took it without looking, swallowed the draught, and continued talking![47]

Perhaps Boy-Żeleński's most interesting work on Rydel is the poem "Z podróży Lucjana Rydla na Wschód czyli Grób Agamemnona" (From Lucjan Rydel's Journey to the East, or The Grave of Agamemnon). Presented as part of a program at the Green Balloon, its subject is a trip Rydel once made to the Middle East.

Young Poland was a period rich in tanslation from the Greek and Roman classics as well as from contemporary European authors. Rydel had translated portions of the *Iliad,*[48] while another young Pole, Edmund Cięglewicz, was gaining a reputation on the strength of his translations of the comedies of Aristophanes. The two were entered in a competition for a prize trip to the East offered as a stipend by the Academy of Science in Cracow. Professor Stanisław Tarnowski, the head of the academy, was fond of Rydel. In his opinion, Rydel was the only one of the younger poets with any real talent. Needless to say, Rydel won the award and went on his trip.

In doing so, he was following in the footsteps of another Polish poet, a far greater talent—Juliusz Słowacki—who in 1836 journeyed the Byronic way to Greece and the Holy Land. Słowacki left an impressive poetic account of his sojourn under the title *Podróz do Ziemi Świętej z Neapolu* (A Journey from Naples to the Holy Land). Inspired by Słowacki, to whom the generation of Young Poland turned with excited new interest,[49] Rydel wrote a cycle of poems, *Mitologie* (Mythologies, 1909), about the ancient glories of the lands he had visited and stories with a classical Greek setting. The conscious emulation of Słowacki, one of the greatest poets in the Polish language, on the part of a writer as personally ludicrous as Rydel appeared to many of his contemporaries, seemed the height of incongruity and prompted Boy-Żeleński to write a parody.[50] As the title indicates, the basis of the parody (and again the irreverence is characteristic) is one of the most powerful poems to result from Słowacki's journey to the Middle East, *Grób Agamemnona* (The Grave of Agamemnon). The poem begins with the lines

Niech fantastycznie lutnia nastrojona
Wtóruje myśli posępnej i ciemnej;
Bom oto wstąpił w grób Agamemnona
I siedzę cichy w kopule podziemnej,
Co krwią Atrydów zwalana okrutną;
Serce zasnęło, lecz śni. Jak mi smutno![51]

(Let the lute tuned with fantasy / Accompany a thought sullen and dark; / For I have entered the Grave of Agamemnon / And sit silent in the subterranean cupola / Stained with the cruel blood of the Atridae. / My heart, though asleep, yet dreams. / How sad am I!)

In the first stanza of his parody, Boy-Żeleński calls attention not only to Rydel's garrulity, but (by the capitalization of "grave") to the fact that it is *Słowacki's* grave that Rydel has entered and defiled:

Niech fantastycznie lutnia nastrojona
Wtóruje pieśni tragicznej i smutnej,
Bo—Rydel wstąpił w Grób Agamemnona
I pysk rozpuścił w sposób tak okrutny,
Że rozbudzone na wpół trupy, z cicha
Szepcą do siebie: "Cóz tam znów, u licha?[52]

(Let the lute tuned with fantasy / Accompany a song tragic and melancholic, / For—Rydel has entered the Grave of Agamemnon / And unleashed his yap so horribly. / The half-awakened corpses murmur / To themselves in low tones: "What the hell's going on now?")

Rydel's bourgeois nature, which stands in so glaring a contrast to the loftiness of his *Mythologies,*[53] is underlined in Boy-Żeleński's last two stanzas:

I gdy tak błądzę po Hellady błoniach,
Dziwne mam wizje przed duszy oczyma:
W tej chwili dają do kolacji w Toniach,
Wszyscy zasiedli—tylko mnie tam nie ma—
Na stole kluski . . . i jajka sadzone. . . .
A dzieci mówią "Pod Twoją Obronę" . . .

I wraz otrząsłem się z pogańskich baśni,
Ukląkłem cicho i złożyłem ręce;
I zaraz w sercu stało mi się jaśniej,
I dziękowałem Najświętszej Panience
Za to, że swoich łask mi wciąż użycza
I mnie wysłała tu—nie Cięglewicz . . ."[54]

(And when I wander through the meadows of Hellas, / I have wondrous visions before my mind's eyes: / At this moment they are serving dinner in Tonie [the name of Rydel's village—HBS], / All are seated—only I am absent. / On the table are noodles . . . and fried eggs . . . / And the children are reciting their prayers. And suddenly I shook myself from these pagan reveries, / Kneeled down silently and folded my hands; / And in my heart it grew suddenly brighter, / And I thanked the Most Blessed Virgin / For blessing me with Her grace / And for sending me here—instead of Cięglewicz.)

Photograph of the *szopka* used in Zielony Balonik (Green Balloon) puppet shows.

A favorite vehicle for the talents of Boy-Żeleński and other regular Green Balloon-ers was the annual *szopka,* or puppet show. The success of shadow and puppet shows in the turn-of-the-century Parisian and other cabarets was an obvious source of inspiration but indeed not the only stimulus to generate the Balloon's interest in this type of entertainment. As a reflection of the general popularity of puppet theater in Europe in the late nineteenth and early twentieth centuries, Polish artists of the time rediscovered the domestic Cracovian *szopka.* This was a type of Nativity puppet show in which wooden rod puppets based on biblical and local characters and made to speak in folkish primitive verse were intermixed on a two-tier miniature stage modeled on the design of the Wawel Castle or that of the late medieval Church of Mary in the Main Marketplace of Cracow.[55] Without doubt, the most brilliant literary adaptation of the *szopka* in turn-of-the-century Poland was the dramatist Stanisław Wyspiański's use of it as the structural basis of his greatest play, *The Wedding.* The artists of the Green Balloon were also not slow to realize the possibilities of the form and eagerly set about mounting their own first

Zielony Balonik (Green Balloon) invitation showing *szopka* and puppet figures. (Biblioteka Jagiellońska, Cracow).

szopka. The dolls which they created with a special zeal provided a splendid opportunity for caricaturing well-known personages, while the traditional *szopka* text became simply a framework for songs and skits rich in allusions to such topical issues as the first international soccer matches or Polish representatives in the parliament in Vienna.

The first *szopka* of the Green Balloon was performed in February, 1906—during the second year of the Carcow cabaret's existence. Like all Green Balloon presentations, it was a closed affair before a select audience and was not repeated. Its success stimulated interest in a second *szopka* the following year. Boy-Żeleński, who had just come into closer contact with the Balloon, was asked to do it, and he worked on it together with Witold Noskowski. It had its premiere in February 1907. Planned on a somewhat larger scale than the first *szopka,* it preserved some songs and skits while reshaping others.[56] The next year, the annual Green Balloon *szopka* was not held in its usual place in Michalik's Lwów

Confectionary, but in the Hotel Pod Różą (Under the Sign of the Rose), which was located not far away on Floriańska Street. It ran for almost three hours—a full evening's entertainment, very much in the style of a Parisian review (Boy-Żeleński is careful to mention, however, a Parisian review as found in an artists' cabaret, not a music hall).

The years 1909 and 1910 saw little activity in the Green Balloon. Noskowski was busy with his journalistic work and could devote little time to the cabaret. Boy-Żeleński, anxious to continue song and *szopka* writing, was able to enlist the cooperation of a very few participants and turned instead to his translations of the comedies of Molière. In his reminiscences, he mentions that in three seasons (1908, 1909, 1910) Green Balloon gatherings fell off to such an extent that he visited Michalik's Cave only a few times a year. How different this was from the excitement the Green Balloon had generated in its first period when shows were staged almost weekly and attendance so good Michalik's shop filled to overflowing. But then the unexpected happened. Michalik announced his intention to enlarge the "cave." A second room was to be built in the courtyard and the artist Frycz was commissioned to decorate it. Interest in the Green Balloon reawakened. Boy-Żeleński and Noskowski directed their energies now to the writing of a spectacular new *szopka* which for the first time would be presented before a paying public. The text of the *szopka*—which attracted a large audience—was published in late 1911 and some thirteen times since.[57]

The success of the newest *szopka* and the obvious signs of renewed energy at the Green Balloon stirred old animosities; before long, fresh attacks were levelled against the Balloon itself and against the phenomenon of cabaret in Poland in general. The literary critic Wilhelm Feldman (1868–1919), now the editor of the monthly *Krytyka* (Criticism), wrote a scathing denunciation of Boy-Żeleński as well as the Green Balloon. Under the title "Piosenkarz Zielonego Balonika" (The Songster of the Green Balloon), it appeared in *Krytyka* in 1910. The Green Balloon, which had a ready model, writes Feldman, "there [Paris-HBS] where originate all fashions, all little thrills, all perversions," is described in these terms:

> . . . a narrow cave, deprived of sun and air, enlivened by the manager with works of art as if it were to symbolize the Polish imprisonment . . . all those who are doing nothing on earth, and who know only how to spit on those who are, all those fair spirits with some kind of muse as wife, goddess, or mistress; all unli-

censed counselors of literature and devotees of art—all those together with the curious and the brotherhood of snobs, deeming the world incomplete without their presence at any performance, rendezvoused in these narrow corners, heated by artistic zeal, at these narrow little tables, and under the tables.[58]

As to Boy-Żeleński, Feldman poses the question, What is a cabaret *chansonnier?,* and answers it himself. He is "a little devil casting not coals in a meaningless gesture . . . holding a concave mirror before every hypocrisy, every Judas."[59] In Boy-Żeleński's work Feldman finds none of the poetry, none of the passion that have made of the French chanson a cultural factor. Boy-Żeleński's satire, in Feldman's view, when compared with that of earlier periods, is without ideas, uncreative, and only destructive.

But despite the vehemence of the assaults of Feldman, and others—motivated, in part, by their consternation over the cultivation of what they regarded as frivolity in the wake of the disastrous consequences of the unsuccessful Russian Revolution of 1905 for Poland—it was already too late to turn the clock back. The Green Balloon had now become a legend and Poland was clearly in the grip of cabaret fever. Cabarets began springing up all over the place ("like mushrooms after a rain," in Boy-Żeleński's words)[60] and before long there was hardly a major Polish city that could not boast of its own. After the Green Balloon in Cracow, the most famous in the pre-World War I period was the Momus in Warsaw (recall that this was the name of Willibald Stilpe's cabaret in Otto Julius Bierbaum's novel *Stilpe*). Founded by Arnold Szyfman, whose principal fame rests on his establishment in Warsaw in 1913 of the most successful theater of interwar Poland, the Teatr Polski (Polish Theater), it opened on December 31, 1908, and lasted until the spring of 1911.[61] Although popular and fashionable in its time, the Momus, unlike the Green Balloon, was conceived and operated strictly as a commercial enterprise.

Despite the enthusiasm aroused by the *szopka* of 1911, the Green Balloon's days were numbered. War was around the corner and with it the dawn of Polish independence after one hundred and twenty-five years of partition. In 1912, the last *szopka* of the Green Balloon appeared, written jointly by Boy-Żeleński and Noskowski. But an undeniable evaporation of spirit was all too evident. A year later, with the activities of the Balloon virtually at a standstill, Boy-Żeleński published a collection of Green Balloon songs and other poetry under the title of *Słówka* (Jottings)—the first book of reminiscences about a cabaret named the Green

Zielony Balonik (Green Balloon) invitation with caricatures of *szopka* rod puppet figures (Biblioteka Jagiellońska, Cracow).

Balloon, certainly one of the more interesting among the many that dotted the map of Europe in the early twentieth century. Adding to the interest of the Polish cabaret is the fact that unlike the overwhelming majority of its counterparts elsewhere in Europe, West and East, the Green Balloon can still be visited at the same address on Floriańska Street, now no longer a cabaret but an active café and informal museum of Poland's most famous cabaret all in one. Its premises, most of its furnishings, many of its pictures and puppets, and even a few of the original green balloons are still intact, preserved much as they used to be, a testament to the very conservatism and traditionalism of old Cracow to which the cabaret arose in sharp protest. Of all the ironies of turn-of-the-century Polish life which the Green Balloon was so fond of touting, this may well be the greatest.

CHAPTER SIX

CABARET IN RUSSIA: MORE BATS, CROOKED MIRRORS, AND STRAY DOGS

The first word of the establishment of a cabaret in Russia—in Moscow, to be exact—came in the form of a modest announcement in the magazine *Russky Artist* (Russian Artist) on March 2, 1908 (9:134):

> On February 29, at 11 P.M., the opening of the intimate circle of the "Letuchaya mysh" (The Bat) took place. The goal of the circle is to be a place of repose for its members and, at the same time, a studio for trying out experiments in the different arts, primarily dramatic since the majority of the members are actors in the [Moscow] Art Theater. But artists from other stages as well as several painters, musicians, singers, and writers have also joined it.
>
> The circle is made up of only 40 members so that the premises are quite small. They consist of a cozy cellar in which there is a sufficiently wide stage and an auditorium with a seating capacity of 60.
>
> The idea of the cabaret belongs to the artist of the Art Theater N. F. Baliev who followed the example of the Parisian cabaret, such as the "Cabaret des Quat'z' Arts" where artists gather together and where after a mug of beer or punch one of the artists mounts the stage and sings couplets about topical issues or declaims verses of his own composition.
>
> The stage here is so convenient that one can use it to try out songs in different styles and then take the successful ones before larger audiences. Of course, all of this lies ahead; in the meantime, a group of artists who banded together some time ago wishes to have its own intimate club without cards or vodka.
>
> The decoration of the club was worked on by the artists Simov, Egorov, the sculptor Andreev, and others. The premises impart a very cozy feeling.
>
> All best wishes for the realization of the circle's ambitions.

The name of the first Russian cabaret—The Bat—at once suggests a conscious emulation of the Vienna Fledermaus. As far as the name of the cabaret is concerned, this may be true; Vienna was, after all, the closest major German-language cultural center to Russia at the time in view of the common borders of the Austro-Hungarian and Russian empires dating from the partitions of Poland in the late eighteenth century. The Hapsburg capital was also well known for its gaiety, its cultural splendor, and its multiethnic character and would have acted as a natural magnet for Russian artists and intellectuals. That turn-of-the-century Austrian culture was reasonably well-known in contemporary Russia is easily established. Interest in the works of Arthur Schnitzler, to take a single example, ran high. The fifth volume of a Russian edition of his complete works by V. M. Sablin had appeared in Moscow already in 1906, while in 1908 A. Budkevich's translations of his three marionette plays (*Marionetten*) were published in St. Petersburg.

In view of the relative proximity of Cracow and the existence of a lively cabaret there since 1905, that is three years before the opening of the Moscow Bat, it might be imagined that the Russians could have been inspired as well by the example of the Green Balloon. This was not the case, however, and there is no real reason why it should have been. Although the Poles were a neighboring Slavic people with whom the Russians had had considerable contact through the centuries (to be sure, most of it unfriendly), they were historically a rival power and now a subjugated nation whose culture seemed to hold little appeal. Just as the Poles at the time found it far more natural to turn for inspiration to Paris, or Munich, or even Vienna, than to Russia, which they despised, so too did Russian artists, writers, and thinkers train their sights on the West. This does not mean that the emergence of a successful cabaret in a major Polish city would have passed completely without notice in Russian circles; just that if Russians had heard anything about it, they would have tended to regard it as a provincial offshoot of something most likely Parisian and let the matter go at that without developing further interest in it.

The name Bat for the Moscow cabaret probably did derive from that of the Vienna Fledermaus, but that is where Russian indebtedness to the Viennese experience ends. As the announcement in *Russky Artist* informs, the first Russian cabaret arose wholly within the context of the contemporary Russian theater; even more specifically, it was the creation, indeed virtually impromptu creation, of members of a single theatrical community, then the most famous in the country, the Moscow Art Theater. From its very inception, Russian cabaret emerged from within the theater and throughout its prerevolutionary history never fully divested itself of that affiliation. When members of the Moscow Art Theater company, led by the minor actor Nikita Baliev (1877–1936), decided to form a cabaret-like intimate circle of their own, they mave have been inspired by what they had heard—or seen—of cabaret life in Vienna and the fame of the Fledermaus. Apart from borrowing the name Bat for their enterprise, however, they went on to shape their cabaret along essentially Russian and theatrical lines owing little to Vienna.

To discover the true roots of the first, and most famous, of prerevolutionary Russian cabarets—beyond the apparent inspiration of Vienna—we have to direct our attention not just to the initiative of members of the Moscow Art Theater from whose ranks its charter members were recruited, but to the Theater's custom, beginning in 1902, of holding so-called cabbage parties (*kapustiniki,* from the Russian word for cabbage, *kapusta*) at the end of each winter season in the *maslenitsa* or Shrovetide period before Lent. For the seven weeks of the Lenten fast all theaters in Russia were closed saved for those offering performances by foreign troupes in foreign languages. Because of the prominence of cabbage in the Russian Lenten diet, the end-of-season theater celebration came to be known as *kapustnik,* or cabbage party. Here is how Konstantin Stanislavsky himself describes the first Moscow Art Theater *kapustnik* to which a paying public was admitted (on February 9, 1910) and which was billed as a benefit for the Theater's needier artists:

> The night before the cabbage party the theatre changed beyond recognition. The seats on the main floor were replaced by tables, at which people had their dinner. The waiters were the young actors and pupils who were not engaged in the performance proper. Under the tables we concealed various lighting effects and rattlers. All the barriers in the auditorium were decorated with picturesque tapestries and garlands; from the ceiling hung lanterns, knick-knacks and garlands; on the balconies we hid two orchestras—string and brass; there were huge baskets with rattlers, whistles and toy balloons. The public gathered at 8 P.M. and the auditorium was gradually plunged into darkness. We gave the audience just enough time to get used to the dark and then filled the hall with din: the trumpets blared, the drums beat, the string instruments sang on their highest notes, the wind instruments wheezed, the cymbals rang, the thunder machines of the theatre roared. In fact, we put our entire sound-effect machinery into effect.

At the same time, together with this bacchanalia of sounds, we switched on all the projectors, blinding the audience. And simultaneously we let loose a shower of confetti, serpentine and multicolored balloons from every corner of the auditorium, from the balconies down and from the main floor up.

The programme that evening was extremely diversified.

We staged *Helen of Troy*—a burlesque of the famous operetta, with Nemirovich-Danchenko as conductor. Vasily Kachalov played Menelaus, Olga Knipper was Helen, Ivan Moskvin was Paris and Leopold Sulerzhitsky was Ajax. By public request Sergei Rachmaninov conducted *The Apache Dance,* which was performed by Alisa Koonen and Richard Boleslavsky. . . .

Wrestling was a great fad in those days and we staged two "matches." In the first, a Frenchman (Kachalov), graceful, thin, in tights and female pantaloons, wrestled with a hefty Russian coachman (Gribunin), dressed in a shirt and rolled up pants. There was no wrestling, of course, just a parody of it, a caricature satirizing unscrupulous judges and wrestlers. . . .

There was also the following number.

A huge cannon was rolled out, followed by little Sulerzhitsky in some unknown foreign uniform made of leather and oilcloth. He made a long speech, parodying the English language. His interpreter explained that the "English colonel was preparing to undertake a dangerous trip to Mars. He would be placed in the cannon and shot into the air." Then came his wife. There were touching and tearful farewells, also supposedly in English.

The fearless hero was approached by Kachalov and Gribunin, allegedly dressed as artillerymen. They had just cleaned and oiled the cannon, and now, with small sewing-machine oilers in their hands, they began to oil his costume so that he might slip into the cannon the more easily. Up in the balcony a large hoop covered with white Indian paper was ready to receive the adventurer. Everything was ready. The farewells were over. The brave colonel made his farewell speech before his long journey. He was lifted to the mouth of the cannon and pushed in. Then Kachalov and Gribunin loaded the cannon with powder and lit the gunwick, from the distance—as a precaution. The audience, and especially the ladies, covered their ears, expecting a thunderous explosion. But to the amazement of all, the shot was no louder than the pop of a toy cracker, although the two artillerymen were thrown to the ground, and the auditorium was filled with Sulerzhitsky's horrible cry. The paper hoop was torn and in the hole was the figure of the brave colonel. The brass band struck a flourish. . . .

And there was another number that created a sensation. On our stage we have a revolving ring. Around it we made a low barrier, as in a circus, and placed several rows of chairs. In the background there was a panorama of a circus filled with people. Opposite the audience was the entrance for the circus artists, and an orchestra above it. In the revolving ring was put a wooden horse on which Burdzhalov, dressed as a female bareback rider, danced the *pas de châle,* leaping through paper hoops. Those who held these hoops stood outside the ring while the horse "ran" in the revolving ring.

Then came my number. I appeared as the ring master, in a tailcoat, in a top hat slightly askew for greater effect, in white breeches, white gloves and black shiny boots, with a huge nose, black moustache, thick black eyebrows and a wide black imperial. The circus attendants in their red uniforms lined up, the band struck up a triumphant march, I entered and bowed to the public. After that the chief equerry handed me a whip, I cracked it (it took me a whole week of hard practice to master that) and a trained stallion, played by Alexander Vishnevsky, flew out into the arena.

The circus number ended with a grand finale cotillon by the whole company, headed by Olga Knipper, Kachalov, Moskvin, Luzhsky and Gribunin, who appeared in the ring on toy *papier-mâché* horses with doll legs while I stood at the entrance with a large bell and rang for changes in figures. The actors danced on their own feet.

It was as a master of ceremonies at our cabbage parties that our actor Nikita Baliev first displayed his unusual talent. His inexhaustible humor, ingenuity and wit, his ability to captivate the audience and to balance on the edge of impudence and merriment, insult and joke, and his ability to stop in time and to turn an insult into a joke—all that made him an interesting performer in a new genre.

Baliev was assisted by Nikolai Tarasov, who thought up many entertaining jokes and numbers.[1]

When the *kapustniki* provided the inspiration for the opening of a cabaret that would enable its participants to carry on their impromptu revelries on a more regular basis and beyond the confines of the Moscow Art Theater, an appropriate location was found in the cellar of a building near the Moscow River within the shadows of the Cathedral of the Savior. The Bat remained here until 1910 when, with the original group of forty now expanded to eighty, it moved to a larger cellar near the Telephone Building. Its last move came in 1913. Already a landmark of Moscow night life, and with the public admitted at the then exorbitant fee of twelve rubles a person, it relocated in a spacious cellar beneath Moscow's largest apartment building just off Tverskaya Street.

Following the practice of cabarets elsewhere, the Bat came to life after midnight. The lateness of the hour was not, however, dictated by fashion. It was a practical necessity in view of the fact that the participants in Bat entertainments were almost all theater people whose professional obligations kept them busy during the evening. It was only after a theatrical performance that the actors and actresses involved in the cabaret would descend into the Bat's cellar there to begin performances of strikingly different character than those they had just concluded.

Although virtually all the leading lights of the Moscow Art Theater

Nikita Baliev, the founder of the Moscow Letuchaya mysh (Bat). (Private collection).

participated in Bat evenings—Moskvin, Sulerzhitsky, Tarasov, Luzhsky, Burdzhalov, Chekhov's wife Olga Knipper, and even Stanislavsky and Nemirovich-Danchenko themselves—it readily became apparent that the bit player Nikita Baliev, whose idea it had been in the first place to establish an after-theater intimate circle of actors and actresses, had a special talent for this type of performance. Short, stocky, round-faced, with heavy nose and lips, marvelously expressive eyes, and a thin covering of dark hair lying flat on his head, Baliev was a dynamo of energy ideally suited to the role he now came to assume at the Bat, that of its *conférencier*. If his place in the distinguished Moscow Art Theater company had been only that of a player of small roles, Baliev now came into his own as a performer: energetic, articulate, spontaneous, and imaginative. He was the consummate *conférencier* and so much the moving spirit of the Bat that the cabaret became unthinkable without him. It was indeed Baliev's Bat.

Initially, Bat evenings conformed to a familiar early cabaret pattern in their highly eclectic and impromptu nature. But before long it was obvious that the performers had a special affinity for parody. This may not be difficult to understand. As actors and actresses, they possessed an obvious talent for mimicry. Most of them were affiliated with the weighty and prestigious Moscow Art Theater. When they descended to the cramped and sparsely decorated cellar premises of the Bat they were usually fresh from performances at the Art Theater and often still in costume and makeup. The temptation to mock the very roles they had just stepped out of must have been as great as the environment of the Bat was felicitous to such irreverent play. Free of the imposing institutional setting of the Art Theater, without a public—and critics—to concern themselves with, and unshackled from the generally serious drama the Art Theater was then staging, the performers might understandably enthuse at the opportunity the Bat afforded them to kick up their heels and entertain themselves into the early hours of the morning by improvising spoofs of the plays in which they had just acted.

As we saw earlier, especially in the case of Max Reinhardt's Schall und Rauch in Berlin, theatrical parody was no stranger to cabaret entertainment. But what took place in the Moscow Bat was something different. The dramatic parodies of Reinhardt, Morgenstern, and others in Germany were not, to begin with, the creations of artists drawn almost wholly from a theatrical milieu. Moreover, they were addressed to currently fashionable artistic movements (naturalism, symbolism) which the cabaret performances found ludicrous for a variety of reasons. At the Bat, however, the targets of the parodies were most often the very plays in which the parodists were appearing at the Art Theater. In a very real sense, then, parody at the Bat became a kind of auto- or self-parody, actors and actresses parodying their own performances as well as the plays in which these performances occurred. It was as if the Bat emerged as an alter ego of the Moscow Art Theater itself, a comic double, so to speak, in the best Gogolian sense. Of course, there were plays—usually related to the Symbolist movement—that seemed to lend themselves to parody, as they did in cabarets elsewhere in Europe. The Moscow Art Theater production of Maeterlinck's *The Blue Bird* was one of them. So was Leonid Andreev's gloomy *Anathema,* which the Art Theater had planned to open on September 19, 1909, and of which the Bat had already conceived its own parody to follow immediately thereafter. On this particular occasion, strenuous ecclesiastical objection to Andreev's allegorical drama of existence succeeded in delaying the play's opening, thus thwarting the Bat's plans, at least for the moment. The parody of *The Blue Bird* had come off more smoothly. The Russian premiere of the Maeterlinck play took place at the Art Theater on September 30, 1908. A week later, on October 5, the Bat unveiled its own parody of it. The Moscow Art Theater's production of *Hamlet,* which Gordon Craig had come to Russia to direct in 1912, provided another golden opportunity for Bat parody, the most memorable feature of which was Vakhtangov's comic imitation of the great Russian actor Kachalov's Hamlet. Other well remembered Bat parodies were inspired by Moscow Art Theater productions of Schiller's *Mary Stuart,* and a stage version of Dostoevsky's novel *The Brothers Karamazov.* In some instances, again in a familiar cabaret pattern, the parodies were staged as puppet shows.[2] This seems to have been the case, for example, with the Bat parody of Maeterlinck's *Blue Bird* in which Stanislavsky and Nemirovich-Danchenko played the lead roles. Since Maeterlinck had designated his early programmatic trilogy of 1893 as being "for marionettes," the Bat decided that perhaps it would be only fitting to try staging all of Maeterlinck's plays as if they were written for puppets; hence the inspiration to do *The Blue Bird* in this style. Getting artists to design and execute the marionettes was no problem since several had already become part of the Bat entourage, including N. N. Andreev, a master of caricature in sculpture.

This parody-oriented, highly informal, and closed-to-the-public period in the Bat's history lasted about a theatrical season and a half, that is through the spring of 1909. As the cabaret expanded to about twice its original membership, with actors and actresses from other Moscow theaters invited to join it, and with its doors ever so slightly opened to members of the public fortunate enough to receive its greyish brown and green cards bearing a picture of a bat and the words "The Bat permits you to visit its cellar sometime," the need was felt for larger premises. These were found in the cellar of a house in the Arbatov district of the city along Milyutin Lane (Milyutinsky Pereulok).

The move to new, slightly larger, and more generously decorated quarters had no appreciable bearing on Bat evenings. Parodies still remained the focus of attention and represented the cabaret's real strength. But there were a few more one-act plays and dramatic sketches, dances (modern and inspired especially by Isadora Duncan), and chansons, giving "programs" a somewhat more conventional cabaret appearance. The spirit of the Bat, and the greatest source of its appeal, lay in improvisation, spontaneity, an overall sense of the impromptu and irreverent, attributes that lost none of their vitality with the passage of time or the change of location. Although the audience now included more people than just the member-performers who in the original premises sat around a single long table which they would get up from when their turn came to perform and to which they would return immediately afterward, the Bat retained its character of an intimate circle of primarily theatrical artists whose self-mocking parodies and other revels outsiders considered themselves privileged to be able to observe. That outsiders were permitted in at all, that tickets (of a sort) priced from ten to twenty-five rubles were distributed through a private and informal distribution system,[3] suggests that on some level thought was being given to the cabaret's transformation into a "little," or "miniature" theater. The inspiration for this need not have been the metamorphosis undergone by Max Reinhardt's Schall und Rauch in Berlin from which the Kleines Theater emerged. The Bat members in all likelihood knew of Reinhardt's Kleines Theater and possibly also that it was the outgrowth of a cabaret similar to their own. But "little," "intimate," "chamber," or "miniature" theaters had already become so much the fashion in the late nineteenth and early twentieth centuries, in Russia as well as Europe as a whole, that the Russians had only to view their own theatrical landscape for models.

The professionalism merely hinted at at the Bat in 1910 became still more evident in 1912. The catalyst for change in this direction may have been Nikita Baliev's fortunes at the Moscow Art Theater. Never more than a bit player in the company, Baliev's star role at the Bat made it obvious to most that what he clearly lacked as a dramatic performer, as an actor, he handsomely made up for with his remarkable talent as a cabaret *conférencier* and entertainer. If he never seemed entirely comfortable at the Moscow Art Theater, he was wholly in his element at the Theater's comic double, the Bat. That Baliev may have come to realize this himself seems evident from his decision to quit the Moscow Art Theater company at the end of the 1911/1912 season. The fact that he had only two small parts to play that entire season, and one of those was without words,[4] could only have convinced him of his own expendability. Yet Baliev was not anxious to make a complete break with the Art Theater. He explained to Stanislavsky and Nemirovich-Danchenko that he wanted to devote more time to the activities of the Bat and that he was thinking of enlarging it, possibly along the lines of a miniature theater, but that he wanted to retain his membership in the Moscow Art Theater company and take part in productions whenever he was asked. Although sympathetic to his goals, both Stanislavsky and Nemirovich-Danchenko refused his request to retain a position at the Moscow Art Theatre while undertaking a more enhanced role at the Bat. It was a question of either/or and the choice was Baliev's to make. By now feeling a greater personal commitment to the Bat, Baliev decided to leave the Moscow Art Theater which he declared his attention to do at the close of the spring season 1912. Simultaneously with the announcement to leave the Art Theater, Baliev announced the opening of a new expanded Bat scheduled for the fall of 1912.

"Expansion" meant little more than a slight enlargement of the premises on Milyutin Lane. A few more tables were added, but chairs were still unnumbered and the intimacy and club-like atmosphere of the original Bat were retained. Before Baliev eventually emigrated from Russia after the Revolution, in 1920, and reestablished The Bat as the Chauve Souris ("bat" in French) at the Théâtre Femina in Paris, the cabaret underwent a final move that completed its gradual transformation into a miniature theater. When the Milyutin Lane location was at last exchanged for one in the basement of the eleven-story Nirensee building in the heart of Moscow, then the tallest building in the city, in the vicinity of the bustling Tverskaya Avenue, the tables that had become virtually a Bat landmark were gone, their place taken instead by neat little rows of numbered chairs. The informal playing area of before was now replaced by something more closely resembling a real, albeit miniature, auditorium with a real stage and curtain and even boxes. A foyer and buffet were also added, outfitted with furniture showing no small influence of

Art Nouveau, and with the walls decorated for the most part with neatly arranged pictures and photographs of members of the Bat company.

The slightly altered premises to which guests descended in the fall of 1912 were but a foretaste of the cabaret's later metamorphosis. More of the public was in evidence as much sought-after tickets to Bat evenings were made available in larger numbers and by means of a more orderly distribution system. Performances began at half past eleven at night, instead of the usual midnight, but within half a year this, too, was changed; the new time was a more commercial half past eight. Some things, however, remained impervious to change. Guests were still greeted by a bubbly Baliev attired in formal black tie with his familiar white chrysanthemum boutonniere and were still expected to sign a huge register.

In terms of its program, the "new" Bat of 1912 was already something of an adumbration of the future miniature theater. Parodies, mostly of theaters, theater persoanlities, and plays rather than of specific productions, remained as prominent and as popular as before. There were also dances, songs, and declamations and with these, as well with the theatrical "numbers," the effort was made to achieve an illusion of the old informality and spontaneity, although planning was obviously now going into performances. The absence of a plainly demarcated auditorium and stage made possible the direct contact between performer and viewer that was at the heart of the early cabaret experience. This, together with the carefully cultivated aura of the unrehearsed, improvised, and amateurish, made the audience feel that they were both privileged onlookers as well as participants in the spontaneous revels of an intimate circle of artists.

Where the Bat gave the greatest indication of the direction in which it was heading and the entertainment with which it would score its greatest fame was in its "living-doll" productions. Since theater-oriented parody had inherent limitations with respect to an ever increasing paying public—the parodies necessitated, after all, a knowledge of what was being parodied, which many in a public audience would simply not have possessed—the Bat had to broaden its theatrical repertoire. Baliev tried to solicit contributions from major contemporary writers such as Blok and Gorky but without success, not because they were disinterested in the Bat but because they were unfamiliar with cabaret theater and uncertain as to what to write for it. By way of a solution to the problem of a repertoire, Baliev and others at the Bat hit upon the idea of adapting short plays from the Russian theatrical tradition to cabaret performance and of creating their own stage versions of classics of Russian literature. In the first category, the short plays by such writers as Turgenev and Chekhov, particularly the latter, offered excellent ready-made material. But it was with works of the second category that the Bat scored some of its greatest successes. Before long, Pushkin's famous story *Pikovaya dama* (The Queen of Spades) and his romantic poem "Bakhchisaraisky fontan" (The Fountain of Bakhchisarai), Lermontov's poem "Kaznacheisha" (The Lady Treasurer), Gogol's comic prose masterpieces *O tom, kak Ivan Ivanovich ssorilsya s Ivanom Nikiforovichom* (How Ivan Ivanovich Quarreled with Ivan Nikiforovich) and *Shinel* (The Overcoat), stories by Chekov, the immensely popular aphorisms by the nineteenth-century parodist and satirist Kozma Prutkov (the pen-name actually of the writers Count Aleksei Tolstoy, 1817–75, and Aleksei Zhemchuzhnikov, 1821–1908), and others became regular items in an expanded Bat repertoire. Dance, song, and music were also often woven into the performances, adding to the audience's visual and auditory pleasure.

A still more original departure for the Bat were its so-called living-doll numbers. These were outgrowths of the cabaret's puppet and shadow shows which originally served as vehicles of theatrical parody. In the "new" Bat of 1912 and afterward similar performances continued to be presented, but they soon gave way to a more visually striking type of entertainment—silent or music-accompanied scenes in which real actors and actresses, pretending to be puppets, marionettes, or dolls, compose an inanimate picture or tableau and then, at a certain point, spring to life, dance, sing, recite dialogue in verse or prose, and then at the end of the production return to their original "lifeless" state. The affinities with Stravinsky's ballet *Petrouchka,* of course, come to mind, but rather than think of influence it would be more productive in this instance to isolate the common source or sources of such closely related phenomena, above all the great contemporary interest among artists in both puppet and marionette.

The living-doll productions of the Bat fell generally into two major categories. One was made up of works of an international, or cosmopolitan, character, not based on anything specifically Russian, such as "Minuet," after a tale by de Maupassant, "Porcelaine de Copenhagen" and

"Porcelaine de Sèvres," in which the actors and actresses represented elaborately costumed china figures (or figurines) that come to life, "The Musical Snuff-Box," "La Granda Opera Italiana," which featured the street performance of an opera as a play-within-a-play, "Under the Eyes of Our Ancestors," based on the old French gavotte "The Scales of Destiny," with an Oriental setting, and the Bat's most famous living-doll number, "The Parade of the Wooden Soldiers," which was staged for the first time in 1911 by Evgeni Vakhtangov.

Since the living-doll productions depended as much for their success on their visual appeal as on the skill with which the performers executed the transition from dolls to living actors and actresses and then back again to dolls, more and more emphasis was placed on colorfulnesss of setting and brilliance of costuming. The outfits of the traditional masks of the Italian commedia dell'arte—Harlequin, Pierrot, and Colombine, above all—were particularly attractive in this regard and provided the inspiration for several productions. So, too, did the period of late eighteenth-century France, of France, that is, of the rococo style. The more the visual became paramount in Bat performances the more the cabaret relied on the cooperation of painters who not only designed costumes, sets, and programs, but whose sketches came to constitute a stunning visual record of productions. Whether because of the great popularity of the Bat, in Russia and later in emigration, or Baliev's personal powers of persuasion—or a combination of both—such well-known figures in early twentieth-century Russian painting as Aleksandr and Nikolai Benois, Nikolai Remizov, Vasili Sukhaev, and Sergei Sudeikin eventually came to enjoy a close affiliation with the cabaret. Decorativeness, love of color, and a certain fairy-tale quality—as if they were executing illustrations for children's books—were characteristic of the style of whatever they did for the Bat. But where this shows up most effectively is in their designs for numbers inspired by native Russian material. It is works of this type that constituted the second major category of Bat living-doll productions. Some of these were based on Russian folk tradition and popular culture, particularly the *lubok,* or cheap print; this was the case, for example, with "Katinka," inspired by an old Russian polka of the 1860s, "Trepak," a Russian ballet dance suggested by Chaikovsky's "Casse-Noisette," "By the Gates of Judgment," originally a story by Count Aleksei Tolstoy, and "Gostinny dvor," with its setting of a bazaar in old St. Petersburg. Others were theatricalized versions of classic paintings such as Repin's *Zaporozhian Cossacks Drafting a Letter to the Sultan* or of recently exhibited and popular canvases such as F. A. Malyavin's *Vikhr* (The Whirlwind), which the Bat staged as a living-doll production under the title of "Baby" (Peasant Women).

As time went on and the Bat was well established now as a theater of miniatures with its own company, the living-doll routines became widely acknowledged as the cabaret's leading attraction. Because their appeal was primarily visual they could easily be enjoyed by non-Russian audiences who needed no knowledge of the language to enjoy the brilliant display of color and costume, the cleverness of conception and virtuosity of execution of many of the living-doll numbers, and the stylized Russian folkishness of the productions overall. When the Bat was reestablished a few years after the Russian Revolution in Paris as the Chauve-Souris, it was precisely because of the universal appeal of the living-doll performances that the cabaret became a success in its new home and indeed went on to achieve international distinction.

Before Baliev's emigration to Paris in 1920 and the complete transformation of the Bat into a theater of visual delight, the living-doll numbers were complemented by several other types of entertainments designed to showcase the talents of newer members of the cabaret's company. Often sharing the duties of *conférencier* along with Baliev himself was the talented and popular raconteur Yakov Yuzhny whose stories about Odessa were among his most popular and who was known especially for his intonation.[5] Another highly successful performer at the Bat was the "singing actor" Viktor Khenkin who sang Russian folk, Georgian, and Ukrainian humorous songs but was esteemed, above all, for his dramatic renditions of the lyrical and satirical songs of the Frenchman Béranger.[6] The master reciter of poetry at the Bat was the veteran actor of the Moscow Korsh Theater, Boris Borisov. Highly regarded for his interpretations of such classic Russian theatrical roles as Famusov (in Griboedov's *Woe from Wit*), the Mayor (in Gogol's *The Inspector General*), and Rasplyuev (in Sukhovo-Kobylin's *Trilogy*), Borisov developed a fascination for cabaret performance and became a member of the Bat troupe without severing his ties to the Korsh Theater. Like Khenkin, Borisov also performed the songs of the popular Béranger, often accompanying himself, like Wedekind, on the guitar. But it was for his acting, especially in dramatizations of Chekhov's stories, and for his declamation of poems by Pushkin, Turgenev (the "poems in prose"), and Nekrasov that he was most admired. Borisov was an impressive theatrical presence, particularly on the small stage of a cabaret. Of above average height, corpulent, and mostly bald, he possessed a large, immensely expressive oval face usually enlivened by a roguish smile. Despite his size, he was exceptionally agile in his movements and brought to his acting, singing, and recitation an impressive range of vocal expression.[7]

On the occasion of the tenth anniversary of the founding of the Bat, N. E. Efros published a copiously illustrated survey of the first decade of artistic work of what he termed "the first Russian theater-cabaret." Entitled *Teatr "Letuchaya mysh" N. F. Balieva* (The "Bat" Theater of N. Baliev), it was published by the journal *Solntse Rossii* (Sun of Russia) in Petrograd in 1918. Judging from Efos' account, the Bat hued to the program format described above virtually to the time of Baliev's flight from the Soviet Union. The only departure from the norm was represented by a few generally successful efforts by the Bat to mount several operatic works of its own invention, among them Pushkin's humorous narrative poem *Graf Nulin* (Count Nulin) set to music as a comic opera, and a special Bat operatic version of Pushkin's *Queen of Spades*. The latter was the less well received of these two more ambitious productions, in Efros' opinion because of the audience's familiarily with and continued loyalty to the Chaikovsky version of the same work.[8]

We may never be able to accurately reconstruct the steps that led to Baliev's decision to emigrate from Russia in 1920, but it is not hard to imagine what may have prompted his flight. After surviving the difficult years of the first World War and then the upheaval of the Revolution of 1917, Baliev might well have reasoned that the bloody civil war between Reds and Whites that followed in the wake of the Revolution and the horrendous economic misery of the country in that strife-torn period created inhospitable conditions for the continued well-being of a cabaret such as the Bat. Had he been able to peer into a crystal ball and see the amelioration of Russian life and the opportunities for entrepreneurs like himself created by the partial and limited free enterprise made possible by the New Economic Policy of 1921–28, he might have had second thoughts about leaving the country. But in 1919, when he apparently had made up his mind to emigrate, conditions in the new Soviet state were dreadful and to Baliev it might well have seemed this was his last chance to make a new life for himself before everything collapsed around him.

From Letuchaya Mysh to Chauve-Souris

Baliev's emigration from the Soviet Union followed a route taken by many in that chaotic period—from European Russia to the Caucasus, thence to Constantinople by boat, and eventual resettlement in Paris. Emigration and the change of cultures in no way seemed to blunt Baliev's drive. By 1921, he had already rounded up some of the best members of the original company such as Deikarkhanovna and Fechtner, recruited new members from among the growing Russian émigré community in Paris, above all the artists Nikolai Remizov and Sergei Sudeikin, contracted for the use of the premises of the Théâtre Femina, and launched the second career of the Bat cabaret under its new name of the Théâtre de la Chauve-Souris.

If not instantaneous, success was anything but slow in coming to the reborn Bat. The large number of Russian émigrés in Paris, many of whom certainly knew the Bat, if only by reputation, eagerly sought out performances which on some level provided contact with the culture they had left behind. But so great was the French interest at the time in the events in Russia and the emergence of a new Russian émigré culture in their midst that the Chauve-Souris was also able to attract respectable numbers of French theatergoers. Whatever language barrier existed was easily surmounted. To be sure, Baliev made a point of introducing more numbers with French dialogue and song. So visual, however, were Chauve-Souris performances that the cabaret indeed spoke a universal tongue of color and movement in which language was a greatly diminished presence and for which translation was unnecessary.

The first Chauve-Souris program in Paris ran seven full weeks and did much to earn the cabaret a secure place in the constellation of Parisian nighttime entertainment. International recognition also followed hard upon the first success in France. Word of the latest sensation in Paris traveled far and wide and invitations to tour other European cities soon arrived. The Chauve-Souris had two enthusiastically greeted visits, for example, to London at the Pavillion and Apollo theaters.

The Bat's first American tour (as the Chauve-Souris, the name it was known best by in this country), which began on February 3, 1922, at the Forty-Ninth Street Theater in New York, may be seen as a logical outgrowth of the cabaret's growing reputation in the West. Only to see it in that light, however, would fail to do justice to the man who arranged the tour, Morris Gest, undoubtedly the most flamboyant impresario in America at the time and a figure cut from the same cloth as the legendary Sol Hurok. Gest was a Russian Jew who had come to America as a boy and had made his name as a booking agent for the Hammersteins. Gest's specialty was the big spectacle production, above all musical, and by the time he came to arrange the Chauve-Souris' first New York engagement he had already acquired an immense reputation for his showmanship and entrepreneurial talent. Gest's search for productions carried him frequently to Europe, with his comings and goings regularly reported as celebrity news in the press. After the Chauve-Souris had begun to catch on in Paris and already had made a successful visit to London, Gest would have lost little time in viewing a performance or two for himself and setting the wheels in motion for a first American tour.

But Gest's interest in a theatrical company such as the Chauve-Souris was motivated not only by commercial considerations. Although he came to the United States as a young boy, Gest carried with him through life a certain nostalgic affection for Russian culture. Once he had become an impresario he had a keen eye out especially for Russian talent and seemed sincere in his desire to make the best of Russian performing arts better known in his adopted land. It was Gest, for example, who first brought the Ballets Russes to the United States and who engaged the brilliant choreographer Michel Fokine for two of his musical extravaganzas, *Aphrodite* and *Mecca*. His major accomplishment in this respect was the first American tour of the Moscow Art Theater which he arranged in 1923. Indeed, in view of the great impact that the Art Theater had, especially on the professional American theatrical community in the 1920s, Gest's place in American stage history has been obscure for too long.

Although the Moscow Art Theater tours achieved greater visibility than those of the Chauve-Souris, the cabaret-theater was very well received in the United States and Gest could again take pleasure from his role in bringing another significant achievement of Russian art (which is how he would have viewed it) before the American public.

The first New York engagement of the Chauve-Souris took place on February 3, 1922 before a "brilliant invited audience" (as the program notes describe it)—invited, it should be pointed out, by Morris Gest himself. The engagement was a huge success. On April 21 that same year the Russian cabaret celebrated its one hundredth performance in the

United States. Another fifty-three performances were to take place before the Chauve-Souris began a special summer engagement on June 3, 1922, at the Century Roof, which was redecorated in Russian style for the occasion at considerable expense.

Despite the flight of Baliev (for Balieff, as his name was always transliterated in the West) from the Soviet Union and the émigré status of the Bat, the cabaret gave benefit performances while in New York for the then popular cause of aid to the homeless and starving in postrevolutionary Russia. On Sunday evening, April 9, 1921, one such benefit raised over $10,000 for the relief of "starving Russian artists of the theatre and their children in Moscow, Petrograd and Odessa, enabling the immediate delivery through Herbert Hoover and the American Relief Administration of over one thousand food parcels, each containing 117 pounds of substantial and wholesome food."[9] Several well-known players of the American stage, among them Ed Wynn, Al Jolson, Lillian and Dorothy Gish, Marilyn Miller, and Leon Errol, participated in the benefit in the capacity of house staff to Baliev and his artists.

Another gala evening took place on April 26 that same year, when the American Committee for Devastated France bought out the entire house for an invitational performance in honor of Marshal Joffre. Special French numbers were added to the program and Baliev conducted most of his part of the program in French out of courtesy to the distinguished visitor.

So popular was the Chauve-Souris in New York that its Century Roof tour continued to be extended, with the result that the cabaret had an unbroken engagement of sixty-five weeks before finally closing on May 8, 1923. Among the more extravagant claims for the impact of the Chauve-Souris was one that attributed to it

> the returning wave of sympathy for the Russian people which is sweeping over this country today and which is taking the form of all kinds of benefits and funds to aid the starving millions and to back up the splendid work which Herbert Hoover and the American Relief Administration are doing. America has a natural kinship with Russia. Both countries and both peoples are extremely democratic.
>
> Today the bond of sympathy and understanding between America and Russia is being knit firmly together again. There is a Russian fad in dressing. There is wide-spread interest in Russian art, in Russian music, in Russian operas, in Russian literature. All these signs point to renewed sympathy and understanding. And the Chauve-Souris should receive much of the credit for this change of heart.[10]

Such enthusiasm became a commonplace in American accounts of tours that took the Chauve-Souris across the length and breadth of the United States in the 1920s. If the praise today strikes us as extravagant, it nevertheless behooves us to remember that the kind of entertainment offered by the visiting Russian cabaret was something new, something fresh and exhilirating in the American theater of the time and audiences and critics responded accordingly. We can see this, for example, in the personal reminiscences of Thoda Cocroft whom Morris Gest hired as press agent for the second tour of the cabaret that carried the group from San Francisco across the country back to New York. Cocroft wrote:

But I knew I had engaged for the tour and next night I was watching Balieff and his Chauve-Souris at the Shubert Theatre in Philadelphia, in the characteris-

The Moscow Bat in Hollywood. Nikita Baliev and Charlie Chaplin. (Private collection).

The Moscow Bat in Hollywood. Baliev (the figure in tails to the right) and his company together with Charlie Chaplin (center rear). (Private collection).

tic daze of intoxicated delight that the crazy, gay, Russian scenery, music and acting and original drill of "The Wooden Soldiers" elicited from audiences everywhere on its first road tour.

Today Russian treatment of color and design is an old story, Russian music is radio-worn, Russian witticisms hackneyed, and the Wooden Soldiers are tiresome vaudeville, bromides. But when Balieff's Chauve-Souris burst brightly on the more or less drab scene, it was absolutely unique and to the American public, utterly enchanting in its variety, color, and humor.[11]

And again, at another point:

After all, it was not vaudeville according to the American tradition, nor was it musical comedy, and yet there was an endless variety of musical numbers, singing, dancing, clowning, pantomime, splashy colorings, haunting gypsy melodies. From the standpoint of charm, interest, and beauty no American vaudeville or cabaret had ever approximated it. The Master of Ceremonies role, assumed by Balieff, which has long since been worn to rags, was fresh and novel then, especially the feature of inducing the audience to join in the spirit of the entertainment and shout aloud in Russian, applaud in a certain manner and take sides against itself. (p. 224)

If imitation is truly the most sincere form of flattery, then the impact of the Moscow Bat / Paris Chauve-Souris on the American theater is best attested by the imitative annual specials known as the *The Grand Street Follies* which became the high point of the New York Neighborhood Playhouse in the 1920s. Alice Lewisohn Crowley, one of the founders of the theater, makes the following comments about the indebtedness of the Playhouse's *Grand Street Follies* to Baliev's Chauve Souris in her book of reminiscences, *The Neighborhood Playhouse: Leaves from a Theatre Scrapbook:*

> *The Chauve-Souris* had made its bow in New York a few months before, and echoes of its whimsical naïve character were often heard at the Playhouse. Balieff was an excellent subject for Helen's wit [Helen Arthur, another leading figure at the Playhouse—HBS], and within ten days *The Grand Street Follies of 1922,* christened by Helen, bubbled fresh, crisp and sparkling.
>
> Apparently sceptical of the homemade brew, the subscribers for whom it was given gratuitously responded at first in small numbers. But the infectious delight of those who came blazed a trail for *The Follies* from one end of the city to the other. The two succeeding performances originally scheduled created almost a panic of excitement. I have never before heard the walls echo with such robust applause. The spontaneity of the playing reached out, capturing the spectators until they too entered the performance, sharing in the refrains of some of the songs as though the theatre contained one large family of players.
>
> . . . *The Follies* had now become an event not merely of local interest; it was received by the satiated critic and Broadway audiences as an innovation which neither the long pilgrimage to Grand Street nor the sweltering heat could mar.[12]

Meanwhile, Back in Moscow

Baliev had emigrated from the Soviet Union in 1920; enough members of the Bat troupe joined him in emigration to enable him, as we have seen, to reestablish the Bat in Paris as the Chauve-Souris. His emigration, however, did not at once end the existence of a Bat cabaret in Moscow. Efforts were made to keep it alive by using the talents of those performers who did not choose to emigrate and by recruiting new performers for it. But the efforts proved unsuccessful and the Letuchaya mysh (Bat) closed in 1922, its premises on Gnezdikovsky Alley now taken over by a new (and lesser) cabaret named Krivoi Dzhimmi (Crooked Jimmy), which itself closed down in May 1924. It was directed at the time by A. G. Alekseev and actually represented a union of the post-Baliev Bat, the Grotesk, and Crooked Jimmy.[13]

Program of the Moscow Bat/Chauve Souris from an American tour in the 1920s. The cover was painted by Sergei Sudeikin. (Private collection).

The inability to sustain a cabaret culture in the Soviet period, manifest in the failures of the post-Baliev Bat, Crooked Jimmy, and several others, was not paralleled in the decade before the Revolution. Because of its brilliant success both in prerevolutionary Russia and, subsequently, abroad, the Bat has tended to become the focus of most of the interest in the pre-Soviet Russian cabaret. But the Bat, for all its brilliance, was not the sum total of early twentieth-century Russian cabaret.

Hardly had the Bat opened its doors in Moscow toward the end of February 1908 when its early success inspired the establishment of other cabaret or cabaret-like theaters. The most important owe much of their stature to the theater personalities associated with them.

Meyerhold's Interludes

The first was the ill-fated Lukomore (Strand) which perhaps the most gifted Russian theater director of the twentieth century, Vsevolod Meyerhold, opened in the former Yusupov Palace on the Liteiny Prospekt in St. Petersburg in 1909. The opening program, which Meyerhold worked on together with the artists M. Dobuzhinsky and I. Bilibin, consisted of five items, chief among them two short Russian dramatic works—*Chest i mest* (Honor and Revenge), a buffonade written by Fyodor Sollogub (1848–1890), and *Petrushka,* a folk farce by the playwright Pyotr Potyomkin—and a Russian stage adaptation of Edgar Allan Poe's *The Fall of the House of Usher.* The evening was essentially one of theatrical parody, in which Meyerhold was becoming increasingly interested. Although elegantly executed and staged, the literary quality of the program was faulty and this according to Konstantin Rudnitsky, Meyerhold's principal Soviet biographer, assured its failure.[14] Whether for this reason or the program's inordinate length—it ran from 8 to 11:30 P.M., coinciding, in this case disadvantageously, with the normal Russian theater hours of the time—Meyerhold's Strand established a record of sorts for the rapidity of a cabaret's demise: it closed within a week.[15]

Chastened by the failure of his Strand, Meyerhold desisted from further initiatives in the area of cabaret theater for another two years. In the autumn of 1910, however, he made a second (and final) foray into the world of the cabaret, opening the Dom intermedii (House of Interludes). Meyerhold then held the position of director of the Russian imperial theaters, which obviously inhibited his ability to engage in the type of avant-garde theatrical experimentation toward which his natural inclinations then gravitated. It was to satisfy these inclinations that he created his alter ego of Dr. Dapertutto (the name derived from a character in E. T. A. Hoffmann's *Adventure on New Year's Eve*), under whose guise he could step outside his official position to conduct theatrical experiments in studios or small theaters. It was in this spirit that the Strand and, two years later, the House of Interludes were established.

After learning some lessons from the Strand failure, Meyerhold gave more careful thought to what he wanted his new outing, The House of Interludes, to conceptualize. In order to achieve a more authentic cabaret environment, he arranged to take over the premises of the very small former Skazka (or Story) Theater, which was also located in St. Petersburg, and to redesign its interior along more familiar cabaret lines. The theater's footlights were removed, small tables replaced rows of chairs, and a staircase was built that extended from the stage into the auditorium. Meyerhold's new undertaking, which enlisted the talents of the contemporary Petersburg theatrical elite, was officially sponsored by the Fellowship of Actors, Writers, Musicians, and Artists of which Meyerhold himself was the principal organizer.

Unlike the Strand, which had performed during regular Russian theater hours, the House of Interludes was conceived of as a late-night cabaret offering not just one-act plays (like the Strand), but a varied repertoire which was to include farces from different periods, comedies of different types, pantomimes, and even operettas.[16] The opening program, which was presented on October 9, 1910, consisted of a musical comedy, a pastorale, a burlesque, and the one memorable production of the night, a version of Schnitzler's pantomime *The Veil of Pierrette* (*Sharf Kolombiny,* Colombine's Scarf, in Russian), with music by Dohnány and settings and costumes by Nikolai Sapunov. Composed of three scenes further subdivided into fourteen brief episodes, Meyerhold's successful effort to use the Schniztler pantomime as the basis for a macabre Hoffmannesque grotesque was dedicated to the poet and dramatist Aleksandr Blok (1880–1921) whose commedia dell'arte-inspired playlet *Balaganchik* (The Fair Booth Show) had been staged by Meyerhold in 1906.

Despite the sinister effectiveness of *Colombine's Scarf* as a pantomime grotesque, Meyerhold still had not hit upon the proper mix of ingredients to fashion a credible cabaret. Significantly, apart from his version of the Schniztler pantomime, the rest of the opening night program made no overwhelming impression on the audience. Sensing perhaps that the House of Interludes was destined to fare only slightly better than the Strand, Meyerhold went ahead with just one more program. It was presented on December 3, 1910, and like the first program was built around a single theatrical centerpiece, Meyerhold's staging of a new comedy called *Obrashchonny prints* (The Transfigured Prince), which was written by a contemporary dramatist, Evgeni Znosko-Borovsky (1884–1954). The production featured designs by Sergei Sudeikin and music by one of Meyerhold's closest and most talented collaborators in this early period of his career, the poet, playwright, and musician Mikhail Kuzmin (1875–1936) who shared Meyerhold's enthusiasm for cabaret. Inspired by the traditional Spanish theater, Znosko-Borovsky's play, like the earlier production of Schnitzler's *Veil of Pierrette,* served essentially as the pretext for a particular Meyerholdian theatrical vision, in this instance a "free composition on the theme of the primitive theater."[17]

Despite the original elements in the productions of *Colombine's Scarf* and *The Transfigured Prince* and their contributions to his personal development as a theatrical innovator, Meyerhold had failed in his two fledgling efforts to create a new Russian cabaret that would rival and perhaps even surpass the success of the Bat. Meyerhold himself was hardly unaware of his failure with both the Strand and the House of Interludes, but his interest in cabaret remained high and not too much time was to elapse before he became involved in yet another, and far more gratifying, attempt to place his own stamp on the Russian cabaret culture of the early twentieth century. Before we take a look at the rise and fall of the St. Petersburg Brodyachaya sobaka (Stray Dog) and Meyerhold's role in its development, let us return to the year 1908, when the Moscow Bat arose, to consider the fate of one of the best known and most interesting Russian miniature theaters—the Krivoe zerkalo (Crooked Mirror)—which was established in St. Petersburg at the same time as Meyerhold's Strand.

The Crooked Mirror

The Crooked Mirror was the brainchild of the prominent theater critic A. R. Kugel (who often used the pseudonym Homo Novus; 1864–1928), the editor of the journal *Teatr i Iskusstvo* (Theater and Art), and his wife, the actress Zinaida Kholmskaya (1866–1936).[18] Obviously inspired by the Moscow Bat as well as by what the Russians were learning at the time about the spread of cabaret in central and eastern Europe, Kugel and Kholmskaya originally conceived of the Crooked Mirror as a combination cabaret and theater in which short plays, generally one-acters, would alternate with various other types of stage entertainment along familiar cabaret lines.

The marked theatrical orientation of the Crooked Mirror from the outset is understandable for two main reasons. First, both Kugel and Kholmskaya were professionally involved in drama and theater and tended to see in cabaret a type of theatrical environment in which they could produce primarily shorter dramatic works that might be difficult, if not impossible, to stage in any regular theaters at the time. Second, as people who lived and breathed theater, both Kugel and his wife, but especially Kugel, were convinced that the contemporary Russian stage was in a state of crisis and that something had to be done to halt further erosion. They were concerned about the quality of contemporary Russian drama, which they saw dominated by the extremes of naturalism and symbolism; they also felt that the time had come to end the hegemony of the conservative tradition-bound imperial theater system to which they attributed restraints on acting and directing that left experimentation the domain principally of small private theaters which had little if any hope of commercial success. Their attitude toward the exaggerated realism of the Moscow Art Theater was one of disdain, but the Symbolist-influenced abstraction of Meyerhold and the Englishman Gordon Craig equally failed to arouse their enthusiasm.

The principal weapons chosen by Kugel and Kholmskaya in their campaign against dramatic and theatrical styles they opposed were parody and satire and it was above all as a platform for such works that the Crooked Mirror was established. That is why, in fact, the theater-cabaret was given its name: the crooked mirror is that grotesque mirror of parody and satire which, by reflecting distorted images, makes fresh vision possible. Writing about the founding of the Crooked Mirror in his book of reminiscences as a theater critic, *Listya z dereva* (Leaves from a Tree) in 1926, Kugel aptly characterized it as a theater of "skepticism and negation."[19]

By a curious stroke of fate, the opening performance of the Crooked Mirror took place on the same day (December 6, 1908) and on the same premises (the St. Petersburg Theater Club on Liteiny Avenue) as Meyerhold's star-crossed Strand. Meyerhold's group performed during the normal theater hours of 8 to 11:30 P.M., and was then followed by the Crooked Mirror which took the stage, more in the tradition of cabaret, from midnight until two in the morning. The opening night program of the Crooked Mirror at once established its parodic-satiric orientation. The principal parody of the evening was based on the play *Dni nashego zhizni* (Days of Our Lives, 1908) by one of the best known Russian playwrights and prose writers of the early twentieth century, Leonid Andreev (1871–1919). Although a popular writer in his time, Andreev's philosophically pretentious but basically shallow plays and symbolically overloaded allegories were held in light regard by his fellow artists. Like D'Annunzio or Maeterlinck, he was a favorite target of dramatic parody. Andreev was a prolific dramatist whose *oeuvre* encompasses a wide range of styles. An early play, *Days of Our Lives,* about the life of a poor student drawn, in part, on Andreev's own experiences as a law student in St. Petersburg and Moscow, still hewed to the realism of the second half of the nineteenth century.

The second major item on the opening night of the Crooked Mirror was a short satirical play by one of the most popular and successful Russian miniaturists of the twentieth century, N. A. Teffi (pseudonym of Nadezhda Buchinskaya, née Lokhvitskaya, 1872–1952). The play, *Lyubov v vekakh* (Love through the Ages), uses its survey of the evolution of love from the apes to the twenty-first century as a means of satirizing the turn-of-the-century obsession with sexuality.

So enthusiastic was the reception of the Crooked Mirror's opening night program that Kugel and Kholmskaya were convinced that the parodic-satiric emphasis of their theater-cabaret was capable of striking responsive chords and that this should continue to be the main line of the Crooked Mirror's development. That this was indeed the case is borne out by the fact that not only did the Crooked Mirror become famous for its dramatic parodies and satires, above all the former, but that not much impact was made by the other items on the programs. As if reflecting the chief interests of Kugel and Kholmskaya themselves, however, even these so to speak secondary program features tended more often to be dramatic rather than musical, choreographical, or narrative.

The basic format of the Crooked Mirror remained essentially unchanged until 1910, that is for two years after its opening, when Kugel and Kholmskaya handed over the direction of the cabaret to Nikolai Evreinov (1879–1953), a dramatist, theorist, and stage director of considerable talent who deservedly ranks as one of the greatest Russian theatrical minds of the twentieth century. When Evreinov assumed direction of the Crooked Mirror in 1910 he accomplished its transformation from a combination theater club and cabaret into a full-fledged, autonomous theater. Evreinov's change was actually less revolutionary than it may at first seem or as it is sometimes presented. Between the time of its founding in 1908 and Evreinov's acceptance of the directorship in 1910, the Crooked Mirror functioned to all intents and purposes more as a miniature theater than as a cabaret. The emphasis was heavily on drama, a fact that in no way was substantially altered by the outward appearance of a cabaret program consisting of several items of different character. Evreinov shared Kugel's and Kholmskaya's views of contemporary Russian drama and theater and was no less committed to the Crooked Mirror's parodic and satiric orientation. He was also not uninformed about or disinterested in cabaret. But he clearly recognized the hybrid nature of the Crooked Mirror and its predominantly theatrical character. Since he was himself more strongly interested in theater than cabaret, in the conventional European sense, and at this stage of his career more interested especially in experimental theater, he merely accelerated a process that one might easily regard as inevitable in the case of the Crooked Mirror; he dropped the less significant, secondary items and concentrated on the theatrical, building an evening's program around three or four miniature theatrical forms including parodies, satires, pantomimes, burlesques, and caricatures. To view the transformation of the Crooked Mirror under Evreinov's direction from another angle, the evolution undergone by the Crooked Mirror was much like that of the Berlin Schall und Rauch which under Max Reinhardt's leadership changed from cabaret into the miniature theater known as the Kleines Theater. There was, in other words, a precedent for such change which Evreinov might well have been aware of and, in fact, used as a model. The difference, however, lay in the fact that unlike Reinhardt, Evreinov did not dispense entirely with the cabaret format of the Crooked Mirror; instead, he preserved the cabaret structure in order to accommodate a program of small, or miniature, theatrical genres.

In considering now the development of the Crooked Mirror before Evreinov took over its directorship, I would like to concentrate on a few of its more outstanding, and representative, productions rather than present a chronicle of all the dramatic and other features presented there between 1908 and 1910.

Although successful from the outset, the Crooked Mirror acquired true renown in January 1908, which was very soon after its opening, with its produciton of a parody of classical opera entitled *Printsessa Afrikanskaya* (The African Princess), but known best by the name of the lead character, the African princess Vampuka. The parody was written in 1900 by Mikhail Volkonsky (1860–1917), a dramatist and writer of prose fiction who for several years also served as editor of the widely read journal *Niva.* Volkonsky had made his debut as a miniaturist and parodist in perhaps the best known of St. Petersburg's small private theaters of the time, the Liteiny. But his real fame as a theatrical parodist rests on two works produced by the Crooked Mirror, the *African Princess* and *Gastrol Rychalova* (Rychalov's Guest Appearance).

The African Princess was an instant hit and did more than anything else to put the Crooked Mirror on the Russian theatrical map. Its original production, under the general direction of A. R. Kugel, was staged by R. A. Unger who did several other Crooked Mirror productions before the advent of Evreinov. Music for the production was composed by another Crooked Mirror regular of the period, Vladimir Erenberg (1875–1923).

Composed of two short acts (the printed text in Russian is just eight pages long)[20] and enlivened with music and dancing, *The African Princess* relates the rivalry between the young man Lodyre and Strofokamil, King of the Ethiopians, for the love of the African princess Vampuka. Just as Lodyre is about to be executed on order of Strofokamil, Vampuka's protector, the European Merinos, appears to save the day. Strofokamil is ordered punished and Lodyre and Vampuka receive Merinos' blessings at the end.

A hilarious parody on commonplaces of Italian opera libretti, in particular, and on the conventions of grand opera, in general, which to the originators of the Crooked Mirror was another musty tradition in need of fresh air, *The African Princess* introduces motifs drawn specifically from Meyerbeer's *The African Woman* and, of course, Verdi's *Aida.* Musical motifs from other works by Meyerbeer can also be identified.

So successful was the Crooked Mirror production of *The African Princess* that before the theater-cabaret ceased to exist, the work was given more than one thousand performances. As further testimony of its extraordinary popularity, the name of the heroine, Vampuka, entered the Russian language for a time as a noun, *vampuknost,* meaning a kind of exaggerated operatic pathos, and as a verb, *vampuchit,* meaning to act in the high operatic manner. The name Vampuka itself has an amusing story behind it. When pupils of the elite Smolny Institute for well-born young women in St. Petersburg presented flowers once to Prince Oldenburgsky on the occasion of his visit, they sang a well-known refrain from the opera *Robert* which in Russian reads: "Vam puk, vam puk, vam puk tsvetov podnosim" (To you, to you, to you we bring a bunch, a bunch, a bunch of flowers). When the wife of the writer P. P. Gnedich asked Volkonsky, the author of *The African Princess,* who related the story, if there really was such a name as Vampuk, mistaking the words "vam puk" as a single word for a person's name, Volkonsky exclaimed with delight that here indeed was the name he was looking for for the heroine of his parody; hence, Vampuka (p. 804).

The great success of *The African Princess,* or *Vampuka,* as the work is best known, inspired Kugel to initiate a series of parodies on foreign classical theatrical forms, including French melodrama, ballet, and the operetta. One of the best of these was a parody on melodrama entitled *Zhak Nuar i Anri Zaverni, ili Propavshy dokument* (Jacques Noir and Henri Zaverni, or The Lost Document). It was written by the actor, director, and playwright Nikolai Urvantsev (1876–1941), with music again by Vladimir Erenberg, and was staged for the first time at the Crooked Mirror in 1909. A one-act melodrama in three scenes, *Jacques Noir* . . . tells the tale of the orphan Marie who was taken in and made a member of the poor but honorable country family of Gaspar Zaverni. She and Gaspar's son Henri fall in love and decide to marry. On his way to the town notary to make arrangements for the marriage, Henri rests by a tree and falls asleep. The demon of the piece, Jacques Noir, a black, comes upon him and steals his papers. He then arrives at the Zavernis insisting that he is their son, Henri, despite the differences in appearance, and that he has the documents to prove it. Moreover, he demands that Marie marry him. When it appears that he will have his way, Marie remembers the medallion she gave Henri to wear for good luck on his journey. She has had the medallion since birth and it identifies her as being of noble birth, even though she does not know whence she comes. When Henri, who is about to be arrested and taken away as Jacques Noir, produces the medallion, which the real Jacques Noir failed to take from him, he is released and the black evildoer is taken into custody. Now united with her true love, Marie seeks no revenge and pleads that Jacques Noir be spared. The police agree and Jacques Noir, beside himself with joy, renounces crime and declares that henceforth he is a reformed man. The notary, who has since come from town to identify the real Henri, recognizes the medallion as one he gave his long lost daughter who, it turns out, had been abducted by Jacques Noir's family. Father and daughter are happily reunited and at the end of the little play, the notary blesses the marriage of Marie and Henri.

Beginning with the year 1910, the Crooked Mirror entered the five-year period of its zenith under the direction of Nikolai Evreinov. Before assuming his new position, Evreinov, together with the actor and director Fyodor Komissarzhevsky (some of whose productions he was later to parody), had launched a season of humorous, sometimes parodic plays in the spring of 1909 under the collective title "Vesyoly teatr dlya pozhilykh detei" (The Merry Theater for Grownup Children). Impressed by what he saw at these performances, Kugel thought that Evreinov would be the ideal person to become the new director of the Crooked Mirror and offered him the job. Evreinov agreed, but on the condition that the Crooked Mirror would become a regular theater, in its own home, rather than a late night cabaret performing on the premises of the St. Petersburg Theatrical Club. Kugel accepted Evreinov's terms and before long the Crooked Mirror was installed in the location it was to occupy for the duration of Evreinov's directorship—the newly refurbished 750-seat Ekaterinsky (Catherine) Theater at no. 60 Ekaterinsky (now Griboedov) Canal.

With Evreinov now in charge, the Crooked Mirror aimed its parody even more concentratedly at the contemporary Russian drama and theater. This is quite evident in several major productions of 1910 and 1911.

Possibly the most notable Crooked Mirror production of 1910 was the parody *Evolutsiya teatra* (The Evolution of the Theater) by the dramatist Boris Geyer (1876–1918), who contributed several pieces to the Crooked Mirror repertoire. Staged by the cabaret for the first time in 1910, *The Evolution of the Theater* reflects the great interest at the time in the so-called crisis of the stage which engaged the energies of some of the outstanding Russian theater personalities of the period, among them such dramatic writers as Aleksandr Blok, Andrei Bely, and Valeri Bryusov, the critic Aleksandr Kugel, and the director Vsevolod Meyerhold. Probably the immediate source of inspiration for Geyer's parody was the book of essays about the contemporary Russian theater published on Meyerhold's initiative in St. Petersburg in 1908 under the title

Teatr: Kniga o novom teatre (Theater: A Book about the New Theater). Among the essays in the book is one by the critic S. Rafalovich entitled "The Evolution of the Theater."

Apart from the cleverness of its parody, the most interesting feature of Geyer's *The Evolution of the Theater* is its structure. It is divided into four small acts, each of which is a parody of the style of a major Russian dramatist of the nineteenth and early twentieth centuries. Thus, the first act, "Pereputannaya nevesta" (The Confused Bride), parodies Nikolai Gogol's famous farce *Zhenitba* (Getting Married); the second act, "Pei, da delo razumei" (Sing if You Want, But Know What You're Doing), takes aim at those plays of the major Russian dramatist of the second half of the nineteenth century, Aleksandr Ostrovsky, which were intended as exemplifications of well-known Russian proverbs; the third act, "Petrov," is a parody of Chekhov's style, and alludes particularly to Chekhov's early play *Ivanov;* the fourth and last act, "Lichiny krika" (The Masks of a Shout), parodies Leonid Andreev's controversial allegory *Anathema* (1909), although the monologue of the character identified as "The Unseen but Visible One" is a clear parody of the Prologue to Andreev's *Zhizn cheloveka* (The Life of Man, 1908) as well as the remarks of the "Someone" in *Anathema.*

The introduction to Geyer's *The Evolution of the Theater,* spoken by the Lecturer, sets the framework for the play's four-sided parody and also reflects the circumstances from which the work itself arose:

> Dear Ladies and Gentlemen! Never have people talked or argued so much about the theater as nowadays.
>
> The theater of immobility (stasis, the theater of flatness [abstraction]), the theater of bas-relief, the theater of the actor, the theater of the director . . . Where are we headed? Why are we headed there? Is theater developing or is this the downfall of theater? And there are still thousands of other questions over which our distinguished critics are breaking their heads. Listening to all of this, I had wanted to deliver a lecture, following the example of many, about the evolution of the theater, but lacking the gift of eloquence, I decided that in place of words I would demonstrate by deed the direction in which the stage is headed, how far it has progressed in a century, how we have gone from coarse, primitive, and unclear forms to the depiction of even the most subtle experiences of the soul, to the most tender of symbols, full of clarity and depth of thought . . . Dear Ladies and Gentlemen! Now there will pass before you four plays by four renowned dramatists of the past century. I shall not announce the names of the dramatists—you will guess them yourselves. Each author represents an epoch in

the history of the theater. And here you will see for yourselves where we are headed and where, God grant, we will not arrive. By a strange set of circumstances, all four plays are written on the same theme and are marked by the same splendid depth and originality. "He" declares his love to another man's wife. The husband comes upon them just at this time. Each author handles the consequences of this in a different way, but this emphasizes all the more the evolution of the theater. And so, I beg your attention and hope that after this visual lecture you will leave here reassured as to the future of our native art.[21]

The format of Geyer's *The Evolution of the Theater,* a parodic play encompassing parodies of several different dramatic or theatrical styles—which Evreinov was soon to follow still more effectively in his famous *Revizor: rezhisserskaya bufonada* (The Inspector General: A Directors' Buffonade, 1911)—was not, to be sure, a distinctly Russian innovation. This type of multidimensional parodic drama had already been established in German cabaret several years earlier. *Don Carlos an der Jahrhundertwende* (Don Carlos at the Turn of the Century), written by Max Reinhardt, Friedrich Kayssler, and Martin Zickel and staged at the Berlin Schall und Rauch in 1901, is a parodic trilogy based on *Don Carlos* in which the authors recast Schiller's classic play as they imagine it in the styles of especially Hauptmann and Maeterlinck. In *Nora,* which Rudolf Bernauer staged at the Berlin cabaret Die Bösen Buben (The Naughty Boys) in 1903, the last scene of the last act of Ibsen's *Doll's House* is presented in the different conceptions of, among others, Frank Wedekind, Maurice Maeterlinck, and Kaiser Wilhelm's favorite dramatist, Joseph Lauff.

Three highly successful productions of 1911 also had theatrical themes: *Gastrol Rychalova* (Rychalov's Guest Appearance), by Mikhail Volkonsky, and Evreinov's *Shkola etualei* (The School of Stars) and *Revizor.*

Rychalov's Guest Appearance, for which Vladimir Erenberg did the music, was written by Volkonsky specifically for the Crooked Mirror. Its subject—the backwardness of the Russian provincial theater—was a frequent butt of jokes in theatrical circles. In Volkonsky's play, a typical Russian provincial theater is getting ready for the production of an opera about the French Revolution in which the big city visiting tenor Rychalov will perform. The first act is set backstage just before Rychalov's arrival. It derives its humor from the lack of sophistication of the provincial theater people who know nothing about the background of the work they are about to perform and Rychalov's dismay over the lack of fanfare upon his arrival. The second and last act of the play is devoted to the opera performance itself. Utter chaos reigns; props fall all over the place, actors and actresses on stage mimic the gestures of an offstage prompter, forget their lines or confuse words, improvise absurdly, begin quarreling among themselves, and so on. Seeing what is happening all around him, Rychalov throws a fit, stamping his feet on the stage and shouting: "I can't take it any more, I can't . . . (Runs out.) [The character playing the role of the papal nuncio continues to bellow. The curtain is lowered. The nuncio bellows behind the curtain. The orchestra plays the concluding finale.]"[22] Needless to say, the operatic part of *Rychalov's Guest Appearance* also provided Volkonsky, and Evreinov, a splendid opportunity to mock the inane conventions of the traditional libretto just as Volkonsky had done before in his *African Princess* (*Vampuka*). The little play, therefore, has two elements to its parody: the Russian provincial theater and traditional opera.

The School of Stars, a "parody-grotesque in one act," was staged by the Crooked Mirror on November 11, 1911. The parody in this case brings us closer to a cabaret milieu; it is now aimed at the modish *café chantant* of the turn-of-the-century period, which had since been imported to Russia, and the training of stars for the cafés. The work is set in a "school of *chansonette*" which also trains "lyrical singers, quick change artists, female tramp types, eccentric dancers, Spaniards [i.e., flamenco dancers—HBS], living pictures, gypsy romance stars, *bébé* [baby star types—HBS], and [Isadora] Duncan-style dancers."[23] The Director of the School alternates between trying to make his unsophisticated pupils grasp what it is they are supposed to do and juggling romantic trysts with some of his charges. The play ends with the manager of a *variété,* who has come to book a trio of *bébé* singers, walking off instead with a country bumpkinish would-be singer who has just come to study at the school.

In the nearly seven years that Evreinov worked as director of the Crooked Mirror under Kugel and Kholmskaya, he staged over one hundred plays, fourteen of which were written by him. Of these fourteen, half were parodies. They include: *V kullisakh dushi* (The Theater of the Soul), *The Inspector General: A Directors' Buffonade, The School of Stars, Kukhnya smekha* (The Laughter Kitchen), *Kolombina segodnya* (Colombine Today), *Vechnaya tantsovshchitsa* (The Eternal Dancer), and *Chetvyortaya stena* (The Fourth Wall). The most famous of these, beyond a doubt, is *The Inspector General: A Directors' Buffonade.*

Staged at the Crooked Mirror for the first time on December 11, 1911, Evreinov's *Inspector General,* like Boris Geyer's *The Evolution of the Theater,* is a multidimensional theatrical parody. But whereas Geyer directed his parody at dramatic styles from Gogol to Andreev, Evreinov bears down on directorial styles. Following the same format as Geyer's *The Evolution of the Theater,* each of *The Inspector General*'s five "constructions" presents a different directorial interpretation of the same first and last scenes from Gogol's great comedy *The Inspector General* as imagined by Evreinov. Before the curtain goes up on the first of the "constructions," an official of the Crooked Mirror appears before the audience to announce that "today's presentation of *The Inspector General* is, in fact, a competitive appearance of directors who have been invited as guest performers by the management [of the Crooked Mirror—HBS]."[24] The official then goes on to explain the purpose of these special "competitive" productions:

> Dear Ladies and Gentlemen! The crisis of the theater is a phenomenon that we have been observing not just since yesterday. The general opinion is that there are no plays. People advise us to turn to the classical repertoire. But does the limited number of classical plays suffice for all theaters and for all the demands of a repertoire? And so, the "Crooked Mirror," taking as its goal the realization of the success of theater by all measures, has resolved to attempt an experiment which, it is hoped, will not pass without consequence; namely, it is determined to quintuple the number of classical plays by presenting them in five different interpretations in such a way that each play is made to yield five different plays.
>
> I shall remain silent concerning the names of those invited to serve as directors in order to impel the audience gathered here to completely impartial judgment about their creative work. It is not a matter of names, of course, but one of the competition of different methods of production, sharply differentiated one from the other and yet at the same time alike in one very important respect: *the original work of the author remains equally unrecognizable in all these methods.*
>
> In this way, if the experiment proposed to the esteemed public succeeds—which you will attest to by your applause—we can have five *Inspector Generals,* five *Woe from Wits,* five *Krechinsky's Weddings,* five *Storms,*[25] and so on. Without bothering you with the figures, I can observe that, by an approximate calculation, the Russian theater will have at its disposal some one hundred and twenty entirely independent, classical works from five Gogols, five Ostrovskys, five Sukhovo-Kobylins, and ten Tolstoys: five Leo Tolstoys and five Aleksei Tolstoys.[26] And this entire harvest of classical works will be collected through the mediation of talented and thoughtful stage direction.

In order to certify before this most esteemed audience that there will actually be presented on stage excerpts from *The Inspector General,* and not some other play having nothing in common with *The Inspector General,* we shall at first present *The Inspector General* in the form in which it has been performed down to the crisis of the contemporary stage. Following this, it will be entirely clear to the audience how far contemporary theatrical direction has gone and how far it can still go if, it is understood, it is not halted.

As concerns the following stagings, in order to simplify for the audience the perception of what is taking place on stage, and, in accordance with the instructions of the management of this theater, I shall introduce before each new version, in compressed form, those facts which each director has presented as the basis for his construction.

And now, the first of the series, an ordinary staging requiring no explanations and no commentaries.[27]

In the first stage direction to the "classical" staging of *The Inspector General,* obviously by a provincial theater, the author (Evreinov, of course) points out that the characters play well, "rendering the text," and without "turning their back to the audience," without "mood pauses" and "other such modernisms" (p. 615). By "rendering the text" Evreinov means remaining faithful to Gogol's text, which in all probability would have been the case with a provincial theater as yet untouched by the innovations taking place in Moscow and St. Petersburg. The references to "turning their back to the audience," "mood pauses," and "other such modernisms" allude unmistakably to characteristic aspects of the playing style of the Moscow Art Theater under Stanislavsky and Nemirovich-Danchenko toward which Evreinov, like Kugel, had a distinct aversion.

The second version of *The Inspector General* to be presented is a "lifelike staging in the spirit of Stanislavsky" in which the meticulous attention to detail and exaggerated realism of the Moscow Art Theater are made the butt of parody. It seems more than likely that it was prompted by an unsuccessful production that the Moscow Art Theater actually mounted in 1908. The Stanislavsky parody, like the three remaining ones, is prefaced with a lengthy explanatory introduction by the same Crooked Mirror official who appeared at the very beginning of the play. In the case of the "Stanislavsky staging" much of the introduction is taken up with a humorous biographical sketch of the guest-director of the Stanislavsky segment and the painstaking care with which the physical setting of *The Inspector General* was researched.

For Evreinov, the most ludicrous aspects of Stanislavsky's style were the frequency of pauses and the importance of mood (*nastroenie*). It is on these two features that the parody of the second segment of the Crooked Mirror's *Inspector General* is concentrated. The preface to the segment sets the tone. The "guest-director" is described as having spent "a year and a half studying mood, two years—the theater, as life, and at night works on pauses. His dissertation, dedicated to Stanislavsky, is titled: 'The Semi-Pause and the Pause of Mood.' Its thesis is—'the square of a mood is in inverse ratio to the distance of the theater from life' " (p. 617). As to the care that went into the Moscow Art Theater productions under Stanislavsky, the Crooked Mirror official has this to say in his introduction to the Stanislavsky segment:

> The greatest care has gone into the setting. It is impossible to enumerate all characteristic details. You will see them yourselves. By way of example, I will point out just a few: thus, Anna Andreevna, raised, according to the author, "on albums," appears with an old album in her hands. Zemlyanika, of whom it is said that he is "an utter swine in a skullcap," actually appears in a skullcap. Tyapkin-Lyapkin, who takes puppies as bribes and is about to present the Mayor "with the natural sister of the male dog that Skvoznik-Dmukhanovsky knows," actually appears with dogs, and so on.
>
> What the weather was on the day the Mayor and Khlestakov meet, the director was unable to elucidate precisely. Nevertheless, if one recalls from *The Inspector General* that "the soldiers were walking through the streets in uniform" but had "nothing on underneath their uniforms," one can suppose that it was a warm, cloudless day. At the end of the play, however, a little rainfall is allowed, like a final artistic touch, in order to create a mood of endless dreariness in accordance with the high artistic traditions of plays with mood in general. (pp. 618–619)

The Stanislavsky segment is followed by a "Grotesque Staging in the Manner of Max Reinhardt" for which Hugo von Hofmannsthal revised the text and Engelbert Humperdinck (the original one) composed the music. This version of Gogol's *Inspector General* has now been recast as a Symbolist play in verse, with appropriate music, a setting in the style of the Munich Secession, and the appearance of allegorical characters representing Laughter, Satire, and Humor. In view of the importance of dance in Symbolist theater, the Max Reinhardt segment is directed by a German who has taught rhythmic gymnastics in school, according to the system of Dalcroze, and who has the characters playing Laughter, Satire, and Humor appear on stage before the curtain is raised to dance a "symbolic dance in the Russian spirit as understood by Humperdinck" (p. 625).

After the Max Reinhardt segment Evreinov brings on a "Miracle Play Staging in the Style of Gordon Craig." In his introduction to it, the Crooked Mirror spokesman alludes to Craig's production of *Hamlet* at the Moscow Art Theater in 1912, referring to Craig as the theater director "who became famous among us for his mystical and cubist production of *Hamlet*" (p. 629). The spokesman goes on to say that the action of the Craig version of *The Inspector General* "takes place at a certain point in infinite interplanetary space. This method itself of staging *The Inspector General,* however, we have decided to keep a secret so that the novelty of the spectacle may be even more striking to the audience. I shall permit myself to say one thing with certainty: the immortal comedy of Gogol, in this staging, is truly capable of bringing forth real tears. (Goes out, moved)" (p. 629).

The fifth and last segment of *The Inspector General: A Directors' Buffonade* is a takeoff on the new medium of the silent film. The segment is entitled "Cinematographic Staging." The Crooked Mirror spokesman explains in his introduction how the film version of Gogol's play came about:

> In accordance with the desire of a cinematographic conference taking place in Moscow this year that the best works of classical literature be staged for the cinematographer, the final production of *The Inspector General* will be presented in purely cinematographic spirit, in the spirit of the well-known Pathé firm. . . . The resulting *tremendously funny comedy, The Inspector General,* has a length of 650 meters, made of the very finest material, and is accompanied by exquisite music from the contemporary repertoire. (p. 632)

The text of the film version of *The Inspector General* is, in fact, a one-paragraph scenario of the play's last scene that calls for the playing of Spanish gypsy dance music and the characters on film running about helter-skelter and finally falling one on top of another after the Mayor's wife, who is in the lead, trips.

Evreinov's multidirectorial buffonade version of Gogol's *The Inspector General* has been discussed at some length here because it was not only the greatest theatrical parody ever staged by the Crooked Mirror, but one of the most effective parodies to have emerged from the entire European cabaret milieu of the early twentieth century. Beyond any doubt, it can easily take its place alongside such gems of German-language cabaret parody as *Don Carlos at the Turn of the Century* and the *Goethe* of Egon Friedell and Alfred Polgar. So highly was the play regarded in Russia in its time, that when the Crooked Mirror went on a tour of the provinces in the spring of 1913, it was requested to mount a special performance of it for the Tsar at the so-called Kitaisky (Chinese) Theater at the imperial residence in Tsarskoe Selo (Imperial Village). The program presented by the Crooked Mirror on this occasion featured not only Evreinov's *Inspector General* buffonade, but also his *Rychalov's Guest Appearance.*

Between the enormous success of his *Inspector General* in 1911 and the triumph of his *Chetvyortaya stena* (The Fourth Wall) in 1915, the year in which he left the Crooked Mirror—and St. Peterburg (now Petrograd)—for a country house in Finland and work on his major theoretical studies of theater, Evreinov mounted, to great public acclaim, the one Crooked Mirror parody written by him to become well-known in the West during his lifetime. That was *V kulisakh dushi* (In the Wings of the Soul, or Backstage of the Soul, or, as it is usually translated into English, The Theater of the Soul). It had its premiere at the Crooked Mirror in October 1912.

The Theater of the Soul is the best example of Evreinov's theory of monodrama. Obviously developed under the strong influence of the subjectivism of much turn-of-the-century art (the plays of Maurice Maeterlinck, for example) and especially by developments in psychology, above all the work of Freud, Evreinov's concept of monodrama proposes a type of theoretical work in which everyone and everything on stage are to be understood by the audience as representing not objective reality, but the subjective perceptions of a central character. The purpose of the monodrama is essentially twofold: it seeks to explore the realm of inner experience and, in doing so, to enable the spectator to enter the private world of the play's central figure and see the phenomenal world through his eyes. In purely theatrical terms, that is apart from his interest in the new trends in psychology, underlying Evreinov's experiments with monodrama was the desire to carry forward the process begun before him, most notably by Meyerhold, to remove the barriers, physical or otherwise, separating spectator from player.

Evreinov had first articulated his ideas about monodrama in a lecture in 1909 entitled "Vvedenie v monodramu" (An Introduction to Monodrama), which he later expanded into a book and published under the same title. His first attempt at writing a monodrama was the play *Predstavlenie lyubvi* (literally, "A Presentation of Love," but usually translated into English as *The Theater of Love* since *predstavlenie* in Russian can also refer to a stage production). Although the three-act work was published in the summer of 1910 in the almanac *Studiya impressionistov* (Studies of Impressionists), Evreinov was unsuccessful in arranging a production of it either by himself or by others. As written by Evreinov, the play would have been technically difficult to bring to the stage in his own time. Three characters appear in it, the central figure identified just as "I," the heroine "She! She!," and the villain of the piece "My Rival." Less important than the characters in the eternal love triangle are Evreinov's stage directions which call for the changing of the play's decor as well as the color and intensity of the stage lighting in conformity with shifts in attitude of the central figure toward the love object. Had the play been shorter, say a one-acter, its chances of production might have been greater. But the subjectivism of the work, in which the love triangle is viewed through the changes in mood and perception of "I," loses its concentration over three acts and becomes tiresome. Furthermore, the need to change sets and lighting over three acts would also have imposed inordinate demands on the capabilities of a theater at the time, apart from any dissipation of audience interest caused by the almost dizzying frequency of the changes themselves.

Evreinov seems to have been aware himself that monodrama might be more effectively accommodated in a shorter play form. In his next attempt, *The Theater of the Soul,* he abandoned the full-length play in favor of a one-acter and succeeded in composing not only one of the best of his short dramatic works but undoubtedly the best known of his plays outside Russia after *Samoe glavnoe* (The Main Thing, or The Chief Thing).

The action of *The Theater of the Soul* takes place in the Soul, and within the space of thirty seconds. Before the curtain is raised, a Professor enters, equipped with blackboard and chalk, to explain to the audience the meaning of the play that it is about to see. Using a large drawing of the heart, which he identifies as the stage on which the Self, or Soul, performs, he goes on to elucidate the several selves of which the Self consists as S_1 (the rational self, or rational aspect of the soul), S_2 (the emotional self), and S_3 (the subconscious self). When the curtain goes up and the play begins, the audience sees three actors representing this tripartite division of the soul. It soon becomes apparent that S_1 and S_2 disagree over the latter's fascination with a café singer identified in the little play as Songstress Image No. 1. At a certain point, S_2 brings her on stage to sing a song (in French) and show how talented and beautiful she really is. S_1 argues that she is only a delusion and to prove his point brings out Songstress Image No. 2, a grotesque caricature who proceeds to remove her wig, falsies, and false teeth just to show how ugly she is in fact. After she leaves, S_1 then brings on Wife Image No. 1, with babe in arms, to convince S_2 how wrong it would be to give up such a lovely wife and child for a tawdry songstress. S_2 rejects this image of his wife as an idealization and to make his point summons Wife Image No. 2 who appears shrill and shrewish. After this, the different images of Wife and Songstress, 1 and 1, then 2 and 2, appear to fight among themselves in the best slapstick fashion. Before long, S_1 and S_2 join the fray. When it appears that S_2 has won and is about to claim Songstress Image No. 1 as his prize, she spurns him saying that she was just teasing and besides, she is more interested in money which he does not have, than love. Distraught, S_2 is about to shoot himself when S_3 (the subconscious), who has been asleep until now, awakens. Before he can intervene, however, S_2 fires the shot that kills him and he falls to the floor dead. As S_3 trembles and stretches nervously a few times, a Conductor enters with a lantern to tell S_3 that they have reached the stop where he is to change. S_3 puts on his hat, picks up his suitcase, and, yawning, follows the Conductor off stage, thus bringing the play to an end.

The Theater of the Soul was a great success when first presented at the Crooked Mirror in 1912. Apart from its more effective exemplification of Evreinov's ideas about monodrama than his previous work in this vein and the obvious elements of both auto-parody (with reference to Evreinov's earlier *Theater of Love*) and parody of Freudian psychology, *The Theater of the Soul* makes clever use of setting. Unlike *The Theater of Love* with its almost kaleidoscopic changes of scenery and lighting, *The Theater of the Soul* gets the maximum effect out of basically a single stage set consisting of a blowup of a human diaphragm complete with heart, lungs, and ribs which correspond to the diagram drawn on the blackboard by the Professor at the beginning of the play. In the original Crooked Mirror production of the play this entire set moved rhythmically throughout the work in time to both the mood of the action on stage and the music. Evreinov obviously sought to achieve the same integration of subject and setting as *The Theater of Love,* but in a much more concentrated and technically feasible way in *The Theater of the*

Soul. The set also added to the humor of this later play, which it did not do in the case of *The Theater of Love.* This is particularly true of the play's ending. When S_2, the emotional self, shoots himself, a gaping hole opens up in the huge heart of the set and red ribbons roll out of it onto the floor of the stage. When S_2 falls to the floor beneath the heart, he drowns in the sea of these ribbons. With his death, the lungs of the set also cease breathing.

As elsewhere in the world of the late nineteenth- and early twentieth century cabaret, literary symbolism and the Symbolist drama in particular were favorite targets of parody and satire. This was especially true of the strongly theater-oriented Russian cabaret, above all the Crooked Mirror. Besides the parodies of Max Reinhardt and Gordon Craig in Evreinov's *The Inspector General: A Directors' Buffonade,* the Crooked Mirror launched another broadside at Symbolist drama the following year, 1912, in the form of witty parody entitled *Litsedeistvo o gospodine Ivanove* (The Hypocrisy Concerning Mr. Ivanov) (Russian text, pp. 588–597), which was written by Nikolai Ventsel (1855–1920; pen names Benedikt, V. B., Furioso, Yurin N., and others), a poet, critic, and dramatist who wrote a number of parodies most of which were staged at the Crooked Mirror. *The Hypocrisy Concerning Mr. Ivanov,* subtitled "A Morality of the Twentieth Century," and written in verse, parodies not only Symbolist drama in general but the plays specifically of the Russian dramatist Fyodor Sologub (the pseudonym of Fyodor Teternikov, 1863–1927), the author of one of the great Russian literary achievements of its time, the grotesque novel *Melky bes* (The Petty Demon, 1907). Ventsel's Crooked Mirror play focuses on the predominance of sexual themes in Sologub's work. The Mr. Ivanov of the play is chafing under the yoke of his marriage and wants to end it in order to be free to find the ideal love of which he dreams. This turns out to be his own daughter who now feels the same way about him. In the meantime, Ivanov's son is beside himself with joy to learn that his father and mother are separating because he is in love with his own mother. When he confesses this love, she too is overjoyed. At the end of the play, the Legal Code appears as a character to pass sentence on Ivanov for his violation of its articles concerning daughters and wives. As Ivanov laments his unlucky fate, the walls of the room begin trembling. He orders the other characters to join him in lying on the floor like lifeless corpses. When they do, the stage scenery comes crashing in on them.

In the fall of 1913, after its successful spring tour, the Crooked Mirror staged another of Evreinov's multipart contrastive parodies. This was the work entitled *Kukhnya smekha* (The Laughter Kitchen) which was staged at the cabaret for the first time on October 23, 1913. The parody this time assumed something of the character of an auto-parody in that it is directed against the mania at the time for short generally one-act plays which were, as we know, the mainstay of the Crooked Mirror.

In *The Laughter Kitchen* (in the writing of which two other dramatists participated, V. A. Azov and S. I. Antimonov), the basis of the parody is a theater-sponsored international contest for short comic plays which the theater itself has few of in its repertoire. The subject of the contest proposed by the theater involves a practical joke devised by one of the bored guests. He bets that he can pull the buttons off someone's coat or jacket and sew them back on in two minutes flat. The bet is accepted by a skeptical Count N. After pulling the buttons from the Count's waistcoat, the jokester loses the bet. Elated that he has won, the Count does not immediately realize that he has become the laughingstock of the other guests because of the torn and shabby appearance of his once elegant waistcoat.

The rest of the Evreinov parody consists of the winning entries chosen by the theater's jury. These include a German version (*Die Bienenliebe,* Bees' Love, by one Georg Meyer—this name, as well as those of other foreign prizewinners are all concoctions of Evreinov and his co-authors), a French version (*Les Boutons d'amour,* The Buttons of Love, by one Jules Corbeau), an American version (*The Betting of Two Red Devils,* by an author named William Midge), and a Russian version (*Schastie Trogloditova,* The Good Fortune of Mr. Troglodyte, by a writer identified as Osip Arkadchinko). The Russian author's name is the only one alluding to real literary figures, in this case two contemporary popular writers of one-act plays and farces, Osip Dymov (1878–1959) and Arkadi Averchenko (1881–1925), hence the name Osip Arkadchinko. The four different versions of the same anecdote parody not only the one-act play form itself, but also national differences in humor. Thus, the German play, representing a "militarization of the anecdote," is characterized also by a "pleasant feeling of love for nature enlivened from time to time by the sounds of a military march" and "concern for the objects of household duties" (pp. 649 and 650). The French play is typically French in that the author "with one bold movement simultaneously tears off clothes, baring not only the lining of the emotions, but also the lining of a dress" (p. 663). One member of the Russian jury held the opinion, however, that the play was insufficiently national in the sense of *grivoiserie* (spiciness), preferring instead another French comedy that had been submitted entitled *Mimi Forgot Her Drawers.* Of particular merit in the American play is the presence of "all the constituent elements of Anglo-Saxon humor—the clever exchange of slaps, the subtle satirical patch on the back part of the dress, and the checkered kerchief into which a huge red nose, filled, so to speak, with irony, is blown." The Russian play also offers all the favorite elements of contemporary Russian wit:

> a drunk appears, with the characteristic psychology of a Russian drunk; such major social disasters as the mother-in-law and the country husband are revealed; the figure of the petty official, complaining about protectionism, casts its mournful shadow; and, of course, a Jew figures in the play, a Jew speaking that special Odessa dialect which Russian humorists have created of elements of the Jewish jargon, the Russian language, and their own imagination. (p. 678)

Alluding to the common practice of Russian writers to base their one-act plays on previously published short stories, such as a few of Chekhov's, for example, the commentary on the Russian play also expresses the regret that

> the esteemed author did not even this time desire to change the custom of all Russian dramatists-humorists who print each of their works first in the form of a short story on the pages of the *Satiricon,*[28] afterward reprint it in one of the organs of the provincial press, later submit it to the almanac of a satirical journal, subsequently insert the story in the next volume of the complete collection of their works, and, finally, include it as "selected" in one of the little books of a cheap library series and only after this long process rework the short story for the stage. But all this is atoned for by the bitter laughter by which in spite of everything and whatever has happened the Russian humorist *tries* to laugh. (p. 679)

The period 1910 to 1915, when Evreinov was artistic director of the Crooked Mirror, was the most brilliant in the theater-cabaret's history. But by 1915 there were signs that it was no longer arousing quite the same degree of excitement and that some of the wind had gone out of its sails. Before the year was over, Evreinov himself would abandon any further activity in it, either as writer or director, preferring instead to retire to a dacha in Finland in order to devote his energies chiefly to the writing of one of his major works on the stage, *Teatr dlya sebya* (Theater for Oneself, 1915–1917).

Prior to his withdrawal from the Crooked Mirror Evreinov brought to its stage his best parody after *The Inspector General, Chetvyortaya stena* (The Fourth Wall). It was first presented on October 22, 1915, and if it was intended as something of a parting shot, it could not have been more effective. The little play was Evreinov's own favorite of the many that he had staged at the Crooked Mirror and it is not hard to understand why. The broad target of the parody was again the preferred whipping boy of Kugel and Evreinov, the Moscow Art Theater and Stanislavsky's obsession with realism on all levels. But *The Fourth Wall* also has two other more immediate and easily identifiable objects of derision. One was the St. Petersburg Theater for Opera, which sought to avoid the excesses of traditional opera by introducing greater realism into its productions. The other was the director Fyodor Komissarzhevsky's production of Goethe's *Faust* at K. Nezlobin's theater in Moscow in September 1912 in which Mephistopheles is presented as Faust's alter ego (pp. 812–813). This same conception of two characters as but two dimensions of the same personality had previously been used in the Moscow Art Theater's production of Dostoevsky's *Brothers Karamazov* in 1910. The role of Ivan Karamazov was played by the great actor Kachalov who transformed Ivan's famous dialogue with the Devil in the novel into an internal monologue, a difficult and impressive theatrical feat (p. 813).

Evreinov's *Fourth Wall* is built around the old stage device of the play-within-a-play or, more properly here, the theater-within-a-theater. The production being mounted by the theater that serves as the setting of the parody is none other than Gounod's *Faust.* The basis of Evreinov's parody is the *reductio ad absurdum.* In its striving for the greatest possible realism in its production, the theater will stop at nothing. The actor playing the lead role of Faust, for example, is made to spend nights in the absolutely authentic medieval setting assembled on stage which includes a medieval bed where he sleeps wearing a medieval nightcap. The actor complains bitterly that while the search for naturalism and "truth" are all right, he has been unable to get to sleep on the stage before three in the morning because of all the rats in the theater. So insistent are the Director and Producter of the production on authenticity that the actor playing Faust is berated for having a copy of a St. Petersburg newspaper in his possession; in another superb touch, the chalice of poison which Faust must hold at one point with trembling hand is actually filled with strychnine mixed with prussic acid. When the actor playing Mephistopheles appears during the rehearsal, the Producer decides to omit him from the production on the grounds that after reading Eckermann he realizes that Mephistopheles is just an aspect of Faust himself, hence there is no need for a separate actor to play the role of Mephistopheles. That Evreinov clearly had the Moscow Art Theater's production of *The Brothers Karamazov* in mind as well as Komissarzhevsky's *Faust* is indicated by the Producer's statements that "Mephistopheles in Faust's tragedy is the same as the devil in the tragedy of Ivan Karamazov," and "If the Moscow Art Theater didn't hesitate to get rid of the devil as a separate character, then we, as the representatives of realistic opera, should have done so long ago" (p. 701).[29]

Absurdity is soon piled on absurdity. Since, as the Producer says, his production of *Faust* is a "realistic opera" and not some *Vampuka,* the verse of the original is abandoned in favor of prose, the transformation of Faust into a young man is dropped as a "childish stunt" and the actor playing the part told that he was engaged for the role not for his voice but for his older age, talking is substituted for singing, and, for still greater naturalism since the characters are supposed to be German, it is decided that they should speak in German and not sing a Russian translation of the opera and that for historical authenticity Faust should speak not contemporary German, but a Middle High German dialect. The issue then arises as to the actor's inability to speak German. The Assistant Director, who has been suggesting the newer more naturalistic changes in the production in a tongue-in-cheek style just to see how far the Producer and Director will go in their search for "realism," solves the problem. He points out that since Faust is no lunatic and therefore cannot conduct monologues or conversations with Mephistopheles as earlier agreed upon, because only a madman does things like that, the role of Faust should be changed from a speaking part to a mimed one. The crowning absurdity is the best parody yet on the "fourth wall" convention of the realistic theater. The Assistant Director has a final brainstorm: for the sake of verisimilitude instead of pretending that a fourth wall exists on stage that has been "removed" so that the audience can peer into the private lives of the characters being portrayed, the theater should erect on stage a *real* fourth wall. The Producer falls for the idea hook, line, and sinker, exclaiming joyously:

A fourth wall! . . . This is a real Columbus' egg! . . . How simple, how clever, and how natural all at once! (Dreamily.) A fourth wall! . . . Here we are, the dawn of a new theater!—A theater free of lies, buffoonery, and the compromises unworthy of pure art! (p. 716)

When the night of the premiere of the new *Faust* arrives, the Director steps before the curtain to tell the audience that the premiere

is the complete liquidation of old-fashioned conventional art, steeped through and through with falseness! Today's premiere is a victorious triumph of unadorned truth in the theater! Today's premiere is the greatest event in the universal history of dramatic art, an event the measure of whose originality can be conveyed perhaps only by the production comprising it. (p. 719)

When the curtain goes up the audience beholds a huge fourth wall, almost at the footlights themselves, constructed in all fidelity to German architecture of the Middle Ages. Although Faust occasionally appears at a window, shedding a tear over the memories of his lost youth, coughing and blowing his nose, the action on stage is concentrated on what takes place in front of the wall. It is pure slapstick: a carousing band of youths passes by, followed by a street urchin who pauses at the wall with the intention of relieving himself against it; a streetsweeper tries to chase him away with a broom and winds up striking the wall and falling down; a woman appears in the window above with a bucket of slops which she had intended for the street urchin but now mistakenly dumps on the streetsweeper; as some typical German villagers from the provinces cross the stage, the auditorium is filled with the stench of salt fish, onions, and pork. As the production continues, the actor playing Faust suddenly stops acting and turning to the audience declares that he can't stand any more of it and then drains the chalice he had been holding containing, as we know, real poison. As he staggers off stage, and tumult erupts in the theater, the Assistant Director, now slightly tipsy, steps before the hastily lowered curtain to announce that "Ladies and Gentlemen, in view of the seriously deranged condition of the actor who plays the role of Faust, the remainder of the opera cannot take place . . ." (p. 723). So ends one of the greatest and possibly the most hilarious theatrical parody ever mounted by the Crooked Mirror in its heyday.

With Evreinov mostly out of the picture after 1915, the Crooked Mirror managed to hold on as best it could until the Civil War created such turmoil in Russia that normal cultural life had to be suspended. The Crooked Mirror closed its doors in 1918. Four years later, with the Civil War at an end, the Bolsheviks in power, and the retrogressive partial capitalism of the so-called New Economic Policy (NEP, 1921–1928) in effect, Aleksandr Kugel tried to resurrect the theater-cabaret, but to no avail. The former premises of the Catherine Theater were unavailable and suitable new ones could not be found. When the Crooked Mirror was reopened once again it was not in St. Petersburg/Petrograd but in Moscow, where the premises of the former Slavyansky Bazaar were turned over to it for the 1923/24 theater season. When the mildly successful season drew to an end, Kugel proposed sending the cabaret on a foreign tour, to Poland, and wanted Evreinov to head it. Evreinov accepted and the company departed for Warsaw in January 1925. The tour proved to be an utter fiasco. It was mercilessly attacked as a Soviet propaganda stunt in the Russian émigré press and Evreinov himself was depicted as little more than a Bolshevik stooge. The attacks of the Russian émigré critics were soon echoed by those of the supportive anti-Communist Polish press. With the first performances of the Crooked Mirror virtually boycotted, Kugel and Evreinov fell to quarreling and soon after parted company for good. Kugel, and his wife Kholmskaya, took the troupe back to the Soviet Union, returning to their native Petersburg (now renamed Leningrad) where they succeeded in installing the Crooked Mirror in the basement of the former Palace Theater which was to be its home for the next six years (that is, until 1931). Evreinov remained abroad, eventually settling in Paris; until his death in the French capital in 1953, he spent his many years away from his homeland working in Russian émigré theater as a playwright and director, writing on the Russian stage, and traveling on occasion to foreign countries (including the United States) in connection with productions of his plays, above all the full-length dramatic work for which he is best known, *The Main Thing,* which he had completed in the Caucasus during the Civil War in 1920. A dramatized distillation of his views on theatricality, on stage and in life, the play also evidences the vitality of Evreinov's parodic gifts; the second act is a very amusing parody of a provincial theater's rehearsal of a stage version of the Polish writer Henryk Sienkiewicz's much acclaimed historical novel *Quo Vadis* conceived in the best tradition of the prerevolutionary Crooked Mirror.

Although the opening of the Crooked Mirror in its new Leningrad location on December 25, 1925, was hardly auspicious, the fertile field for satire created by conditions in the Soviet Union in the time of the New Economic Policy created a felicitous climate for the theater-cabaret as well as providing it with new material. With a combination of old "classics" and new satires and parodies on Soviet themes, the Crooked Mirror managed to survive until 1931. Kugel himself died in 1928 and although Kholmskaya survived him, the cabaret lost much of its drive after his death. The passing of Kugel, followed by the curtailment of the cultural liberalism of the NEP period and the mounting evidence of less tolerant internal policies made the demise of a theater-cabaret whose stock in trade was mockery only a matter of time. That time came definitively in 1931.

The Stray Dog

The next, and, to all intents and purposes, the last chapter in the history of the early twentieth-century Russian cabaret was written by the Brodyachaya sobaka (The Stray Dog) which opened its doors in Petersburg on the last day of the year 1911, within a year after the founding of the Crooked Mirror in the same city.

To anyone familiar with the rarified literary ambience for which the Stray Dog became justifiably famous in its relatively short history, it may indeed seem that at least one major Russian cabaret had succeeded in resisting the theatrical imperative of Russian cabaret life as a whole. If one speaks of the Stray Dog of 1913 and 1914, when it was the center of Petersburg literary life and the Russian literary avant-garde in general, the impression is essentially correct. By the time of its closure by the imperial police in March 1915 on the basis of a harch censorship code in force during World War I, the Stray Dog had become a true literary haunt, frequented by virtually every major figure in the development of Russian literary modernism. The list of habitués, which would be quite long indeed, would include—to mention just several of the better known names—Anna Akhmatova (1889–1966), Aleksandr Blok (1880–1921), Nikolai Gumilyov (1886–1921), Georgi Ivanov (1894–1958), Aleksei Kruchonykh (1886–1969?), Mikhail Kuzmin (1885–1922), Velimir Khlebnikov (1885–1939), Benedikt Livshits (1881–1939), Osip Mandelshtam (1891–1938), and Vladimir Mayakovsky (1893–1930), who came to Petersburg from Moscow in the autumn of 1912.

In the beginning, the Stray Dog was of a rather different character than what it became. The brainchild of the former actor and director Boris Pronin (1875–1946), a friend and sometime collaborator of Vsevolod

Meyerhold, the cabaret emerged from yet another artistic grouping with which Meyerhold was closely identified, the Artistic Society of the Intimate Theater (Khudozhestvennoe Obshchestvo Intimnogo Teatra). Its charter members included, besides Pronin and Meyerhold, such well-known theater people as Nikolai Evreinov and Fyodor Komissarzhevsky; the artists Sapunov and Sudeikin, who figured prominently in early twentieth-century Russian cabaret life; the poet, dramatist, and musician Mikhail Kuzmin, with whom Meyerhold had collaborated on a few productions, among them Blok's *The Fairbooth Show* (1906) and Znosko-Borovsky's *The Transfigured Prince* (1910); the Symbolist writer Aleksei Remizov (1877–1957); the composers Ilya Sats (1875–1912) and Valter Nuvel (1871–1949) of the famous *Mir Iskusstva* (World of Art) circle, and the music critic Alfred Nurok (1860–1919); the actor Aleksandr Mgebrov (1884–1966); David Krants, one of the founders and publishers of the important literary-artistic journal *Apollon;* the aristocrat Prince Georgi Sidamonov-Eristov (1885–after 1931), a patron of the arts and one of the most loyal backers of the Stray Dog.

In order to better understand Meyerhold's part in the establishment of the Stray Dog, a look at chronology is useful. Meyerhold's own cabaret theater, the House of Interludes, which he had launched with Kuzmin and Sapunov, had lasted, as we have seen, just a year, from 1910 to 1911. This was the same short life span as Evreinov's and Komissarzhevsky's Merry Theater for Grownup Children. When Evreinov was offered the artistic direction of the Crooked Mirror in 1910, the opportunity to work with a theater of small forms of greater potential negated the value of the Merry Theater, leaving that enterprise moribund.

The closing of the House of Interludes, however, left Meyerhold with no similar outlet and his enthusiasm as Dr. Dapertutto for the experimental possibilities of cabaret theater was too great at the time to remain long ungratified. The solution came in the context of Meyerhold's friendship with Boris Pronin, whose entrepreneurial eagerness to establish his own cabaret or intimate theater was matched by Meyerhold's desire to secure a "laboratory" for the experiments of his alter ego, Dr. Dapertutto. What resulted was the founding of the Artistic Society for the Intimate Theater whose premises in the neglected cellar of the old Dashkov mansion on the corner of Italyanskaya Street and Mikhailovsky Square would soon become known as the Stray Dog.[30]

Charged with new energy, Meyerhold threw himself into the endeavor with obvious delight. Oblivious to the dust, cold, and dampness of the place, he joined Pronin and other members of the Artistic Society and friends in transforming the murky former wine cellar into what the actor Mgebrov, a participant in the frenzied activity of renovation, compares to the kind of Faustian tavern so clearly depicted by Goethe. Before long, "fantastic huge fireplaces" were erected in its small cave-like vaulted rooms[31] and its once bare walls now bore frescoes painted by such outstanding artists of the time as Sapunov, Sudeikin, Aleksandr Yakovlev, and Boris Grigorev, among others. When everything was ready, the Stray Dog, so-called now to suggest a place where all the "stray dogs" on the different roads of contemporary Russian art could come together and be welcome, opened its doors on December 31, 1911, just in time for the New Year revels.

Pronin's original desire, his dream, in fact, was to establish a serious "theater of masks and Colombines"[32]—another temple, in other words, of the Italian *commedia dell'arte* and pantomime which had figured so prominently in Dr. Dapertutto's theater experimentation of 1909, 1910, and 1911. Pronin was not to see the dream fulfilled at the Stray Dog. Theatrical works were, of course, presented at the cabaret, among them two popular works by Kuzmin, his "pantomime-grotesque" *Vybor nevesty* (The Choice of a Bride) and a puppet Nativity play which was performed on January 6, 1913, to very favorable response.[33] There was also an evening (January 13, 1913) devoted to the memory of Kozma Prutkov, presided over by Prince Baryatynsky and carried out "entirely in the spirit of that naive tomfoolery with which the work of that distinguished poet [Kozma Prutkov—HBS] is permeated."[34] But the cramped basement quarters of the Stray Dog and the cabaret's tiny stage were not particularly conducive to theatrical numbers, less so even than other cabarets whose premises were also small. This may explain two developments that occurred even before the cabaret's first year of existence was at an end. One was Meyerhold's early withdrawal from active participation in the Stray Dog. Possibly disappointed that the new venture was not going to be as fulfilling theatrically as he had expected, and would have liked, Meyerhold soon transferred his enthusiasm from the Artistic Association of the Intimate Theater, which may be regarded as the parent organization of the Stray Dog, to his new Fellowship of Actors, Writers, Musicians, and Artists which was created in June 1912 at the seaside town of

Terioki just over the border in Finland. With Meyerhold as artistic director, the Fellowship, which consisted of a group of theater-oriented artists assembled by Meyerhold and the director and theater critic Vladimir Solovyov, lived communally on the grounds of a large estate at Terioki giving performances once in a while at the nearby Casino theater.[35] It was while he was at Terioki that Meyerhold succeeded in completing his well-known essay "Balagan" (The Fairground Booth), which was published along with other writings on the theater in a collective volume entitled *O teatre* (On Theater) in 1913. Further distancing Meyerhold from the Stray Dog were his acceptance in March 1913 of an invitation by Ida Rubinstein to come to Paris to direct her in a production of *La Pisanelle, ou la mort parfumée,* a weak verse-drama written as a showcase for her by an admiring D'Annunzio—the production was staged in June of that same year—and his opening in September 1913 of his own permanent theater-studio at 18 Troitskaya Street in Petersburg.

The other factor contributing to the change of character of the Stray Dog from what Pronin and Meyerhold may originally have had in mind was its rapid transformation into a type of literary salon.

Virtually from the outset, admission to the Stray Dog was limited to the kinds of "stray dogs" Pronin and company had in mind when they created the cabaret: artists, writers, musicians, and their friends. It was this exclusivity as well as the chance to have a common meeting ground that proved so attractive to Petersburg's artistic and intellectual elite. As word spread about the Stray Dog, its clientele and the exciting ambience of the place, an aura developed around it that made it irresistible to the public. The more the Stray Dog became the favorite gathering place of the Petersburg literati and Bohème, the more sought after it became by outsiders anxious to gawk at and rub shoulders with the celebrities known mostly by name.

While Pronin had no desire to open the doors to the cabaret to the public at large, he was not hostile to the idea of letting in a certain number of "outsiders" each night (the cabaret began to function usually only after midnight), but on payment of an outlandishly high admission fee, which could be as high as twenty-five rubles, no mean sum at the time. Hewing to the tradition of Rodolphe Salis, Aristide Bruant, and other cabaret entrepreneurs who came around to admitting the public, for the most part on a limited basis, but all the while heaping scorn on it, Pronin made a point of distinguishing between the artists who clustered in the

Stray Dog and the *farmatsevty* (pharmacists), or bourgeois public, he condescendingly let in for a price.

Although highly enthusiastic about the Stray Dog in the beginning and, in fact, in the years 1909 to 1911 when the cabaret still existed only in Pronin's dreams, the actor Mgebrov soon became disenchanted with it, as he writes in his memoiristic *A Life in the Theater:* "The official 'Stray Dog,' apart from the spring of 1912, lost much of its charm for me. When another era began, when it became less a romantic cellar than a commercial undertaking, I broke almost for good with Pronin."[36]

The evidence is, admittedly, circumstantial, but it is quite possible that Meyerhold's surprisingly early withdrawal from the Stray Dog was precipitated by a reaction similar to Mgebrov's concerning Pronin's increasing commercialism. Given his expectations as to what the cabaret might be able to achieve in the area of theatrical experimentation, Meyerhold is likely to have felt thwarted by the direction in which he saw the Stray Dog heading and so invested his hopes instead in the new Terioki undertaking with Solovyov.

With the Stray Dog well on its way to becoming not a theater-cabaret on the order of the Crooked Mirror but a semi-public literary salon, literary activities quickly took precedence over anything theatrical, so much so that by 1913 and 1914, the cabaret had an overwhelmingly literary character. Much of this transformation—apart from the physical limitations of the premises and Meyerhold's withdrawal—is attributable to the fact that the cabaret's emergence as the center of the Petersburg Bohème coincided with the emergence of the two most prominent avant-garde poetic camps of early twentieth-century Russia—futurism (Khlebnikov, Mayakovsky, Livshits) and acmeism (Akhmatova, Gumilyov, G. Ivanov). Before long, the Stray Dog became one of the principal battlegrounds between the two groups, enhancing the cabaret's aura as the most fashionable literary milieu of the time and turning its vaulted cellar premises into a forum for heated debates that often dragged on into the early hours of the morning.

Benedikt Livshits, one of the Stray Dog habitués during this period, offers some characteristic views of it in his book of memoirs entitled *Polutoroglazy strelets* (The One and a Half-Eyed Archer):

> I don't know what the "Stray Dog" was supposed to be according to the original conception of its founders when they established it in conjunction with the Artistic Society of the Intimate Theater. But in 1913 it was the only islet in noc-

turnal Petersburg where the literary and artistic youth, without a cent to their name as a general rule, felt at home.

The "Stray Dog" opened around midnight . . . Hither, like a hot dish in a thermos prepared at the other end of the city, they bore by coach, taxi, or tram a freshly baked triumph which people wanted to prolong, to savor over and over again while it still had not acquired the rancid taste of yesterday's success.

Making one's way past the cloud of stench which struck one squarely in the nose from the cesspit located nearby, everyone who did not succeed in removing his top hat on the threshold wound up breaking it against the low ceiling.

Covered in black silk, with a huge oval cameo on her belt, in floated Akhmatova, pausing at the entrance in order, on the insistence of Pronin who rushed forward to greet her, to inscribe in his "piggy book" [the cabaret guest book so called—HBS] her latest verses out of which the simpleminded "pharmacists" made conjectures that tickled only their curiosity.

In a long frock-coat and black boater's hat, without leaving a single attractive woman unnoticed, Gumilyov stepped back, retreating between the tables either observing courtly etiquette this way or fearing the "dagger" glance in the back.

Glistening of pomade which had not yet run down their faces, the Georgi Adamoviches furtively kissed the sweaty hands of the Georgi Ivanovs and squeezed each other's lustful knees beneath the table.

Beaming, as if fresh from communion, in came Pyast, who had just parted with Blok, and the sheen of his threadbare jacket seemed a glimmer of unexpected joy.

In the pose of a wounded gladiator, Mayakovsky lay on a Turkish drum striking it each time the figure of a Futurist who dropped in for a chat appeared at the door and a pickled Acmeist, not understanding what was going on, proclaimed from a dark corner, "Hommage! Hommage!"[37]

The style of the Stray Dog was informal, eclectic, and impromptu. There was a great deal of spur-of-the-moment recitation and argumentation, all the more impassioned for the lateness of the hour when they took place. But whatever the fervor of rival artistic viewpoints, the atmosphere was one of an almost carnivalesque gaiety and cameraderie. Mikhail Kuzmin, whose own association with the Stray Dog was so close, captures much of this spirit in the mock "hymn" of the Stray Dog that he wrote in late 1912; I shall quote only the first stanza of the well-known poem in the original (in transliteration):

Ot rozhdeniya podvala
Proletel lish bystry god,
No "Sobaka" nas svyazala
V tesno-druzhny khorovod.
Chya dusha pechal uznala

Opuskaites v glub podvala
Otdykhaite (3 raza) ot nevzgod . . .[38]

(From the birth of the cellar/ Barely a year has flown by,/ But the "Dog" has bound us together/ In a merry-go-round of close friendship./ If your spirit is burdened with care,/ Descend into the depths of the cellar/ And there rest from your woes./

We pull no long faces;/ We're ready ever to drink and to sing./ You'll find here singers, ballerinas,/ And artists of all sorts./ Pantomimes and shows/ Are performed for no reason by Général de Kroughlikoff.[39]/

Our maidens and our ladies,/ What a delight for eye and mouth!/ A guild of poets—all "Adams"[40]/ Each one pleasant and not crude./ Don't be afraid of the dog pit,/ Even Sologub drops in/ On our hubbub and racket./ Our artists, who are anything but savage,/ Decorate the walls and fireplaces./ Here are Belkin and Meshchersky,/ And the Cubist Kulbin.[41]/ The insolent Mr. Sudeikin himself/ Takes command as if leading a company of grenadiers./

And our prestige has not fallen/ As long as Podgorny-Birdie,/ Kolya Peter, Gibshman,[42]/ And the captivating Bobish[43]/ Are alive./ The spirit of music has not fallen,/ We are still in Apollo's good graces./ You won't surprise us with anything!/

Ah! . . . / And Pallas Athena[44] hasn't been forgotten/ In this titled circle./ Like an ancient dryad/ Who gambols about in a meadow,/ Love is a sheer delight to her,/ And, where necessary,/ She'll never answer, "I can't!")

Anna Akhmatova, like Kuzmin a denizen of the Stray Dog, also contributed to its literary lore. In one of her best known poems of 1913, the text of which follows in translation, she extrapolates from her own experience as one of the cabaret's stellar female attractions to portray the uninhibited, theatrical, and faintly libertine atmosphere of the Stray Dog as irresistibly decadent and, because of this, foredoomed:

We're all revellers here, and harlots./ How unjoyful we are all together!/ On the walls flowers and birds/ Drift languidly along clouds./ You smoke a black pipe,/ How strange the smoke about her./ I put on a narrow skirt/ In order to seem all the more shapely./ Little windows boarded up forever:/ What's out there, hoarfrost or a storm?/ Your eyes resemble those of a cautious kitten./ Oh, how anxious is my heart!/ Am I not awaiting the hour of my death?/ And she, who is now dancing,/ Will unfailingly end in hell./[45]

Undoubtedly, Akhmatova's greatest literary work associated with the Stray Dog milieu is the *Poema bez geroya* (Poem Without a Hero). It was begun in 1940 and was completed only in 1962, when a longstanding ban on publication of Akhmatova's "decadent" poetry in the Soviet Union was lifted and her literary "rehabilitation" begun. A work of undeniably deep personal meaning, the poem was inspired by the suicide of the minor poet Vsevolod Knyazev in 1913. For several years the lover of the homosexual Kuzmin, Knyazev fell in love with the reputedly beautiful and talented actress Olga Glebova, the wife of the painter Sudeikin. Unable to find a satisfactory way out of his bisexual impasse, Knyazev took his own life in 1913. A close friend of Olga Glebova as well as of Kuzmin, Akhmatova was profoundly touched by the senseless death of the handsome young poet and brooded over the event as a tragic fulfillment of the foreboding expressed in her earlier poem "We're all revellers, harlots . . . " It was as if the poet had uncovered the dark underside of the cabaret's carnivalesque surface.

Poetry readings as well as lectures on literature and language—the latter an area of great contention in view of the far-reaching experiments with poetic language then being undertaken by the Futurists, Acmeists, and others—were staples at the Stray Dog. Nikolai Kulbin lectured on "The New World View," Vladimir Pyast on "The Theater of the Word and the Theater of Movement," and the drama critic Sergei Auslender on "Theatrical Dilettantism," which went to the very heart of cabaret art with its carefully cultivated illusion of nonprofessional, spontaneous performance. The fine literary scholar and co-founder of the Formalist movement, Viktor Shklovsky (1893–1984), then a young man and a self-proclaimed Futurist,[46] delivered an important talk on "The Place of Futurism in the History of Language" (Mesto futurizma v istorii yazyka) which in published form in 1914 was hailed as the first clear pronouncement of formalism. In his lecture Shklovsky addressed himself primarily to the language of poetry; he distinguished between the old art of the word and the new, underscored the value of "estrangement" (*strannost*) as a weapon in the battle against ordinariness, and identified the chief task of futurism as the "resurrection of things, the return to man of the experience of the world" (zadacha futurizma—voskreshchenie veshchei, vozvrashchenie cheloveku perezhivaniya mira).[47] Shklovsky recalls that there were few people in attendance at his lecture, that they argued a great deal over it, and that the poet Voldemar Shileiko (1891–1930), who was a well-known specialist in the Sumero-Akkadian language, arose to dispute his contentions.[48] Vladimir Pyast, who was in the audience at the time, offers his own account of the occasion in his book *Vstrechi* (Encounters), which was published in Moscow in 1929:

only at one in the morning in the "Dog" does the philological-linguistic lecture of the young Shklovsky on the "Resurrection of the Word" begin. (From the view-point of the Philistines, of all possible subjects, it would be hard to think of a more boring one!) The point of departure for the learned young scholar's heated talk is language as reanimated by Velimir Khlebnikov [one of the leaders of the Russian Cubo-Futurists—HBS]. He presented in the hard shell of a learned nut the quintessence of the most difficult thoughts of Aleksandr Veselovsky and [Aleksandr] Potebnya[49] already penetrated by the rays of his own "inventions," as they used to say at the time. By virtue of his own powerful, truly resurrected, living language, he compels the large audience,[50] now become very still, to lis-ten. Almost half the audience was made up of the "evening-dress crowd" or women in low-necked dresses. At half past two, discussions began. The tuxedos and décollétes, of course, having nothing to say.[51]

Another informative inside view of Stray Dog literary lectures and dis-cussions comes from Mikhail Kuzmin who published a short account in the *Sini Zhurnal* (Blue Journal) in 1914 of a lecture that he himself gave at the cabaret. The account is titled "How I Gave a Lecture at the 'Stray Dog' " (Kak ya chital doklad v "Brodyachey sobake"). The account is short enough to quote almost in full:

Not long ago I gave a lecture on the premises of the "Stray Dog" about con-temporary Russian prose. It was more in the nature of an intimate and candid talk not so much about prose exclusively as about the state of contemporary Russian literature after the victory of modernism in the '90s and the discontinu-ance of a special publication. After *The Scales* [*Vesy,* the leading Symbolist journal—HBS] there was no bulwark of modernism and all writers went not to the nation, but to the public, contributing to big and small journals alike and thereby bringing about the assimilation of the old and new ones. The necessity to free criticism not only from social and political viewpoints, but also from a bias toward the service of one particular school. The results of all schools should be technical; the inconvenience, almost the impossibility of idealistic bases for literary schools. The need for the individual personality of the author. Complete confusion in the division into groups, with the results that F. Sologub and Z. Gippius show up in the group of Ego-Futurists, as participants in the *Enchanted Wanderer* [*Ocharovanny putnik*]. The sole criterion can be only the technical analysis of language and verse. Three paths open to prose: the path of simplicity (Pushkin), that of Russian floweriness and sumptuousness (Gogol through Leskov), and the path of the filtered language of the intelligentsia (Turgenev through Chekhov). . . . The services rendered by acmeism and fu-turism (liberation of the word). New energies can be expected only from the Futurists and the "wild ones" [*dikikh*]. In conclusion, excerpts from a novel by V. Modzalevsky, V. Khlebnikov's *Death of Burnwater* [*Smert Palivody*], and chapters from Yuri Yurkun's novel *The Swedish Gloves* [*Shvedskie perchatki*],[52] which was then in press, were read.

The discussion as well as the lecture was chaired by T. G. Shenfeld. Rebuttals came from N. Kulbin, B. Mosolov, N. Zdanevich, M. Moravskaya, N. Gumilyov, Mr. Demchinsky and Mr. Velyanson. N. Kulbin expatiated on the theory of the liberation of the word. N. Zdanevich demonstrated the need for schools as instruments of conflict and polemics and attributed great significance to the novelty of technical devices, supporting his view with excerpts from Yurkin's novel. M. Moravskaya stressed the necessity of trend and found the contemporary trend in a turning to the simpler and folkish. She recalled E. Guro.[53] N. Gumilyov attested to the isolation of the public and writers with respect to each other, considered literary schools necessary, like labels and a passport without which, in the view of the rebuttalist, a person is only half a person and in no way a citizen. He found the contemporary trend to be a striving toward spiritual nakedness and he imagines that it is entirely of short duration. . . . After the discussions, M. Kuzmin, Ryurik Ivnev, M. Moravskaya, and D. Tseizor read poems.[54]

Pyast notes further in *Encounters* that these "serious lectures" (*seryoznye doklady*) at the Stray Dog, which began usually at one in the morning, fascinated not only the Futurists, who seemed to take a particular interest in them, but also poets who belonged to no group. Toward the end of a designated "season," it became the custom at the Dog to present a serious lecture each Monday night. Pyast remembers that "Professor A. A. Smirnov gave a talk on 'Simultaneity' (in painting and partly in declamation). How young and how elegant at the time was the artist G. B. Yakulov who had just arrived from Paris where he became impregnated with just this trend! He demonstrated a narrow stripe, painted with the colors of a rainbow, only not in the order of a spectrum. And the entire stripe, which you held in your hands, seemed to be continuously moving before your eyes. Such were the qualities of such a combination of colors."[55]

Besides lectures, discussions, and readings of poetry and prose, the Stray Dog also organized special evenings and sometimes weeks in honor of outstanding domestic and foreign artists. One of the evenings, for example, which was held on March 26, 1914, was dedicated to the great Russian ballerina Tamara Karsavina. This is how she describes the event, and the Stray Dog itself, in her own book of reminiscences, *Theatre Street:*

Comparatively few amongst the artists had been sent to the Front. We still continued to meet at the *Wandering Dog* [the "Stray Dog"—HBS], an artistic club, distinctly Bohemian, as its name suggests. Artists of a permanent job and steady habits, relative Philistines of the caste, patronized but little the *Wandering Dog*. Actors hectically making a precarious living, musicians of prospective fame, poets and their muses, and a few aesthetes gathered there every night. And when I say "Muses," I would like to warn off any possible misconception towards this lovable species, some of unusual attire, but not failing to give expression to a distinct personality; there was no affectation and no tiresome *cliché* in the manner of the fair members of the club, whether of some social standing or none.

I had been brought there for the first time by a friend, a painter, in the year before the war. My reception on this occasion had a certain solemnity. I was hoisted up in my chair and, slightly embarrassed, acknowledged the cheers. This ritual was equivalent to bestowing on me the freedom of the cellar; and, though not qualified for a Bohemian, I felt the place congenial. It was a cellar of a big house, and originally used for storing firewood; Soudekine had decorated it—Tartaglia and Pantalone, Smeraldina and Brigella [Italian commedia dell'arte figures—HBS] and Carlo Gozzi himself smiled and grimaced from the walls. For the most part the entertainments were unrehearsed ones. Acclaimed, an actor would come forward and give of what his mood suggested, if at all in a mood for doing so. The poets, always amenable, recited their new poems; and some nights nothing happened on the stage. Then the host would take a guitar and sing, and when he came to a favourite song all joined in the refrain: "Oh, Maria, oh, Maria, how sweet is this world."

I danced for them one night to the music of Couperin, the Cuckoos and Dominos and the Chimes of Cytherea, not on the stage, but in the midst of them, within a small space encircled by garlands of fresh flowers. The choice had been mine; in those days I dearly loved all the sweet futility of hoops and patches and the sound of harpsichord like a glorified choir of insects. My friends responded by the "Bouquet," that day straight from the Press. In this almanack the poets had written their madrigals to me, and some fresh ones were made and recited at supper. "*Quelle floraison vous faites éclore, Madame,*" summed up a man of the world; for in their zeal to make this evening select the *Wandering Dog* had invited some distinguished guests, amongst them a great friend of mine, whose British dislike of the demonstrative kept him looking at his watch, while my poets exerted themselves in recitations, and asking me how long I meant to stay with these microbes. The *Wandering Dog* lingered through the war, dragging its impecunious existence up to the second year of the Revolution.[56]

Among the "special" weeks celebrated at the Stray Dog were those in honor of such non-Russian artists as the founder of Italian futurism, Filippo Tommaso Marinetti (1876–1944), the French balladeer Paul Fort (1872–1960), and the highly popular French comic actor known best under the assumed name of Max Linder (1883–1925), all of whom visited St. Petersburg in the period of the Stray Dog and became guest stars of the cabaret for the duration of their stay there.

The excitement of the Futurists over the visit of Marinetti to Russia, and to St. Petersburg in particular, lent a special glow to the week held in his honor at the Stray Dog. Since they felt that the literary atmosphere of the cabaret was more hospitable to the Acmeists than themselves and that Boris Pronin looked down his nose at them, the Futurists believed that a visit by the respected high priest of Italian futurism would improve their image and send their stock soaring.

Marinetti's eagerly awaited visit to Russia began with great fanfare in Moscow at the beginning of February 1914. Arriving after a long and tiring train trip that began in Berlin and carried him through Warsaw, the Italian poet was obviously gratified by his reception but not entirely comfortable—or uncritical—of his new surroundings. He recalls in typical Futurist prose style that

After a deep sleep I wake in the austere barren frozen Moscow railroad station feeling like a piece of lost luggage that's been found but there's no key and so it must await its owner while pretty customs inspectresses gather round solicitously ugly if they speak Russian but better if they speak French while their men pickled in alcohol curse the cameras and magnesium flare popping all over the place laughter and great bouquets of flowers while criticism and praise of Futurism multiply on all sides the Futurism safely back in Milan not the real me approaching the great cold frightening heart of Moscow.[57]

Although partially compensated for whatever discomfort he may have experienced by what he would have us believe was his extraordinary success with Russian women, Marinetti's public appearances in Moscow were not without mishap. On one occasion, he writes

In the packed amphitheater lecture hall of the university I use a large portrait of the Tsar to explain the absurdity of *verismo* when all of a sudden a group of officers and soldiers with bayonets at the ready begins moving toward the speaker's stand but fortunately are stopped by my usual female admirers excitedly explaining over and over again in Russian that I didn't mean anything revolutionary or disrespectful but just an artistic explanation.

Standing to receive their enthusiastic applause and the repeated comment "Yes you are the great Futurist not these stupid sensation-mongering Russian Futurists. (p. 347)

Controversy flared up all around him as rival groups of Russian Futurists took the occasion of his visit to intensify their hostilities. Marinetti himself was well aware of what was happening, as his further account of the Moscow visit makes clear:

My lectures provoke arguments between the group of Russian Futurist painters known as the "Donkey's Tail" headed by Larionov[58] and the group of Futurist writers called "Ferment" who decides to protest against the Italian poet by leaving Moscow.

A third group crops up known as "Bouquets to Marinetti" headed by Tatseven but he turns out to be a peculiar supporter and impresario having written about me in the most solemn and deadly terms saying that "Futurist depravation is a force and therefore a glory to desire cripple the defeated and woe to the woman who feels pity for a man's tears she must kill him immediately unless she wants to debase herself below the basest whore."

In all the bookstores and smart shops there's a caricature of me in the window showing me half bombarded by rotten fruit and half colonized by feminine hearts.

My raging success with women arouses the ire of the "Donkey's Tail" group whose leader after he had denounced me as a traitor to Futurism in an article introduces me affectionately into the most important literary circle and eating drinking and talking in French with his Russian wife Goncharova[59] I'm allowed to attend an important meeting.

We stand in the back of the packed room and discover that a violent argument is raging on stage between university professors and poets about Futurism and me. (p. 347)

Marinetti's arrival in St. Petersburg on February 4 (1914) was, to judge from his own account, even more spectacular than the one in Moscow:

At St. Petersburg the station is jammed picturesquely with the wildest most luxurious furs monumental white bearskin hats mustaches of iced Bernini proportions and all through this enthusiastic reception I keep thinking with every arctic blast about having my triumphs in some cave somewhere. (p. 357)

Hardly did he arrive in St. Petersburg when Marinetti was swept up in the embrace of the local avant-garde and rushed off for exhibit at the Stray Dog like some rare specimen. Again, his own punctuation-less recollection of the events is worth quoting:

A peculiar avant-garde this one different from the French and even from the avant-garde of Moscow bringing together shabby poets beautiful actresses loaded with pearls grand dukes Futurist painters dancers cartoonists industrialists engineers electrical technicians Siberian prisoners ship commanders from Odessa policemen university professors sculptors and Italian architects who swarm around me with too many ribbons and blasts of wind and I'm swallowed into a downstairs place called Sabacha [meaning the Brodyachaya Sobaka, or Stray Dog—HBS] which means wild dog.

> Luxurious enough but I still feel like a wild dog forced to bark for his supper no matter how tired and longing for sleep and Italian solitude. (p. 357)

Describing the Stray Dog as "made up of about seven rooms painted and draped with a variety of materials velvets and purple brocades and many portraits of me done by Kulbin and Larionov" (p. 357).[60] Marinetti made the cabaret the focus of most of his activity in St. Petersburg.

For two nights in a row he regaled his admirers with readings of his own works and those of his friends and with impromptu explanations—in the French in which he was so fluent—of his literary and aesthetic beliefs. The Futurists, of course, were beside themselves with joy. "Our sense of unity with him," wrote Vladimir Pyast, "notwithstanding the hostile receptions with which his closest Russian brothers-in-arms, i.e. the Futurists, the Ego-Cubists, were greeted, was so complete that everyone as if instantly and suddenly without difficulty grasped the French language (in which, and not Italian, he wrote and declaimed) . . . And indeed in Marinett's mouth this language was entirely comprehensible. He accompanied himself with gestures which made clear the concepts tossed out by him to his auditors. His poems consisted entirely of nouns, whether subjects or spoken in 'resurrected language,' that is, 'onomatopoetic' (giving their contents in the sounds themselves)."[61]

To Benedikit Livshits, another eyewitness to Marinetti's visit, the Italian was a model of self-composure, unruffled by the strangeness of his surroundings, who used every occasion to speak or declaim from his own works in order to advance the cause of futurism:

> Here, in this cellar, where the most interesting lectures were drowned out by the noise of forks and knives, where a month later Paul Fort, thrown into confusion by the surroundings, wore down the far from innocent "pharmacists" with his *conférences,* Marinetti did not deliver a single lecture, did not make a single report, although at any time of the day or night he could speak endlessly on the subject of futurism which had clearly become the sole content of his life.[62]

As Livshits' remarks suggest, Marinetti was a hard act to follow, as Paul Fort must have discovered, to his disappointment. For Pyast, Fort's visit was more in keeping with the Stray Dog's spirit. The Parisian poet was, after all, a Socialist; he had recently (in 1912) been crowned the "prince of poets," and he was the founder and editor of a modernist journal, *Vers et Prose,* which had an extremely limited circle of subscribers. Of Fort's visit to the Stray Dog, Pyast writes:

He was the last representative of that Parisian Bohème which goes back centuries in time. He himself ran a similar night café in Paris, the "Closerie de Lilas" (The Croft of Lilacs). About it, and about all its forerunners—about all the Parisian "Stray Dogs," in other words, beginning with the fifteenth century—Fort delivered a most learned lecture the program of which, decorated with elegant graphics, he gave as a present to the proprietor of the "Petersburg Dog" as a memento. He read an endless quantity of his evidently colorless and in any case completely incomprehensible (unlike Marinetti's) *poèmes.*

Sometimes his voice gave out—or perhaps it was for some other reason—and his place was taken by a woman whom he called "Mademoiselle" Germaine d'Orfer, who came with Fort to Russia—HBS who got up from his table and performed while he remained seated. I've forgotten her name. She was very tender, her voice sounded soft and deep. If the texts continued to remain incomprehensible, when "M-lle" performed hearing and sight, nevertheless, were stroked. I remember how she blushed gratefully when one of the audience paid her a compliment in French: "Quand vous récitez ces vers, vous êtes vous même comme une poème" [When you recite these verses, you yourself are like a poem].[63]

The visit by Max Linder was still less of a success, despite his enormous popularity in Russia, if we are to judge from Vladimir Pyast's account:

Plans were made to hold a "Max Linder week." But nothing came of it. As soon as the harried small fellow entered the "Dog" . . . you could at once feel to what degree he bore with him a foreign, petit bourgeois tone. (The poor artist eventually wound up a tragic suicide.) Kulbin immediately noticed this in his speech, which was delivered, it's true, in the Russian dialect, but with the insertion of the "Dog's" favorite French word, *hommage* . . . The only *hommage* that we allow our guest to be shown, said Kulbin, will be that you, Boris [Pronin—HBS] will not take any money from him for admission.

And we, the artistic Bohème, suddenly as if buttoned ourselves up tight in the presence of this element that was foreign to us, as if it were an alien body that fell into our boullion saturated with compatible bacteria. Linder sat in a corner, and two elegantly dressed ladies who were little known to us occupied him with sedate conversation. Linder established no contact at all with the entire auditorium at the entrance to which it used to be announced: "All know each other."[64]

The Comics' Halt

The establishment of the Prival komediantov (Comics' Halt), the immediate successor to the Stray Dog, which was closed by police order in 1915, followed the pattern of the latter's founding in terms of Meyerhold's involvement and the cabaret's theatrical orientation.

The first glimmer of the appearance of a successor to the Stray Dog came in the announcement in the second issue of the journal *Apollon* for 1916 that a new cellar theater named Zvezdochot would open in late March of that year, with a fresh production of Schnitzler's pantomime *The Veil of Pierette* (*Sharf Kolombiny,* Colombine's Scarf, in Russian) by Dr. Dapertutto (Vsevolod Meyerhold, of course) with sets and costumes by Sergei Sudeikin. Again uniting the talents of Meyerhold and Pronin, the original plan called for a Teatr podzemnykh klassikov (Theater of Underground Classics) whose repertoire would include plays by Claudel, Maeterlinck, Tieck, Strindberg, Kuzmin, the Russian authority on the Italian commedia dell'arte Konstantin Miklashevsky, and others.

With the production of the Schnitzler pantomime in April 1916, which received only lukewarm review, Meyerhold's collaboration with the enterprise promptly ceased. The old official designation, carried over from Stray Dog days, of the Society of the Intimate Theater remained, but the cabaret, now headed by Evreinov and N. V Petrov, a young director at the Aleksandrinsky Theater, bore the name of the Comics' Halt.[65]

The premises of the new cabaret were larger and more ornate than those of the Stray Dog and featured, above all, decorations by Sergei Sudeikin in honor of the spiritual forebears of the cabaret, the late eighteenth-century Italian dramatist Carlo Gozzi, who attempted a revival of the commedia dell'arte and a synthesis of the improvised tradition of the commedia and literary comedy, and the great German Romantic story writer E. T. A. Hoffmann after both of whom the central hall of the Comics' Halt was named.[66] In contrast to the Stray Dog, the atmosphere of the Comics' Halt was restrained and commercial. But like the reborn Crooked Mirror of 1922, which closed its doors forever in 1931, it found the postrevolutionary environment of Soviet Russia less hospitable to the spirit that had prevailed earlier and shut down in 1919.

The continued existence of a Crooked Mirror and attempts to preserve a cabaret-like art notwithstanding, the brilliant era of the early twentieth-century Russian cabaret—the period from 1908 to 1919—was over. The emigration of Nikita Baliev together with other members of the Bat and the reestablishment of the first Russian cabaret in Paris in 1920 as the Chauve-Souris patently symbolized the end of that era.

Writing of what he regarded as the failure of Russian society to preserve an authentic artistic cabaret, free from commercialization and the inroads of the bourgeois, the actor A. A. Mgebrov, whose two-volume book of memoirs, *A Life in the Theater,* contains valuable comments especially on the Stray Dog, held Russia's lack of culture principally responsible:

Russia still lacked sufficient culture to create something similar to Montmartre. Pharmacists and burghers, the bourgeois and predators, of whom there have always been and still are so many in our country, indeed have a great idea—the unification of artists of all branches. But they very quickly destroyed the idea and the artists themselves with it. And that is why for me the "Stray Dog" in later years almost ceased to exist.[67]

Had he been able to view the development of the cabaret in Europe as a whole in the late nineteenth and early twentieth centuries, Mgebrov's judgment would doubtless have been more benign. That is because the commercialization he decried with respect to the Russian cabaret was the fate of cabaret virtually throughout Europe. The intensity with which the spirit of cabaret was entered into, above all by the participating artists, in the early history of the phenomenon, made it all but impossible to sustain the momentum for long periods of time, hence the frequent openings and closings of cabarets. And even if this had not been the case, it can only be a matter of conjecture how long it might have been possible to preserve the artistic "purity" and integrity of the cabarets without the eventual admission of a paying public in ever larger numbers in view of the costs of even modest productions and the notorious business sense of so many of the people associated with cabarets.

What stands out so strikingly in the case of the Russian cabaret in the decade 1908 to 1918 is not so much the capitulation to the bourgeois as the inability of the Russians to develop a cabaret of the archetypical Western pattern for any but the briefest period. The extreme reactionary nature of the state and the ever present police surveillance made the kind of social and political satire typical of much Western cabaret (including that of Germany, particularly Munich, where repressive conditions also prevailed) difficult if not impossible. Even had they so desired it (and there is really nothing to indicate that they did), the Russians were thus denied an important dimension of cabaret culture common in the West. There were also specific forms resistant to transplantation in Russian soil, above all the Parisian chanson or the type of chanson-like macabre and corrosive *Moritaten* for which Frank Wedekind was renowned in Munich in the early years of the century. The Russian cabaret, in fact, produced no outstanding singers or poets with a distinct cabaret identification, in yet another depature from Western experience. What remained was theater and theatrical spectacle, on the one hand, and the heated atmosphere of conflicting avant-garde literary groups, on the other; it was principally from these two sources that the major Russian cabarets drew their greatest inspiration and sustenance.

The predominance of theater in the cabarets was understandable in light of the great ferment in Russian theatrical culture of the time and the virtual impossibility of experimenting and innovating within the world of the imperial theater system. When a great new theater came into being in the late nineteenth century, the Moscow Art Theater, the style for which it became world famous was regarded as an anachronism by the avant-garde and they turned on it with the kind of disdain reserved previously for the old imperial theaters. Against this background, the overwhelming preoccupation with theater on the part of the authors of cabaret satires and parodies should come as no surprise. If it is proper to speak of a certain theatricalization of Russian life in the early twentieth century, a theatricalization by which the community of artists and intellectuals responded to the greater social and political unreality around them, then the Russian cabaret of the early twentieth century deserves consideration as another aspect of that theatricalization, of that making life a carnival before the imminent descent into the abyss.

CHAPTER SEVEN

ZURICH: DADA VOLTAIRE

Tom Stoppard's scintillating play *Travesties* (1974) evokes a vivid picture of Zurich during the Great War. As a refuge from the madness of a war that was to transform the political map of Europe, the picturesque city on the banks of the Limmat was a natural magnet for expatriates of every stripe: draft dodgers, revolutionaries, pacifists, agents, and artists who needed some island of relative sanity and stability in which to pass the events taking place around them through the prism of a consciousness no longer content with traditional forms. It was that motley community of expatriates, clustered mostly in the old town of narrow streets and cobblestone roads that rises up from the banks of the Limmat but a short distance from the city's commercial center, that gave an otherwise placid Zurich so much of its political and artistic dynamism during the war.

In *Travesties,* Stoppard has his central character, the British consular official Henry Carr, note with special delight that one of the streets in the Old Town, Spiegelgasse, was the hatching ground of two revolutions:

Now here's a thing: two revolutions formed *in the same street.* Face to face in Spiegelgasse! *Street of Revolution!* A *sketch.* Meet by the sadly-sliding chagrinned Limmat River, strike west and immediately we find ourselves in the Old Town, having left behind the banking bouncing metropolis of trampolines and chronometry of all kinds for here time has stopped in the riddled maze of alleyways and by the way you'd never believe a Swiss redlight district, pornographic fretwork shops, vice dens, get a grip on yourself, sorry, sorry, second right, third left—Spiegelgasse!—narrow, cobbled, high old houses in a solid rank, number 14 the house of the narrow cobbler himself, Kammerer his name, Lenin his tenant—and across the way at Number One, the Meierei Bar, crucible of anti-art, cradle of Dada!!! Who? What? Whatsisay Dada?? You remember Dada!—historical halfway house between Futurism and Surrealism, twixt Marinetti and André Breton, 'tween the before-the-war-to-end-all-wars years and the between-the-wars years—Dada!—down with reason, logic, causality, coherence, tradition, proportion, sense and consequence . . .[1]

Whether Lenin's presence there for a time during the Great War justifies regarding Zurich as a "hatching ground" of the Russian Revolution remains for historians to decide. But that the great Swiss city became the cradle of the revolution in art known as Dada is beyond question. Since the emergence of Dada is inseparable from the rise and fall of the Cabaret Voltaire, it is to that most famous cabaret in Swiss history that we now turn our attention.

Among the expatriates who sought out Zurich primarily as a refuge from war was the young German poet Hugo Ball (1886–1927), who was to become the founder of the "Cabaret Voltaire" and a principal architect of Dada. Ball's interest in cabaret was an outgrowth of his serious involvement in theater which antedated his resettlement in Zurich. Between 1910 and 1914, for example, he was enrolled as a student in the Max Reinhardt school of acting and directing in Berlin in order to acquire the training that would enable him to make a career in the theater. Later writing of his passion for the stage in this period of his life in his memoiristic *Die Flucht aus der Zeit* (Flight Out of Time), Ball wrote: "Between 1910–1914 the theater was everything to me: life, society, love, morality. To me the theater signified elusive freedom."[2] Although he failed as an actor, Ball was more successful as a director and for a while in 1913 held the directorship of the Munich Kammerspiele.

Ball's natural inclination toward café literary society and the artistic Bohème of the time resulted in two of the most significant encounters of his life. At the famous Café des Westens in Berlin, the gathering place of the capital's intelligentsia and literati, he met another poet, Richard Huelsenbeck, with whom he was to renew his acquaintance in Munich in 1912 and who was to join him as one of the central figures of Zurich Dada and the Cabaret Voltaire. In Munich, whence his theatrical and artistic interests led him after Berlin, Ball ventured into the popular Simplicissimus cabaret one night in the autumn of 1913 and it was there that he met Emmy Hennings, a performer at the cabaret and the woman who was to become not only the great love of his life but the greatest single influence on it as well.

When war broke out, Ball volunteered for military service convinced as so many of his fellow artists were that war was the inferno through which the rotten society of contemporary Europe had to pass in order to be reborn. But he was rejected for medical reasons and when he tried to enlist on two other occasions, he was again rejected. Intensely curious about the war, the more so for having been thrice rejected for military service, Ball, on his own, took a trip to Belgium in November 1914 to witness the conflict firsthand. What he saw turned him so vehemently against the war that he conceived a profound loathing for the German militarism that he held accountable for it. On New Year's Day 1915, he took part in an antiwar demonstration in Berlin and not long afterward resolved to leave Germany altogether.

With forged papers and an assumed name, he and Emmy Hennings crossed into Switzerland in May of that year to join the growing colony of expatriates of different nationalities. Although the Swiss authorities eventually caught on to his ruse and briefly imprisoned him until the true facts of the matter could be established, Ball was permitted to remain in Switzerland. But his and Emmy Henning's life there was one of considerable want and discomfort. As unregistered aliens neither of them was allowed by Swiss law to work except on a part-time basis, which limited them for the most part to menial jobs. Ball continued to write concentrating especially on a "fantastic novel" begun earlier[3] and a book about German culture intended to explore the ruthlessness and folly of Prussian militarism. But the prospects of earning an income from such writing were anything but reassuring. Indeed, the first break in their luck came when Ball was taken on as a pianist by a vaudeville troupe called the Flamingo, an experience not without bearing on his subsequent activity as a cabaretist and which he transmogrified into the adventures of the titular character of his second (and only other) novel, *Flametti oder vom Dandysmus der Armen* (Flametti, or The Dandyism of the Poor), published in 1918.

The absence of regular employment in Ball's early period in Switzerland left ample time not only for writing but also for the avid study of politics in which he had become seriously interested as the result of his stance toward the war and his enmity for the system that had produced it. By now a convinced pacifist, Ball was also attracted for a while to the philosophy of anarchism and immersed himself in the works especially of the Russians Bakunin and Kropotkin. The attraction did not prove durable, however; Ball found himself at odds with what he regarded as the essential utopianism of the anarchists and soon repudiated the movement for a more abiding interest in the spiritual and mystic. As the war dragged on longer and the privations and frustrations of his personal life mounted, Ball delved deeper into the metaphysical and occult. His quest for inner peace was aided and abetted by the religious pieties of Emmy Hennings which her conversion to Roman Catholicism in 1920, the year in which she and Ball finally married, only intensified.

Ball's political and spiritual views ripened into two major prose works which he wrote after *Flametti* and at a time when he had largely withdrawn from further active participation in the Dada movement. The first was the mystical *Byzantinisches Christentum* (Byzantine Christianity, 1923), about the lives of the ascetic saints John Climacus, Dionysius the Areopagite, and Simeon Stylites; the second was a withering assault on German society and the German religious, political, and intellectual heritage originally titled *Zur Kritik der deutschen Intelligenz* (Toward a Critique of the German Mind, 1919), later expanded and retitled *Die Folgen der Reformation* (The Consequences of the Reformation, 1924). Death came to the anguished, spiritually questing Ball in 1927 at the age of forty-one. Before the end, he had managed to complete two more prose works, a biography of the writer Herman Hesse, with whom he and Emmy Hennings had developed a friendship, on the occasion of Hesse's fiftieth birthday, and a personal memoir, *Die Flucht aus der Zeit* (Flight Out of Time, first published in 1947), which, in view of Ball's state of mind at the time, was aptly titled.

The Cabaret Voltaire

Ball's entry into the world of cabaret and the establishment of the Cabaret Voltaire in 1916 did not come about by chance. His enthusiasm for the theater together with his growing anti-establishment feelings and especially his relationship with Emmy Hennings, herself a talented cabaret performer, stimulated his interest in cabaret and eventually inclined him in that direction. Furthermore, his association with the Flamingo troupe brought him into direct contact with variety theater and vaudeville and taught him lessons about the art of *Kleinkunst*—albeit in this instance on a lower popular level—that he would remember and to some extent try to incorporate into the programs of the Cabaret Voltaire.

Although these formative experiences and influences must be taken into account when tracing the genesis of Ball's active participation in cabaret, the growing expatriate community in wartime Zurich probably weighs heaviest in an assessment of those factors that set him on this course. As the colony of expatriates grew to include more artists and malcontents like himself, as well as such friends as Leonhard Frank and Richard Huelsenbeck, Ball must have felt an irresistible impulse to find some way of bringing as many of these people together as possible, both to share experiences and views and to break out of the isolation imposed on them by Swiss law and custom.

Once Ball had conceived the idea of opening a literary and artistic cabaret, he approached Jan Ephraim, an old Dutch seaman and the proprietor of a café known as the Hollandische Meierei located at No. 1 Spiegelgasse, with the proposition that he allow him to establish his new cabaret on the premises of his café. Once assured that the enterprise would bring in different clientele than he was used to and, more importantly, that his business would improve, Ephraim agreed. The cabaret was on its way. Not much refurbishing was necessary, or possible. The Meierei already had a small stage, a piano, and enough tables to hold upwards of fifty people. Ephraim himself was not going to put up any money for new furniture or decorations and Ball and the other expatriates who were soon to join him in the cabaret hardly had the means to make any investment of their own.

When he was ready to launch his undertaking, Ball decided to make an official press announcement of the opening of the new cabaret. He named it after Voltaire both in honor of Voltaire's Swiss residence and to convey a rationalistic unmystical attitude toward life. Richard Huelsenbeck mentions Ball's interest in and sense of kinship with Voltaire in his *Memoirs of a Dada Drummer:*

> Ball characteristically dubbed his cabaret "Voltaire." Voltaire, who, as we know, was one of the most violent opponents of the Catholic church, had already fascinated Ball in Berlin. Ball, like all of us, was an "enlightener," a liberal, who expected the salvation of mankind to come from the mind and the intelligence rather than from metaphysics.[4]

The announcement, which appeared on February 2, 1916, read:

> Cabaret Voltaire. Under this name a society of young artists and writers has been formed whose aim is to create a center for artistic entertainment. The idea of the cabaret will be that at daily gatherings musical performances will be presented by artists who will appear as guests. The young artists of Zurich, without

consideration of any particular orientation, are hereby invited to come along with suggestions and contributions.[5]

The response was swift, and gratifying. Ball gives an account of it in his entry for February 5 in *Flight Out of Time:*

> The place was jammed; many people could not find a seat. At about six in the evening, while we were still busy hammering and putting up futuristic posters, an Oriental-looking deputation of four little men arrived, with portfolios and pictures under their arms; repeatedly they bowed politely. They introduced themselves: Marcel Janco the painter, Tristan Tzara, Georges Janco, and a fourth gentleman whose name I did not quite catch. [Hans] Arp happened to be there also, and we were able to communicate without too many words. Soon Janco's sumptuous *Archangels* was hanging with the other beautiful objects, and on that same evening Tzara read some traditional-style poems, which he fished out of his various coat pockets in a rather charming way (p. 50)

Programs in the early days of the Cabaret Voltaire were as eclectic as the paintings, sketches, and other wall decorations with which the premises of the old Hollandische Meierei came to be decorated, as eclectic, to be sure, as programs tended to be elsewhere in the early history of the cabaret. Ball's own diary (*Flight Out of Time)* and Huelsenbeck's *Memoirs of a Dada Drummer* are still the best sources of what the first programs of the Cabaret Voltaire were like. In his entries for February 6, 7, 26, 27, and 28 (pp. 51–52), Ball mentions the reading of poems by Kandinsky, Else Lasker-Schüler, Wedekind ("Donnerwetterlied," Thundersong), Aristide Bruant's classic "A la Villette," Blaise Cendrars, Jakob van Hoddis, Franz Werfel ("Die Wortmacher der Zeit," The Wordmakers of the Time, and "Fremde sind wir auf der Erde alle," Strangers Are We All Upon the Earth), Morgenstern, Lichtenstein, Max Jacob (from "La Côte," The Coast, read by Tristan Tzara), and Erich Mühsam's "Revoluzzerlied" (Revolutionary Song). Prose readings and musical performances also took place, among them a short story, "Der Selbstsüchtige" (The Self-Addict), by a young worker named Ernst Thape, Liszt's *Thirteenth Rhapsody,* a berceuse by Debussy, Turlet's *Sambre et Meuse,* and humoresques by the pianist-composer Max Reger (1873–1916).

Ball's enthusiasm for Russian culture was not limited just to the anarchist philosophy of Bakunin or Kropotkin. He had a good knowledge of Dostoevsky and was familiar with Leonid Andreev's gloomy quasi-Symbolist putdown of bourgeois materialism, *The Life of Man,* which he and

The Cabaret Voltaire, painting by Marcel Janco. (Kunsthaus Zürich).

Emmy Hennings read on February 29. Ball comments on the play that "it is a distressing mythic play that I like a lot. Only the two central characters seem to be men of flesh and blood; the others are all dreamlike marionettes. The play begins with a birth scream and ends in a wild dance of gray shadows and masks. Even the commonplace verges on horror. At the climax of his life, surrounded by wealth and glory, the artist is respectfully called 'Mr. Man' by the mummers sitting around him. That is all he achieves" (pp. 52–53). Without identifying who they were, Ball recalls that on February 7 there were a lot of Russians in the cabaret (could Lenin have been among them? after all, he lived just across the street at No. 14 Spiegelgasse at the time) and that "they organized a balalaika orchestra of about twenty people and want to be regular customers" (p. 51). The Russians, whoever they may have been, took full advantage of the informality of the cabaret as well as Ball's obvious interest in things Russian to perform also on other occasions; on February 27, for example, Ball notes that they gave a choral rendering of what he calls in German "Die rote Sarafan" (The Red Smock) (p. 52), while on March 4 a Russian Soirée was organized, which Ball describes as follows:

> A short, good-natured gentleman, Mr. Dolgalev, was applauded even before he got on the stage; he performed two humorous pieces by Chekhov, then he sang folk songs. (Can you imagine singing folk songs to Thomas or Heinrich Mann?)
>
> An unknown lady reads "Yegorushka" by Turgenev and poems by Nekrasov.
>
> A Serbian (Pavlovac) sings impassioned soldiers' songs to a roar of applause. He took part in the retreat to Salonika.
>
> Piano music by Skryabin and Rakhmaninov. (pp. 54–55)

Other nationalities also had soirées at the Voltaire on the model of the Russian. The French one on March 14 presented Tzara reading poems by Max Jacob, André Salmon, and Jules Laforgue; Oser and Rubinstein played the first movement of the *Sonata for Piano and Cello op. 32* by Saint-Saens; Arp read from Jarry's *Ubu Roi* in place of the translations Ball had intended to read from Lautréamont but was unable to because the volume he had ordered did not arrive in time; and finally, Madame Leconte, who sang at the cabaret and was also known under the name of Madame le Roy, did a rendition of "A la Martinique" and other French songs (pp. 56–57).

A day had also been set aside for the Swiss (Sunday, March 7), but as Ball notes in *Flight Out of Time:* "the young Swiss are too cautious for a cabaret. A splendid gentleman paid tribute to the current climate of freedom and sang a song about the 'Schöne Jungfer Lieschen' (Beautiful Virgin Lise); it made us all blush and look down. Another gentleman performed "Eichene Gedichte" (Poems of Oak)" (p. 55).

In a diary entry for March 2 in *Flight Out of Time,* Ball not only articulates the energizing effect of the success and challenge of the cabaret, but the importance the oral recitation of poetry has begun to assume for him, a fact of some significance in assessing the "sound poems" that represent his major contribution to the Dadaist direction of the Cabaret Voltaire:

> Our attempt to entertain the audience with artistic things forces us in an exciting and instructive way to be incessantly lively, new, and naive. It is a race with the expectations of the audience, and this race calls on all our forces of invention and debate. One cannot say exactly that the art of the last twenty years has been joyful and that the modern poets are very entertaining and popular. Nowhere are the weaknesses of a poem revealed as much as in a public reading. One thing is certain: art is joyful only as long as it has richness and life. Reciting aloud has become the touchstone of the quality of a poem for me, and I have learned (from the stage) to what extent today's literature is worked out as a problem at the desk and is made for the spectacles of the collector instead of for the ears of living human beings. (p. 54)

Although other singers performed at the Voltaire from time to time, Emmy Hennings was the resident chanteuse. If no actual record of the songs she sung at the cabaret exists, Richard Huelsenbeck's description of her performances in *Memoirs of a Dada Drummer* provides a good picture of what they were like. The description is also valuable for what it conveys of the ambience of the Cabaret Voltaire in general:

> That first evening, as I entered the cabaret after my fateful trip from Germany, Hugo was sitting at the piano, playing classical music, Brahms and Bach. Then he switched over to dance music. The drunken students pushed their chairs aside and began spinning around. There were almost no women in the cabaret. It was too wild, too smoky, too way out.
>
> Hugo had written against war and murderous insanity. Emmy recited it, Hugo accompanied her on the piano, and the audience chimed in, with a growl, murdering the poem. During this period, I saw Tzara for the first time (a little man with a monocle), as well as his friend Janco and Janco's brothers. Plus René Schickele, Werfel, and J. C Heer, a Swiss poet celebrating his native soil (the mountains weighed down his heart).
>
> The furnishings of the cabaret were inconceivably primitive. Emmy, on whose success or failure as a singer the existence of the cabaret hinged, had no dressing room. She would change behind a trestle over which a canvas was stretched with holes as big as your fist. There was little of the prima donna about Emmy, but she delighted in showing me the different costumes that belonged to the different numbers. These songs, known only in Central Europe, poke fun at politics, literature, human behavior, or anything else that people will understand. The songs are impudent but never insulting. There is no intention of hurting anyone, only the desire to express an opinion. Sometimes they are erotic, treating old farce themes such as the cuckold or the ignorance of the bride on her wedding

night. The intellectual level is low but not unpleasantly so. Usually, they subsist on refrains and popular music, but Ball made up the melody for every song he wrote.

The songs created the "intimate" atmosphere of the cabaret. The audience liked listening to them, the distance between us and the enemy grew smaller, and finally everyone joined in. The students rocked on their chairs, and the Dutchman, our landlord, stood in the doorway, swaying to and fro.[7]

Huelsenbeck's first appearance at the cabaret on February 11, 1916, may have acted as something of a catalyst for its turn away from the eclecticism of other cabarets in their early phases of development toward its Dadaist transformation, above all in the area of poetry and language.

As an artistic movement, Dada represented a repudiation, even more a negation, of traditional European values, the values of Western civilization, brought on by a profound disenchantment with those values which were now held ultimately responsible for the brutal and, to the Dadaists, mad war then raging in Europe. The war was seen as the great cataclysm that would at last bring to ruin the corrupt, tottering edifice of the bourgeois nineteenth century.

None of the values of traditional European society meant anything any more to the Dadaists; they had all become debased. Institutional religion was a mockery of true faith intent on buttressing the existing social and economic order for its own advantage; art had become stultified in outworn conventional forms; language was unreliable as an instrument of communication because hypocrisy, cynicism, and venality had robbed it of its authenticity and vigor.

As the Dada movement cohered, it assumed the characteristics of revolution, negation, and purification at one and the same time. In its active negation of traditional values and structures, it was a revolt against content as well as form. In looking about itself it saw unmistakable signs of disintegration and fragmentation and danced in celebration of chaos. By emphasizing art as play, as boisterous, irreverent, mocking play, Dada sought to strip the hollow structures of the past of any meaning still clinging to them. But in striving to hasten the demise of the traditional and outworn, Dada was not merely negation, a childish romp (as Hans Arp once put it). It saw itself also as an agent for the purification that society and its institutions and values had to undergo if a new system was to be reborn out of the chaos of the destruction of the old. This is surely what the outstanding Dada poet and sculptor Hans Arp had in mind when reacting against what he regarded as the simplistic and inaccurate assessment of Dada as a kind of self-titillating adult childishness he wrote in his short essay "Dada Was No Childish Romp":

> Madness and murder vied with each other when, in 1916, in Zurich Dada rose out of the depths. The people who did not participate directly in the terrible madness of World War acted as if they were unable to comprehend what was going on all around them. Like lost sheep they stared at the world with glazed eyes. Dada sought to jolt men out of their wretched unconsciousness. Dada detested resignation. Those who only describe the farcical and fantastical side of Dada and do not penetrate into its heart, its transcendent reality, offer only a worthless fragment. Dada was no childish romp.[8]

The Dadaist negation of Western civilization was accompanied by an enthusiasm for primitive art and culture common to much of the turn-of-the-century avant-garde. In the case of Dada, the primitive was equated, to a great extent, with the black African. Richard Huelsenbeck, who had once recited "Negro poems" (*Negerlieder*) of his own concoction during an expressionist evening in Berlin, seems to have been the first to introduce the genre at the Cabaret Voltaire. On his first visit to the cabaret, Huelsenbeck met Jan Ephraim who regaled him with stories of his days at sea. As if to demonstrate his own familiarity with the exotic, Huelsenbeck then recited some Negro poems that he had made up himself. Ephraim listened patiently, but when the recitation was over he motioned Huelsenbeck outside where, according to Huelsenbeck, he told him:

> They sound very good . . . but unfortunately they're not Negro poems. I spent a good part of my life among Negroes, and the songs they sing are very different from the ones you just recited." He was one of those people who take things literally, and retain them verbatim. My Negro poems all ended with the refrain "Umba, umba,"[9] which I roared and spouted over and over again into the audience.[10]

Hugo Ball, who was present at the time, suggested that perhaps Huelsenbeck ought to recite something authentic. Huelsenbeck turned to Ephraim for advice and a few days later the Dutchman brought him a sheet of paper on which he had scribbled the words:

Trabadja La Modjere
Magamore Magagere
Trabadja Bobo

Huelsenbeck recalls:

> I read the lines through slowly while Ephraim sat there smiling, and I ended up liking them. . . . I recited my new "authentic" Negro poems, and the audience thought they were wonderful. Naturally, no force on earth could have gotten me to leave out the "Umba" at the end of every verse, although my Dutchman shook his head disapprovingly. He wanted everything to be "authentic," literal, factual, just as he had heard it in Africa and the South Seas.[11]

To enhance the authenticity of Huelsenbeck's Negro poems, the big kettle drum which often accompanied Dada recitations at the Cabaret Voltaire was banged during his performance. Thereafter, both the Negro poems—and the drum accompaniment—became regular features of Huelsenbeck's appearances at the cabaret, so much so in fact that Ball noted in his diary entry for February 11, 1916, that Huelsenbeck "pleads for stronger rhythm (Negro rhythms). He would prefer to drum literature into the ground" (p. 51). Lines such as the following from Huelsenbeck's *Phantastische Gebete* (Fantastic Prayers, 1916), parts of which were also recited by him at the Cabaret Voltaire, demonstrate how the integration of the quasi-African lines into the stream-of-consciousness German was meant to achieve a newness of expression in sound and rhythm as well as image:

Schmierling in Haut gepurpur schwillt
        auf Würmlein und Affe
hat Hand und Gesass
O tscha tschipulala o ta Mpota
        Mengen
Mengulala mengulala kulilibulal
Bamboscha bambosch
es schliesset der Pfarrer den
        Ho-osenlatz rataplan rataplen den
Ho-osenlatz und das Haar steht ihm
            au-aus den Ohren
Tschupurawanta burruh pupaganda
        burruh
Ischarimunga burruh den Ho-osenlatz
        den Ho-osenlatz
kampampa kamo katapena kara
Tschuwuparanta da umba da umba
        da do
da umba da umba da umba hihi . . .[12]

(Grease[paint] in the hide swells purpled
    on a little worm and a monkey
  has hands and buttocks . . .
  The parson closes his fly . . .
    and hair sticks out of his ears . . .)

It might be mentioned at this point en passant that Huelsenbeck's later fortunes took him to Africa. Although his very active literary career, which included employment as a newspaper correspondent, would seem to have allowed little time for it, Huelsenbeck was a medical doctor by profession. In 1925 and again in 1927, he did two stints as a ship's surgeon, on the second trip sailing around Africa. The voyage resulted in one of his most acclaimed books, a combination travelogue and novel entitled *Afrika in Sicht* (Africa in Sight).[13]

Because of Huelsenbeck's interest in them, Negro poems became a more or less regular feature of Cabaret Voltaire performances. Even proprietor Ephraim had a hand in them, as Ball relates in his diary entry for March 30, 1916. The high point of the evening was the first performance at the Cabaret Voltaire of a *poème simultané* (simultaneous poem). Recited by Huelsenbeck, Janco, and Tzara in German, English, and French respectively, the poem was entitled "L'amiral cherche une maison à louer" (The Admiral is Looking for a House to Rent) and was eventually included in the *Cabaret Voltaire* anthology which was published in June 1916, principally on Tzara's initiative. Ball was immensely enthusiastic about the new genre of simultaneous poetry, seeing in its unintelligible cacaphony a reflection of man's situation in contemporary society and another weapon in the assault on traditional concepts and forms of poetry. He recorded his impressions of it in *Flight Out of Time:*

> All the styles of the last twenty years came together yesterday. Huelsenbeck, Tzara, and Janco took the floor with a *poème simultané.* That is a contrapuntal recitative in which three or more voices speak, sing, whistle, etc., at the same time in such a way that the elegaic, humorous, or bizarre content of the piece is brought out by these combinations. In such a simultaneous poem the willful quality of an organic work is given powerful expression, and so is its limitation by the accompaniment. Noises (an rrrrr drawn out for minutes, or crashes, or sirens, etc.) are superior to the human voice in energy.
>
> The "simultaneous poem" has to do with the value of the voice. The human organ represents the soul, the individuality in its wanderings with its demonic companions. The noises represent the background—the inarticulate, the disastrous,

the decisive. The poem tries to elucidate the fact that man is swallowed up in the mechanistic process. In a typically compressed way it shows the conflict of the *vox humana* [human voice] with a world that threatens, ensnares, and destroys it, a world whose rhythm and noise are ineluctable. (p. 57)

Writing about the simultaneous poem in *En Avant Dada: Eine Geschichte des Dadaismus* (En Avant Dada: A History of Dadaism) in 1920, Richard Huelsenbeck related it to the concept of *simultaneità* of the Italian Futurists and proposed a less impressionistic definition of it than Ball:

Simultaneity (first used by Marinetti in this literary sense) is an abstraction, a concept referring to the occurrence of different events at the same time. It presupposes a heightened sensitivity to the passage of things in time, it turns the sequence a=b=c=d into an a-b-c-d, and attempts to transform the problem of the ear into a problem of the face. Simultaneity is against what has become, and for what it is becoming. . . . Simultaneity is a direct reminder of life, and very closely bound up with bruitism. Just as physics distinguishes between tones (which can be expressed in mathematical formulae) and noises, which are completely baffling to its symbolism and abstractionism, because they are a direct objectivization of a dark vital force, here the distinction is between a succession and a "simultaneity," which defies formulation because it is a direct symbol of action. And so ultimately a simultaneous poem means nothing but "Hurrah for life!"[14]

Although Ball, despite enthusiasm for it, never experimented directly with simultaneous poetry, the genre remained of considerable interest to the Dadaists. Tristan Tzara composed a simultaneous poem called "Lumière Froide" (Cold Light) which was read by seven people at the Third Dada Soirée on April 28, 1917, and Arp, Tzara, and another Cabaret Voltaire regular, Walter Serner, wrote a cycle of simultaneous poems under the German title *Die Hyperbel vom Krokodilcoiffeur und dem Spazierstock* (The Hyperbole of the Crocodile's Hairdresser and the Walkingstick).[15]

The performance of the first simultaneous poem at the Cabaret Voltaire was followed by two more Negro poems which Ball refers to as "Chant nègre I and II" and which were also being performed for the first time. "Chant nègre (or funèbre) No. 1," writes Ball in his diary entry for March 30, 1916, "was especially prepared and was performed as if in a Vehmic court in black cowls and with big and small exotic drums. The melodies for Chant nègre II were composed by our esteemed host, Mr. Jan Ephraim, who had been involved in African business for some time a while ago, and he was helping eagerly with the performance like an instructive and stimulating prima donna" (pp. 57–58).

The enthusiasm for "Negro," African or African-sounding poems on the part of Huelsenbeck, Ephraim, Arp, and others associated with the Cabaret Voltaire in 1916 and 1917 reflected the fascination with the primitive that was common, in general, among the avant-gardists of the late nineteenth and early twentieth centuries. Primitivism was in a sense an alternative as well as an antidote to the Western civilization whose values these artists felt they could no longer relate to and which most of them held in contempt. But among poets, the lure of what they regarded as primitive language was also closely linked to their disenchantment with traditional poetic language and their belief that the languages of their own societies had become so corrupted they were no longer effective vehicles of communication. Throughout the development of the literary avant-garde of the turn-of-the-century, traditional language was seen as in a state of crisis because of the social and political situation and efforts were made to renovate language, to breathe new life into it in a variety of ways. For literature, language was the central concern of the avant-garde revolution explaining the many experiments with language, particularly poetic language, that engaged the energies of writers from one end of Europe to the other.

The Dadaists were among the most daring experimenters and innovators in the area of poetic language. In the context of the Cabaret Voltaire, a clear line of development exists between the Negro poems of Huelsenbeck, Ephraim, and Arp, and the sound poems of Hugo Ball. Sound poems, or *Lautgedichte* in German, were not, to be sure, the invention of Ball. The poet Paul Scheerbart had included one entitled "Kikakoku" in his collection *lch liebe Dich!* (I Love You!), published in Berlin in 1897. Christian Morgenstern, one of the leading poets of the early Berlin cabaret, as we saw earlier, also wrote a sound poem called "Das grosse Lalula" (The Big Lalula), which became a part of the *Galgenlieder* (Gallows Songs) collection of 1905.

The principal difference between Ball and those German poets who preceded him in the sound poem was that before Ball there was no serious consistent effort to cultivate the sound poem as a genre. Sound poems were at best isolated phenomena. This is clearly the case with Scheerbart and Morgenstern, while Ball's fellow participants in the Cabaret Voltaire such as Arp and Huelsenbeck either wrote sound poems only very occasionally or interspersed lines of phonemic poetry (*poesia fonemica,* as Laura Mancinelli terms it in her Italian study *Il messagio razionale dell'avanguardia*)[16] and German verse. In the late nineteenth or early twentieth centuries, the sound poem—as written by Scheerbart or Morgenstern—was a harbinger of the avant-garde. Since the sound poem lacked sense in terms of meaning it could be regarded as nonsensical, hence another aspect of the world of the child from which so much of the perspective of the avant-garde was fashioned. In this respect, the sound poem was a kind of child's play with language which, lacking meaning, was reduced just to sound and rhythm. As a form of play, the early sound poems also became another weapon in the avant-gardists' arsenal against the traditional and conventional. With Huelsenbeck and Arp, a certain change of emphasis occurs. Still intended to shock, provoke, and disturb, the sound poem now suggested not so much childish gibberish and play as the sounds and rhythms of the "primitive" speech of black Africans whose "primitivism" was the main determinant of their appeal to European poets happily dancing around the bier of Western civilization. If the sounds in the sound poems of Morgenstern and Huelsenbeck, for example, are compared, it is easy to see that Huelsenbeck was clearly attempting to approximate a European's sense of what a typical African language sounds like. Proprietor Ephraim's presence at the Cabaret Voltaire was also an assurance of at least a semblance of accuracy in view of the Dutchman's familiarity with Africa and supposed acquaintance with at least the sounds and rhythms (if not the grammar) of African languages.

Ball, therefore, did not come out of a vacuum, despite his desire to create the impression that the sound poem originated with him at the Cabaret Voltaire. He must surely have known Scheerbart's and Morgenstern's sound poems as well as what Huelsenbeck alone or together with Ephraim recited at the Voltaire. But if not the originator of the sound poem, Ball must be recognized as the most innovative practitioner of the form.

Altogether Ball composed six sound poems, all of which were recited at the Cabaret Voltaire and represent one of his most important contributions to the Dadaist transformation of the cabaret. Since they have seldom been reprinted as a group and the scholarly literature on Ball includes citations just of individual lines or stanzas, I have thought it best to give the complete texts of the poems:

Wolken

elomen elomen lefitalominai
wolminuscaio
baumbala bunga
acycam glastula feirofim flinsi

elominuscula pluplubasch
rallalalaio

endremin saxassa flumen flobollala
feilobasch falljada follidi
flumbasch

cerobadadrada
gragluda gligloda glodasch
gluglamen gloglada gleroda glandridi

elomen elomen lefitalominai
wolminuscaio
baumbala bunga
acycam glastala feirofim blisti
elominuscula pluplusch
rallabataio

Katzen und Plauen

baubo sbugi ninga gloffa

siwi faffa
sbugi faffa
olofa fafamo
faufo halja finj

sirgi ninga banja sbugi
halja hanja golja biddim

ma ma
plaupa
mjama

pawapa baungo sbugi
ninga gloffalor

Totenklage

ombula
take
biti
solunkola
tabla tokta tokta takabla

taka tak
Babula m'balam
tak tru - ü
wo - um
biba bimbel
o kla o auw
kla o auwa
la - auma
o kla o ü
la o auma
klinga - o - e - auwa
ome o-auwa
klinga inga M ao - Auwa
omba dij omuff pomo - auwa
tru - ü
tro-u-ü o-a-o-ü
mo-auwa
gomum guma zangaga gago blagaga
szagaglugi m ba-o-auma
szaga szago
szaga la m'blama
bscigi bschigo
bschigi bschigi
bschiggo bschiggo
goggo goggo
ogoggo
a - o - auma

Gadji beri bimba

gadji beri bimba glandridi laula lonni cadori
gadjama gramma berida bimbala glandri galassassa laulitalomini
gadji beri bin blassa glassala laula lonni cadorsu sassala bim
gadjama tuffm i zimzalla binban gligla wowolimai bin beri ban
o katalominai rhinozerossola hopsamen
bluku terullala blaulala loooo

zimzim urullala zimzim urullala zimzim zanzibar zimzalla zam
elifantolim brussala bulomen brussala bulomen tromtata
velo da bang bang affalo purzamai affalo purzamai lengado tor
gadjama bimbalo glandridi glassala zingtata pimpalo ogrogoooo
viola laxato viola zimbrabim viola uli paluji malooo

tuffm im zimbrabim negramai bumbalo negramai bumbalo tuffm i zim
gadjama bimbala oo beri gadjama gaga di gadjama affalo pinx
gaga di bambalo bumbalo gadjamen
gaga blung

Karawane

jolifanto bambla o falli bambla
grossiga m'pfa habla horem
egiga goramen
higo bloiko russula huju
hollaka hollaia
anlogo bung
blago bung blago bung
bosso fataka
ü üü ü

schampa wulla wussa olobo
hej tatta gorem
eschige zunbada
wulubu ssubudu uluwu ssubudu
tumba ba-umf
kusa gauma
ba - umf

Seepferdchen und Flugfische

tressli bessli nebogen leila
flusch kata
ballubasch
zack hitti zopp

zack hitti zopp
hitti betzli betzli
prusch kata
ballubasch
fasch kitti bimm

zitti kitillabi billabi billabi
zikko di zakkobam
fisch kitti bisch
bumbalo bumbalo bumbalo bambo
zitti kitillabi
zack hitti zopp

tressli bessli nebogen grügrü
blaulala violabimini bisch
violabimini bimini bimini
fusch kata
ballubasch
zack hitti zopp[17]

As can be seen from the texts, they are "pure" sound poems; that is, no quasi-macaronic intermingling of phonemic lines and German (or any other European) verse occurs. Although the poems obviously lack sense in terms of semantic meaning, as indeed they were intended to, they are not a haphazard, random collection of sounds. Patterns of repetition and stanzaic division clearly indicate some concept of structure. In the first poem "Wolken" (Clouds), for example, the first stanza reappears in the last with just the change of the last word "flinsi" to "blisti." The second stanza is similarly repeated after the first in the poem's final lines this time with the last word of the first line "pluplubasch" shortened by a "syllable" to "pluplusch" and the end word changed from "rallalalaio" to "rallabataio." The third and fourth middle stanzas both have common repetitive elements. In the third stanza the first two words are followed by six, all of which begin with the letter "f" and two of which contain the syllable "basch" which repeats the third syllable of the word "pluplubasch" in the preceding stanza. The same pattern (more or less) occurs in the fourth stanza. Here, after an opening word, a series of seven words appears each beginning with the letter "g" (the next after "f" in the alphabet) and with one of them containing the now familiar "(b)asch" phoneme ("glodasch") Minor variations on themes are also played within the alliterative parts of stanzas three and four: "flumen" "flumbasch" (stanza three), "gligloda" "gloglada" (stanza four). Note, additionally, the elements of linkage between stanzas other than those already mentioned. The word "wolminuscaio" in the first stanza has the same ending as the final words of the second ("rallalalaio") and last ("rallabataio") stanzas. The second line of the third stanza and the last line of the fourth stanza have a partial rhyme ("follidi," "glandridi"). The opening word of the second stanza, "elominiscula," appears to have a "grammatical" connection with the opening and twice repeated "elomen." The syllables "min" or "men" (as a variant) appear in several words: "elomen," "lefitalominai," "wolminuscaio," "elominiscula," "endremin," "flumen," "gluglamen." Similarly, the words "wolminuscaio" in the first stanza and "elominuscula" in the second are almost identical.

It is also interesting to observe the carrying over of certain words from one poem to another either whole or with only slight changes. Thus, the poem "Gadji beri bimba" contains the words "glandridi" and "laulitalomini." "Laulitalominai" is obviously a variation of "lefitalominai" as is "katalominai" in the same poem. The ending "men" also appears in "Gadji beri bimba" in "hopsamen," "bulomen," "gadjamen," and in

"Karawane" (Caravan) in "goramen." The "assa" phoneme is also productive. It appears in "Clouds" in "saxassa," in "Gadji beri bimba" in "galassassa," "blassa," and "glassala," and in the variants "brussala" and "rhinozerossola," and in "Caravan" in "wussa" and "russula." The phonemes "asch" or "basch" also appear as the last part of a word in more than one poem. We find "pluplubasch," "feilobasch," "flumbasch," and "glodasch" in "Clouds" and "ballubasch" in "Seepferdchen und Flugfische" (Seahorses and Flying Fishes). Ball is also fond of words that seem to be related by declension or conjugation: the stanza "siwi faffa / sbugi faffa / olofa fafamo / faufo halja finj" in "Katzen and Pfauen" (Cats and Peacocks); "szaga," "szago," "szagaglugi" and "bschigi," "bschigo" in "Totenklage" (Funeral Lament); "cadori," "cadorsu," "zimzin," "zimzalla," "zam," "bling," "blong," "blung" in "Gadji beri bimba"; "hollaka," "hollala," "wulubu," "ssubudu," "uluwu" in "Caravan."

Although Ball has left conventional language far behind in his sound poems, some elements of real words are discernible. The first syllable of the title of "Clouds"—"wol" (from German *Wolken*) appears in "wolminuscaio"; the "kla" repeated several times in "Funeral Lament" suggests the German *Klage* (lament), as in the original title of the poem "Totenklage"; the lines "tru - ü / tro-u-ü o-a-a-ü / mo-auwa" and "szaga" in the same poem may have been suggested by the German *Traum, Traüme* (dream, dreams) and *Sarg* (coffin), respectively. "Rhinozerossola" obviously derives from "rhinoceros," "zimbrabim" hints at "zebra," and "negramai" is certainly "negroes" in "Gadji beri bimba"; "jolifanto," in "Caravan," identifies the subject of the poem as elephant or elephants.

Onomatopoeia also figured in the composition of the sound poems. The third stanza in "Cats and Peacocks"—"ma ma / piaupa / mjama"—echoes the meowing of cats with "piaupa" a spinoff of the German for "peacock" (*Pfau*). The "o," "auw," and "ü" sounds in "Funeral Lament" both independently and in the combinations in which they appear in the poem were obviously intended to evoke sepulchral associations. The whole of "Caravan" is commonly interpreted as suggesting through sound and rhythm the passing of a parade of elephants, while the rhythm of "Seahorses and Flying Fish," especially in the lines "flusch kata / ballubasch / zack hitti zopp," conveys the flipping and flopping of fish.

While Huelsenbeck's (and Ephraim's) Negro songs form a link with

Ball's sound poems, the Ball works are not at all consistently African. "Clouds" and "Seahorses and Flying Fish" are virtually without any recognizably African linguistic elements; "Cats and Peacocks" and "Funeral Lament" have a few African sounding words—"siwi," "sbugi," "ninga," "babula m'balam," "m'blama." "Gadji beri bimba" and "Caravan" are the most African of the poems. While many of the words in the poems have no particular African sound patterns, such items as "rhinozerossola," "negramai, and "zanzibar" are meant to establish an African coloration. In "Caravan," beginning with the very first line with its opening "jolifanto"—"jolifanto bambla o falli bambla"—the entire sound instrumentation of the poem and its rhythm conjure up a picture of a passing caravan of lumbering, swaying elephants coming close to the viewer and then passing by him.

Although Ball's first public presentation of the sound poems (*Lautgedichte*), or poems without words (*Verse ohne Worte*), at the Cabaret Voltaire dates from June 23, 1916, earlier entries in *Flight Out of Time* establish the growth of an attitude toward language and poetry that would eventually express itself in something as bold, outlandish, and abstract as the sound poems. On March 5, 1916, for example, Ball observed, referring to the example of Kandinsky, whom he greatly admired, that

> The image of the human form is gradually disappearing from the painting of these times and all objects appear only in fragments. This is one more proof of how ugly and worn the human countenance has become, and of how all the objects of our environment have become repulsive to us. *The next step is for poetry to do away with language for similar reasons* [italics mine—HBS]. These are things that have probably never happened before. (p. 55)

A week later, Ball noted down a programmatic imperative of considerable relevance for much of his work in general and for his cabaret poetry in particular:

> Adopt symmetries and rhythms instead of principles Oppose world systems and acts of state by transforming them into a phrase or a brush stroke.
>
> The distancing device is the stuff of life. Let us be thoroughly new and inventive. Let us rewrite life every day.
>
> What we are celebrating is both buffoonery and a requiem mass. (p. 56)

In his entry for June 18, Ball deals wholly with language and as his remarks make clear was already on the threshold of the sound poems:

We have now driven the plasticity of the word to the point where it can scarcely be equaled. We achieved this at the expense of the rational, logically constructed sentence, and also by abandoning documentary work (which is possible only by means of a time-consuming grouping of sentences in logically ordered syntax). Some things assisted us in our efforts: first of all, the special circumstances of these times, which do not allow real talent either to rest or mature and so put its capabilities to the test. Then there was the emphatic energy of our group; one member was always trying to surpass the other by intensifying demands and stresses. You may laugh; language will one day reward us for our zeal, even if it does not achieve any directly visible results. We have loaded the word with strengths and energies that helped us to rediscover the evangelical concept of the "word" (logos) as a magical complex image. (p.68)

In the next paragraph in the same entry, Ball differentiates between his own experiments with language and those of the founder of Italian futurism, Filippo Tommaso Marinetti, whose influence on him and other Dadaists was considerable. Ball writes:

With the sentence having given way to the word, the circle around Marinetti began resolutely with *parole in libertà* [literally, "words in freedom"—HBS]. They took the word out of the sentence frame (the world image) that had been thoughtlessly and automatically assigned to it, nourished the emaciated big-city vocables with light and air, and gave them back their warmth, emotion, and their original untroubled freedom. We others went a step further. We tried to give the isolated vocables the fullness of an oath, the glow of a star. And curiously enough, the magically inspired vocables conceived and gave birth to a new sentence that was not limited and confined by any conventional meaning. Touching lightly on a hundred ideas at the same time without naming them, this sentence made it possible to hear the innately playful, but hidden, irrational character of the listener; it awakened and strengthened the lowest strata of memory. Our experiments touched on areas of philosophy and of life that our environment—so rational and so precocious—scaracely let us dream of. (p.68)

Ball had indeed gone beyond Marinetti and the Futurists in his sound poems. Whereas the Futurists had sought the liberation of the word from the tyranny of syntax in order to restore an acoustical and semantic resonance they believed had been lost—the concept underlying the slogan *parole in libertà*—Ball aimed at a greater degree of abstraction and purification, the liberation of the word from meaning. Words in the sound poems are clusters of sounds, phonemic clusters, in other words, which alone or in sentences of such concoctions are meant to reach an auditor's subconscious in the same way as ritual chants and incantations. The surface aspect of play is deceptive. Underlying what may at first appear to be no more than typical cabaret irreverence and spoofing, this time at the expense of conventional language, is a striving to "cleanse" and renovate a much abused vehicle of human communication by reenacting the evolution of language beginning with primitive sounds. The end result, it was hoped, would be the same fresh perspective on language, on words, on the individual sounds that make up words, that visual artists such as the Cubists, for example, sought to achieve by means of a calculated distortion of view, angle, and plane. In other words, Ball's experiments with the word as sound alone ought to be regarded as a corollary to the anti- and non-representational experiments of the avant-garde visual artists of the period. Ball's approach to sound in language can also be compared with the centrality of color in the painting of such early twentieth-century artists as Gauguin, Van Gogh, Matisse, Braque, Kandinsky, Chagall, the German Expressionists, and the Fauvists. The French painter Robert Delaunay once declared that "color is form and subject"; Ball could have said as much with respect to sound in language. Ball also invested verbal sound with the same power of enchantment, the same capacity for working magic that the visual artists of the early twentieth century attributed to color. This is borne out by his remarks about his first recitation of sound poems on June 23, 1916, in *Flight Out of Time:*

> I have invented a new genre of poems, "Verse ohne Worte" or *Lautgedichte,* in which the balance of the vowels is weighed and distributed solely according to the values of the beginning sequence. I gave a reading of the first one of these poems this evening. I had made myself a special costume for it. My legs were in a cylinder of shiny blue cardboard, which came up to my hips so that I looked like an obelisk. Over it I wore a huge coat collar cut out of cardboard, scarlet inside and gold outside. It was fastened at the neck in such a way that I could give the impression of winglike movement by raising and lowering my elbows. I also wore a high, blue-and-white-striped witch doctor's hat.
>
> On all three sides of the stage I had set up music stands facing the audience, and I put my red-penciled manuscript on them; I officiated at one stand after another. Tzara knew about my preparations, so there was a real little premiere. Everyone was curious. I could not walk inside the cylinder so I was carried onto the stage in the dark and began slowly and solemnly:
>
> gadji beri bimba
> glandridi lauli lonni cadori
> gadjama bim beri glassala . . .
>
> The stresses became heavier, the emphasis was increased as the sound of the consonants became sharper. Soon I realized that, if I wanted to remain serious (and

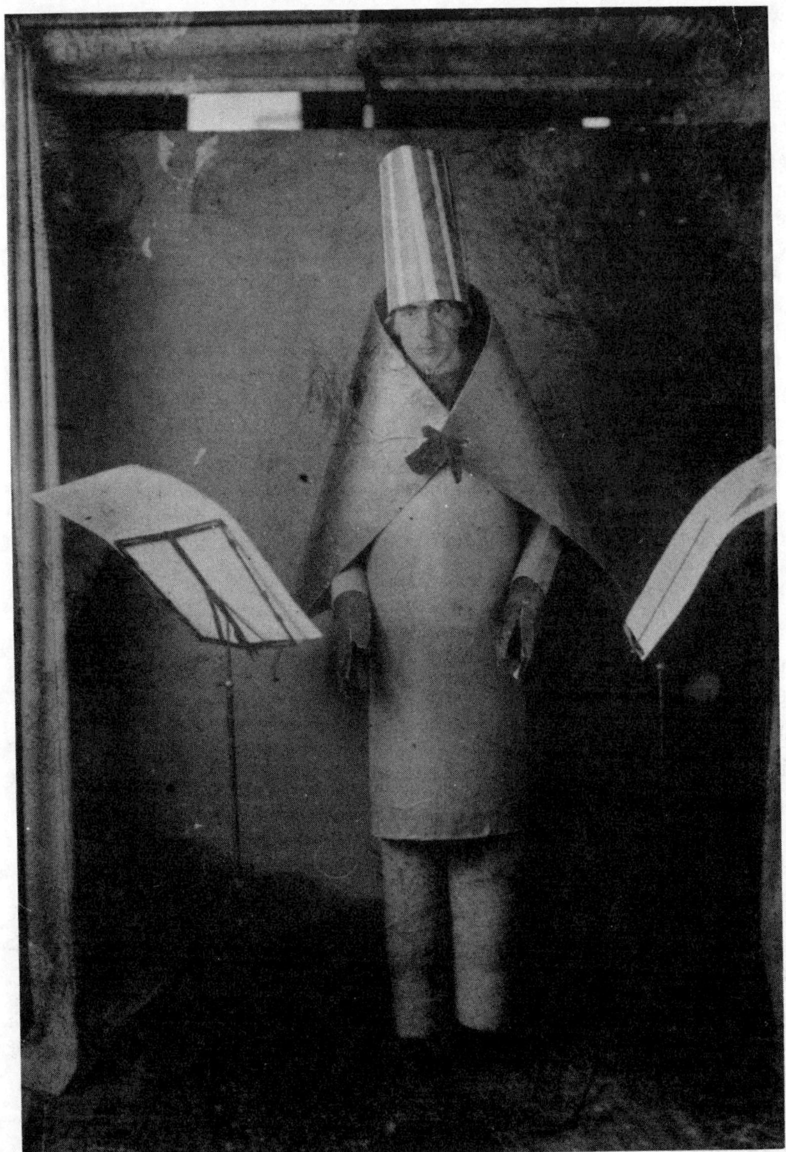

Hugo Ball in the "Cubist" costume in which he recited his "verses without words" at the Cabaret Voltaire in 1916. (Kunsthaus Zürich).

I wanted to at all costs), my method of expression would not be equal to the pomp of my staging. I saw Brupbacher, Jelmoli, Laban, Mrs. Wigman in the audience.[18] I feared a disgrace and pulled myself together. I had now completed "Labadas Gesang an die Wolken" [Labada's Song to the Clouds, shortened just to "Wolken" in most editions of Ball's works—HBS] at the music stand on the right and the "Elefanten-karawane" [Elephant Caravan, or just "Karawane," Caravan—HBS] on the left and turned back to the middle one, flapping my wings energetically. The heavy vowel sequences and the plodding rhythm of the elephants had given me one last crescendo. But how was I to get to the end? Then I noticed that my voice had no choice but to take on the ancient cadence of priestly lamentation, that style of liturgical singing that wails in all the Catholic churches of East and West.

I do not know what gave me the idea of this music, but I began to chant my vowel sequences in a church style like a recitative, and tried not only to look serious but to force myself to be serious. For a moment it seemed as if there were a pale, bewildered face in my cubist mask, that half-frightened, half-curious face of a ten-year-old-boy, trembling and hanging avidly on the priest's words in the requiems and high masses in his home parish. Then the lights went out, as I had ordered, and bathed in sweat, I was carried down off the stage like a magical bishop. (pp. 70–71)

The church allusions in Ball's description of his recitation point up not only his own spiritual proclivities, which intensified as time went on, but also the almost mediumistic mood into which he slipped as he recited his sound poems. What Ball experienced was what, perhaps not wholly consciously, he wanted his auditors to experience. The strange, unfamiliar sounds of the poems seemed as if by their very nature to demand a similarly distancing and extraordinary method of articulation. Without initially intending to (at least that is how he would have us understand it), Ball infused his recitation with the rhythms and cadences of incantation. The performance became then a kind of primitive religious rite in keeping with the primitive sound of the "language" of the poems. Ball's Futurist-inspired costume with its tall cone-like hat (a "witch doctor's," as Ball describes it) and the limitations forced on his movements because of it suggested an austere priestly figure who had come before his flock to lead them in some form of primitive worship. As if emerging from a mystic transport, or a possession, Ball was so drained by the experience that he needed help in leaving the stage of the cabaret.

It was, to be sure, his last appearance at the Cabaret Voltaire. Moreover, it signaled the end of the cabaret itself. Proprietor Ephraim had for some time been receiving complaints from neighbors about the noisy goings-on in his establishment and had already given thought to closing it down. Finances were also in a mess. Since no one connected with it paid much attention to such mundane matters as expenses and admissions, the cabaret was allowed to fall into a state of bankruptcy. Rowdiness was also not mere gossip. Boisterous students are known to have raised havoc with the furniture on more than one occasion and funds were lacking for replacements. Sensing, after Ball's near collapse following his June 23 performance, that the time might be propitious for a closure of the Voltaire, Ephraim seized the moment and chose discretion as the better part of valor. The Cabaret Voltaire had run its brief but tumultuous course. Dada, however, was now on the threshold of a life of its own and Ball's involvement in the movement continued for nearly a year after the Cabaret Voltaire ceased to exist.

Even before his fateful last appearance at the cabaret on June 23, 1916, Ball had spent most of May of that year preparing a *Cabaret Voltaire* anthology ("Recueil littéraire et artistique") which appeared in an edition of five hundred copies on June 14. With an introduction by Ball, it contained literary and artistic selections by Ball, Arp, Tzara, Janco, Huelsenbeck, Emmy Hennings, Picasso, Modigliani, Kandinsky, Apollinaire, Francesco Cangiullo, Otto van Rees, Jacob van Hoddis, Marcel Slodki, Max Oppenheimer, and Blaise Cendrars. The anthology also carried the announcement that the artists represented in it intended to publish an international review which would be called *Dada*.

Historically, this was the first appearance of the name "Dada" in print. Debate over who originated it has continued down to the present. Ball claims credit for its invention, and Huelsenbeck has backed him up saying that when he and Ball were looking through a German-French dictionary for a stage name for the singer Madame Le Roy, they hit upon the French word for a hobby- or rocking-horse (dada). Arp, on the other hand, has insisted that the term was Tristan Tzara's invention and that it was taken from the Romanian word for "yes" (*da*), which cropped up frequently in an emphatic doubling (*da, da*) in conversations in their native tongue between Tzara and Janco. Be that as it may, the name "Dada" won instant acceptance and has been used ever since to designate that avant-garde movement in the arts that began with the Cabaret Voltaire.

When the new *Dada* journal made its first appearance only in July 1917, however, Ball and Huelsenbeck had already left Zurich and Tzara had effectively assumed leadership of the movement. A "Collection

Dada," a kind of Dada series, which Ball and the others had already planned, did succeed in issuing its first volume in July 1916. Significantly, it featured a work by Tzara, *La première aventure céleste de M. Antipyrine* (The First Celestial Adventure of Mr. Fever Fighter).

After the physically and emotionally exhausting final appearance at the Cabaret Voltaire on June 23, 1916, and the swirl of post-Voltaire activities connected with the launching of Dada in July and culminating in the famous first Dada evening in Zurich's Zunfthaus zur Waag on July 14, Ball, desperately in need of rest, quit Zurich for the peace and quiet of the village of Vira-Magadino in the Swiss Ticino region. It was only in late November that he was back in Zurich again for a longer stay.

Ball's long absence, followed by Huelsenbeck's departure from Zurich in January 1917 thence to plant the seeds of Dada in Berlin, left Tzara the uncontested leader of Zurich Dada. One of his first acts in this capacity was the organization of the first public Dada exhibition on the Bahnhoffstrasse premises of the Galerie Corray which its owner, Hans Corray, made available to Tzara and his group for this purpose. Spurred by the success of the exhibition, Tzara, Janco, and Arp decided that they should open a Dada gallery for further shows of Dada artists. Ball had already returned to Zurich and, on Tzara's urging, made an effort to again become active in the movement by taking part in the new venture. That this indeed required some effort on Ball's part seems incontrovertible. As late as September 15, 1916, in a letter to Tzara from Ascona, apologetic for being out of touch and beseeching Tzara for news from Zurich and elsewhere, Ball clearly indicated a desire to break with Dada and other "isms." "I declare herewith," he wrote, "that expressionism, dadaism, and other isms are the worst kind of bourgeoisie. Bad, bad, bad." In another letter to his sister, Maria Hildebrand-Ball, on November 28, 1916, that is after he and Emmy Hennings had returned to Zurich, Ball left no doubt as to the definitiveness of his break with cabaret: "Ascona, and even more so Vira, were very pleasant after the strains of the cabaret. I want nothing more to do with cabaret, despite the fact that we could live very well. I prefer instead to write. That was always my goal."[19]

Such declarations to the contrary, Ball was genuinely enthusiastic about the opening of the Galerie Dada, seeing in it, as he writes in *Flight Out of Time,* "a continuation of the cabaret idea of last year" (p. 100). With the closing of the Cabaret Voltaire and the emergence of Dada, the resettlement of the former partisans of the cabaret, now Dadaists, in a gallery of their own certainly made sense. Ball's view of the Galerie Dada as an extension of the Cabaret Voltaire was indeed logical. The Dadaists were not the first, however, to effect such an extension. The precedent had been established much earlier when the Four Cats in Barcelona moved into the gallery of the Sala Parés for purposes of exhibition.

The inaugural exhibition of the Galerie Dada, which ran from March 17 through April 7, featured works by such members of the Sturm group as Campendonk, Jacob van Heemskerck, Kandinsky, Paul Klee, Carlo Mense, and Gabriele Münter. Additionally, there were works by the Dadaists themselves as well as examples of Negro art. The more Ball became involved in the Galerie Dada and its exhibitions, or soirées, as they chose to call them, the more he regarded the Galerie not only as an extension of the cabaret but a progressive step forward. The day after the Galerie Dada's opening he spoke of it, as we have seen, as "a continuation of the cabaret idea of last year," but four days later, on March 22, he declared that "we have surmounted the barbarisms of the cabaret. There is a span of time between 'Voltaire' and the 'Galerie Dada' in which everyone has worked very hard and has gathered new impressions and experiences" (p. 101).

In conjunction with the Galerie Dada's first soirée, a series of lectures was planned in which the Dadaists were to speak on aspects of art or on artists of greatest interest to them. The series began with a talk by Tzara on expressionism and abstract art and concluded with one by Ball on Kandinsky.

Ball's interest in Kandinsky and the Russian's influence on him merit some attention in light of the development of Ball's thought and his experiments at the Cabaret Voltaire.[20] Ball had met Kandinsky in Munich in 1912 and his admiration for him ran deep. What he was most impressed by in Kandinsky's work was the Russian artist's ideas on abstraction, above all with respect to color in art, on the purity of sound of the human voice unobscured by the word, on which Kandinsky's "mystic drama" *The Yellow Sound* was based, on the "inner sound" of words, and, finally, on the spiritual capacity of art to overcome the materialism and utilitarianism of the age, to which parts of Kandinsky's well-known essay *Über das Geistige in der Kunst* (usually translated under the title *On the Spiritual in Art,* 1912) were devoted.

Apart from the demonstrable impact of Kandinsky's ideas on Ball's writings and experiments with sound in the "poems without words," Ball also had the opportunity to voice his thoughts about Kandinsky directly in the lecture that he delivered at the Galerie Dada on April 7, 1917.[21]

Equating Kandinsky with "liberation, solace, redemption, and peace" (p. 226), Ball drew extensively from Kandinsky's *On the Spiritual in Art, Rückblicke* (Reminiscences, 1913), and *Der Blaue Reiter* (The Blue Rider) anthology of 1912 to define the measure of his subject's greatness and uniqueness. Of relevance clearly for his own art, Ball identified the "whole secret of Kandinsky" in his being the first painter to reject . . . everything representational as impure, and to go back to the true form, the sound of a thing, its essence, its essential curve" (p. 226). Paraphrasing *On the Spiritual in Art,* Ball took note, among Kandinsky's "three levels of pictorial expression, each corresponding to a way of treating external nature at different degrees of intensity . . . improvisations, which are mainly unconscious and sudden expressions of something internal, expressions of the inner nature" (p. 230).

Of great importance to Ball both personally and artistically was Kandinsky's spirituality. "With these two artists [Rembrandt and Wagner—HBS] he shares the Christian evangelical element, everything Parsifal stands for, purity and pathos. He is more pure in spirituality than his two predecessors . . . He applauds in primitive Christianity the participation of the weakest in the spiritual struggle. He concludes his stage composition *Der gelbe Klang* with the figure of a great upright cross" (p. 233). Ball also saw Kandinsky's spirituality present in the painter's poetry. Writing of the collection *Klänge* (Sounds, or Resonances), Ball declared that "In poetry too he is the first to present purely spiritual processes. By the simplest means he gives shape in *Klänge* to movement, growth, color and tonality, as in the text 'Fagott' (Bassoon). The negation of illusion occurs here again by the juxtaposing of illusionistic elements, taken from conventional language, which cancel each other out. Nowhere else, even among the Futurists, has anyone attempted such a daring purification of language. And Kandinsky has even extended this ultimate step. In *Der gelbe Klang* he was the first to discover and apply the most abstract expression of sound in language, consisting of harmonized vowels and consonants" (p. 234).

In his introduction to the English translation of Ball's *Flight Out of Time,* John Elderfield suggests that besides Kandinsky's own direct impact on Ball's advanced poetry in the areas of abstraction, sound, and the spiritual, Kandinsky might also have served as a conduit for information about the experiments with verse and poetic language of the Russian Futurists (p. xxvii). Elderfield mentions only the poet Velimir Khlebnikov (1885–1922), a leader of the Russian Cubo-Futurists whose poetics derived from a primitivistic theory of language according to which the roots of words and certain groupings of sounds contain basic meanings. These meanings could be uncovered in a poetry made up of speech reduced to its constituent elements. This was, in essence, the principle of *zaumny yazyk,* trans-sense language ("za" in Russian means "beyond," and "um," sense or rational intellect). In poetry, "trans-sense language" expressed itself either in speech sounds alone—the pattern of Ball's sound poems—or in neologisms, "etymologisms" (the use of words not in familiar meanings, but in "original" meanings retrieved by the poet), puns, recurrent sound patterns, and metaphoric and metonymic associations, and so on. In line with the artistic primitivism of the period, Khlebnikov took, as Victor Terras terms it, "a magic view of language, believing that there exists a deep organic link between the truth of language, as revealed to the poet, and the cosmic truth of the universe."[22] That Ball, knowingly or otherwise, shared this magical concept of language with Khlebnikov is evident from a few of his diary entries. On June 15, 1916, he declared that

> two thirds of the wonderfully plaintive words that no human mind can resist come from *ancient magical texts* [italics mine—HBS]. The use of "grammalogues," of magical floating words and resonant sound characterizes the way we [he and Huelsenbeck—HBS] both write. Such word images, when they are successful, are irresistibly and hypnotically engraved on the memory, and they emerge again from the memory with just as little resistance and friction. It has frequently happened that people who visited our evening performances without being prepared for them were so impressed by a single word or phrase that it stayed with them for weeks. (pp. 66–67)

The day after his recitation of his sound poems at the cabaret on June 23 [1916], Ball noted that "In these poems we totally renounce the language that journalism has abused and corrupted. *We must return to the innermost alchemy of the word, we must even give up the word too, to keep for poetry its last and holiest refuge* [italics mine—HBS]. We must give up writing secondhand; that is, accepting words (to say nothing of sentences) that are not newly invented for our own use" (p. 71).

Khlebnikov's most famous poem, "Zaklinanie smekhom" (Incantation by Laughter), the composition of which owes much to elements of Russian folklore (as indeed do many of Khlebnikov's works), is a superb example of "trans-sense" poetry. Only twelve lines long, the poem consists entirely of words derived from the root "sme- " (laugh) and was intended to demonstrate the poetic potential of morphological derivations permitted by the structure of the Russian language.

Very closely related to Khlebnikov in the development of early twentieth-century Russian "trans-sense" language was the poet Aleksei Kruchonykh (1886–1969?), whose career began with painting and the graphic arts. To Kruchonykh, "trans-sense" language would be the means to achieve the liberation of nineteenth-century poetry from the bondage of social concern and philosophy and in that sense he hailed his most famous "trans-sense" poem, "Dyr bul shchyl," as "more Russian in spirit than all of Pushkin's poetry."[23] In poems sometimes closer to Ball's experiments than those of Khlebnikov, Kruchonykh used meaningless but emotionally suggestive sound sequences and, like Huelsenbeck and Arp, composed poems in which "trans-sense" and meaningful language were intermixed. Kruchonykh's typographical experiments, reminiscent of those of Marinetti and other Italian Futurists, had little resonance, however, among the Dadaists of the Cabaret Voltaire circle.

It seems unlikely that Ball had any direct knowledge either of the poetry of Khlebnikov or Kruchonykh or of their jointly authored Cubo-Futurist programmatic pamphlet *Slovo kak takovoe* (The Word as Such, 1913). Nevertheless, the possibility certainly exists that in view of his serious interest in Russian culture—his reading of the anarchist writings of Kropotkin and Bakunin, his familiarity with the works of Gogol, Turgenev, Nekrasov, Pisarev, Dostoevsky, Tolstoy, Merezhkovsky, Andreev, Evreinov, Rozanov, and Solovyov, as well as his contact with and admiration for Kandinsky—mention by Kandinsky (or anyone else for that matter) of the theories of language and experiments with verse of Khlebnikov and Kruchonykh might have encouraged Ball to learn more about these Russian poets with whom he shared certain affinities, as he did indeed with Kandinsky himself. While it is tempting to imagine that it was Kandinsky who introduced Ball to Khlebnikov and Kruchonykh, it has not been established that Kandinsky knew these poets personally or the extent to which he may have been familiar with their works. However, given Ball's enthusiasm for Kandinsky, the prominence of Kandinsky in Ball's writing and cabaret work, and the undeniable influence of Kandinsky on Ball, the likelihood of Kandinsky's having shared with Ball whatever he knew of Khlebnikov and Kruchonykh seems strong.

The special cylindrical costume worn by Ball for the recitation of his sound poems, and in which he was photographed for what has become the most frequently reproduced picture from the Cabaret Voltaire after Marcel Janco's painting *Cabaret Voltaire* (1917), was undoubtedly inspired by the cabaretists' interest in mask. This interest received its greatest stimulus from the masks Marcel Janco created for one of the cabaret's evenings. When he first saw them, the masks reminded Ball of the Japanese or ancient Greek theater, but yet they seemed to him at the same time to be wholly modern. As soon as Janco appeared with the masks, Ball and the others at the cabaret rushed to put them on. Once they did, they succumbed to a strange, "magical" reaction which Ball describes this way:

> Not only did the mask immediately call for a costume; it also demanded a quite definite, passionate gesture, bordering on madness. Although we could not have imagined it five minutes earlier, we were walking around with the most bizarre movements, festooned and draped with impossible objects, each one of us trying to outdo the other in inventiveness. The motive power of these masks was irresistibly conveyed to us. All at once we realized the significance of such a mask for mime and for the theater. The masks simply demanded that their wearers start to move in a tragic-absurd dance. (p. 64)[24]

Although the mask assumed no particular significance in other earlier cabarets, by the time the Cabaret Voltaire came into existence during the Great War in 1916 and in turn gave rise to the Dada movement, previous negative feelings about society and the age among cabaretists had darkened into a bleak vision of man and his constructs. Ball's remarks about "The Age" in his lecture on Kandinsky at the Galerie Dada on April 7, 1917, summed up the feelings of many of his contemporaries:

> God is dead. A world disintegrated. I am dynamite. World history splits into two parts. There is an epoch before me and an epoch after me. Religion, science, morality—phenomena that originated in the states of dread known to primitive peoples. An epoch disintegrates. A thousand-year-old culture disintegrates. There are no columns and supports, no foundations any more—they have all been blown up. . . . The meaning of the world disappeared. The purpose of the world—its reference to a supreme being who keeps the world together—disappeared. Chaos erupted. Tumult erupted. The world showed itself to be a blind

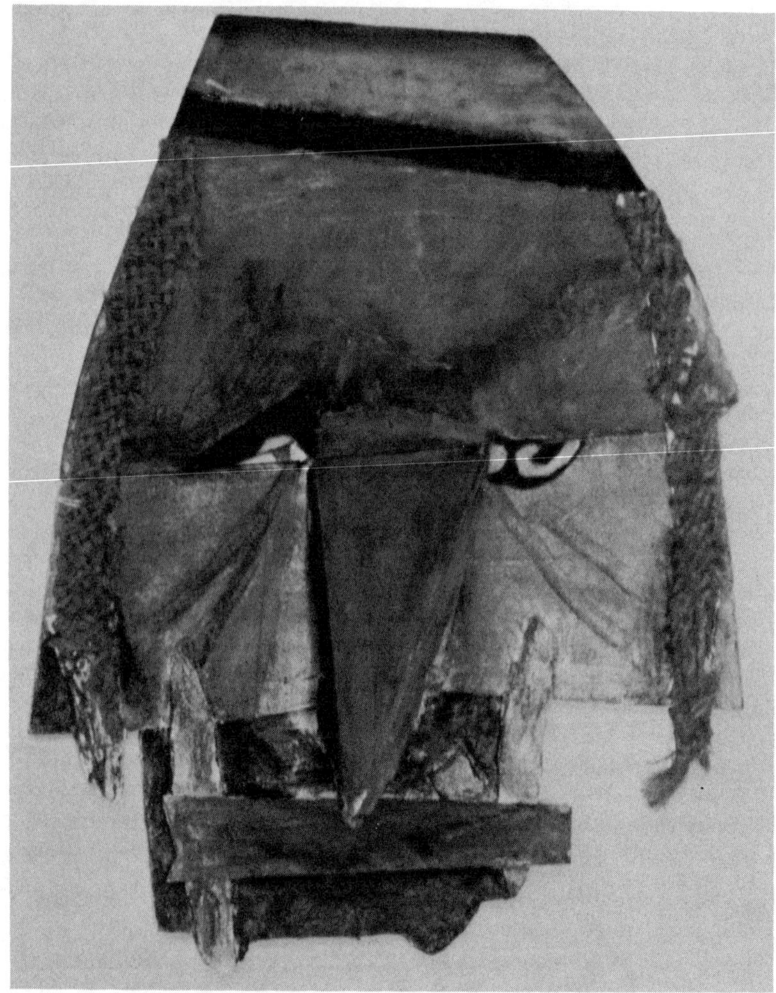

Dada mask designed by Marcel Janco for Cabaret Voltaire performances. (Janco-Dada Museum, Israel).

juxtapositioning and opposing of uncontrolled forces. Man lost his divine countenance, became matter, chance . . . Man lost the special position that reason had guaranteed him. . . . Man, stripped of the illusion of godliness, became ordinary, no more interesting than a stone . . . (pp. 223–224)

The mask, like the marionette, had served *fin-de-siècle* art well with its abstraction and symbolic suggestiveness. Dada negation, so passionately articulated by Ball in his Kandinsky lecture, now found in the mask a proper substitute for the lost divine countenance of man. Not only could the mask hide the disintegrating and fragmenting face of man, but it could also provide a link with the primitive world of essences which Dada sought to regain. In their struggle against the madness of their age, nowhere more irrefutably exemplified than in the war, artists discovered affinity, as Ball declares in the same essay on Kandinsky, "with the dread masks of primitive peoples, and with the plague and terror masks of the Peruvians, Australian aborigines, and Negroes" (p. 225). When Janco brought his masks to the Cabaret Voltaire and Ball and the others donned them for the first time, a sensitive chord in the Dada psyche was touched. If the mask concealed, it also liberated, and Ball's account of the effect of the masks on their wearers easily conveys a sense of both possession and psychic release.

That the donning of strange and exotic masks would produce a kind of demonic posession that would express itself in what Ball describes as a "tragic-absurd dance" comes as no surprise in the context of an artistic upheaval that had as one of its principal goals the restoration of primordial vigor to language. The more the avant-gardists of the late nineteenth and early twentieth centuries pressed their indictment of conventional language and sought various ways of pumping fresh blood into its communicative arteries, the more the instinctual and spontaneous rhythms of the body came to be seen as an equal if not superior system of communication. As the early history of the cabaret elsewhere in Europe has demonstrated, the desire of artists to break with the traditional, the conventional, the academic, and the classical embraced the entire spectrum of creativity, even shaping attitudes toward something as basic as language itself.

Dance was very much in the main arena of the artistic transvaluation. Repudiation of classical ballet and other traditional dance forms opened the way to the revolution of modern dance. But besides the liberation, the unfettering that modern dance represented, dance as rhythmic movement, as a system of human communication of its own directly related to the contemporary crisis of language. As spoken language came more and more to be regarded as debased, a shift of emphasis occurred from verbal language to the language of the body. The programmatic elimination of logical meaning from words, the transformation of words into an arbitrary arrangement of sounds, as in the experiments of Ball and other

Dadaists, for example, was often accompanied by spontaneous rhythmic movement of the body as if inspired by primitive dance. The primitive and archetypal were indeed common denominators of developments in poetic language, on the one hand, and in dance and theater, on the other. By moving beyond meaning into the sphere of pure sound, Ball, the Dadaists, and Russian Cubo-Futurists such as Khlebnikov and Kruchonykh sought the retrieval of a lost primordial wonderment and purity in language.

In view of the place of dance in primitive society, of the importance of dance to folk rites and rituals, of its role in the development of drama, it was natural that cabaret primitivist experiments with language would be accompanied by or at the least encourage exploration of the natural rhythms of the body as an organically related or alternative semantic system. That this occurred as if by instinct or another kind of alchemy when Ball and the others at the Cabaret Voltaire put on Marcel Janco's striking masks would have reenforced attitudes toward dance already evolving.

Another reason for an interest in dance on the part of the Cabaret Voltaire, apart from the impact of Janco's masks on the primitivist proclivities of the Dadaists, was the presence in Zurich at the time of one of the leaders of the modern dance movement, Rudolf von Laban (real name, R.L. von Váralya, 1879–1958). A highly regarded choreographer and theorist of dance, Laban directed a dance academy in Zurich that counted among its students such gifted dancers of the time as Mary Wigman (Marie Wiegmann, 1886–1958), a pioneer of modern dance in Europe who later operated her own schools in Germany and published extensively on the dance, and Sophie Taeuber (1889–1943), a talented artist as well as dancer, particularly in the field of applied art, whom Hans Arp met in Zurich in 1915 and subsequently married in 1922.

The ferment in the dance world, represented by the activities in Zurich of such outstanding exponents of modern dance as Laban, Wigman, and Taeuber, would hardly have passed unnoticed at the Cabaret Voltaire, even without direct contact. But the dancers visited the cabaret, knew the poets and painters who performed there and, with other creative people in Zurich who frequented it, contributed to the Voltaire's artists' circle ambience. More importantly, however, the experiments of Laban and his followers constituted an avant-garde transformation of dance that paralleled the avant-garde experiments with poetic language of the Dadaists of the Cabaret Voltaire. Laban's famous system of dance notation, named "Labanotation" after its inventor, was, after all, an attempt to construct a language for dance viewed as a vehicle of expressive communication. Dada primitivism and the spirituality of an artist such as Hugo Ball were echoed in the inspiration that Mary Wigman, for example, drew from primitive religious rituals. Appropriately, her dances bore such names as "Dance to the Virgin Mary," "Sacrifice" (consisting of "Dance for the Sun," "Summons of Death," "Dance for the Earth," and "Dance to Death"), and "The Celebration" (composed of "The Temple," "The Mark of Darkness," and "Festive Clamor"). Abstraction, the striving for the essential and archetypal, figured as prominently in the theories and experiments of the artists of the dance of the time as they did in those of the artists of the word, or of the canvas. The Expressionist, Futurist, and Dadaist concern for the retrieval of the putatively lost essence of the word was matched by the dancers' emphasis on the rediscovery and reconquest of the body, to borrow Mary Wigman's terms in her essay "The Philosophy of Modern Dance."[25]

The first appearance of Rudolf von Laban and members of his dance academy at the Cabaret Voltaire came on April 2, 1916, as Hugo Ball notes in *Flight Out of Time:* "Frank [Leonhard Frank—HBS] and his wife visited the cabaret. Also Mr. von Laban with his ladies" (p. 58). Since Sophie Taeuber and Hans Arp were already a couple, it is fair to assume that she as well as Mary Wigman were among Laban's "ladies" on this occasion. On June 23, 1916, when Ball recited his sound poems for the first time at the cabaret, Laban and Wigman were among the spectators before whom Ball feared "a disgrace" (p. 70).

Evidence of an increase in contact with Laban and his dancers comes in the same diary entry (March 18, 1917) in which mention of the opening of the "Galerie Dada" is made. Ball notes that on the previous Sunday there was a costume party at Mary Wigman's at which, among other things, poems by Hans Arp were read. The opening of the Galerie was formally celebrated on March 29, an occasion marked by still greater participation of the Zurich modern dance circle in the activities of the Voltaire Dadaists. While Rudolf von Laban and Mary Wigman joined others in the audience, Sophie Taeuber and another dancer named Claire Walter perfomed dances as part of the celebration's entertainment, Taeuber dancing what Ball characterizes as "abstract dances" and Walter "expressionist dances." Ball took a particular interest in Sophie Taeuber's dances; his reflections about abstract dances in *Flight Out of*

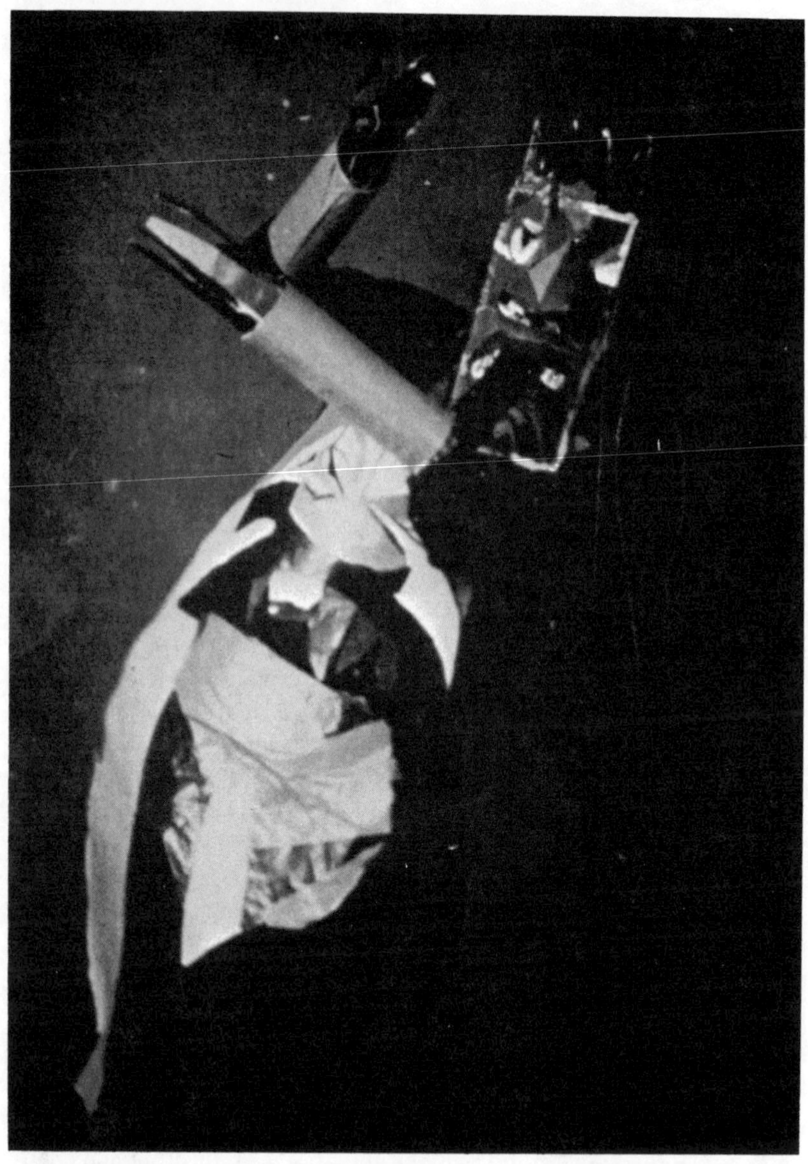

Sophie Taeuber-Arp in an "abstract dance" at the Cabaret Voltaire, 1916. (Kunsthaus Zürich).

Time prompted by them offer ample evidence of the impact of the modern dance phenomenon on him and his ability to reconcile it with his own experiments with sound in verse language:

> Abstract dances: a gong beat is enough to stimulate the dancer's body to make the most fantastic movementts. The dance has become an end in itself. The nervous system exhausts all the vibrations of the sound, and perhaps all the hidden emotion of the gong beater too, and turns them into an image. Here, in this special case, a poetic sequence of sounds was enough to make each of the individual word particles produce the strangest visible effect on the hundred-jointed body of the dancer. From a "Gesang der Flugfische und Seepferdchen" [Song of the Flying Fish and Sea Horses. One of Ball's sound poems—HBS] there came a dance full of flashes and edges, full of flames and edges, full of dazzling light and penetrating intensity. (p. 102)

As his remarks indicate, Ball found in the dancer's reactions vindication of his belief in the ability of rhythmic patterns of expressible but logically meaningless sounds to reach something deep and basic in the human psyche. Indeed, for Ball, this interaction of verbal sound and physical movement became a reenactment of the primitive origins of language and art. This is probably what he had in mind when he wrote of the dance that, "as an art of the closest and most direct material," it is "very close to the art of tattooing and to all primitive representative efforts that aim at personification; it often merges into them" (p. 103).

The more enthusiastic Ball and the other Dadaists became about dance, the more they saw the realization of Kandinsky's concept of the monumental art work of the future within their grasp. In his Kandinsky lecture of April 7, 1917, Ball discussed Kandinsky's critique of Wagner's ideas about the total work of art, the *Gesamtkunstwerk,* in *The Blue Rider.* He pointed out that the Russian artist's notion of a monumental stage composition was based not on an externalization of each of the arts, as in Wagner, but instead envisaged "a symphonic composition in which every art, reduced to its essentials, provides as an elementary form no more than the score for a construction or composition on the stage. Such a composition would allow each individual art its own material mode of operation, and it would create the future monumental work of art from a blend of the refined materials" (p. 233). To Ball, Kandinsky's stage works *The Yellow Sound* and *Violet Curtain* represented Kandinsky's efforts to put his theory into practice. The day after his lecture on Kandinsky, Ball noted in his diary that at least he himself had realized "a favorite old plan of mine. Total art: pictures, music, dances, poems—now we have that"(p. 104). What Ball is referring to is not just the interplay of a dancer and his sound poems, but the entire program for the celebration of the opening of the Galerie Dada which he inferentially takes credit for devising. The program included, in addition to the dances of Sophie Taeuber and Claire Walter, poems by Ball himself, Emmy Hennings, Hans Arp (read, as at Mary Wigman's previously referred to costume party, by Arp's friend H. L. Neitzel, since Arp tended to shun public performances), and Frédéric Clauser, Negro poems by Hans Heusser, prose by Mynona read by Olly Jacques, new music by Mme. Perrottet, and masks by Arp. This celebration program, from Ball's point of view, had all the cohesion and integrity of the ideal *Gesamtkunstwerk*, as defined above all by his most admired artist, Kandinsky.

How far Ball had progressed in his thinking about dance is manifest in his preparations for the ("Sturm") soirée of the Galerie Dada that was to open on April 14 (1917). Working now not just with Sophie Taeuber and Claire Walter, but with five "Laban-ladies," Ball began on April 10 rehearsing a new dance in which the dancers from Laban's academy would appear as Negroes in long black caftans and wearing face masks. Again, the association of modern dance with the primitive suggested by the Negro or African element and by mask should be noted. Ball planned for the dance of his Negroes to have symmetrical movements with strongly emphasized rhythm. "The mimicry," he observed in his diary, "is of a studied, deformed ugliness" (p. 104). Ball explained what he meant by this essentially Cubist notion in the rest of his diary entry for April 10:

> The consciousness of beauty comes first. How can we save it? Ugliness awakens the consciousness and finally leads to recognition—of one's own ugliness.
>
> The aesthete needs ugliness as a contrast. The moralist tries to get rid of it. Is there a helping, healing beauty? Maybe according to the principal that everything shall be beautiful, not only the Ego? How can we bring the aesthete into harmony with the moralist?
>
> Our present stylistic endeavors—what are they trying to do? To free themselves from these times, even in the subconscious, and thus to give the times their innermost form. (pp. 104–105)

The program for the second soirée, as presented on Saturday, April 14, 1917, had more than a single curious item. Ball's dance number with the five "Negresses" was formally billed as "Negro Music and Dance, performed by five persons with the help of Mlles. Jeanne Rigaud and

Maria Cantarelli" (p. 105).[26] The face masks planned for the dancers were finally designed by Marcel Janco, who by now had become the premier artist of mask of the cabaret/gallery. The program for the soirée was divided into three parts. The "Negro Music and Dance" was performed as the last item on the first part of the program. The third part of the program contained the second most striking number, a production of Oskar Kokoschka's *Sphinx and Strawman,* which by now enjoyed the status of a cabaret classic. The production of *Sphinx and Strawman* was not the only surprise of the third part of the program. Two of the performers in the production were none other than Hugo Ball, as Mr. Firdusi, and Emmy Hennings, as Female Soul, Anima. The production itself was directed by Marcel Janco who also designed masks for it. This is how Ball recalls the production and Janco's masks in *Flight Out of Time:*

> The play was performed in two adjoining rooms; the actors wore body masks. Mine was so big that I could read my script inside it quite comfortably. The head of the mask was electrically lighted; it must have looked strange in the darkened room, with the light coming out of the eyes. Emmy was the only one not wearing a mask. She appeared as half sylph, half angel, lilac and light blue. The seats went right up to the actors. Tzara was in the back room, and his job was to take care of the "thunder and lightning" as well as to say "Anima, sweet Anima!" parrot fashion. But he was taking care of entrances and exits at the same time, thundered and lightninged in the wrong places, and gave the absolute impression that this was a special effect of the production, an intentional confusion of backgrounds (p. 106)

Ball's appearance in *Sphinx and Strawman* at the Galerie Dada on April 14, 1917, was followed by his participation, in less prominent roles, in two other soirées (the third and fourth) on April 28 and May 12, respectively. The fourth Dada soirée of May 12, which was devoted to "old and new art," was a private affair. Ball and Emmy Hennings joined Tzara, Janco, Arp, and others in reading selections from the works of medieval and Baroque writers, among them Jacopone da Todi and Jakob Böhme. Music was provided by the composer Hans Heusser (1892–1954), who had taken part in the soirée of April 14 at which Ball performed in *Sphinx and Strawman.* The evening of "old and new art" was repeated on May 19. Six days later, the Galerie Dada held its last event, an evening's recital by Hans Heusser of his own compositions.

Even though his active involvement in the Galerie Dada had ended on May 12, Ball remained in Zurich and in touch with his fellow Dadaists through May 27.[27] But then, succumbing again to the need for distance and tranquillity, he bolted from Zurich and returned to Magadino. His state of mind at the time recalls the exhaustion that overtook him during the recitation of his "poems without words" at the Cabaret Voltaire on June 23, 1916. In a letter to Tristan Tzara from Magadino, dated May 28 (1917), Ball apologizes for his hasty departure from Zurich, saying that "I was at the end of my strength. There was nothing more I could do for the Galerie. . . . I could not remain any longer. My circumstances no longer permitted it. I did for the Galerie what lay within my power to do, and more, since I could have taken responsibility for other obligations which I had assumed already previously.[28]

Ball's links with Dada in the creation of which he had played such a pivotal role were now at best tenuous. Most of the summer of 1917 he spent in virtual seclusion with Emmy Hennings on the Brussada Alp in the Maggia Valley completing the writing of his novel *Flametti* and beginning his work on the Russian revolutionary Bakunin. *Flametti,* which was published in 1918 and was dedicated to Emmy Hennings, describes the adventures and eventual downfall of the leader and chief performer of a troupe of artists who entertain in a variety of bars and cafés. The novel draws heavily on Ball's own experiences in Zurich both before and during his time at the Cabaret Voltaire. That it is a settling of scores with his own cabaret period and the Dada movement that ushered from it is beyond question. Ball relives in the novel all the privations of his early days in Zurich, the excitement of the founding of the Cabaret Voltaire, the joys and frustrations of creative experimentation there, the emergence of a new movement in the avant-garde (Dada), and the dissolution of a once close knit circle of artistic rebels through a sense of unreality, financial hardship, internal dissension, and, finally, a draining of spiritual resources. If *Flametti* is a retrospective view of the birth of the Cabaret Voltaire and Dada, it is written in a straightforward, almost conventional manner free of the avant-garde techniques of Dada and thus in its very style signaling Ball's deliberate act of self-exile from the movement.

As if further separating himself from anything related to Dada, Ball and Emmy Hennings resettled in Bern rather than Zurich in the fall of 1917 after leaving the serenity of the Maggia Valley. Ball was well aware of the symbolism of his new location. He noted in *Flight Out of Time* on September 7, 1917, that "Now I feel really forsaken in this strange city. Aesthetics in Zurich; politics here; but I feel so divided in my interests that I am actually at the point of sacrificing the aesthete to politics" (p. 133). Ball's preference for Bern over Zurich was as much practical as symbolic. It was in Bern that he believed he had the best chance of finding a publisher for *Flametti* and his work on Bakunin and where he found employment at the *Freie Zeitung* newspaper.

Once *Flametti* and the Bakunin book were out of the way and the Cabaret Voltaire-Dada phase of his life was firmly behind him, Ball spent the next few years writing two works of deep personal meaning to him, *Byzantine Christianity* (published in Munich in 1923) and *Toward a Critique of the German Mind* (published in Bern in 1919). Probably more under the influence of Emmy Hennings than at any time earlier in their relationship, Ball also devoted much of his time now to religious and spiritual questions. In July 1920, with the considerable encouragement of Emmy Hennings whom he had at last married on February 20 of that year, he reentered the Roman Catholic church. He made his last entry in *Flight Out of Time* on September 29, 1921, and then undertook the rewriting of the entire diary from 1924 to 1927. In October 1921 Ball and Emmy Hennings returned to Germany, to Munich, where they remained for a year, thereafter returning to Switzerland. Except for an eighteen-month stay in Italy and occasional trips to Germany, Ball spent his final years in his adopted Switzerland. He died there in 1927 not long after the publication of a book on the German writer Herman Hesse, with whom Ball believed he shared spiritual affinities, and the revision of *Flight Out of Time*. Emmy Hennings survived him by eighteen years.

With Ball out of the picture from the late spring of 1917, Tristan Tzara presided over Zurich Dada like its anointed high priest. The appearance of the first issue of the periodical *Dada* in July 1917 heralded, for Tzara, the "official" launching of the Dada movement. When the Parisian-born Cuban artist Francis Picabia (1879–1953), the originator, in Barcelona, of an extreme Dadaist periodical named *391* (in memory of *291*, the periodical of the Alfred Stieglitz group with whom Picabia had worked on his visits to New York in 1913 and 1915) arrived in Zurich during the autumn of 1918, the way was prepared for the internationalization of the Tzara-led Zurich Dada. With much happening within the span of just a few months, 1919 was clearly a "year of the miracle." In February of that year Picabia, Tzara, and others collaborated on a Zurich issue of *391*. It was followed in May by the last number (4–5) of the *Dada* review to be produced in Switzerland with its title page designed, significantly, by

Picabia. The next issue of *Dada,* nos. 6 and 7, while still under Tzara's editorship, would appear in Paris.

The great event of 1919 for Zurich Dada, which represented both the apogee of the movement in Zurich and its end there, took place in the Saal zur Kaufleuten on the evening of April 9, 1919. The artist Hans Richter (1888–1976), a participant in the event, describes it in detail in the chapter "Finis Dada Zurich" in his book *Dada: Art and AntiArt.* In somewhat shortened form, this is Richter's account:

[Viking] Eggeling [1880–1925—HBS] appeared first . . . and delivered a very serious speech about elementary *Gestaltung* and abstract art. This only disturbed the audience insofar as they wanted to be disturbed but weren't. Then followed Susanne Perrottet's dances to compositions by Schönberg, Satie and others. She wore a Negroid mask by Janco, but they let that pass. Some poems by Huelsenbeck and Kandinsky, recited by Kathe Wulff, were greeted with laughter and catcalls by a few members of the audience. Then all hell broke loose. A *poème simultané* by Tzara, performed by twenty people who did not always keep in time with each other. . . . Shouts, whistles, shouting in unison, laughter . . . all of which mingled more or less antiharmoniously with the bellowing of the twenty on the platform. . . .

I started the second half with an address, "Against, Without, For Dada" . . . In this address I cursed the audience with moderation, and ourselves in a modest way, and consigned the audience to the underworld.

Then followed music by Hans Heusser, whose tunes or antitunes had accompanied Dada since its inauguration at the Cabaret Voltaire. Some slight opposition. A little more greeted Arp's "Wolkenpumpe" (Cloud Pump), which was interrupted from time to time, but not often, with laughter and cries of "Rubbish." More dances by Perrottet to the music of Schönberg and then Dr. Walter Serner, dressed as if for a wedding in immaculate black coat and striped trousers, with a gray cravat. This tall, elegant figure first carried a headless tailor's dummy on to the stage, then went back to fetch a bouquet of artificial flowers, gave them to the dummy to smell where its head would have been, and laid them at its feet. Finally he brought a chair, and sat astride it in the middle of the platform with his back to the audience. After these elaborate preparations, he began to read from his anarchistic credo, *Letzte Lockerung* (Final Dissolution). At last! This was just what the audience had been waiting for.

The tension in the hall became unbearable. . . . Then the cat-calls began, scornful at first, then furious. "Rat, bastard, you've got a nerve!" until the noise almost entirely drowned Serner's voice . . .

That really did it . . . . But the young men, most of whom were in the gallery, leaped on to the stage brandishing pieces of the balustrade . . . chased Serner into the wings and out of the building, smashed the tailor's dummy and the chair, and stamped on the bouquet. The whole place was in an uproar. . . .

> . . . the third part of the programme . . . resumed after a breathing-space of twenty minutes. It was in no way less aggressive than the second part, but it reached its end without incident. This was all the more remarkable since the ballet *Noir Kakadu,* with Janco's savage Negro masks to hide the pretty faces of our Laban-ese girls, and abstract costumes to cover their slender bodies, was something quite new, unexpected and anti-conventional. Even Serner was permitted to return to the stage, and his poems, no less provocative than before, were received without protest. So were Tzara's poems, and his highly provocative *Proclamation 1919.* The evening was concluded by some compositions by Hans Heusser which left no tone unturned.[29]

With this final parting salvo at the sensibilities of the bourgeois, Dada was prepared to leave the smug nest from which it had issued thence to begin its tumultuous trek across Europe and, transoceanically, to New York. Three years later, in 1922, its frenzy exhausted, it was finally declared dead as a movement. By then, however, what had begun as a wartime émigré cabaret in the safe haven of neutral Zurich had cohered into the most dynamic repudiation of reason, logic, convention, and tradition in the whole history of the early twentieth-century avant-garde. As Willy Verkauf puts the appeal and meaning of the Cabaret Voltaire so well in *Dada. Monograph of a Movement:*

> People came not for amusement, but to take part in that wonderful atmosphere of mental regeneration. Intelligence and youth refurbished their resistance and their ideology whilst at the same time taking up the comfortable nourishment offered to their palates by the poets and thinkers. It was an unforgettable experience, in an era of shortages of all kinds and in the withdrawn corner of a little Zurich alley, to find oneself in the presence of free thought, the expression of the free conscience of man in face of a culture that had gone bankrupt.[30]

NOTES

INTRODUCTION

1. The term *cabaret,* of uncertain origin, was recorded in French as early as the late thirteenth century in the meaning of a drinking establishment, a tavern, perhaps, or wine cellar. For a well-illustrated survey of cabaret from its beginnings through the early 1960s, see Lisa Appignanesi, *The Cabaret.* The book, however, excludes the development of the cabaret in Spain, East Central Europe, and Russia.

2. Hans-Peter Bayerdörfer argues persuasively for the contribution of the cabaret to the development of the avant-garde, particularly in drama and theater, in his article "Überbrettl und Überdrama: Zum Verhältnis von literarischem Kabarett und Experimentierbühne," in *Literatur und Theater im Wilhelminischen Zeitalter,* 292–325.

3. F. T. Marinetti, *Teoria e invenzione futurista,* 100.

4. "In Italia una tradizione cabarettistica non si è mai affermata, a parte sporadici tentativi. . ." (A tradition of cabaret never asserted itself in Italy, apart from sporadic attempts), *Enciclopedia dello spettacolo* (Rome: Casa Editrice Le Maschere, 1954), 2:1,430.

5. Augustus John's book of reminiscences, *Chiaroscuro: Fragment of an Autobiography* sheds some light on his relationship with Frida Strindberg and his participation in her Cabaret Theatre Club.

6. Violet Hunt, *I have This to Say: The Story of My Flurried Years,* 116.

7. For reproductions of a poster and at least one wall decoration for the Cave of the Golden Calf by Wyndham Lewis, see Walter Michel, *Wyndham Lewis: Paintings and Drawings,* with an introductory essay by Hugh Kenner, Plates 14, 15, 16. On Lewis and the Cave, see also 56 and 334 in the same book.

8. Wyndham Lewis, *Rude Assignment: A Narrative of My Career Up-to-Date,* 124–125.

9. Sir Osbert Sitwell, *Great Morning,* 229.

10. See Walter Michel, Plate 16.

11. In her memoirs, Violet Hunt mentions the singing of lieder and the performance of amateur plays. See *I Have This to Say,* 116.

12. *The Letters of Wyndham Lewis,* 46.

13. *Ibid.,* 53–54.

1. PARIS: BLACK CATS AND REED PIPES

1. *Le Chat Noir,* May 27, 1882, samedi, No. 20 bis, 4. "Sapeck" (Marie-Félicien Bataille), Émile Goudeau, and Clovis Hugues were contemporary poets who were prominent in Parisian bohemian and cabaret circles.

2. Anne de Bercy and Armand Ziwès, *A Montmartre . . . le soir,* 15–16. See also Michel Herbert, *La Chanson à Montmartre,* 58–59.

3. On Willette's relationship with Salis and the Chat Noir, see his book of reminiscences *Feu Pierrot 1857–19 ?,* 135–149. Willette's major work of art for the Chat Noir was his huge painting *Parce Domine* (Lord Have Mercy) which depicts a frenzied carnival-like procession of figures meant to symbolize the contemporary Bohème and Montmartre cabaret world.

4. Bercy-Ziwès, 17–18.

5. Émile Goudeau, *Dix Ans de Bohème,* 255–256.

6. A good study devoted just to the Hydropathes is Raymond de Casteras, *Avant le Chat Noir: Les Hydropathes 1878–1880.* See also the discussion of Goudeau and the Hydropathes in the context of the Parisian Bohème of the time in Jerrold Siegel, *Bohemian Paris: Culture, Politics, and the Boundaries of Bourgeois Life, 1830–1930,* 215–241 ("Publicity and Fantasy: The World of the Cabarets").

7. Quoted in Anne de Bercy and Armand Ziwès, *A Montmartre . . . le soir,* 10–11.

8. Charles Cros, *Le Coffret de santal,* 173–174.

9. Alphonse Allais, *Oeuvres posthumes,* 1:122.

10. Paul Verlaine, *Oeuvres en prose complètes,* 814.

11. Jules Lévy, *Les Hydropathes: Prose et Vers,* 61.

12. *Ibid.,* 69.

13. *Ibid.,* 71.

14. Texts in Jules Lévy, 34–35, 36–37, respectively.

15. *Ibid.,* 226–228.

16. *Ibid.,* 74.

17. *Ibid.,* 159.

18. *Ibid.,* 156–157.

19. *Ibid.*

20. *Ibid.*

21. Maurice Rollinat, *Oeuvres,* 2:266–267.

22. Maurice Rollinat, 95.

23. On Richepin's career in general, see Howard Sutton, *The Life and Work of Jean Richepin* Geneva: Libraire E. Droz; Paris: Libraire Minard, 1961).

24. Jules Lévy, 197–199.

25. Jean Richepin, *Choix de Poësies,* 93.

26. There is a good account of this period in the life of the Hydropathes in Anatole Jakovsky, *Alphonse Allais "Le Tueur à gags,"* 53.

27. Goudeau briefly describes the encounter with Salis in his *Dix Ans de Bohème,* 251–252.

28. *Ibid.*, 254.
29. Charles Cros, *Oeuvres complétes,* 606.
30. *Ibid.*, 341–342.
31. Émile Goudeau, *Poèmes ironiques,* 15–16.
32. Jules Lévy, *Les Hydropathes: Prose et Vers,* 177.
33. See Alphonse Allais, *Oeuvres posthumes,* vols. 1 and 2.
34. For works published in *Le Chat Noir* and assigned to Allais, though they do not bear his name, see Alphonse Allais, *Oeuvres posthumes,* 1:135–162.
35. Alphonse Allais, *Oeuvres posthumes,* 1:157–159.
36. Alphonse Allais, *Oeuvres posthumes* 1:333–335.
37. On the chanson in turn-of-the-century France, see especially Horace Valbel, *Les Chansonniers et les Cabarets Artistiques* and Michel Herbert, *La Chanson à Montmartre.* There is also good material in Walter Rösler, *Das Chanson in deutschen Kabarett 1901–1933,* 15–53 ("Das Chanson in den Anfängen des französischen Kabaretts").
38. For an attractive survey of the turn-of-the-century Parisian *café-concert,* music halls, and other types of popular entertainment, see Charles Rearick, *Pleasures of the Belle Epoque: Entertainment & Festivity in Turn-of-the-Century France.* On the Chat Noir and other cabarets, see 55–74.
39. Maurice Donnay, *Mes Débuts à Paris,* 229 and 235.
40. Jules Jouy, *Les Chansons de l'Année,* 5.
41. *Ibid.*, 19–20. The chanson, like other works of Jouy, is dedicated to the poet Jean Richepin.
42. Jules Jouy, *Les Chansons de l'Année,* 14.
43. *Chansons du Chat Noir par Mac-Nab.* Musique nouvelle ou harmonisée par Camille Baron (Paris, Au Ménestral 2bis rue Vivienne: Henri Hengel), 15–18.
44. A reference to a member of the royal house that ruled Portugal from 1640 to 1910.
45. The nickname of Napoléon Joseph Charles Paul Bonaparte (1822–1891).
46. Napoléon Victor Jérôme Frédéric Bonaparte (Victor Bonaparte; 1862–1926).
47. Émile Basly (1854–1928), founder in 1883 of French miners' union and later its president. Eventually became actively involved in cabaret.
48. Léon Say (1826–1896), French economist and statesman.
49. Maurice Boukay, *Chansons rouges,* 117.
50. An untranslatable pun in the original French based on the similarity of sound between *ventre-un* (belly-one), etc. and *vingt et un* (twenty-one), *vingt-deux* (twenty-two), *vingt-trois* (twenty-three).
51. Léon Xanrof, *Chansons à rire* (Paris, n.d.), 6.
52. Léon Xanrof (Léon Fourneau), *Chansons sans-gêne,* 61–63.
53. Michel Herbert, *La Chanson à Montmartre,* 211–212.
54. Of the literature on Bruant two useful introductory texts, both in French, are Alexandre Zévaès, *Aristide Bruant,* and Mouloudji, *Aristide Bruant.* The lat-

ter also contains a representative selection of Bruant's chansons. In English, see Lisa Appignanesi, *The Cabaret,* 26–30 and Raymond Rudorff, *The Belle Epoque: Paris in the Nineties,* 74–81.

55. Michel Herbert, *La Chanson à Montmartre,* 253.
56. Henri Perruchot, *Toulouse-Lautrec,* 113–114.
57. Aristide Bruant, *Dans la Rue* (Paris, 1889), 13.
58. Arthur Symon, *Colour Studies in Paris,* 67–68.
59. Bruant, 179.
60. On Séraphin, Lemercier de Neuville, and the history of the shadow show in France, see Denis Bordat and Francis Boucrot, *Les Théatres d'ombres: Histoire et techniques,* 77–101, 119–129.
61. Michel Herbert, *La Chanson à Montmartre,* 160.
62. Maurice Donnay, *Autour du Chat Noir,* 17–18.
63. Maurice Donnay, *Mes Débuts à Paris,* 212–213.
64. *Ibid.,* 205–206.
65. Jules Lemaître, *Impressions de Théâtre,* 322–324.
66. Maurice Donnay, *Mes Débuts à Paris,* 207–208.
67. Maurice Donnay, *Autour du Chat Noir,* 109.
68. Michel Herbert, *La Chanson à Montmartre.,* 237.
69. Maurice Donnay, *Mes Débuts à Paris,* 223.
70. Michel Herbert, 164.
71. Alphonse Allais, *Oeuvres posthumes,* 2:344.
72. *Centenaire du Cabaret du Chat Noir, Musée de Montmartre,* 3.

2. BARCELONA: FOUR MORE CATS

1. For a survey of the history of Catalonia in English, see Victor Alba, *Catalonia: A Profile.*
2. On Prat de la Riba's life and career, see especially J. M. Ainaud de Lasarte and Enric Jardí, *Prat de la Riba: Home de govern,* and Enric Prat de la Riba, *Prat de la Riba: Propulsor de la llengua i la cultura* (*Articles i parlaments*).
3. The best edition of the text in the original Catalan is Enric Prat de la Riba, *La Nacionalitat Catalana.* Another important source for Prat de la Riba's views on language is his communication to the First Congress of the Catalan Language of October 1906, "Importància de la Llengua dins el concepte de la Nacionalitat"; it is available in *Prat de la Riba. Propulsor de la llengua i la cultura* (*Articles i parlaments*), 63–71.
4. On Catalonian modernism and its place in the development of late nineteenth- and early twentieth-century Catalonian cultural nationalism, see especially J. F. Rafols, *Modernismo y modernistas;* A. Cirici Pellicer, *El arte modernista catalan;* the same author's *1900 en Barcelona* (Barcelona; 1967); Francesc Fontbona, *La crisi del modernisme artistic;* Joseph Phillip Cervera, *Modernismo: The Catalan Renaissance of the Arts;* and J. M. Infiesta, ed., *Modernisme a Catalunya,* 1.

5. Jaime Sabartés, *Picasso: An Intimate Portrait,* 52.

6. Apart from the material in Marilyn McCully's *Els Quatre Gats: Art in Barcelona around 1900,* there is a small essay on his career by Catherine Banlin Lacroix, "Miquel Utrillo i Morlius," in Jean Fabris, *Utrillo: Sa Vie, son oeuvre,* 12–16.

7. The most complete account of the Quatre Gats is Enric Jardí Casany's *Història de Els Quatre Gats.* For the best work on the subject in English, see Marilyn McCully, *Els Quatre Gats;* this is actually a catalogue written for an exhibition of Els Quatre Gats held at the Princeton University Art Museum in 1978. It is superbly illustrated and has been of great value to my own work. Additional views on the Quatre Gats appear in: Rafael Benet, "La revisión de la época de Els Quatre Gats," *Goya:* Revista de Arte (Madrid, 1954–55), 1–6; *Quatre Gats.* Primer Salón "Revista" (Barcelona, 1954). The work is subtitled "La Exposición Homenaje al grupo Quatre Gats presentada por "Revista," fué inaugurada en la Salá Parés de Barcelona el día 15 de mayo de 1954." See especially Rafael Benet's introduction, "Los 'Quatre Gats' y su época," 7–12; José Maria Garrut, *Dos siglos de pintura catalana* (*XIX–XX*), 374–376; Francesc Fontbona, *La crisi del modernisme artístic,* 64–66; Josep Pla, *Santiago Rusiñol i el seu temps,* 187–202; J. F. Ràfols, *Modernisme i modernistes* (Barcelona; 1982), 113–130; this work is a Catalan translation of the author's *Modernismo y modernistas.*

8. On Suzanne Valadon, see especially John Storm, *The Valadon Drama: The Life of Suzanne Valadon.*

9. On Sitges, Catalonian modernism, the *festes,* and Rusiñol's role in them, see Ramon Planes, *Llibre de Sitges,* and *El modernismo a Sitges.*

10. On Rusiñol and Cau Ferrat, see Ramon Planes, *Rusiñol i el Cau Ferrat.*

11. Santiago Rusiñol, "El reino de las sombras," "Desde el molino," *Obres Completes,* 1915.

12. For a detailed account of Quatre Gats art exhibitions, see Marilyn McCully's *Els Quatre Gats.*

13. McCully, 30.

14. Jaime Sabartés, 54–55.

15. On Picasso and Barcelona during this period, see Josep Palau i Fabre, *Picasso en Cataluña,* especially the illustrations on 45–53, and Josep Palau i Fabre, *Picasso per Picasso,* 83 in particular.

16. McCully, 33.

17. *Ibid.*

18. *Ibid.,* 35.

19. Santiago Rusiñol, "El reino de las sombras," 1915.

20. The text of the poem appears in Joan Maragall, *Obres Completes: Obra Catalana,* 202–204.

21. Ezequiel Vigues, *Teatre de Putxinel-lis;* Xavier Fabregas, introd., 6. Vigues (1880–1960), known also as Dido, was a popular Catalonian puppeteer in the 1930s, one of whose puppet plays, *El convidat* (1937), was dedicated to the Four Cats. See *Teatre de Putxinel-lis,* 55–59. On puppetry in Catalonia,

see also J. E. Varey, "Los títeres en Cataluña, en el siglo XIX," *Estudios Escenicos,* 5, 45–78.

22. The front cover of *El Teatre catalá,* Any 1, No. 26, August 24, 1912, has a photograph of Pi and his puppets. An article about him, "En Pi, titellaire dels IV Gats," by Avelí Artis, appears on 10–12 of the same journal.

23. Avelí Artís, "En Pi, titellaire," *El Teatre catalá* (August 24, 1912), Any 1, No. 26, 11.

24. Rowland Thirlmere, *Letters from Catalonia and Other Parts of Spain,* 1:366, 368–369.

25. Rubén Darío, *España contemporanea,* 35.

26. *Ibid.,* 36–38.

27. Enric Jardí Casany, *Història de Els Quatre Gats,* 63–64.

28. *Ibid.,* 64. For an introduction to Frègoli's career, see Jean Nohain and Fr̨ancois Caradec, *Frègoli* (*1867–1936*): *Sa Vie et ses secrets.*

29. Quoted in Jardí Casany, 113–114.

30. On the contest, see *ibid.,* 111–112.

31. See *Pel & Ploma,* nos. 62 and 63, October 15, 1900, and November 1, 1900: no. 88, May 20, 1901, 364–365, and 370–371, respectively.

32. Santiago Rusiñol, "En Pere Romeu," *Obres Completes,* 2:652–653.

3. BERLIN AND MUNICH: FROM SUPERSTAGE TO EXECUTIONER'S BLOCK

1. For a brief reminiscence of Drachmann on the occasion of a later visit to Munich, see Ludwig Thoma, *Gesammelte Werke,* 1:234–238.

2. On Drachmann's influence, the early Scandinavian cabaret, and the history especially of the Norwegian Chat Noir, see Odd Bang-Hensen, *Chat Noir og Norsk Revy.*

3. Oskar Panizza, "Der Klassizismus und das Eindringen des Variété," *Die Gesellschaft. Monatschrift für Litteratur, Kunst u. Sozialpolitik* 12:1253, 1254, 1255, and 1256.

4. *Ibid.,* 1270. For further information on Panizza's life and career as well as other works by him, see Oskar Panizza, *Das Liebeskonzil und andere Schriften.*

5. On Otto Julius Bierbaum and his contribution to the development of the German cabaret, see especially Franz Blei, *Erzählung eines Leben,* 327–329, and Hannsludwig Geiger, *Es war um die Jahrhundertwende,* 142–149.

6. Otto Julius Bierbaum, *Stilpe,* 165–166.

7. Otto Julius Bierbaum, *Deutsche Chansons,* viii ff.

8. Wolzogen's work for the theater includes such plays as *Die Kinder der Excellenz* (1890), a four-act comedy; *Ein unbeschriebenes Blatt* (A Blank Page, 1896), a three-act comedy; *Die hohe Schule* (The Upper School, subtitled "Five Acts from the Life of a Girl of Talent: A Play about Munich," 1899); and *Feuersnot* (Fire Emergency, 1901), a "song poem" (Singgedicht), with music by Richard Strauss.

9. Perhaps Wolzogen was not as unlikely a founder of the German cabaret as may appear at first glance. Before establishing his Überbrettl (Superstage) he lived in the bohemian quarter of Munich, the Schwabing district, where in addition to occasionally contributing poems and chansons (once the form began to take root in Germany) to the famous Munich satirical magazine *Simplicissimus,* with which Frank Wedekind, among others, was associated, he also founded a literary and theatrical society known as the *Literarische Gesellschaft.* On this society and his role in it, see Ernst von Wolzogen, *Verse zu meinem Leben,* 89, and *Wie ich mich ums Leben brachte,* 189.

10. Wolzogen notes in his memoiristic *Wie ich mich ums Leben brachte* (194): "In the winter of 1899–1900, suggestions came to me from different quarters, verbally and in writing, that I introduce the French cabaret into Germany."

11. In *Wie ich mich ums Leben brachte* (195), Wolzogen clearly attributes the coinage of the term "Überbrettl" to himself: "And the second experience was my unfortunate invention of the term Überbrettl as a designation for the German artistic cabaret."

12. Wolzogen acknowledges his indebtedness to Nietzsche in this and other respects in *Wie ich mich ums Leben brachte,* 197. See also his remarks on how he came to found the Überbrettl in "Wie ich das 'Überbrettl' erfand," in Helga Bemmann, ed., *Mitgelacht—dabeigewesen: Erinnerungen aus sechs Jahrzehnten Kabarett,* 13–16.

13. Ernst von Wolzogen, *Wie ich mich ums Leben brachte,* 196–197.

14. *Ibid.,* 199.

15. Ernst von Wolzogen, *Ansichten und Aussichten,* 14.

16. Ernst von Wolzogen, *Wie ich mich ums Leben brachte,* 197.

17. *Ibid.,* 204.

18. He speaks of this expectation in *Wie ich mich ums Leben brachte* (205–206). Wolzogen's public relations work in behalf of his enterprise helped create an unmistakable air of curiosity about it which the linkage with the Goethe festivity, as in the following announcement from the *Berliner Tageblatt* of January 5, 1901, could only heighten: "In the interest of artistic effect, both the Goethe performances and Wolzogen's Überbrettl will be held in the hall of the Berlin Philharmonic. Eventually, the entire presentation will be repeated." How new the idea of cabaret was in Germany and the uncertainty and yet curiosity concerning it comes through clearly in the same announcement in the paper's "Literary Review" (Literarische Rundschau) section: "The idea of an aesthetic *Überbrettl* or variety theater, or however one calls the thing, in which modern art and the old honky-tonk (*Tingel-Tangel*) come together, seems really to be in the air."

19. Ernst von Wolzogen, *Wie ich mich ums Leben brachte,* 205.

20. *Ibid.,* 206.

21. *Ibid.,* 207.

22. *Ibid.,* 209.

23. Rudolf Presber, *Ich gehe durch mein Haus,* 289–290. For other interesting although brief comments on the early Berlin cabaret, see 288–296. Presber

himself, incidentally, was the author of a short parody of Maeterlinck, *Das Eichhörnchen* (The Squirrel), which was performed by Wolzogen's Überbrettl (292). Further information on the opening night program can be found in the generally favorable review of the event published in the January 19 (1901) Saturday morning edition of the *Berliner Tageblatt* (30 Jg., Nr. 33).

24. For the first program as a whole, see Rudolf Hösch, *Kabarett von gestern,* 57–58.

25. Rudolf Presber, 290.

26. For the most recent edition in German, see *Die Schallmühle: Grotesken und Parodien.* For a good introduction to Morgenstern's life and career in English, see Erich P. Hofacker, *Christian Morgenstern,* Hofacker mentions the successful staging of a few of Morgenstern's sketches at Wolzogen's Überbrettl (37) and also that Morgenstern's *Galgenlieder* were also first presented at the cabaret by Wolzogen (45).

27. Christian Morgenstern, *Die Schallmühle,* 131–132.

28. *Ibid.,* 131.

29. See Wolzogen's letter to Morgenstern of January 20, 1901, in *Christian Morgenstern: Ein Leben in Briefen,* Margareta Morgenstern, ed., 116–117.

30. Kayssler's letter to Morgenstern of January 21, 1901, in *Ibid.,* 115. In another letter dated January 27 that same year, Kayssler requested more material from Morgenstern, suggesting perhaps a Maeterlinck piece, "short and funny" (kurz und ulkig), something in the spirit of [Max Reinhardt's] "Carlos" but not another Schiller parody (117).

31. *Simplicissimus,* 6 (1901/1902), no. 39: 307.

32. Text in Otto Julius Bierbaum, *Irrgarten der Liebe,* under the title "Er fühlt sich Lustiger Ehemann," 245.

33. Leonhard M. Fiedler, *Max Reinhardt,* 29, points out that despite the success of a few numbers in the cabaret's program, above all Bierbaum's "Lustige Ehemann," the program as a whole lacked vitality, was inorganic, and has to be considered, in the final analysis, as an unsuccessful attempt at an "ennobled" or elevated *variété.*

34. When, in an obvious attempt to put as much distance as possible between himself and the whole cabaret fad, Bierbaum later wrote: "Who really knows my poetry knows that *from the very beginning* alongside what you call too much '*Kling-Klang-Gloribusch,*' there were also what you termed 'the beginnings of a symbolic celebration.' And he knows, too, that whatever of mine had any success in the 'Überbrettl' (much too much and, in this respect, undeserved) had already appeared, in fact, *long before* the cabaret arose and that I always took offense to the cabaret itself as well as to the tasteless name of 'Überbrettl' whenever the idea of a lyrical *variété* theater in part was attributed to me. Certainly, then, also the *Deutsche Chansons,* which appeared shortly before Wolzogen's venture, made no small contribution to the 'Überbrettl.' But this book was never any idea of mine. It was not I, to be sure, but Mr. [Alfred Walter] Heymel who was most pleased with the great material success of this book." From a letter of

Bierbaum to Fritz Mauthner, dated Munich, February 11, 1904, the text of which appears in Hanns-Ludwig Geiger, *Es war um die Jahrhundertwende,* 164–170. The original of the above passage appears on p. 168.

35. Ludwig Thoma, *Ein Leben in Briefen* (*1875–1921*), 67.

36. *Ibid.*, 71.

37. Letter to Viktor Pröbstl, June 27, 1901; letter to Langen, July 4, 1901, 83; letter to Langen, July 17, 1901, 84; in Ludwig Thoma, *Ein Leben.*

38. *Ibid.*, 103, 105.

39. For the text of *Die Medaille* and other dramatic works by Thoma, see Ludwig Thoma, *Theater,* Hans-Reinhard Müller, ed. (Munich: R. Piper, 1964). *Die Medaille* appears on pp. 209–246. In his revue of the play for the *Münchner Neueste Nachrichten,* Hans von Gumppenberg referred to it as a "highly spiced farce" best suited for performance in a cabaret. See Thoma, *Theater,* 658–659.

40. For his own recollection of the episode, see Ludwig Thoma, *Erinnerungen,* 204–205.

41. On Reinhardt's early days in Berlin and especially the establishment of Die Brille, see Gusti Adler, *Max Reinhardt,* 33–37.

42. Speaking of the parodic mainly one-act plays presented by Die Brille and Reinhardt's successor cabaret, Schall und Rauch, Klaus Budzinski makes the point that throughout the cabaret's existence they remained the essential component of programs. See Klaus Budzinski, *Die Muse mit der scharfen Zunge: Vom Cabaret zum Kabarett,* 76.

43. For a photograph of the entrance to the Schall und Rauch at its new Unter den Linden location, see Max Reinhardt, *Schriften,* Hugo Fetting, ed. (Berlin: Henschelverlag Kunst und Gesellschaft, 1974), opposite 64.

44. Like the Chat Noir in Paris and the later Elf Scharfrichter in Munich, Schall und Rauch also published the texts of some of the major dramatic works presented at the cabaret, among them *Don Carlos an der Jahrhundertwende in drei Stilarten* (Don Carlos at the Turn of the Century, in Three Different Styles), *L'Interieur oder Das Intime Theater* (The Interior, or The Intimate Theater), subtitled "An Internal and External Event," about an unsuccessful effort to found an intimate theater and alluding obviously to Maeterlinck, and three skits by Reinhardt himself: *Diarrhoesteia des Persiflegeles* (Persiflegel's Diarrhea), subtitled "A Flop in Several Acts"; *Das Regie-Kollegium* (The School of Directing), also known as *Die Theaterprobe* (The Rehearsal); and *Ein böhmischer Fremdenführer* (A Bohemian Tourist Guide). On Reinhardt's dramatic writing during this period, see especially Gusti Adler, *Max Reinhardt,* 3–37.

45. On Munich during this period, see, among others, Hanns Arens, *Unsterbliches München: Streifzüge durch 200 Jahre litterarischen Lebens der Stadt,* and Manuel Gasser, *München um 1900.*

46. Marc Henry wrote extensively about himself and his experiences in and impressions of Germany. His books *Au Pays des Maîtres-Chanteurs, Trois Villes: Vienne-Munich-Berlin,* and *Villes et paysages d'Outre-Rhin* remain the principal sources of information about him.

47. Marc Henry, *Trois Villes: Vienne-Munich-Berlin,* 152.

48. *Ibid.,* 153, 156.

49. *Ibid.,* 157.

50. Marc Henry, *Au Pays des Maîtres-Chanteurs,* 118.

51. *Ibid.,* 7. On the establishment of the Elf Scharfrichter and especially Marc Henry's role in it, see Hanns von Gumppenberg's memoirs, *Lebenserinnerungen: Aus dem Nachlass des Dichters,* 280–282.

52. Marc Henry, *Au Pays des Maîtres-Chanteurs,* 7.

53. The quotations follow the text as it appears in Helga Bemmann, ed., *Immer um die Litfasssaüle rum: Gedichte aus sechs Jahrzehnten Kabarett,* 26–27.

54. On Marya Delvard's background, see Klaus Budzinski, *Die Muse mit der scharfen Zunge,* 55. Hösch, *Kabarett von gestern,* 113, states that Marc Henry first discovered Delvard in an amateur production of Courteline's *Boubouroche,* in which she appeared on stage for the first time.

55. Hans Carossa, *Der Tag des jungen Arztes,* 136–137. Also quoted by Heinz Gruel in his *Elf Scharfrichter,* 28.

56. Max Brod, ed., *The Diaries of Franz Kafka, 1910–1913,* 47.

57. Frank Wedekind, *Dramen 2: Gedichte,* 404. Also, Frank Wedekind, *Gedichte und Chansons,* 28–29.

58. L. Achim von Arnim and Clemens Brentano, eds., *Des Knaben Wunderhorn:Alte deutsche Lieder,* 2: 222–223.

59. Quoted by Heinz Gruel in his *Elf Scharfrichter,* 25.I have been thus far unable to consult the original source, possibly because so many of Von Maassen's casual pieces were published in magazines and journals, many of which are difficult to locate without specific reference. There is the additional problem of Von Maassen's having written satirical verses and other "light" works under the pseudonyms Jacobus Schnellpfeffer and Wilhelm Heinrich Schollenheber. On Von Maassen himself, whose role in turn-of-the-century Munich cultural life was by no means insignificant, see especially Herbert Günther, "Carl Georg von Maassen," *Die Literatur.* Monatschrift für Literaturfreunde, Heft 9 (Stuttgart, June 1931), 495–498, and the same author's *Drehbühne der Zeit: Freundschaften. Begegnungen. Schicksale,* 153–163.

60. Franz Blei, *Erzählung eines Lebens,* 343. For Blei's comments on the Elf Scharfrichter in general in the same book, see 341–345 ("Die Scharfrichter—Ein Theaterprogram").

61. On Lautensack's life and work, see Wilhelm Lukas Kristl, *Und morgen steigt ein Licht herab: Vom Leben und Dichten des Heinrich Lautensack.* The best collection of Lautensack's works is Heinrich Lautensack, *Das verstörte Fest. Gesammelte Werke.* Of Lautensack's several plays, the best known and most successful is *Die Pfarrhauskomödie* (The Parsonage Comedy, written 1911).

62. I am quoting the text of the poem as it appears in W. L. Kristl, *Und morgen steigt ein Licht herab,* 13.

63. Hanns Arens makes an important point of this motivation on Wedekind's

part in his monumental *Unsterbliches München: Streifzüge durch 200 Jahre literarischen Lebens der Stadt,* 294.

64. Wolfdietrich Rasch, ed., *Der vermummte Herr: Briefe Frank Wedekinds aus den Jahren 1881–1917,* 132.

65. *Ibid.,* 134.

66. *Ibid.,* 145.

67. *Ibid.,* 145–146.

68. Hanns Arens, 294; see also Walter Rösler, *Das Chanson im deutschen Kabarett 1901–1933,* 103.

69. German text from Frank Wedekind, *Gedichte und Chansons,* 95.

70. John Willett, ed. and tr., *Brecht on Theatre: The Development of an Aesthetic,* 3–4.

71. Heinrich Mann, *Essays,* 247.

72. Franz Blei, *Erzählung eines Lebens,* 343.

73. The complete title of Lautensack's requiem to Wedekind is: "Ein Requiem. Grablegung Frank Wedekinds, des grössten deutschen Dramatikers, im Waldfriedhof in Müchen, Dienstag, den 12. März 1918. Pantomime für den Film—Flammen wie bei Homunculus." The text appears in Heinrich Lautensack, *Das verstörte Fest: Gesammelte Werke,* 475–479. The excerpt quoted here appears on 476.

74. On the Schwabinger Schattenspiele, see Hans Brandenburg, *München leuchtete: Jugenderinnerungen,* 173, 174; Rolf von Hoerschelmann, *Leben ohne Alltag,* 111–139; *In Memoriam Alexander von Bernus.*

75. Hanns von Gumppenberg, *Lebenserinnerungen: Aus dem Nachlass des Dichters,* 286.

76. Hanns von Gumppenberg, "Die Verlobung," *Überdramen,* Vol. 1, 18, 21, and 22.

77. *Die Kritik des Wirklich-Seienden: Grundlagen zu einer Philosophie der Wirklich-Seienden* (Berlin, 1892) and *Grundlagen der wissenchaftlichen Philosophie* (Munich, 1903). In 1910, Gumppenberg also began publishing in Munich a weekly art and poetry magazine called *Licht und Schatten: Wochenschrift für Schwarzweiss-Kunst und Dichtung.*

78. Hanns von Gumppenberg, *Lebenserinnerungen,* 285.

79. Falckenberg describes the stage of the Elf Scharfrichter in some detail in his book *Mein Leben—Mein Theater,* 108–109. For Falckenberg's other comments on the Elf Scharfrichter see 102–146.

80. Wedekind already had acting experience before joining the Eleven Executioners. In 1895, in Lenzburg and Zurich, he gave readings of plays by Ibsen under the pseudonym of Cornelius Minehaha, and in June 1898, after his pseudonymous appearance as Dr. Schön in the Leipzig premiere of *Earth Spirit,* he accepted employment at the Munich Schauspielhaus as *dramaturg, regisseur,* and actor. It was in the latter capacity that he played the role of Gerardo in his own play *Der Kammersänger* (The Chamber Singer) at the Schauspielhaus.

81. For an overview of Wedekind's pantomime writing, see Artur Kutscher, *Wedekind: Leben und Werk,* 100–103, and Sol Gittelman, *Frank Wedekind,* 57–63.

82. "Zirkusgedanken," *Neue Zürcher Zeitung,* June 29, 30, 1887; "Im Zirkus," *Neue Zürcher Zeitung,* August 2,5, 1888. The texts are reprinted in Frank Wedekind, *Prosa,* 153–162, 163–169.

83. Texts in Wedekind, *Prosa,* 281–331 and 188–190, respectively.

84. Frank Wedekind, *Ausgewählte Werke,* 1:xxxviii.

85. On pantomime in turn-of-the-century Paris, in the context of an evolving avant-garde, see especially John A. Henderson, *The First Avant-Garde 1887–1894: Sources of the Modern French Theatre,* 120–122.

86. Frank Wedekind, *Dramen 2: Gedichte,* 763. This same edition also includes the complete text of *Die Kaiserin von Neufundland.* See 343–378.

87. Wedekind mentions his pleasure at the successful outcome of the first production of *The Empress of Newfoundland* in a letter to Beate Heine from Munich on August 5, 1902: "The performance of my *Empress of Newfoundland,* naturally without extras and with a musical potpourri arranged by me, brought me the greatest joy. The impression it created was, however, wholly artistic, since the two main roles were played so well. I couldn't have hoped for anything better from any big stage." *Der vermummte Herr: Briefe Frank Wedekinds aus den Jahren 1881–1917,* 146.

88. Walter Rösler, *Das Chanson im deutschen Kabarett 1901–1933,* 105.

89. *Der vermummte Herr: Briefe Frank Wedekinds aus dem Jahren 1881–1917,* 156–158.

90. Klaus Budzinski, *Die Muse mit der scharfen Zunge,* 72.

91. Peter Jelavich, *Munich and Theatrical Modernism: Politics, Playwriting, and Performance 1890–1914,* 245.

92. Hanns von Gumppenberg, *Lebenserinnerungen,* 293–294.

93. Censored items included a dialogue by Wedekind, *Hanns und Hanne,* on the theme of sadomasochism, the Austrian writer Hermann Bahr's anti-monarchic satire "Unter sich" (Among Ourselves), and the first act of Heinrich Leopold Wagner's *Kindermörderin* (The Child Murderess, 1776). See Jelavich, *Munich and Theatrical Modernism,* 181–182.

94. Otto Falckenberg, *Mein Leben—Mein Theater,* 137–138.

95. For a good introduction to the *Bänkelsänger* and *Moritaten* tradition, see the copiously illustrated anthology *Das Moritatenbuch,* Mia Geimer-Stangier and Karl Riha, eds. Riha's afterword (505–515) is particularly useful. On Wedekind as a cabaret singer with links to the *Bänkelsang* and *Moritat* traditions, see Edward P. Harris, "Freedom and Degradation: Frank Wedekind's Career as a Kabarettist," in Gerald Chapple and Hans Schulte, eds., *The Turn of the Century: German Literature and Art, 1890–1915,* 493–506.

96. Texts of Brecht's own *Moritaten* can be found in Geimer-Stangier and Riha, *Das Moritatenbuch.* See also the collection by Helga Bemmann, ed.,

Leute höret die Geschichte: Bänkeldichtung aus zwei Jahrhunderten, 5–13, 286–293.

97. Kenneth C. Lindsay and Peter Vergo, eds. *Kandinsky: Complete Writings on Art,* 1:264, 260, and 264, respectively.

98. *The Yellow Sound* was scheduled for production in Munich in 1914, in Berlin in 1922, and at the Bauhaus under Oskar Schlemmer. None of the productions materialized.

99. Max Halbe, *Jahrhundertwende: Erinnerungen an eine Epoche,* 339.

4. VIENNA: NIGHTLIGHTS AND BATS

1. For an excellent introduction to *fin-de-siècle* Vienna, see Carl E. Schorske, *Fin-de-Siècle Vienna: Politics and Culture.*

2. For a good overview of turn-of-the-century Viennese art and literature, see Gotthart Wunberg, with Johannes J. Braakenburg, eds. *Die Wiener Moderne: Literatur, Kunst und Musik zwischen 1890 und 1910.* The work is essentially an anthology of well-chosen texts by virtually every major figure of the period.

3. Egon Friedell, ed., *Das Altenberg-Buch,* 214. The best accounts of Altenberg's life are Gisela von Wysocki, *Peter Altenberg: Bilder und Geschichten des befreiten Lebens,* and Hans Christian Kosler, ed., *Peter Altenberg: Leben und Werk in Texten und Bildern.* See also Mara Gelsi's Italian study, *Peter Altenberg: La Strategia della rinuncia.*

4. *Fremden-Blatt,* Nr. 104, Sunday, April 15, 1906, 25. All my references are to the one page on which the interview appears.

5. Quoted by Hans Weigel in *Karl Kraus oder Die Macht der Ohnmacht,* 8. Müsahm's entry is dated April 30, 1906.

6. Arthur Schnitzler, *Jugend in Wien: Eine Autobiographie,* 269.

7. Peter Haage, ed., *Egon Friedell, Wozu das Theater? Essays, Satiren, Humoresken,* 166.

8. Egon Friedell, ed., *Das Altenberg-Buch,* 152.

9. The only biography of Friedell of which I am aware is the popular study by Peter Haage, *Der Partylöwe, der nur Bücher frass: Egon Friedell und sein Kreis.*

10. Carl E. Schorske, *Fin-de-Siècle Vienna: Politics and Culture,* 9.

11. *Ibid.,* 152.

12. Werner J. Schweiger, ed., *Das grosse Peter Altenberg Buch,* 329–330. The text first appeared in Altenberg's *Bilderbögen des kleinen Lebens* (Berlin: S. Fischer, 1908).

13. Felix Salten, *Das Österreichische Antlitz: Essays,* 111–112.

14. Werner J. Schweiger, ed., *Das grosse Peter Altenberg Buch,* 65–66 and 94–95.

15. *Fledermaus,* opening program, 1907.

16. Elisabeth Pablé, ed., *Rote Laterne / Schwarzer Humor,* 41.

17. Peter Altenberg, *Ausgewählte Werke in zwei Bänden,* 1:165 and 166.

18. Werner J. Schweiger, ed., *Das grosse Peter Altenberg Buch,* 333–334.

19. *Ibid.,* 336–337.

20. The play was published as a separate text in 1908: Egon Friedell and Alfred Polgar, *Goethe: Eine Szene.*

21. *Ibid.,* 179, 180.

22. *Ibid.,* 186.

23. *Ibid.,* 188.

24. *Das grosse Peter Altenberg Buch,* 338. The remark appears in Altenberg's review of the February program of the 1908/1909 season.

25. On Kokoschka's *The Spotted Egg,* see also Gerhard Johann Lischka, *Oskar Kokoschka: Maler und Dichter,* 58–60.

26. Max Mell, *Gesammelte Werke,* vol. 4.

27. Both *Sphinx and Strawman* and Kokoschka's play *Mörder—Hoffnung der Frauen* (Murder—The Hope of Women) were first presented at a Bat matinee on March 29, 1908, in Kokoschka's own stage designs. Unfortunately, none of the sketches for the productions nor even descriptive material concerning them have been preserved. From literature on Kokoschka, we know only that the costume and mask of the leading actress were done in the style of Aubrey Beardsley. On Kokoschka's *Sphinx and Strawman* and *Murder—The Hope of Women,* see also the remarks by Donald E. Gordon in his article "Oskar Kokoschka and the Visionary Tradition," in Gerald Chapple and Hans H. Schulte, eds., *The Turn of the Century: German Literature and Art 1890–1915,* 23–52.

28. The version of *Sphinx and Strawman* performed at the Cabaret Voltaire is available in English translation in Victor H. Miesel, ed., *Voices of German Expressionism* (Englewood Cliffs, N.J.: Prentice-Hall, 1970), 119–125.

29. Oskar Kokoschka, "Sphinx und Strohmann. Komödie für Automaten," 148.

30. *Ibid.*

31. Gerhard Lischka, *Oskar Kokoschka: Maler und Dichter,* 56.

32. See the remarks on this also of J. M. Ritchie, *German Expressionist Drama,* 43–47.

33. The *Wiener Allgemeine Zeitung* of January 8, 1908, 3, contains the announcement of the Bat's "artistic *Maskredouten*" beginning January 20 under the motto of *Moderne Redoute,* evenings at 10.

34. Gertrud Pott, *Die Spiegelung des Sezessionismus im österreichischen Theater,* 143.

35. This is mentioned by Peter Altenberg in a review in the *Wiener Allgemeine Zeitung,* February 4, 1908, 2.

36. The most outstanding of the sisters was clearly Grete Wiesenthal (1885–1969). On her, see the *Neue österreichische Biographie ab 1815* (Vienna and Munich: 1977), 19:140–145. Grete Wiesenthal began her career as a dancer on an open-air stage in a garden performing *The Dancer and the Marionette* (based on

a poem by Max Mell and arranged by Gustav Klimt, Kolo Moser, and Josef Hofmann). She became a star performer at the Fledermaus, dancing solo in such numbers as a Chopin waltz, Strauss' *Danube Waltz,* and Beethoven's *Allegretto.* Besides professional tours throughout Europe, she also performed in the United States. Grete Wiesenthal was also the author of a book about her own career, *Die erste Schritte* (The First Steps, 1947), and a novel about the dance entitled *Iffi: Roman einer Tänzerin* (Iffie: The Novel of a Dancer, 1951).

37. Gertrud Pott, 152.

38. Gertrud Pott, 152.

39. *Ibid.,* 150.

5. CRACOW: LITTLE GREEN BALLOONS

1. For a good general history of Poland, see Norman Davies, *God's Playground: A History of Poland,* 2 vols. (New York: Columbia University Press, 1982).

2. One of the most interesting accounts of Cracow in the late nineteenth and early twentieth centuries is Tadeusz Boy-Żeleński's *Znasz-li ten kraj;* see *Pisma,* 2:7–185. See also the memoirs of Zygmunt Leśnodorski, *Wspomnienia i zapiski.* For factual information on turn-of-the-century Cracow, helpful works are the collective *Kraków w XIX w.,* vols. 1 and 2, and Stefan Kieniewicz, *Galicja w dobie autonomicznej* (*1850–1914*).

3. In 1894, Stanisław Szczepanowski, the author of *Nędza Galicji* (Galicia's Poverty, 1888), published a strongly worded attack against the new literary currents under the title *Dezynfekcja prądów europejskich* (The Disinfection of European Currents). The moralist and historian of literature Marian Zdziechowski (1861–1938) joined him, insisting that the young writers of the day were disinterested in the fate of the nation and had little talent. The attacks of Szczepanowski and Zdziechowski were answered by Ludwik Szczepański (1872–1954), who in 1897 had become the editor of the influential journal *Życie* (Life), the leading poet of the time Kazimierz Przerwa-Tetmajer (who wrote under the name Szyldkret), and one of the foremost publicists of the period, Artur Górski (1870–1959). Górski penned a series of articles (under the pseudonym Quasimodo) defending the "new art." It was in these articles that the term "Young Poland" was used for the first time. Excerpts from Szczepanowski's articles appear on pages xxv and xxvii of Boy-Żeleński's *Młoda Polska: Wybór poezyj;* from Górski's reply, xxvii–xxix.

4. Boy-Żeleński, *Pisma* 6:234, in the article "Wstęp do Antologii Młodej Polski."

5. On Polish Romantic drama, see Harold B. Segel, *Polish Romantic Drama* (Ithaca, N.Y., and London: Cornell University Press, 1977).

6. Tadeusz Boy-Żeleński, "Mes Confessions," *Pisma* 2:507.

7. The author, principally, of the plays *W sieci* (In the Net, 1899) and

Karykatury (Caricatures, 1899). For an introduction to Kisielewski's life and work, see Roman Taborski's introduction to Jan August Kisielewski, *Dramaty;* on Kisielewski's sojourn in Paris and his project for a Polish cabaret, see especially XLII–LII.

8. Jan August Kisielewski, *Panmusaion,* 165–166. The essay was originally published in the journal *Wędrowiec* in 1904.

9. Jan August Kisielewski, *Życie dramatu,* 155–156.

10. *Ibid.,* 158–159.

11. For reproductions of Green Baloon invitations, see Boy-Żeleński, *Pisma,* 2:412 (this one drawn by Boy-Żeleński himself), 418, 453, 457, 461, 467; Jan Paweł Gawlik, *Powrót do Jamy* and Tomasz Weiss, *Legenda i prawda Zielonego Balonika.* These two last publications contain many reproductions of Green Balloon invitations.

12. A boisterous, gaudy, slapstick kind of theatrical improvisation named for its principal German practitioner, the actor and director Adolf Ernst (1846–1927).

13. Zenon Przesmycki, "Nadsceny," *Myśl teatralna Młodej Polski,* Irena Sławińska and Stefan Kruk, eds., 111–112.

14. Boy-Żeleński, *Pisma,* 1:232.

15. The *maxixe,* or *maxixa,* a Brazilian instrumental dance characterized by voluptuous movements. It was introduced in Paris in 1904 under the name *matchiche* (or *mattchiche*), and remained popular until about 1913. The dance's popularity in Poland at the time may be gauged by other references to it in Boy-Żeleński. Cf., for example, his Green Balloon songs "List otwarty kobiety polskiej" (Open Letter of a Polish Woman) and "Kuplet posła Battaglia" (The Couplet of Deputy Battaglia).

16. Boy-Żeleński, 228–231.

17. *Ibid.* 1:230.

18. One of the most famous works of art to be displayed in Michalik's shop was Kazimierz Sichulski's *Kabaret szalony* (The Mad Cabaret), which the artist painted on an ungrounded sheet. Its subject was a trip to the moon by members of the Balloon. When they arrive, they are greeted by Master Twardowski, a wizard-like character in Polish folklore, wearing the traditional cloak (*kontusz*) of a Polish squire and with the traditional squire's sword at his side. The painting was also the subject of a poem, "Kabaret szalony," by the popular "Young Poland" poet Edward Leszczyński (1880–1921), who was also a translator of Musset and Claudel.

19. Boy-Żeleński, 1:231.

20. For a chronicle of Boy-Żeleński's life and work, see *Pisma,* 1:9–46. This is followed (47–70) by Jan Kott's introductory article "Satyryk i pamiętnikarz Młodej Polski" (A Satirist and Chronicler of "Young Poland"). For other works on Boy-Żeleński, see: Andrzej Stawar, *Tadeusz Żeleński* (*Boy*); Andrzej Z. Makowiecki, *Tadeusz Żeleński* (*Boy*); Wojciech Natanson, *Boy-Żeleński.* There is also valuable material on Boy-Żeleński in the general books on the Green Bal-

loon previously referred to: Jan Pawel Gawlik, *Powrót do Jamy,* and Tomasz Weiss, *Legenda i Prawda Zielonego Balonika.*

21. See especially his *Znasz-li ten kraj?,* published in 1930, and the *Młoda Polska* anthology for which Boy-Żeleński wrote an illuminating introduction.

22. *Latarnik,* in Polish; one of Sienkiewicz's best stories, about an old Polish emigré, a lighthouse keeper off the coast of Panama, far from his native land, who finds some beauty in his lonely existence in a copy he manages to obtain of the greatest work of poetry in the Polish language, *Pan Tadeusz* (Master Thaddeus, 1834) by Adam Mickiewicz (1798–1855).

23. Boy-Żeleński, *Pisma,* 1:434. See also his article "Echa piosenki," *Pisma,* 2:340–345.

24. "Mes Confessions," *Pisma,* 2:504–506. Boy-Żeleński expressed very much the same sentiments in his article "Śladami piosenki, "written in 1925 and included in *Pisma* 16:82–88.

25. "Kaprys" (Caprice) *Pisma* 1:161–162 [*Les Petits Paves];* "Piosenka megalomana" (Song of a Megalomaniac), 163–164 [*Exil d'amour];* "Piosenka sentymentalna, której jednak nie trzeba brać zanadto serio" (A Sentimental Song Which Should Not, However, Be Taken Too Seriously), 259–260 (*Envoi des fleurs*); "Piosenka przekonywająca" (A Persuasive Song), 287–288 (*Petit chagrin*); "Piosenka wzruszająca" (A Moving Song), 287–288 (*Fleurs et pensées*).

26. Boy-Żeleński's irreverent treatment of Polish literary "greats" was legendary. In "List otwarty kobiety polskiej" (An Open Letter from a Polish Woman) *Pisma,* 1:134–137, Mikołaj Rej z Nagłowic, a major sixteenth-century writer and the first of importance to use the vernacular Polish language instead of Latin, is described as "the old boor from Nagłowice" (*stary gbur z Nagłowic*). In "Replika kobiety polskiej" (Rejoinder of a Polish Woman), 138–141, the reader learns that Zosia (the idealized young heroine of Adam Mickiewicz's *Pan Tadeusz*) and others like her were dreamt up by Mickiewicz over his *bigos* (a Polish national dish of stewed cabbage and meats). Many other examples of the same sort of thing can be found in Boy-Żeleński's works.

27. Rajchman was gaining a reputation at the time by his attempts to build the treasury of the Philharmonic by whatever means. It was with this goal in mind, for example, that he organized "mystic evenings"—which proved rather popular—during which, by "mood" light, musical productions, declamations, and other entertainments were offered. This is the meaning of the line "Słyną Warszawy mistyczne wieczory / I ich subtelny nastrojowy cień" (Warsaw's mystic evenings and delicate shade of mood are renowned) in Boy-Żeleński's poem "Song of Our Capitals and How Providence Endowed Them."

28. Boy-Żeleński, *Pisma,* 1:349–350.

29. Boy-Żeleński, 1:302–303. The "Raphael," obviously an imitation, was quite the cause célèbre in its time. For some contemporary discussion of the painting, see the collective article "Galerya miejska we Lwowie," *Lamus* (1908–1909), 217–229.

30. Boy-Żeleński, *Pisma,* 1:307–309 and 283–284.

31. "Zielony Balonik—Muzeum Narodowemu," *ibid.*, 278.

32. *Ibid.*, 87–91.

33. Comte Pierre Jacques Etienne Cambronne (1770–1842). A Napoleonic general who won distinction in the campaigns of 1812, 1813, and 1814, later accompanying Napoleon to Elba. He commanded the Old Guard at Waterloo in 1815 and, when invited by the British to surrender, reportedly answered with a vulgarity that has since become famous as the *mot de Cambronne.*

34. In *Also sprach Zarathustra.*

35. Boy-Żeleński, *Pisma,* 1:90.

36. The text of Boy-Żeleński's *Bodenhain* appears in *Pisma,* 1:367–379.

37. Hoesick figures in several of Boy-Żeleński's works: "Dedykacja" (Dedication), *Pisma,* 1:175–176; "Pieśń o naszych stolicach" (Song about Our Capitals), 242–244; "Dzień p. Esika w Ostendzie" (Mr. Esik's Day in Ostend), 248–253; "Rozkosze życia" (The Pleasures of Life), 261–263; "Hoesick w poezji polskiej" (Hoesick in Polish Poetry), *Pisma,* 2:405–409.

38. An interesting review of Hoesick's biography of Tarnowski by the respected literary scholar Józef Kallenbach appeared in the monthly *Biblioteka Warszawska* (1907), 1:583–593. Boy-Żeleński also took advantage of the opportunity to poke fun at the biography in the *szopka,* or puppet play, which he wrote for the Green Balloon in 1907–1908. The Biographer (Hoesick) asks Tarnowski for a photograph of him when he was two years old because he wants to write his biography. The following dialogue ensues:

TARNOWSKI: I don't intend to object,/ Although I shake from fear,/ Because I dread, quite frankly,/It all won't turn out well.
HOESICK: Don't be afraid, dear fellow,/ There is no cause to quake,/ The reader can swallow a lot/ And on occasion be fooled.
TARNOWSKI: Polish patience is well known,/But you must realize/ That, if I may be forgiven for saying so,/ you have taxed it to excess.
HOESICK: I'll describe you exactly;/ It's little work for me,/ Because I seldom ever think,/ And the better for it write.
TARNOWSKI: To think—how bad a habit,/ I have been preaching this for many years./ Our world today is stubborn/ And heeds me not, alas . . .

39. This is an obvious allusion to Hoesick's interest in the love affairs of famous personalities, particularly writers. In addition to his *Love in the Life of Zygmunt Krasiński,* he later published a book entitled *Miłość i miłostki w życiu sławnych ludzi* (Love and Love Affairs in the Lives of Famous People, 1917).

40. The title and first line of the poem are borrowed from a popular poem by the nineteenth-century Polish poet Wincenty Pol (1807–1872). Boy-Żeleński, *Pisma,* 1:130.

41. *Ibid.*, 126.

42. *Ibid.*, 130.

43. In *Wyspiański żywy* (London, 1957), there is an interesting little article entitled "Bronowice dzisiaj" (114–118), by Jadwiga Tetmajer-Naimska, in which the author traces the destinies of the prototypes of the characters in

Wyspiański's *The Wedding* and describes the way the village of Bronowice looks at the time the article was written.

44. *Lamus* (1908–1909), 493–508.

45. For Boy-Żeleński's humorous account of the courtship and wedding, see his article "Plotka o 'Weselu' Wyspiańskiego," *Pisma,* 3:129–161.

46. In his article "Na początku była chuć," *Pisma,* 2:100, Boy-Żeleński quotes a letter of "Sewer" (the popular novelist Ignacy Maciejowski, 1839–1901) to Eliza Pareńska, the wife of a well-known doctor and professor, in which Rydel's courtship is mentioned as follows: "Włodzio Tetmajer came to us here and tells amusing stories about Lucek's contest for Jaga's hand in Bronowice Małe. How Lucek flies around barefoot with his pince-nez on his nose, how he digs potatoes, binds sheaves, how he woos, how he is feeling, sentimental, etc., etc., he relates with humor, and superbly imitates Lucek, his gestures, his expressions. Nonetheless, he is very fond of Lucek and laughs when he tells me that from now on I must address correspondence to him: Rydel's brother-in-law. . ."

47. "Zatarg bohatefow 'Wesela'," *Pisma,* 3:187–188.

48. At this time Rydel's translations from Homer were considered the best since Słowacki (who had translated parts of Songs 1, 17, and 21 of the *Iliad.* See Juliusz Słowacki, *Dzieła* (Wrocław, 1949), 3:583–609.

49. In addition to books on Słowacki by Hoesick (*O Słowackim, Krasińskim i Mickiewiczu,* On Słowacki, Krasiński, and Mickiewicz, 1895; *Życie Juliusza Słowackiego na tle współczesnej epoki,* The Life of Juliusz Słowacki against the Background of His Age, 1896–1897), Tretiak (a two-volume study which appeared in 1904), and others (Pawlikowski, Kleiner), there were countless articles in such literary journals as *Sfinks, Lamus, Krytyka, Ateneum, Biblioteka Warszawska,* and *Pamiętnik Literacki.*

50. Because he was considered ludicrous, Rydel was seldom ever taken seriously and his true worth as a writer remained long unappreciated. Two articles deal with the matter: Edmund Jańkowski, "Rydel—poeta zaśmieszony," *Przegląd Humanistyczny* (Warsaw, 1959), 2:133–139, and Jan Zygmunt Jakubowski, "O Lucjanie Rydlu," *Polonistyka* (Warsaw, 1959), 3:47–49.

51. Juliusz Słowacki, *Dzieła,* 3:71.

52. Boy-Żeleński, *Pisma,* 1:142.

53. This excerpt, in translation, from "Syreny" (Sirens), one of the poems in *Mythologies,* is typical: "The sea, the green sea in measureless expanse, / And above it the moon milky (white) in the azure / Pellucidity; / One luminous stream after another / Flows from afar / White with foam, sparkling with flashes of beams."

54. Boy-Żeleński, *Pisma,* 1:143.

55. On the Cracow *szopka,* see Zygmunt Leśnodorski, *Wspomnienia i zapiski,* 45–59, and Jan Krupski, *Szopka krakowska.* Krupski's book is especially valuable because it contains complete *szopka* texts.

56. For excerpts, see: "Z niewydanej 'szopki' krakowskiej na rok 1907 i 1908," Boy-Żeleński, *Pisma,* 1:310–321.

57. For excerpts, see: "Z 'szopki krakowskiej' na rok 1911 i 1912," Boy-Żeleński, *Pisma,* 1:325–359.

58. Wilhelm Feldman, "Piosenkarz Zielonego Balonika," *Krytyka* (Warsaw, 1910), 330, 328. The complete text of the article appears on 327–334.

59. *Ibid.,* 330.

60. See his article "Z tryumfalnych dni polskiego kabaretu," *Pisma,* 1:382–392.

61. For a good monograph on Momus, see Helena Karwacka, *Warszawski Kabaret Artystyczno-Literacki Momus.* Additional material of interest, mostly in the form of excerpts from reminiscences and texts, related to Momus as well as to the Green Balloon and other Polish cabarets of the pre- and post-World War I periods, can be found in Kazimierz Rudzki, ed., *Dymek z papierosa czyli wspomnienia o scenach, scenkach i nadscenkach.* On the interwar Polish cabaret in particular, see especially Ŕyszard Marek Groński, *Jak w przedwojennym kabarecie: Warszawski Kabaret 1918–1939.*

6. CABARET IN RUSSIA: MORE BATS, CROOKED MIRRORS, AND STRAY DOGS

1. Konstantin Stanislavsky, *My Life in Art,* G. Ivanov-Mumjiev, tr., 415–417. For the Russian original of the entire text, see: K. S. Stanislavsky, "Kapustniki i 'Letuchaya Mysh,' " *Moya zhizn v teatre,* 432–444.

2. N. E. Efros, *Teatr "Letuchaya Mysh" N. F. Balieva,* 24.

3. L. Tikhvinskaya, "Letuchaya mysh," *Teatr,* 3:107.

4. *Ibid.*

5. The text of one of Yuzhny's best Odessa stories, "Kefal" (Grey Mullet), about the love of Odessa Greeks for the fish of the title, appears in *Sini Zhurnal* (St. Petersburg, April 30, 1914), 17:10. The story is part of an article on Bat performers under the title "Gospoda odessity."

6. On Khenkin at the Bat, see Evgeni Kuznetsov, *Iz proshlogo russkoi estrady,* 304–305.

7. On Borisov and the Bat, see Kuznetsov, 305–308. See also Borisov's book about his own career, *Istoriya moego smekha* (Moscow; Teakinopechat, 1929).

8. N. E. Efros, 46.

9. *Balieff's Chauve-Souris of Moscow.* American Season under the Direction of F. Ray Comstock and Morris Gest. Original program. Undated (probably 1921), 8.

10. *Ibid.,* 9.

11. Thoda Cocroft, *Great Names and How They Are Made,* 223–224.

12. Alice Lewisohn Crowley, *The Neighborhood Playhouse: Leaves from a Theatre Scrapbook,* 116–117, 119. There are also some interesting remarks on the Chauve-Souris in America by Mary Cass Canfield in her book *Grotesques and Other Reflections on Art and Theatre* (New York and London: Harper, 1927).

13. E. D. Uvarov, ed., *Russkaya sovetskaya estrada 1917–1929: Ocherk istorii,* 344.

14. Konstantin Rudnitsky, *Meyerhold the Director,* 137.

15. On the failure of the Strand, see also Edward Braun, *The Theatre of Meyerhold: Revolution on the Modern Stage,* 90.

16. On Meyerhold and the House of Interludes, see Rudnitsky, *Meyerhold,* 146–147, and Braun, 90–91 and 101–102.

17. On the second, and last, production of the House of Interludes, see Braun, 105–107.

18. For a brief survey of the Crooked Miror in English, see C. Moody, "The Crooked Mirror."

19. A. R. Kugel, *Listya z dereva,* 100.

20. In the collection *Russkaya teatralnaya parodiya XIX-nachala XX veka,* M. Ya Polyakov, ed., 523–531.

21. *Russkaya teatrainaya parodiya XIX-nachala XX veka,* 569–570.

22. *Ibid.,* 555.

23. *Ibid.,* 640.

24. *Ibid.,* 613.

25. *Woe from Wit,* a masterpiece of nineteenth-century Russian satiric comedy dating from 1823 and written by Aleksandr Griboedov; *Krechinsky's Wedding,* the first play in a satirical-philosophical trilogy on the inhumanity of the imperial Russian bureaucracy and police written between 1854 and 1869 by Aleksandr Sukhovo-Kobylin; *Storm,* the major work by the greatest Russian dramatist of the second half of the nineteenth century, Aleksandr Ostrovsky.

26. Aleksei Tolstoy (1817–1875), a Russian writer best known for such costume dramas as *The Death of Ivan the Terrible* (1866), *Tsar Fyodor* (1868), and *Tsar Boris* (1870).

27. *Russkaya teatralnaya parodiya XIX-nachala XX veka,* 613–614. Page references hereafter given parenthetically in text.

28. A popular satirical journal of the time.

29. For a good translation of *The Fourth Wall,* see Laurence Senelick, ed. and tr., *Russian Satiric Comedy,* 75–99.

30. The best source of information on the Stray Dog is the richly annotated collection of programs published by A. E. Parnis and R. D. Timenchik under the title "Programmy 'Brodyachei sobaki' " in *Pamyatniki kultury: Novye Otkrytiya,* 160–257. Unfortunately, this volume reached me too late to be of maximum use. There is also good material on the Stray Dog in A. A. Mgebrov, *Zhizn v teatre 11,* 157–173.

31. *Ibid.,* 158.

32. *Ibid.,* 159.

33. There are some interesting remarks on *The Choice of a Bride* and on Kuzmin at the Stray Dog in general in Anatoli Snaikevich's "Peterburgskaya Bogema (M. A. Kuzmin)"—an excerpt from his book *Most vzdokhov cherez Nevu* (The Bridge of Sighs across the Neva)—published in the literary almanac *Orion* (Paris, 1947), 136–143. For an enthusiastic description of the perfor-

mance of Kuzmin's Nativity play (*Vertep kukolny,* in Russian), see Sergei Auslender's review in *Apollon* (February 1913), No. 2, 66–67.

34. *Apollon,* No. 2, 67.

35. These included works by Cervantes, Strindberg, and Solovyov himself who was the author of a popular one-act harlequinade called *Harlequin, the Marriage Broker,* which was first performed in Petersburg on November 8, 1911.

36. A. A. Mgebrov, 160.

37. Benedikt Livshits, *Polutoraglazy strelets,* 177–178 [translation my own—HBS]. For a complete translation of the work into English, see Benedikt Livshits, *The One and a Half-Eyed Archer,* John E. Bowlt, tr. (Newtonville, Mass. Oriental Research Partners, 1977).

38. M. A. Kuzmin, *Sobranie stikhov,* 3:455. The complete poem appears on 455–456. Besides this poem, Kuzmin was also the author of a novel set in and about the Stray Dog—*Plavayushchie puteshesvuyushchie* (Travelers by Sea and by Land); the Stray Dog appears under the thinly disguised name of Sova (The Owl).

39. Kuzmin means either Nikolai Kruglikov (1861–1920), an engineer and state dignitary, or his sister, the artist Elizaveta Kruglikova (1865–1941), who spent much time at the Stray Dog where she drew silhouettes of some of the regulars there, including Kuzmin, Gumilyov, and Sudeikin.

40. The reference is to Gumilyov's Guild of Poets and the Acmeists, who were also called Adamists.

41. Venyamin Belkin (1884–1951), a painter; Nikolai Meshchersky (d. 1914), an amateur painter; Nikolai Kulbin (1866–1917), an army doctor, artist, and patron of the avant-garde.

42. Vladimir Podgorny (1887–1944), an actor with close ties to Evreinov and Meyerhold; Kolya Peter (Nikolai Petrov, 1890–1964), a producer and conductor; Konstantin Gibshman (b. 1884), an actor who also appeared frequently in the cabaret as a storyteller and *conférencier.*

43. The reference is to the dancer Boris Romanov (1891–1957). As an émigré, he was very active as a dancer and choreographer in New York.

44. Kuzmin is referring to the poet and Petersburg society lady Pallada Gross (d. 1964), who was a Stray Dog habitué. As an author, she is remembered most for her collection of poems published in Petrograd in 1914 under the title *Amulety* (Amulets).

45. Russian original in Anna Akhmatova, *Stikhotvoreniya i poemy,* 57. The poem is dated January 1, 1913.

46. Viktor Shklovsky, *Zhili-byli. Vospominaniya. Memuarnye zapisi: Povesti o vremeni: so kontsa XIX v. po 1962,* 259.

47. I am quoting from Shklovsky's own account of the lecture in *Zhili-byli,* 259.

48. *Ibid.,* 258.

49. Aleksandr Veselovsky (1838–1906), a professor at the St. Petersburg University and an outstanding pioneer in the field of comparative folkloristics. He

also wrote extensively on poetics and aesthetics. Aleksandr Poetbnya (1835–1891), a professor at Kharkov University and a distinguished linguist and philologist.

50. Shklovsky himself later recalled only a small crowd.

51. Vladimir Pyast, *Vstrechi,* 250.

52. Yuri Yurkun (1895–1938), a writer and habitué of the Stray Dog.

53. Elena Guro (1877–1913), a well-known poet and painter of the period with close ties to the Futurists.

54. M. Kuzmin, "Kak ya chital doklad v 'Brodyachei sobake.' "

55. Vl. Pyast, 266.

56. Tamara Karsavina, *Theatre Street,* 312–314.

57. R. W. Flint, ed., R. W. Flint and Arthur A. Coppotelli, trs., *Marinetti: Selected Writings,* 346.

58. The painter Mikhail Larionov (1881–1964).

59. Natalya Goncharova (1883–1962), a painter and member of the Donkey's Tail group.

60. There are other interesting remarks about Marinetti's visit to St. Petersburg and the Stray Dog in an article in the Trieste paper *Piccolo* which Marinetti quotes in his own piece, "Il Futurismo in Spagna, a Londra, Parigi, Berlino, Mosca." See F. T. Marinetti, *Teoria e invenzione futurista: Manuscritti Scritti politici Romanzi Parole in libertà,* 515.

61. Vl. Pyast, *Vstrechi,* 268.

62. Benedikt Livshits, *Polutoraglazy strelets,* 156.

63. Vl. Pyast, *Vstrechi,* 268–269.

64. *Ibid.,* 267.

65. An announcement in the newspaper *Rech* for Wednesday, April 20, 1916, Nr. 107, 5, gives April 18 as the date of the official opening of the Comics' Halt.

66. There are several illustrations of Sudeikin's commedia dell'arte-inspired decorations for the Comics' Halt accompanying V. N. Solovyov's article on Sudeikin in the journal *Apollon* (October–December 1917), Nr. 8–10, 15–29.

67. A. A. Mgebrov, *Zhizn v teatre 11,* 198–199.

7. ZURICH: DADA VOLTAIRE

1. Tom Stoppard, *Travesties,* 24–25.

2. Hugo Ball, *Flight Out of Time: A Dada Diary,* 5.

3. *Tenderenda der Phantast* (Tenderenda the Fantasist), written between 1914 and 1920 but published for the first time only in 1967.

4. Richard Huelsenbeck, *Memoirs of a Dada Drummer,* 4.

5. Hugo Ball, *Flight Out of Time,* 50. Hereafter page references will be given parenthetically in the text.

6. *Ibid.*

7. Richard Huelsenbeck, *Memoirs,* 9–10.

8. R. W. Last, *Hans Arp: The Poet of Dadaism,* 77–78.

9. Huelsenbeck may or may not have been aware of it, but *umba* is the Swahili verb meaning to create and is commonly used when speaking of divine creation.

10. Richard Huelsenbeck, *Memoirs,* 9.

11. *Ibid.*

12. Richard Huelsenbeck, *Dada: Eine literarische Dokumentation,* 201–202.

13. Richard Huelsenbeck, *Memoirs of a Dada Drummer,* xxiii.

14. Richard Huelsenbeck, "En Avant Dada," in Robert Motherwell, ed., *The Dada Painters and Poets: An Anthology,* 35–36. *En Avant Dada: Eine Geschichte des Dadaismus* was originally published by Paul Steegman Verlag, Hannover, Leipzig, Vienna, Zurich, in 1920.

15. This poem, together with other simultaneous poems by Arp, Serner, Tzara, and Huelsenbeck are included in the collection *Dada Gedichte: Dichtungen der Gründer* (Dada Poetry: Poems of the Founders), a separate publication of the poetry chapter in the volume *Die Geburt des Dada: Dichtung und Chronik der Gründer* (The Birth of Dada: The Poetry and a Chronicle of the Founders), which was assembled by Peter Schifferli together with Arp, Huelsenbeck, and Tzara and published by "Die Arche" in Zurich in 1957. See 69–79. The collection also contains (70–71) Arp's preface to the simultaneous poems, which sheds still further light on the Dadaists' attitude toward simultaneous poetry and which I quote in translation:

> In the Café de la Terrasse, Tzara, Serner and I wrote a cycle of poems entitled *Die Hyperbel* . . . The Surrealists later christened this kind of poetry "Automatic Poetry." Automatic poetry springs directly from the poet's bowels or other organs, which have stored up reserves of usable material. Neither the Postillion of Longjumeaun or the hexameter, neither grammar nor aesthetics, neither Buddha nor the Sixth Commandment, should hold him back. The poet crows, curses, sighs, stutters, yodels, as he pleases. His poems are like Nature. Unregarded trifles, or what men call trifles, are as precious to him as the sublimest rhetoric; for, in Nature, a tiny particle is as beautiful and important as a star. Man was the first who presumed to judge what was beautiful and what was ugly.

16. Mancinelli, *Il messagio razionale,* 34–49.

17. The texts have been taken from *Dada Gedichte: Dichtungen der Gründer,* Hans Arp, et al., 28–34.

18. Fritz Brupbacher (1874–1945), Swiss political theorist, author of a book on Marx and Bakunin, who advised Ball during his own work on Bakunin; Franz Anton Jelmoli (1851–1928), prominent Zurich department store owner. Rudolf von Laban and Mary Wigman are discussed later in this chapter.

19. Hugo Ball and Emmy Hennings, *Damals in Zürich: Briefe aus den Jahren 1915–1917,* 98, and 112.

20. John Elderfield has some interesting remarks about Kandinsky's influence on Ball in his introduction to the English translation of *Flight Out of Time,* xxvi–xxvii.

21. An English translation of the complete lecture appears in *Flight Out of Time,* 222–234.

22. Victor Terras, ed., *Handbook of Russian Literature* (New Haven and London: Yale University Press, 1985), 223.

23. A. Kruchonykh and V. Khlebnikov, *Slovo kak takovoe,* 9.

24. Janco's masks, which were eventually used to adorn the walls of the Cabaret Voltaire, are described by Richard Huelsenbeck as blood-red in color and "extremely beautiful." See Richard Huelsenbeck, *Memoirs of a Dada Drummer,* 22.

25. Excerpts of the essay in English appear in Roger Copeland and Marshall Cohen, eds., *What is Dance? Readings in Theory and Criticism.* See especially 305–307.

26. An illustration of the program for the Second (*Sturm*) Soirée appears on p. 107 of the English edition of Ball's *Flight Out of Time.*

27. In a letter to his old friend August Hofmann, dated June 26, 1917, Ball mentions that he was the "Director" of a Galerie Dada from March 17 to May 27. See Hugo Ball and Emmy Hennings, *Damals in Zürich,* 150.

28. Hugo Ball and Emmy Hennings, 143.

29. Hans Richter, *Dada: Art and Anti-Art,* 77–80.

30. Willy Verkauf, *Dada: Monograph of a Movement,* 30.

BIBLIOGRAPHY

Late nineteenth- and early twentieth-century newspapers, journals, and cabaret publications used in preparation of this book, and in many instances unavailable in this country, are cited in notes and are not included in the bibliography.

Adler, Gusti. *Max Reinhardt.* Salzburg: Festungsverlag, 1964.

Ainaud de Lasarte, J. M. and Enric Jardí. *Prat de la Riba: Home de Govern.* Barcelona: Editorial Ariel, 1973.

Akhmatova, Anna. *A Poem Without a Hero.* Carl Proffer with Assya Humesky, trs. Ann Arbor, Mich.: Ardis, 1973.

——*Requiem and Poem Without a Hero.* D. M. Thomas, tr. Athens: Ohio University Press, 1976.

——*Stikhotvoreniya i poemy.* Leningrad: Izdatelstvo "Sovetsky Pisatel," 1976.

Alba, Victor. *Catalonia: A Profile.* New York: Praeger, 1975.

Allais, Alphonse. *Oeuvres posthumes.* Vols. 1 and 2. François Caradec and Pascal Pia, eds. Paris: La Table Ronde, 1966.

Allen, Ann Taylor. *Satire and Society in Wilhelmine Germany: Kladderadatsch & Simplicissimus 1890–1914.* Lexington, Kentucky: The University Press of Kentucky, 1984.

Alpár, Ágnes. *A fövárosi kabarék Müsora 1901–1944.* Budapest: Magyar Színházi, 1978.

Altenberg, Peter. *Ausgewählte Werke in zwei Bānden.* Vol. 1. Munich: Carl Hanser Verlag, 1979.

Appignanesi, Lisa. *The Cabaret.* New York: Universe Books, 1976.

Arens, Hanns. *Unsterbliches München: Streifzüge durch 200 Jahre literarischen Lebens der Stadt.* Munich and Esslingen: Bechtle Verlag, 1968.

Argo, A. *Svoimi glazami.* Moscow: Sovetsky Pisatel, 1965.

Arnim, L. Achim von and Clemens Brentano. *Des Knaben Wunderhorn: Alte deutsche Lieder.* 3 vols. Leipzig: Insel-verlag, 1910. [A reproduction of the original edition of 1806–08].

Arp, Hans et al. *Dada Gedichte: Dichtungen der Gründer.* Zurich: Verlag die Arche, 1957.

Bab, Julius. *Das Theater der Gegenwart*. Leipzig: Verlagsbuchhandlung von I. J. Weber, 1928.

Ball, Hugo. *Flight Out of Time: A Dada Diary*. John Elderfield, ed.; Ann Raimes, tr. New York: Viking, 1974.

Ball, Hugo and Emmy Hennings. *Damals in Zürich: Briefe aus den Jahren 1915–1917*. Zurich: Im Verlag der Arche, 1978.

Bang-Hensen, Odd. *Chat Noir og Norsk revy*. Oslo: Cappelen, 1961.

Bass, Eduard. *Letáky-Satiry, verše, písničky*. Prague: Československý spisovatel, 1955.

Bathille, Pierre. *Maurice Donnay: Son Oeuvre*. Paris: Éditions de La Nouvelle Revue Critique, 1932.

Bayerdörfer, Hans-Peter. "Überbrettl und Überdrama. Zum Verhältnis von literarischem Kabarett und Experimentierbühne," *Literatur und Theater im Wilhelminischen Zeitalter*. Hans-Peter Bayerdörfer, Karl Otto Conrady, and Helmut Schanze, eds. Tübingen: Max Niemeyer Verlag, 1978.

Bemmann, Helga, ed. *Immer um die Litfasssaüle rum: Gedichte aus sechs Jahrzehnten Kabarett*. Berlin: Henschelverlag, 1965.

——*Leute, höret die Geschichte: Bänkeldichtung aus zwei Jahrhunderten*. Berlin: Verlag der Nation, 1976.

——*Mitgelacht—dabeigewesen: Erinnerungen aus sechs Jahrzehnten Kabarett*. Berlin: Henschelverlag, 1967.

Bercy, Anne de and Armand Ziwès. *A Montmartre . . . le soir*. Paris: Bernard Grasset, 1951.

Bierbaum, Otto Julius. *Deutsche Chansons* (*Brettl-Lieder*). Berlin and Leipzig: Schuster & Loeffler, 1900.

——*Irrgarten der Liebe*. Leipzig: Insel-Verlag, 1906.

——*Stilpe. Ein Roman aus der Froschperspektive*. Munich/Zurich: Droemersche Verlaganstalt Th. Knaur Nachf., 1982.

Bigsby, C. W. E. *Dada and Surrealism*. London: Methuen, 1972.

Blei, Franz. *Erzählung eines Leben*. Leipzig: Paul List Verlag, 1930.

Bordat, Denis and Francis Boucrot. *Les Théatres d'ombres: Histoire et techniques*. Paris: L'Arche, 1956.

Boukay, Maurice. *Chansons rouges*. Paris: Ernest Flammarion, Éditeur, 1896.

Boy-Żeleński, Tadeusz, ed. *Młoda Polska: Wybór poezyj*. 2d ed. Wrocław: Zakład Narodowy im. Ossolińskich, 1947.

Brandenburg, Hans. *München leuchtete: Jugenderinnerungen*. Munich: Verlag Herbert Neuner, 1953.

Braun, Edward. *The Theatre of Meyerhold: Revolution in the Modern Stage*. New York: Drama Book Specialists, 1979.

Brod, Max, ed. *The Diaries of Franz Kafka, 1910–1913*. New York: Schocken, 1949.

Bruant, Aristide. *Chansons et monologues*. 3 vols. Paris: E. Geffroy, 1896–1897.

——*Dans la Rue: Chansons & Monologues*. Paris: Aristide Bruant Auteur Editeur, 1889.

——*Dans la Rue.* 2d ed. 2 vols. Paris: Au Mirliton, 1895.

——*Dans la Rue.* Nouvelle Édition. Paris: Eugène Rey, Libraire-Éditeur, 1924.

Budzinski, Klaus. *Die Muse mit der scharfen Zunge: Vom Cabaret zum Kabarett.* Munich: Paul List Verlag, 1961.

——*Pfeffer ins Getriebe: Ein Streifzug durch 100 Jahre Kabarett.* Munich: Wilhelm Heyne Verlag, 1984.

Budzinski, Klaus, ed. *So weit die scharfe Zunge reicht: Die Anthologie des deutschsprachigen Cabarets.* Munich, Bern, Vienna: Scherz Verlag, 1964.

Caradec, François. *Frègoli (1867–1936): Sa Vie et ses secrets.* Paris: La Jeune Parque, 1968.

Carco, Francis. *La Belle Époque au temps du Bruant.* Paris: Gallimard, 1954.

Carossa, Hans. *Der Tag des jungen Arztes.* Wiesbaden: Insel-Verlag, 1955.

Casteras, Raymond de. *Avant le Chat Noir: Les Hydropathes 1878–1880.* Paris: Éditions Albert Messein, 1945.

Casteret, Norbert. *Une Vie de Chauve-Souris.* Paris: Didier, 1945.

Centenaire du Cabaret du Chat Noir. Paris: Musée de Montmartre, 1981.

Červený, Jiří. *Červená sedma.* Prague: Orbis, 1959.

Cervera, Joseph Phillip. *Modernismo: The Catalan Renaissance of the Arts.* New York and London: Garland Publishing, Inc., 1976.

Chapple, Gerald and Hans H. Schulte. *The Turn of the Century: German Literature and Art, 1890–1915.* Bonn: Bouvier Verlag Herbert Grundmann, 1981.

Cirici Pellicer, A. *El Arte modernista catalán.* Barcelona: Aymá, Editor, 1951.

——*1900 en Barcelona.* Barcelona: Ediciones Polígrafa, S. A., 1967.

Cocroft, Thoda. *Great Names and How They Are Made.* Chicago, New York, London: Dartnell Press, 1941.

Copeland, Roger and Marshall Cohen, eds. *What Is Dance? Readings in Theory and Criticism.* New York: Oxford University Press, 1983.

Coquelin ainé and Coquelin cadet. *L'Art de dire le monologue.* Paris: Paul Ollendorff, Éditeur, 1884.

Crauzat, E. de. *L'Oeuvre Gravé et Lithographié de Steinlen.* Paris: Société de Propagation des Livres d'Art, 1913.

Cros, Charles. *Le Coffret de santal.* Paris: Gallimard, 1972.

——*Oeuvres complètes.* Louis Forestier and Pascal Pía, eds. Paris: Pauvert, 1964

Crowley, Alice Lewisohn. *The Neighborhood Playhouse: Leaves from a Theatre Scrapbook.* New York: Theatre Arts Book, 1959.

Dario, Rubén. *España contemporanea.* Madrid: Afrodisio Aguado, S. A., 1950.

Donnay, Maurice. *Autour du Chat Noir.* Paris: Bernard Grasset, 1926.

——*Mes Débuts à Paris.* Paris: Libraire Arthème Fayard, 1937.

Driver, Sam N. *Anna Akhmatova.* New York: Twayne, 1972.

Efros, N. E. *Teatr "Letuchaya Mysh" N. F. Balieva.* Petrograd: "Solntse Rossii," 1918.

Ericson, John D. *Dada: Performance, Poetry, and Art.* Boston: Twayne (G. K. Hall), 1984.

Ewers, Hanns Heinz. *Das Cabaret.* Berlin and Leipzig: Schuster & Loeffler, 1904.

Fàbregas, Xavier. *Història del teatre català.* Barcelona: Editorial Millà, 1978.
Falckenberg, Otto. *Mein Leben—Mein Theater.* Wolfgang Petzet, ed. Munich, Vienna, Leipzig: Zinnen-Verlag, 1944.
Fiedler, Leonhard M. *Max Reinhardt in Selbstzeugnissen und Bilddokumenten.* Hamburg: Rowohlt, 1975.
Fink, Werner. *Witz als Schicksal, Schicksal als Witz.* Hamburg: Schröder, 1966.
Flint, R. W., ed. *Marinetti: Selected Writings.* R. W. Flint and Arthur A. Coppotelli, trs. New York: Farrar, Strauss and Giroux, 1972.
Fontbona, Francesc. *La crisi del modernisme artístic.* Barcelona: Curial, 1975.
Forestier, Louis. *Charles Cros l'homme et l'oeuvre.* Paris: Minard, 1969.
Friedell, Egon, ed. *Das Altenberg-Buch.* Leipzig and Vienna: Verlag der Wiener Graphischen Werkstätte, 1922.
Friedell, Egon and Alfred Polgar. *Goethe: Eine Szene.* Vienna: Carl Wilhelm Stern, 1908.
Garrut, José María. *Dos siglos de pintura catalana (XIX–XX).* Madrid: Iberico Europea de Ediciones, S. A., 1974.
Gasser, Manuel, *München um 1900.* Munich: Wilhelm Heyne Verlag, 1981.
Gawlik, Jan Paweł. *Powrót do Jamy.* Cracow: Wydawnictwo Artystyczno-Graficzne, 1961.
Geiger, Hannsludwig. *Es war um die Jahrhundertwende.* Munich: Albert Langen-Georg Miller, 1953.
Geimer-Stangier, Mia and Karl Riha, eds. *Das Moritatenbuch.* Frankfurt am Main: Insel Verlag, 1981.
Gelsi, Mara. *Peter Altenberg: La Strategia della rinuncia.* Rome: Edizioni Dell'Ateneo, 1982.
Gittelman, Sol. *Frank Wedekind.* New York: Twayne, 1969.
Goudeau, Émile. *Dix Ans de Bohème.* Paris: A La Libraire Illustrée, n.d.
——*Paris qui consomme.* Paris: Imprimé pour Henri Beraldi, 1893.
——*Poèmes ironiques.* Paris: Paul Ollendorff, Éditeur, 1884.
Groński, Ryszard Marek. *Jak w przedwojennym kabarecie: Kabaret warszawski 1918–1939.* Warsaw: Wydawnictwo Artystyczne i Filmowe, 1978.
Gruel, Heinz. *Elf Scharfrichter.* Zurich: Sanssouci Verlag, 1962.
——*Bretter, die die Zeit bedeuten: Die Kulturgeschichte des Kabaretts.* 2 vols. Munich: Deutsche Taschenbuch Verlag, 1971.
Gumppenberg, Hanns von. *Lebenserinnerungen: Aus dem Nachlass des Dichters.* Berlin and Zurich: Eigenbrödler-Verlag, 1929.
——*Überdramen.* 3 vols. Berlin: Verlag von Th. Mayhofer Nachf., 1902.
Günther, Herbert. "Carl Georg von Maassen." *Die Literatur. Monatschrift für Literaturfreunde* (Stuttgart: June 1931), 9:495–498.
——*Drehbühne der Zeit: Freundschaften. Begegnungen. Schicksale.* Hamburg: Christian Wegner Verlag, 1957.
Haage, Peter. *Der Partylöwe, der nur Bücher frass: Egon Friedell und sein Kreis.* Hamburg and Düsseldorf: Claassen Verlag, 1971.
——*Ludwig Thoma: Eine Biographie.* Munich: C. Bertelsmann Verlag; Vienna: Gütersloh, 1975.

Haage, Peter, ed. *Egon Friedell: Wozu das Theater? Essays, Satiren, Humoresken.* Munich: Deutscher Taschenbuch Verlag, 1969.

Hadamowsky, Franz. *Richard Teschner und sein Figurenspiegel: Die Geschichte eines Puppentheaters.* Vienna and Stuttgart: Wancura, 1956.

Haight, Amanda. *Anna Akhmatova: A Poetic Pilgrimage.* New York and London: Oxford University Press, 1976.

Hakel, Hermann. *Mein Kollege der Affe: Ein Kabarett mit Fritz Grünbaum, Peter Hammerschlag, Eric Mühsam, Fritz Kalmar, Anton Kuh, Mynona.* Vienna: Sefer-Verlag, 1959.

——*Wigl Wogl: Kabarett und Variété in Wien.* Vienna, Hannover, Bern: Forum, 1962.

Halbe, Max. *Jahrhundertwende: Erinnerungen an eine Epoche.* Munich and Vienna: Langen Müller, 1976.

Hayböck, Eva Maria. "Der Wiener Simplicissimus 1912–1974: Versuch einer Analyse des Kabaretts mit längster Bestandzeit in deutschen Sprachraum." Typescript. Vienna, 1976.

Henderson, John A. *The First Avant-Garde 1887–1894: Sources of the Modern French Theatre.* London: George G. Harrap, 1971.

Henningsen, Jürgen. *Theorie des Kabaretts: Abriss des deutschsprachigen Kabaretts.* Ratingen: Henn, 1977.

Henry, Marc (Achille Georges d'Ailly-Vaucheret). *Au Pays des Maîtres-Chanteurs.* Paris: Payot, 1916.

——*Trois Villes: Vienne-Munich-Berlin.* Paris: Payot, 1917.

——*Villes et paysages d'Outre-Rhin.* Paris: Payot, 1919.

Herbert, Michel. *La Chanson à Montmartre.* Paris: La Table Ronde, 1967.

Heuschele, Otto, ed. *In Memoriam Alexander von Bernus: Ausgewählte Prosa aus seinem Werk.* Heidelberg: Verlag Lambert Schneider, 1966.

Hevesi, Ludwig. *Altkunst-Neukunst Wien 1894–1908.* Vienna: Verlagsbuchhandlung Carl Konegen, 1909.

Hinck, Walter, ed. *Handbuch des deutschen Dramas.* Düsseldorf: Bagel Verlag, 1980.

Hippen, Reinhard and Ursula Lücking, eds. "*Sich fügen—heisst lügen:*" *80 Jahre deustches Kabarett.* Mainz: Deutsches Kabarett Archiv, 1981.

Hoerschelmann, Rolf von. *Leben ohne Alltag.* Berlin: Wedding-Verlag, 1947.

Hofacker, Erich P. *Christian Morgenstern.* Boston: Twayne (G. K. Hall), 1978.

Hösch, Rudolf. *Kabarett von gestern: Nach zeitgenössischen Berichten, Kritiken und Errinnerungen.* Vol. 1. 1900–1933. Berlin: Henschelverlag, 1967.

Huelsenbeck, Richard. *Dada: Eine literarisache Dokumentation.* Hamburg: Rowohlt, 1964.

——*Memoirs of a Dada Drummer.* Hans J. Kleinschmidt, ed., with introduction, notes and bibliography; Joachim Neugroschel, tr. New York: Viking, 1969.

Hunt, Violet, *I Have This To Say: The Story of My Flurried Years.* New York: Boni and Liveright, 1926.

Infiesta, J. M., ed. *Modernisme a Catalunya.* Vol. 1. Barcelona: Edicions de Nou Art Thor, 1981. Castilian edition, 1976.

Ivanov, Georgi. *Peterburgskie zimy*. New York: Chekhov Publishing House, 1952.

Jakovsky, Anatole. *Alphonse Allais "Le Tueur à gags."* Aubin Ligugé (Vienne): Les Quatre Jeudis, 1955.

Jardí Casany, Enric. *Història de Els Quatre Gats*. Barcelona: Editorial Aedos, 1972.

Jardí, Enric. *Història del Cercle Artístic de Sant Lluc*. Barcelona: Edicions Destino, 1976.

Jelavich, Peter. *Munich and Theatrical Modernism: Politics, Playwrighting, and Performance 1890–1914*. Cambridge, Mass. and London, England: Harvard University Press, 1985.

John, Augustus. *Chiaroscuro: Fragments of an Autobiography*. New York: Pellegrini & Cudahy, 1952.

Jourdain, Francis. *Un grand imagier: Alexandre Steinlen*. Paris: Éditions Cercle d'Art, 1954.

Jouy, Jules. *Les Chansons de l'Année*. Paris: En Vente Chez Bourbier et Lamoureux, 1888.

Just, Vladimír. *Proměny malých scén*. Prague: Mladá fronta, 1984.

Kamp, J. E. van de. *Mens, durf te leven! Grote Figuren uit het cabaret in en om Amsterdam tot 1940*. Amsterdam: Stadsdrukkerij, 1978.

Kandinsky, Wassily. *Sounds*. Elizabeth R. Napier, tr. New Haven and London: Yale University Press; 1981.

Karwacka, Helena. *Warszawski Kabaret Artystyczno-Literacki Momus*. Warsaw: Państwowe Wydawnictwo Naukowe, 1982.

Karsavina, Tamara. *Theatre Street*. London: William Heinemann, 1931.

Keiser, César. *Herrliche Zeiten 1916–1976: 60 Jahre Cabaret in der Schweiz*. Bern: Benteli Verlag, 1976.

Kerr, Alfred. *Sätze meines Lebens: Über Reisen, Kunst und Politik*. Berlin: Buchverlag Der Morgen, 1978.

Kieniewicz, Stefan. *Galicja we dobie autonomicznej (1850–1914)*. Wrocław: Zakład Narodowy im. Ossolińskich, 1952.

Kisielewski, Jan August. *Dramaty*. Roman Taborski, ed. Wrocław, Warsaw, Cracow: Zakład Narodowy im. Ossolińskich, 1969.

——*Panmusaion*. Lwów: Nakładem Towarzystwa Wydawniczego; Warsaw: E. Wende, 1906.

——*Życie dramatu*. Lwów: Nakładem Towarzystwa Wydawniczego, 1907.

Knapp, Bettina and Myra Chipman. *That was Yvette: the Biography of Yvette Guilbert, The Great Diseuse*. New York, Chicago, San Francisco: Holt, Rinehart and Winston, 1964.

Kokoschka, Oskar. "Sphinx und Strohmann. Komödie für Automaten." *Wort in der Zeit. Österreichische Literaturzeitschrift* (March 1956), 2: 145–148.

Kosler, Hans Christian, ed. *Peter Altenberg: Leben und Werk in Texten und Bildern*. Munich: Matthes & Seitz Verlag, 1981.

Kraków w XIX w. 2 vols. Cracow: W. L. Anczyc, 1932.

Kristl, Wilhelm Lukas. *Und morgen steigt ein Licht herab: Vom Leben und Dichten des Heinrich Lautensack.* Munich: Der Tukankreis, 1962.

Kruchonykh, A. and V. Khlebnikov. *Slovo kak takovoe.* Moscow: privately printed, 1913.

Krupski, Jan. *Szopka Krakowska.* Cracow: Nakładem Tow. miłośników historyi i zabytków Krakowa, 1904.

Kugel, A. R. *Listya z dereva.* Leningrad: 1926.

Kutscher, Arthur. *Wedekind: Leben und Werk.* Karl Ude, ed. Munich: Paul List Verlag, 1964.

Kuzmin, M. A. "Kak ya chital doklad v 'Brodyachey Sobake.' " *Sini Zhurnal* (1914), 18:6.

——*Plavayushchie puteshestvuyushchie.* Petrograd: M. Semyonov, 1915.

——*Sobranie stikhov.* Vol. 3. John Malmstad and Vladimir Markov, eds. Munich: Fink Verlag, 1977.

Kuznetsov, Evgeni. *Iz proshlogo russkoi estrady.* Moscow: Gosudarstvennoe izdatelstvo "Iskusstvo," 1958.

Lacroix, Catherine Banlin. "Miquel Ultrillo i Morlius." Jean Fabris, *Utrillo: Sa Vie, son oeuvre.* Paris: Editions Frédéric Birr, 1982.

Last, Rex W. *Hans Arp: The Poet of Dadaism.* Chester Springs, Pa.: Dufour Editions, 1969.

——*German Dadaist Literature: Kurt Schwitters, Hugo Ball, Hans Arp.* New York: Twayne, 1975.

Lautensack, Heinrich. *Das verstörte Fest: Gesammelte Werke.* Wilhelm Lukas Kristl, ed. Munich: Carl Hanser Verlag, 1966.

Lemaître, Jules. *Impressions de théatre.* Deuxième Série. Paris: Libraire H. Lecène et H. Oudin, 1888.

Leśnodorski, Zygmunt. *Wspomnienia i zapiski.* Cracow: Wydawnictwo Literackie, 1959.

Lévy, Jules. *Les Hydropathes. Prose et Vers.* Paris: André Delpeuch, Éditeur, 1928.

Lewis, Wyndham. *Rude Assignment: A Narrative of My Career Up-To-Date.* London: Hutchinson, 1950.

Lindsay, Kenneth C. and Peter Vergo, eds. *Kandinsky: Complete Writings on Art.* Vol. 1. London: Faber and Faber, 1982

Lischka, Gerhard Johann. *Oskar Kokoschka: Maler und Dichter.* Bern: Herbert Lang; Frankfurt / M.: Peter Lang, 1972.

Livshits, Benedikt. *Polutoraglazy strelets.* New York: Chekhov Publishing House, 1978.

Makowiecki, Andrzej Z. *Tadeusz Żeleński (Boy).* Warsaw: Wiedza Powszechna, 1974.

Mancinelli, Laura. *Il messaggio razionale dell'avanguardia.* Turin: Giulio Einaudi Editore, 1978.

Mann, Heinrich. *Essays*. Hamburg: Claassen Verlag, 1960.

Maragall, Joan. *Obres Completes: Obra catalana*. Barcelona: Editorial Selecta, 1960.

Marinetti, F. T. *Teoria e invenzione futurista: Manuscritti Scritti politici Romanzi Parole in libertà*. Luciano de Maria, ed. Verona: Arnoldo Mondadori Editore, 1968.

Markov, Vladimir. *Russian Futurism: A History*. Berkeley and Los Angeles: University of California Press, 1968.

McCully, Marilyn. *Els Quatre Gats: Art in Barcelona around 1900*. Princeton, N. J.: Princeton University Press, 1978.

McCully, Marilyn, ed. *A Picasso Anthology: Documents, Criticism, Reminiscences*. London: The Arts Council of Great Britain, in association with Thames and Hudson, 1981.

Mell, Max. *Gesammelte Werke*. Vol. 4. Vienna: Amandus-Verlag, 1962.

Mgebrov, A. A. *Zhizn v teatre*. Vol. 2. Moscow and Leningrad: Academia, 1932.

Michel, Walter. *Wyndham Lewis*. Paintings and Drawings, with an introductory essay by Hugh Kenner. Berkeley and Los Angeles: University of California Press, 1971.

Moody, C. "The Crooked Mirror." *Melbourne Slavic Studies* (1972), 7:25–37.

Moore, George. *Memoirs of My Dead Life*. London: William Heinemann, 1906.

Morgenstern, Christian. *Die Schallmühle: Grotesken und Parodien*. Basel: Zbinden Verlag, 1976.

Morgenstern, Margareta, ed. *Christian Morgenstern: Ein Leben in Briefen*. Wiesbaden: Insel-Verlag, 1952.

Motherwell, Robert, ed. *The Dada Painters and Poets: An Anthology*. New York: Wittenborn, Schultz, 1951.

Mouloudji. *Aristide Bruant*. Paris: Éditions Pierre Seghers, 1972.

Mühsam, Erich. *Publizistik: Unpolitische Erinnerungen*. Ausgewählte Werke. Vol. 2. Berlin: Verlag Volk und Welt, 1978.

Natanson, Wojciech. *Boy-Żeleński: Opowieść biograficzna*. Warsaw: Ludowa Spółdzielnia Wydawnicza, 1977.

Neatrour, Elizabeth Baylor. "Miniatures of Russian Life at Home and in Emigration: The Life and Works of N. A. Teffi." Ph.D. dissertation, Indiana University, 1972.

Pablé, Elisabeth, ed. *Rote Laterne / Schwarzer Humor*. Salzburg: Residenz Verlag, 1964.

Palau i Fabre, Josep. *Picasso en Cataluña*. Barcelona: Editorial Aedos, 1961.

——*Picasso i els seus amics catalans*. Barcelona: Editorial Aedos, 1971.

——*Picasso per Picasso*. Barcelona: Editorial Aedos, 1970.

Panizza, Oskar. "Der Klassizismus und das Eindringen des Variété. Eine Studie über zeitgenössischen Geschmack." *Die Gesellschaft. Monatschrift für Litteratur, Kunst u. Sozialpolitik* (Leipzig, 1896), 12:1252–1274.

——*Das Liebeskonzil und andere Schriften*. Neuwied am Rhein and Berlin-West: Luchterhand, 1964.

Parnis, A. E. and R. D. Timenchik, "Programmy 'Brodyachei sobaki,' " *Pamyatniki Kultury. Novye otkrytiya.* Ezhegodnik 1983. Leningrad: "Nauka," 1985.

Perruchot, Henri. *Toulouse-Lautrec.* Humphrey Ware, tr. New York: Collier Books, 1962.

Pianzola, Maurice. *Théophile-Alexandre Steinlen.* Zurich: Editions Rencontre Lausanne, 1971.

Pignotti, Lamberto and Stefania Stefanelli. *La scrittura verbo-visiva: Le avanguardie del novocento tra parola e immagine.* Rome: Espresso Strumenti, 1980.

Pla, Josep. *Santiago Rusiñol i el seu temps.* Barcelona: Edicions Destino, 1981.

Planes, Ramon. *LLibre de Sitges.* Barcelona: Editorial Selecta, 1952.

——*El Modernisme a Sitges.* Barcelona: Editorial Selecta, 1969.

——*Rusiñol i el Cau Ferrat.* Barcelona: Editorial Pòrtic, 1974.

Polgar, Alfred. *Auswahl: Prosa aus vier Jahrzehnten.* Bernt Richter, ed., Siegfried Melchinger, intro. Hamburg: Rowohlt, 1968.

Polyakov, M. Ya., ed. *Russkaya teatralnaya parodiya XIX-nachala XX veka.* Moscow: Isskustvo, 1976.

Pott, Gertrud. *Die Spiegelung des Sezessionismus im österreichischen Theater.* Vienna: Wilhelm-Braumüller Universitäts-Verlagsbuchhandlung, 1975.

Prat de la Riba, Enric. *Prat de la Riba: Propulsor de la llengua i la cultura* (*Articles i parlaments*). Jordi Rubió i Balaguer, Enric Jardí, and Jordi Sali, eds., Barcelona: Editorial Selecta, 1974.

——*La Nacionalitat Catalana.* Barcelona: Editorial Barcino, 1977.

Presber, Rudolf. *Ich gehe durch mein Haus.* Stuttgart and Berlin: Deutsche Verlags-Anstalt, 1935.

Pyast, Vladimir. *Vstrechi.* Moscow: Federatsiya, 1929.

Ráfols, J. F. *Modernismo y modernistas.* Barcelona: Ediciones Destino, 1949.

Rainer, Otto and Walter Rösler. *Kabarettgeschichte: Abriss des deutschsprachigen Kabaretts.* Berlin: Henschelverlag, 1977.

Rasch, Wolfdietrich, ed. *Der vermummte Herr: Briefe Frank Wedekinds aus den Jahren 1881–1917.* Munich: Deutscher Taschenbuch Verlag, 1967.

Rearick, Charles. *Pleasures of the Belle Epoque: Entertainment & Festivity in Turn-of-the-Century France.* New Haven: Yale University Press, 1985.

Reisner, Ingeborg. "Kabarett als Werkstatt des Theaters; Literarische Kleinkunst im Wien vor dem 2. Weltkrieg." Typescript. Vienna, 1961.

Richepin, Jean. *Les Blasphèmes.* Paris: Bibliothèque-Charpentier, 1913.

——*Choix de Poésies.* Paris: Bibliothèque-Charpentier, 1926.

Richter, Hans. *Dada: Art and Anti-Art.* David Britt, tr. New York and Toronto: Oxford University Press, 1965.

Riha, Karl. *Moritat, Bänkelsong, Protestballade: Kabarett-Lyrik und engagiertes Lied in Deutschland.* 2nd ed. rev. Frankfurt am Main: Athenäum, 1979.

Ripellino, Angelo Maria. *Il trucco e l'anima: I maestri della regia nel teatro russo del Novecento.* Turin: Giulio Einaudi Editore, 1965.

Ritchie, J. M. *German Expressionist Drama.* Boston: Twayne, 1976.

Roda Roda's Geschichten. Gregor von Rezzori, ed. Hamburg: Rowohlt Taschenbuch Verlag, 1956.

Rollinat, Maurice. *Oeuvres I: Dans les brandes:* Georges Lubin, preface; Régis Miannay, ed. Paris: Minard, 1971; *Oeuvres II: Les Névroses.* Régis Miannay, ed. Paris: Minard, 1972.

Rose, W. K., ed. *The Letters of Wyndham Lewis.* London: Methuen, 1963.

Rösler, Walter. *Das Chanson im deutschen Kabarett 1901–1933.* Berlin: Henschelverlag, 1980.

Rudnitsky, Konstantin. *Rezhisser Meierkhold.* Moscow: Izdatelstvo "Nauka," 1969.

——*Meyerhold the Director.* George Petrov, tr. Ann Arbor, Mich.: Ardis, 1981.

Rudorff, Raymond. *The Belle Epoque: Paris in the Nineties.* New York: Saturday Review Press, 1973.

Rudzky, Kazimierz. *Dymek z papierosa czyli wspomnienia o scenach, scenkach i nadscenkach.* Warsaw: Iskry, 1959.

Rusiñol, Santiago. "Desde el molino," *Obres Completes.* 2d ed. Barcelona: Editorial Selecta, 1956.

——"En Pere Romeu," *Obres Completes.* Vol. 2. Barcelona: Editorial Selecta, 1976.

Sabartés, Jaime. *Picasso: An Intimate Portrait.* Angel Florés, tr. New York: Prentice-Hall, 1948.

Sackett, Robert Eben. *Popular Entertainment, Class, and Politics in Munich, 1900–1923.* Cambridge, Mass. and London, England: Harvard University Press, 1982.

Salten, Felix. *Das Österreichische Antlitz: Essays.* Berlin: S. Fischer Verlag, 1910.

Schaefer, Camillo. *Peter Altenberg.* 2d ed., rev. Vienna: Freibord sonderreihe nr. 10, 1980.

Schnitzler, Arthur. *Jugend in Wien: Eine Autobiographie.* Vienna, Munich, Zurich: Verlag Fritz Molden, 1968.

Schorske, Carl E. *Fin-de-Siècle Vienna: Politics and Culture.* New York: Knopf, 1980.

Schweiger, Werner J., ed. *Das grosse Peter Altenberg Buch.* Vienna and Hamburg: Paul Zsolnay Verlag, 1966.

Seehaus, Gunter. *Frank Wedekind und das Theater.* 2d ed. Remagen-Rolandseck: Verlag Rommerskirchen, 1973.

Sempoliński, Ludwik. *Wielcy artyści małych scen.* Warsaw: Czytelnik, 1968.

Senelick, Laurence, ed. and tr. *Russian Satiric Comedy.* New York: Performing Arts Journal, 1983.

Shapirovsky, E. *Konferans i konferense.* Moscow: "Iskusstvo," 1970.

Shattuck, Roger. *The Banquet Years: The Origins of the Avant-Garde in France. 1885 to World War I.* Rev. ed. New York: Vintage, 1968.

Shklovsky, Viktor. *Zhili-byli: Vospominaniya. Memuarnye zapisi. Povesti o vremen: s kontsa XIX v. po 1962.* Moscow: Sovetsky Pisatel, 1964.

Siegel, Jerrold. *Bohemian Paris: Culture, Politics, and the Boundaries of Bourgeois Life, 1830–1930.* New York: Viking, 1986.

Simonetta, Umberto. *La patria che ci è data: I testi comici del cabaret italiano.* Milan: Bompiani, 1974.

Sitwell, Sir Osbert. *Great Morning.* Boston: Little, Brown, 1947.

Sławińska, Irena and Stefan Kruk. *Myśl teatralna Młodej Polskiej: Antologia.* Warsaw: Wydawnictwa Artystyczne i Filmowe, 1966.

Stanislavsky, Konstantin. *Moya zhizn v teatre.* Moscow: Izdatelsvto "Iskusstvo," 1962.

——*My Life in Art.* G. Ivanov-Mumjiev, tr. Moscow: Foreign Languages Publishing House, n. d.

Stawar, Andrzej. *Tadeusz Żeleński (Boy).* Warsaw: Państwowy Instytut Wydawniczy, 1958.

Steinbruckner, Bruno F. *Ludwig Thoma.* Boston: Twayne (G. K. Hall), 1978.

Steinke, Gerhardt Edward. *The Life and Work of Hugo Ball: Founder of Dadaism.* The Hague and Paris: Mouton, 1967.

Stoppard, Tom. *Travesties.* New York: Grove Press, 1975.

Storm, John. *The Valadon Drama: The Life of Suzanne Valadon.* New York: E. P. Dutton, 1958.

Strindberg, Freda. *Marriage with Genius.* London: Jonathan Cape, 1937.

Styan, J. L. *Max Reinhardt.* Cambridge: Cambridge University Press, 1982.

Symons, Arthur. *Colour Studies in Paris.* New York: E. P. Dutton, 1918.

Teffi, N. A. *Pesy.* Paris: Vozrozhdenie, 1934.

Thirlmere, Rowland (John Walker). *Letters from Catalonia and Other Parts of Spain.* Vol. 1. London: Hutchinson, 1905.

Thoma, Ludwig. *Ein Leben in Briefen (1875–1921).* Munich: R. Piper & Co. Verlag

——*Gesammelte Werke.* Vol. 1. Munich: Albert Langen, 1922.

——*Erinnerungen.* Munich: Albert Langen, 1931.

Tikhvinskaya, L. "Letuchaya mysh." *Teatr* (Moscow, March 1982), 3;102–112.

Uvarov, E. D., ed. *Russkaya sovetskaya estrada 1917–1929: Ocherk istorii.* Moscow: Isskustvo, 1976.

Valbel, Horace. *Les Chansonniers et les Cabarets Artistiques.* Paris: E. Dentu, Éditeur, 1895.

Varey, J. E. "Los títeres en Cataluña, en el siglo XIX." *Estudios Escenicos* (Barcelona, 1960), 5; 45–78.

Veigl, Hans. *Lachen im Keller: Von den Budapestern zum Wiener Werkel: Kabarett und Kleinkunst in Wien.* Vienna: Löcker Verlag, 1986.

Verdone, Mario, ed. *Teatro Contemporaneo.* Vol. 1. *Teatro Italiano.* Rome: Lucarini Editore, 1981.

Verkauf, Willy. *Dada: Monograph of a Movement.* New York: G. Wittenborn, 1957.

Verlaine, Paul. *Oeuvres en prose complètes.* Jacques Borel, ed. Paris: Gallimard, 1972.

Vigues, Ezequiel. *Teatre de Putxinel-lis.* Publicacions de l'Institut del Teatre. Barcelona: Edicions 62, 1st ed., 1975; 2d ed., 1976.

Waissenberger, Robert, ed. *Vienna 1890–1920.* New York: Rizzoli, 1984.

Wagener, Hans. *Frank Wedekind.* Berlin: Colloquium Verlag, 1979.

Wedekind, Frank. *Ausgewählte Werke.* Fritz Strich, ed. Munich: Georg Müller, 1924.

——*Dramen 2: Gedichte.* Manfred Hahn, ed. Berlin and Weimar: Aufbau-Verlag, 1969.

——*Gedichte und Chansons.* Munich. Wilhelm Goldmann Verlag, 1979.

——*Prosa.* Berlin and Weimar: Aufbau-Verlag, 1969.

Weigel, Hans. *Karl Kraus oder Die Macht der Ohnmacht.* Vienna, Frankfurt, Zurich: Verlag Fritz Molden, 1968.

Weiss, Tomasz. *Legenda i prawda Zielonego Balonika.* Cracow: Wydawnictwo Literackie, 1976.

Wenng, Walter, ed. *Das schiefe Podium: Ein buntes Brett'l Buch.* Berlin: Dr. Eysler, 1921.

Weys, Rudolf. *Literatur am Naschmarckt: Kulturgeschichte d. Wiener Kleinkunst in Kostproben.* Vienna: Cudek, 1947.

——*Cabaret und Kabarett in Wien.* Vienna and Munich: Jugend & Volk, 1970.

Die Wiener Werkstätte. Modernes Kunsthandwerk von 1903–1932, 22. Mai bis 20 August 1967. Österreichisches Museum für Angewandte Kunst. Dr. Wilhelm Mrazek, gen. ed. Vienna, 1967.

Das Wiener Kaffeehaus. Von den Anfangen bis zur Zwischenkriegszeit. 66 Sonderausstellung des Historischen Museums der Stadt Wien, Karlsplatz 12. 12. Juni bis 26. Oktober 1980. Reingard Witzmann, gen. ed. Eigenverlag der Museen der Stadt Wien.

Wien um 1900. Ausstellung Veranstaltet vom Kulturamt der Stadt Wien. 5. Juni bis 30. August 1964. Vienna: Brüder Rosenbaum, 1964.

Willett, John, ed. and tr. *Brecht on Theatre: The Development of an Aesthetic.* New York: Hill and Wang, 1964.

Willette, A. *Feu Pierrot. 1857–19 ?.* Paris: H. Floury, Éditeur, 1919.

Winkler, Michael. *Einakter und kleine Dramen des Jugendstils.* Stuttgart: Philipp Reclam Jun., 1974.

Winklowa, Barbara. *Tadeusz Żeleński* (*Boy*): *Twórczość i życie.* Warsaw: Państwowy Instytut Wydawniczy, 1967.

Wittlin, Jerzy, ed. *Warschau, abends halb zehn: Polnisches Kabarett.* Berlin: Henschelverlag Kunst und Gesellschaft, 1979.

Wolzogen, Ernst von. *Ansichten und Aussichten.* Berlin: F. Fontane, 1908.

——*Verse zu meinem Leben.* Berlin: F. Fontane, 1907.

——*Wie ich mich ums Leben brachte: Erinnerungen und Erfahrungen.* Braunschweig and Hamburg: Verlag von Georg Westermann, 1922.

Wunberg, Gotthart and Johannes J. Braakenburg. *Die Wiener Moderne: Literatur, Kunst und Musik zwischen 1890 und 1910.* Stuttgart: Philipp Reclam Jun., 1981.

Wysocki, Gisela von. *Peter Altenberg: Bilder und Geschichten des befreiten Lebens*. Munich and Vienna: Hanser Verlag, 1979.

Xanrof, Léon (Léon Fourneau). *Chansons sans-géne*. Paris: G. Ondet, Éditeur, 1890.

——*Chansons à Rire*. Paris: E. Flammarion, n. d.

——*Pochards et Pochades. Histoires du Quartier Latin*. Paris: Libraire Marpon & Flammarion, n. d.

Zampogna, Domenico. *Charles Cros dal "Parnasse" al Simbolismo*. Messina: Peloritana Editrice, 1968.

Zévaès, Alexandre. *Aristide Bruant*. Paris: Éditions de La Nouvelle Revue Critique, 1943.

Żeleński (Boy), Tadeusz. *Pisma*. 28 vols. Warsaw: Państwowy Instytut Wydawniczy, 1956–1975.

Zolotnitsky, D. *Zori teatralnogo oktyabrya*. Leningrad: Iskusstvo, 1976.

INDEX